The Decline of Privilege

THE MODERNIZATION OF
OXFORD UNIVERSITY

The Decline of Privilege

THE MODERNIZATION OF OXFORD UNIVERSITY

JOSEPH A. SOARES

Stanford University Press
Stanford, California
1999

Stanford University Press, Stanford, California

© 1999 by the Board of Trustees of the
Leland Stanford Junior University

Printed in the United States of America

CIP data appear at the end of the book

For my parents

Preface

Ever since Max Weber wrote his celebrated essay on the affinities between seventeenth-century Calvinism and the ethos of modern capitalism, scholars have inquired into the economic effects of cultural forces. The inspiration that launched this book came from a twist on Weber's problem. At the onset my thoughts were influenced by a controversy on the economic decline of Britain for which many assigned much of the blame to cultural factors. The culture that once nourished aggressive entrepreneurs had allegedly been supplanted by a mandarin ethos uncongenial to wealth creation. Historians and, most important, politicians placed considerable responsibility for the decline on apostles of English culture. University academics, especially those identified as Oxbridge, were seen by critics as having been particularly at fault. The miseducation of Britain's most carefully selected talent must have drained away the nation's competitive spark. British governing elites stood accused of having become soft-hearted, more concerned with social expenditures than with profitable reinvestments.

Initially, the claim that in the welfare-capitalist state there was an imbalance between public goods and the requirements of private capital did not trouble me. Granting for the moment the diagnosis, I was disinclined to see the condition as diseased. Britain did not have high poverty or illiteracy rates. It was a society with a national health service, where tuition fees were paid by taxpayers whether the student was in primary school or university. It was a land without motorway billboards, where even leatherclad youths sporting body jewelry would use the word "please" when requesting a drink in a pub. All told, it did not seem an infirm place to me. In the decline debate, where some affixed blame, I hoped to award distinction.

If intellectuals played an important role in the crafting of Britain's civil society, then perhaps my work on that issue could contribute to the discussion of public culture in the United States? Imagine my disappointment when, after months of field work, the complexity of the situation revealed that the actors and institutions portrayed in the debate were caricatures. Then the terms of my inquiry changed. The story became less about the relation of culture to the economy and more about the symbolic role of the university at the center of the controversy. Thus this book became a sociologically informed monograph on Oxford University since the Second World War. I hope to have captured germane aspects of the external dynamics, climate of ideas, and internal politics that have shaped Oxford's history—and to have said something worthwhile about the nature of an elite university's autonomy in a modern society.

I want to express my thanks to the two foundations that made my years abroad possible: the Krupp Fellowship program at Harvard's Center for European Studies and the Jacob Javits Fellowship program of the U.S. Congress. A cordial acknowledgment is owed to those Harvard professors who advised me during the dissertation phase of this project. To Daniel Bell, without whose letters of introduction this work would have been infeasible, my deepest gratitude for nurturing in me something of his sense of scholarly standards. To the wise and liberal David Riesman, unsurpassed exemplar in the field of the sociology of education, I am especially grateful. Also Nathan Glazer and Peter Hall were unfailingly encouraging mentors.

At Oxford University, I was graced by the friendship of Alan and Nibby Bullock, traditional humanists, ever generous with time and knowledge, who opened all doors. Thanks are owed to Professor A. H. Halsey, for the invitation to join, as a visiting member, the Senior Common Room of Nuffield College. From Dr. Brian Harrison's project on the history of Oxford University, I am indebted to Daniel Greenstein and Mark Curthoys.

My most sincere gratitude goes to every person who graciously granted me an interview. And I would like to thank the Harvard Faculty of Arts and Sciences for selecting my thesis to win the De Lancey K. Jay Prize.

From the Department of Sociology at Yale, I want to thank Professor Deborah Davis for recommending the publisher and for her unflagging moral support. Professors Kai Erikson and Charles Perrow provided thoughtful suggestions at various stages of the project. And they all joined with other colleagues, especially Professor Debra Minkoff, to offer timely amounts of good cheer.

A special appreciation must go to the friends who helped keep me happy over the intervening years, especially: Fiona Carter, Madeline Dymsza, Thomas Garside, David Morgan, Ann Mullen, Felicitas Opwis, Ian Robinson, and Tim Scoones.

Finally, I want to express my gratitude to the editors at Stanford University Press, Muriel Bell and Laura Comay, who saw merit in publishing this book; and to the press's readers, Sheldon Rothblatt and Steven Brint, whose valuable comments guided me through the final draft of this composition.

J.A.S.

Contents

Tables and Figures

The Decline of Privilege

THE MODERNIZATION OF
OXFORD UNIVERSITY

Introduction

Oxford University has played a unique role in the cultural and political life of Britain. In addition to being the place where most of the kingdom's national leaders were educated, it has been, and is, a symbol of many things peculiarly English. This book is about controversies spun around Oxford over its qualities and its contributions, real and imagined, to the character of British society in the second half of the twentieth century; it is about how Oxford modernized and yet continued to be widely perceived as antiquated.

Throughout much of its history, Oxford has had a mythical stature. In recent times, even outside the book-reading public, Oxford's image was the stuff of romantic fancy. Even most contemporary Americans would likely believe that at Oxford today the majority of students are from wealthy families, attended elite private schools such as Eton and Rugby, and plan to dabble in the liberal arts before going into politics or banking. But if you told those same people that most Oxford students have modest social backgrounds, receive public financial assistance, pursue degrees in the natural sciences and technology before joining industry and commerce, and are taught by a faculty chiefly engaged in research in the natural sciences, they might wonder if you had had one too many at the local bar.[1] An account of Oxford as a meritocratic science university would be difficult to believe because the image of Oxford as steeped in stuffy traditions and upper-class networks has become almost too perva-

I

sive to shake. Nevertheless, the first image is an outdated one, and the reasons why are the substance of this book.[2]

Oxford's association with the qualities of English culture that form the national temperament has long been both well known and a source of trouble.[3] There were times when the nation's sense of identity was called into question, memories were contested, and people engaged in a form of collective soul searching. Whether that reevaluation of beliefs and institutions was born from a feeling of revival, such as Britain's celebrated end of postwar rationing, or evolved from a sense of decline, as in Britain's experience in the 1970s, there were periods when scholars and journalists, politicians and citizens participated in a debate on the national heritage and its prospects.

Since the Second World War, the British have engaged in at least two such debates. First, after the war, there was a discussion of how to make Britain a more open and affluent society. Policy makers and journalists spoke of a "new Jerusalem," where poverty, meager health care, and the confines of class would no longer mangle people's lives. During this period much of the British welfare state was built, the national health service was put into place, and the Butler Education Act was passed with the belief that an expanded educational system would open up Britain's class structure.

Many individuals inside Oxford, during and after the war, contributed to this optimistic spirit of social reform. It was widely believed, especially in political and intellectual circles, that the forces that had vanquished Hitler and were building a better Britain represented vindications of British institutions, including Oxford. There was an air of mutual congratulation. The sounds of contentment were such that Edward Shils, then a sociologist at the London School of Economics, wrote in *Encounter*, "Great Britain on the whole . . . seemed to the British intellectual of the early 1950s to be fundamentally all right and even much more than that. Never had an intellectual class found its society and its culture so much to its satisfaction" (Shils 1972: 137). Oxford's intellectual community was not suffering much angst.[4]

The honeymoon could not last. By the early 1960s the reformist spirit had struck Oxford. The university's traditional manner of self-governance was disparaged by an official parliamentary commission in 1963 as incompatible with public support (Committee on Higher Education 1963a: 224, para. 687). The Conservative Party in control of the government ratified the report. And the Labour Party, in the run-up to the 1964 general elections, took the opportunity to denounce Oxford as an incorrigible haven for sons of bankers and bosses. As I describe in Chapter 5, Oxford felt compelled to defend itself, and it did so very effectively in the form of a major public self-examination. But things did not rest there.

About a decade later, in the late 1970s, a second debate began after it became clear that a prosperous and classless society had failed to materialize and that Britain was headed down a slope of economic deterioration. The partisans in that quarrel, especially supporters of Margaret Thatcher's Conservative administration, sought to arrest the forces culpable for British decline and to uncover the means for national renewal.

The debate on the economic decline of Britain extended through the 1980s (see Collins and Robbins 1990). At the time, many politicians and historians claimed that British decadence was due to the miseducation of elites at anti-industrial private boarding schools, known as "public schools,"[5] and at Oxbridge.[6] And, adding weight to that charge, Margaret Thatcher's education minister, Sir Keith Joseph, issued a broad policy report that admonished certain unspecified universities for being anti-business and snobbish.[7] As the editor of Oxford's faculty magazine noted in a review of the university's relationship with the Conservative government: "An important aspect of the 1979 government's analysis of what it saw as a national crisis was that the universities—and especially Oxbridge, and Oxford more than Cambridge—bore a vital part of the responsibility for national 'decline.' They represented, it was thought, an anti-entrepreneurialism" (Reed 1994: 1). Thatcher's manner toward universities was less abrasive than her technique for breaking up trade unions—but not much less.

To punish British universities as a whole for their Oxbridge pretensions, Thatcher's government, while preaching laissez-faire, pushed through the greatest centralization of governmental powers over higher education in modern British history. Universities received most of their funds from the state, so Thatcher legislated strict governmental controls. Block grants were replaced by line-item funding on a contractual basis, which was subject to repayment if targets were missed. The body that had stood between the government and universities and had been responsible for allocating public money, the University Grants Committee (UGC), was eliminated. Tenure, which supplied the legal basis for academic job security and freedom from external coercion, was abolished for all new faculty appointments. Thanks to Thatcher, in the future the state would have the machinery and the statutory right to impose its will directly upon universities. After 1988, the celebrated autonomy of university dons was just a nostalgic memory.[8]

In the controversies of the 1960s and 1980s, advocates of reform denounced the cultural ethos of the "establishment." Both the political old left and the political new right agreed that the establishment's customs were among the nation's prevailing maladies. For members of the Labour Party, established cultural conventions propped up Britain's rigid class structure; they were an obstacle to social justice. And, according to free-market Conservatives, traditional gentlemanly habits sapped Britain's economic competitiveness by nourishing an anti-entrepreneurial culture.

During those two disputes, modernizing critics had several potential targets. The establishment (in addition to its various military, economic, and media branches) also included four prominent institutions of medieval lineage that were saturated with custom and ritual; they were the monarchy, the Church of England, the House of Lords, and Oxbridge with its feeder schools. Yet the institution that politicians, journalists, and intellectuals disproportionately criticized and targeted for reform was Oxbridge. Why should Oxbridge receive so much attention? Why have public debates on the national heritage repeatedly involved claims about the qualities of Oxbridge?

The short answer is that throughout the second half of the twentieth century the monarchy, as a symbol of national unity, continued to be too popular to invite widespread criticism (although members of the royal family may yet change that). According to a poll taken in 1987, the monarchy held first place in the British public's mind as a source of national pride (Topf, Mohler, and Heath 1989: 125–29). Secularization left the Church of England looking too frail to effectively shape the nation for good or ill; its membership by the 1980s was down to 3.8 percent of the adult population, about one-third of its prewar high (Brierley 1988: 540, table 13.13). And the House of Lords was too subordinate to the House of Commons to take independent blame for anything. But Oxbridge was just right. It was symbolic without being untouchable, and it performed an obviously important function. It educated people. While the populace may not have felt entitled to evaluate the obscure functions of the monarchy, the Church, and the House of Lords, it had little difficulty believing that educational institutions should function to promote equality of opportunity and economic growth. When there was a public perception that individual choices and economic prosperity were not what they should be, it was not long before fingers started pointing at schools and universities. During periods of national soul searching, educational institutions are easy targets. They appear malleable enough to tempt social engineering, and blame placed on them is blame deflected from business leaders and politicians.

Yet Oxford, more than any other educational institution, was singled out and attacked for reasons that went beyond its status as a university. It was identified as being especially responsible for nurturing Britain's unwholesome qualities for two reasons. The first was Oxford's historical association with politics.

Since the Middle Ages, Oxford has served as a doorway for those seeking entry to the corridors of power. Until the late nineteenth century, Oxford was literally part of the British state. Along with the monarchy, Parliament, and the Church of England, Oxford was a branch of the governing establishment; as such, it prepared men for positions of social authority.[9] One could say that Oxford was Britain's candidate training school for its officer corps. Over the past hundred years more high-level politicians and civil servants have passed through Oxford than through all other universities combined, including Cambridge (Commission of Inquiry 1965a: 11; Guttsman 1963).

The preponderance of Oxbridge graduates within the power elite was widely known, but Oxford's disproportionate share was appreciated less well. Yet in British cabinets in the twentieth century, Oxford men and women outnumbered Cambridge graduates nearly two to one. From 1900 to 1985, of the 972 ministers with a university education, 455 went to Oxford and 276 to Cambridge. Of eleven prime ministers counting back from Tony Blair, eight were undergraduates at Oxford, and none were at Cambridge. And Oxford's lead in Parliament has been similarly commanding. On average, between 1951 and 1970, 48 percent of the Conservative members of the House of Commons and 30 percent of the Labour members with university experience were at Oxford, while the respective figures for Cambridge are 34 and 14 percent. Oxford has been second to none as a gatekeeper to the political elite.[10]

Because of the remarkable number of politicians and civil servants who had personal experience at Oxford, that university has been ever-present in the governing class's collective memory. In policy debates and their postmortems, Oxford provided the unstated background for presumptions about higher education.

The second reason Oxford was singled out for attack was the symbolic role it played for the professional middle classes. For many who pursued careers in education or literature, Oxford epitomized old England.

Academics and novelists have viewed Oxford as the quintessential English university. In surveys of academic opinion, people have overwhelmingly identified Oxford with the ideal of English education (Halsey and Trow 1971: 67). And authors who portray universities in their novels, as Ian Carter's definitive study of British university fiction since 1945 demonstrated, have been attracted to Oxford by a huge majority. Of the 204 novels written between 1945 and 1988 that featured British academic life, 119 depicted Oxford; Cambridge, with 26 appearances, came in a distant second place; other British universities provided the settings for the remaining 59 books. Carter showed that fictional Oxford signified those values thought to epitomize English society: tolerance, civility, pluralism, and democracy (Carter 1990: 4, 263). To judge from novels on academic life, one would surmise that England's soul dwelled in Oxford.[11]

Because of its relation to the power elite and its hold on the middle-class imagination, Oxford often provided the mental landscape for national self-examination. As one bemused Oxford don put it: "Not the least of the services which the University of Oxford performs for a harassed nation is that of moral scapegoat, or lightning conductor for the electric discharges from storms in the national conscience" (Griffin 1966: 220). Yet nearly always in these storms, the light cast on Oxford was deceptive.

When Oxford was portrayed by Labour as home ground to the Conservative enemy or by the Tories as a country estate responsible for seducing the business classes away from the entrepreneurial frontiers, their image of Oxford was really just a variant of Evelyn Waugh's *Brideshead Revisited* (1945).[12] The Brideshead depiction presented Oxford as a garden society for the idle rich and those who aspired to a similarly elevated social station. The vision was of a place where undergraduates strolled around intoxicated on wine and brandy, carrying teddy bears, staying out until all hours, and sneaking into college after the gates were locked, to the amusement of Oxford's faculty, themselves eccentrics or sycophants who did very little if any teaching or research. This privileged world was then seen by the critics as responsible for giving the upper classes the passkey to career advancement, relying on old-boy patronage networks to close ranks against non-Oxbridge parvenus. This landed-gentry culture left the upper classes totally unprepared to run British corporations or the affairs of state. Oxford, its critics alleged, nurtured generation after generation of leaders who had no technical skills whatsoever for modern management.

From the preceding, one might conclude that to many critics Oxford represented upper-class privilege. They objected that its concentration of academic talent was an entitlement bequeathed to children of the upper classes through their parents' economic and cultural resources. But the children-of-privilege explanation of Oxford's bad reputation was already outdated by the 1960s. Unlike the United States' Harvard, Oxford was not after 1946 an expensive private university with an undergraduate population drawn primarily from the top of the economic pyramid. Besides, in the British context, the upper class has been defined less by economic criteria than by honorific titles. The Brideshead upper-class element largely disappeared from Oxford after World War II. Shirley Williams, a former Labour Cabinet secretary of state for education and science, told me that the upper class tends "to think of Oxbridge as being very academic . . . and those less academically inclined children [of the upper class] either leave school at eighteen [or they] go to the Plate-glass universities which were acceptable to them . . . Sussex and York," in particular (Williams interview 1987).[13] Since the 1960s, Oxford has been a middle-class institution with a substantial contingent of students from working-class families; by 1963, it had approximately five times the number of undergraduates with blue-collar backgrounds as Harvard.[14] In the second half of the twentieth century, Harvard was more plutocratic than Oxford, but unlike Oxford it escaped being a focus of debate on the responsibility of institutions for social inequality.[15]

The other major charge against Oxford was that it was biased toward the liberal arts, that it was anti-science and unconcerned with contributing to economic growth. As we shall see in Chapter 3, there was substance to this criticism before World War II, but there has not been since then. As Michael Sanderson, a historian of British universities and industry, noted, "Oxford, the rightful object of contempt for its neglect of science . . . had emerged during the war as playing a very major role indeed in physical science" (1972: 348). In the fields of natural scientific research and education, between the war and the 1950s, Oxford went from the rear to the front ranks. In Britain, it caught up with Cambridge University, and it surpassed sister institutions abroad, such as Yale University.

How was it that Oxford could change so considerably on matters of upper-class privilege and commitments to the natural sciences and yet find itself for decades still the target of attacks aimed at precisely those issues? Politicians, journalists, and authors in the 1950s and 1980s were caught in a culture lag, recycling 30-year-old images of Oxford. More than just Oxford's position in the collective memory was at issue. The Conservative government in the 1980s effectively managed to manipulate myths associated with Oxford to justify its overpowering of academia. It is not an accomplishment that inspires one with confidence in the cognitive abilities of elites.

The rest of this book is divided into two parts: first, Oxford's transformation, and second, its experiences with political adversity. The rest of this chapter is a brief overview of the nature and timing of Oxford's metamorphosis, with a summary of the main forces responsible, including the names and dates of the most important university and government reports and legislative acts.

First, a few comments on the historical context and forces that drove Oxford's institutional transformation. The controversial issues and a spectrum of potential responses were in circulation well before the Second World War, yet the catalyst and finances came during and soon after the war. They were part of the modernizing reforms ushered in by the fight against Hitler and postwar reconstruction efforts. Although there have been controversies over the extent to which one should view the war as responsible for the reformist trend or whether there ever really was a broad consensus in favor of welfare extensions, there is no disputing the postwar expansion of the public-service state (see Glennerster and Low 1990: 11–15). From 1944 forward, Tory paternalism and Labour's social reformism in Parliament legislated various extensions of social rights and public culture (see Marshall 1950). Universal health care and other welfare benefits expanded the scope of citizens' social entitlements; government grants of taxpayers' money, on an unprecedented scale, to undergraduates and universities substantially enlarged public culture.

The major movements in the government's orchestration of student entitlements and plentiful budgetary outlays for universities included: the Butler Education Act of 1944, which set the framework for the modern British education system; the University Grants Committee and the Treasury Department's compact in 1945 to double the total amount of public funds distributed to universities; the Anderson Report and Education Act of 1962, which provided full tuition awards and means-tested stipends to every United Kingdom undergraduate; and the Robbins report of 1963, which ratified and prolonged a period when new universities were built and existing ones expanded. Finally, there was one piece of legislation that did not directly involve public funding but that did give impetus to a reevaluation of gender roles. In 1975, Parliament passed the Sex Discrimination Act, which, among other effects, made gender segregation in education illegal.

One can classify Oxford's changes into three categories: finance, social composition, and academic activities. On finance, the key shift came in the late 1940s, when the share of the taxpayers' contribution to Oxford's budget grew from approximately one-fourth to more than one-half of its annual expenses. In the 1940s Oxford became a hybrid institution, more public than private because of its sources of funds.

On social composition, a proverbial silent (and occasionally not so silent) social revolution worked through Oxford after the war. Those not-very-academic sons of wealthy gentlemen were bumped aside by merito-cratic scholars, often from middle- or working-class homes. Eventually, those male scholars were joined by large numbers of women.

The important social changes clustered together during three periods: the late 1940s, the early 1960s, and the late 1970s. In the 1940s, young men from state schools and the working class gained entry to Oxford in significant numbers for the first time. An army of lower-class, state-educated students broke through the lines of the privileged and privately schooled youths who had dominated the university. In 1938, state-school alumni contributed only 19 percent of Oxford's freshmen; by 1948 their ranks had grown to 35 percent. A closely connected development was the increase in the number of undergraduates whose parents were working class. The contingent of sons with blue-collar fathers, between the late 1940s and early 1960s, increased from approximately 10 to 20 percent of Oxford's undergraduates. In reverse, sons of the British peerage, future members of the House of Lords, who found Oxbridge's new emphasis on academic performance tedious, discovered a fashionable taste for New universities. As late as the 1950s, nearly half of the peerage's eldest sons of university age were in Oxbridge colleges; by the late 1960s and early 1970s, they constituted just 20 percent. At the same time, their propor-tion in higher education, but not at Oxford or Cambridge, went up from 12 to 32 percent. Also, the aristocracy of the male sex was undermined when, with Parliament's help, Oxford's men's colleges realized the virtues of including female students and faculty. After 1975, women were no longer limited to approximately 18 percent of undergraduates; by the late 1980s, female enrollment had more than doubled, to 38 percent.

Academically, Oxford was recast by a dramatic increase between 1953 and 1963 in its natural science faculty. During those years, senior mem-bers who engaged in scientific research or instruction grew from approx-imately 28 to 40 percent of Oxford's staff. Virtually the entire expansion was funded by the state. Students specializing in the sciences swung in line with faculty interests; between 1951 and 1971, science undergradu-ates jumped from just 26 to over 39 percent of Oxford's junior members. And last, between 1958 and 1963 the number of postgraduate students (the British synonym for graduate students) went from 15 to 21 percent of Oxford's total student population.

Oxford's altered social composition and shift toward the natural sci-ences were promoted by its traditions of democratic self-governance. Faculty committees conducted investigations and stimulated dialogue until Oxford's democratic assemblies in the university and in the colleges took action. The most important internal inquiries were: the Chilver report of 1960, which brought about the elimination of the Latin language requirement for science students; the Hardie report of 1962, which effectively closed the separate admissions door for gentlemen, forcing everyone through the difficult entryway for scholars; and the Franks report of 1966, which sought to equalize the admissions opportunities of state-school and privately educated students. The cultural chasm between the humanities and the natural sciences was bridged, after much discontent and discussion, by integrating scientists into the college system. The work of assimilation was done by three committees, which produced the Harrison report of 1962, the Norrington report of 1964, and, again, the Franks report of 1966.

Many newcomers were given homes through the creation, between 1950 and 1965, of six modern Oxford colleges: St. Antony's, Nuffield, St. Catherine's, Linacre, St. Cross, and Wolfson. For undergraduates there was St. Catherine's, which excelled in recruiting state-educated science students, often from northern working-class families. For senior natural scientists, Oxford built St. Cross and Wolfson colleges; social science faculty had St. Antony's and Nuffield. All but St. Catherine's were exclusively for postgraduate students and faculty. Those six colleges were material expressions of Oxford's modernization.

If public subsidies and a broad climate of reform made Oxford's transformation possible, by themselves those factors were insufficient to complete the process. Either the government could impose modernization, or it could have advocates inside the university. The internal camp of reform was on most things a jump ahead of government—the glaring exception was female equality. The partisans and allies of modernization were from a new generation of socially progressive college dons and university scientists. Dons concerned about social justice and those with Labour Party sympathies made common cause with meritocrats, often scientists, who saw little point to continuing Oxford's prewar indulgence of the wealthy classes. With the opportunities provided by government funds, those dons sought to make good the university's ideal promise to be purely a community of scholars. And there was a contingent, yet formidable, affinity between meritocratic admissions and the swing toward modern science subjects. In addition, modernizers could rely on unfavorable comparisons with Oxford's sister universities, especially those in the United States, to help make their case. And they received indispensable assistance from some well-positioned elder statesmen. A few of those elders were reform-minded themselves, but others deferred pragmatically to change because it resonated with their conservative instinct that institutional preservation was impossible without innovation.

In the late 1940s, Oxford stopped being a privately funded university; by the early 1960s, it had ceased to be an upper-class club; in the 1950s and 1960s, Oxford moved into the sciences and postgraduate education; and by the late 1970s, women were no longer relegated to the margins.

While Chapters 1 through 4 document and reconstruct Oxford's transformation, Chapters 5 and 6 look at Oxford under attack by its critics in the worlds of education and politics. The 1960s threat began with fervor. The specter of a Royal Commission and parliamentary legislation was raised and then safely spirited into progressive internal reforms. In contrast, the challenge from the political right arrived in 1980 like an overdraft notice from the bank. It quickly became a full financial audit, complete with embarrassing public scenes, and resulted in the paymaster placing all universities under a form of legal receivership. The second part of this book explores the distinctions between the threats of the 1960s and 1980s, examines why the outcomes were different, and creates a balance sheet on the dilemmas of the academic profession at the end of the twentieth century.

Part One

THE TRANSFORMATION
OF OXFORD

1.

Academic Autonomy and Money Matters

OXFORD GOES PUBLIC

Universities have always had to find ways to harmonize the freedoms claimed by academics with the constraints of covering their expenses. Unless academics take a vow of poverty and retreat to countryside communes, the life of the mind rarely feeds, clothes, and shelters itself. Modern research in the natural and social sciences is a very expensive proposition. And in 800 years, there has not been a university in Europe or America with sufficient income-earning resources of its own not to have to rely on donations from benefactors, or grants from external authorities, to pay its bills. Academics have always counted on the cash nexus to deliver their needs.[1]

Scholars and scientists may be economically dependent, but they are not servile. Like other professionals, academics believe their expertise entitles them to the privileges of self-regulation. Since nonspecialists are unable to judge the particular merits of intellectual labors, they are allegedly served best if the process of oversight and regulation is left to the academic peer group. Consequently, there is at least a rhetorical connection between how academics organize their mutual relations and their claims on material resources. The organization of the profession, the way it governs itself, may help to justify the confidence of those to whom academics turn for remuneration.

This chapter explores, in relation to Oxford's modernization, the relevant aspects of the two preceding problems: the challenge of acquiring resources, and the matter of domestic arrangements from the end of the Second World War to the 1960s. The 1970s and 1980s are covered in the second part of the book.

After 1945, shifts in the sources and scale of financing available for British universities made Oxford's metamorphosis possible. Before the war, Oxford was a private liberal arts university with an exceptionally privileged social-class composition and ethos; by the end of the 1950s, Oxford was effectively a state institution, heavily committed to the natural sciences, with a middle-class constituency and a meritocratic ethos. Of the factors responsible for the metamorphosis, none was more important than Oxford's switch from mostly private to mainly public sources of financing.

Oxford's distinctive form of academic organization heavily influenced the way the state and universities institutionalized their financial relations. Academics and politicians viewed the Oxford model of a university as requiring democratic self-government and institutional independence. Public authorities could give money to universities, but academics determined how that money would be spent. In addition, self-governance provided the arena in which the politics of adaptation and transformation played itself out. The claim is not that without democratic assemblies Oxford would not have changed at all, but that the pace and character of innovation would have been different. To understand the peculiarities of Oxford's evolution, as well as the noninterventionist posture adopted by the government, one needs to know about Oxford's organizational traditions.

The move of British universities from relative financial independence to dependence on public funds reflected a contingent mix of powers and opportunities that is best understood in comparative-historical and sociological terms.

RESOURCES AND PROFESSIONAL PRIDE

In his collective biography of English intellectuals, Noel Annan wrote, "The years 1945–75 were the golden age of the don" (1990: 377).[2] During the era when the Treasury man held open the public's purse to universities, Oxford was for English academics very near to heaven. A don's life appeared to embody all of those freedoms and dignities desired by members of the profession. A fellow of an Oxford college had job security, a place to dine and converse, a vote on college and university affairs, a respectable amount of social prestige, and a constant flow of students.

The basic terms of his existence were comfortably set. One imagines that for nearly a half-century financial anxieties were a rare topic of lunchtime conversation.

The subject of donnish reticence on financial matters was touched upon by Noel Annan at a 1986 conference in London on higher education. He commented that while dons might look down upon American academics for their pecuniary appetites, as confederates in the "American national vice of materialism," the English suffered from the adverse maladies of snobbery and hypocrisy (Annan 1986). Money was a subject American academics could speak about without embarrassment, but not the British.

Dons may have had complex and infrequently acknowledged motives for eschewing conversations on cash, but they also had a reason to take pride in the polite habit. Not having to worry about lucre was one of the ways dons understood the virtues of university autonomy. Modern academic traditions in Oxford included the belief that the special mission of the university, the disinterested discovery and transmission of knowledge, was safeguarded by keeping it aloof from market pressures. The life of the mind required freedom of inquiry and expression, peer-group evaluation, and collegial self-governance. It was thought that intellectual excellence flourished within protected sanctuaries. Tenure stood at the center as the castle keep, providing shelter from breaches in the outer walls by men with political power or wealth. Academic freedom, the argument went, rested on institutional autonomy and occupational security from fiscal anxiety. Insouciance toward money matters could be a don's way of affirming his membership in the profession. The attitude, from a certain vantage point, reflected pride in collective accomplishments that rested upon centuries of effort.

The struggle for academic dignity was usually viewed as providing a cord of continuity between contemporary faculty and those scholars who created the vocation. European universities were twelfth-century inventions that furnished livelihoods for members of an intellectual guild.[3] Medieval scholars had to maneuver for working space with religious, aristocratic, and civic powers. On this Alan Cobban, a historian of medieval Oxbridge, has written: "The universities had their genesis in conflict, and struggle punctuated every stage in their evolution . . . as they fought first to win and then to defend an acceptable degree of autonomy vis-à-vis a range of ecclesiastical and secular authorities" (Cobban 1988: 9). Universities were most often urban communities of bachelors who vied with church and public authorities for legal rights to practice their trade.

The work of Jacques Le Goff has shown that the basic rights of the medieval university included "jurisdictional autonomy . . . the right to strike and to secede; and the monopoly of conferring university degrees" (1993: 75). Certainly the most defining academic power was the legal monopoly on scholastic certification. Then, as now, a central project of the university was to attract and prepare undergraduates for careers. A degree had vocational value, designating the bearer as having sufficient literacy and competence in a few areas (such as Latin, law, or rudimentary accounting) for him to be employable by ecclesiastic, city, or aristocratic powers (Le Goff 1980: 141).

With a monopoly on intellectual credentials under its control, scholars could strive for ancillary rights, ranging from economic privileges (such as reduced rents, tax exemptions, first pick in local food markets) to full legal jurisdiction over university members (ibid.: 135–49). Students in Heidelberg, Germany, for example, could not be tried and punished by city authorities for civil disturbances—until the twentieth century, only the university had that power.

Over time, in their dealings with external authorities as well as in their relations with undergraduates, the faculty found it useful to make special status claims. As summarized by Le Goff, "Academics . . . sought to define themselves as an *intellectual aristocracy*, endowed with . . . [a] specific morality and code of values" (ibid.: 144–45). For this intellectual nobility, nothing was more important than autonomy. Autonomy, self-rule, was a demand for the right to exist made by a nascent academic community against external authorities, and it was also a scholar's way to describe the preferred conditions for the performance of his craft. If authorities and clients placed any value on the fruits of intellectual labor, then one could argue that the best products came from scholars who controlled their own small worlds. But no matter how logical and eloquent the plea, sovereignty was a hard case to win.

Medieval university autonomy, like that enjoyed by cities, was conditional. In exchange for a space in which to conduct their activities, both universities and cities honored their duties to aristocratic and religious authorities. Cities, like Nuremberg, Germany, might have had only one external master, but all of the first universities had to serve two: Rome and the local authorities. Obligations could be met with services or money, but they almost always included granting the power to overlords to make some academic appointments.

Le Goff revealed that since universities were unable to support themselves solely from student fees, external authorities furnished a large portion of their operating funds. In exchange, they often decided who would hold positions in the universities. Le Goff has written that, for universities:

> The bulk of their remuneration, apart from ecclesiastical benefices, came, therefore, from the salaries and grants afforded them by cities, princes, or sovereigns. In return, the public powers claimed the right—which went with patronage—to sponsor candidates for university positions. As a result, the academic corporation did not fully enjoy one of the basic privileges of all other guilds, the right of *self-recruitment*. Yet the academics seem to have accepted this limitation. (Le Goff 1980: 140)

Academics could award credentials, and at their own risk strike or split away, as Oxford did from Paris, and Cambridge from Oxford. But they were too financially dependent to completely control which individuals gained entry into their profession.

In two respects, self-governance and the power of self-selection, academic autonomy fared somewhat better in England than on the Continent. Oxford and Cambridge were ultimately just as dependent on king and Church as their brethren abroad; nonetheless they managed to receive more freedoms of self-rule.

The architects of academic democracy in Oxford built a structure with two tiers: independent and self-governing colleges on one level, and university-wide parliamentary assemblies called Congregation and Convocation on the other. The historian Alan Cobban (a former fellow of Trinity College, Cambridge) has informed us that "the typical English medieval college was a self-governing community of fellows organized on democratic lines" (Cobban 1988: 124). The fellows elected all of the college's officers, and they chose most of their own members. In contrast to medieval French and German practice, autonomy in Oxford included the powers of self-selection and self-administration.

Originally colleges were for faculty, not students. Undergraduates lived throughout, and university activities percolated across, the city of Oxford. To regulate the life of the university as a whole, the fellows needed something other than a college governing body—for that they had Congregation. It was a democratic assembly "composed of masters and doctors in all of the faculties" (ibid.: 97). Academic powers in Oxford went beyond collective control inside the colleges to include governance of the university as well.

The colleges, then, began as small academic guilds, run by democratic councils, with elected heads. The university-wide general assembly was

Congregation. Within and between the two, the balance of power fluctuated. The external interventions of public authorities often determined who had the upper hand.

For centuries, Oxford was embroiled in one court, parliamentary, or religious controversy after another. Those conflicts greatly affected Oxford's internal democracy. Tudor and Stuart authorities, from Cardinal Wolsey to James II, intervened in Oxford's internal life to make both the university and the colleges more pliant in response to royal command. The court, rather than negotiate with what must have seemed to them a mob of young masters in Congregation, encouraged oligarchy by working through the heads of halls and colleges (*Oxford University Gazette* 1964: 27). The democratic powers of Congregation were overturned by a series of political interventions that culminated in the Laudian statutes of 1636. (These were put into effect the same year as Harvard's founding, and both events were reverberations of royal machinations.) Drawn up under the authority of Archbishop Laud, the new statutes took all residual democratic powers out of the hands of resident scholars and gave control to heads of houses. Paradoxically, those interventions both undermined Oxford's medieval democratic arrangements and established the colleges as the locus of academic life; the erosion of donnish democracy was unfortunate, yet the strength of college independence since then has been hailed as one of Oxford's glories.

Oligarchy ruled Oxford from 1636 forward. The civil war changed little of Oxford's formal organization; but it certainly affected Oxford's wealth and religious monuments. The king set up court at Oxford's Christ Church College and then plundered all the precious metals his men could find. And when Oliver Cromwell's parliamentary forces occupied the university, the iconoclasts among them went around knocking the heads off religious statues. The university cleverly protected what was left of its resources by electing Cromwell its chancellor.

There were other episodes of outside intervention, but the next significant exchange came in the Victorian era. In 1854, a Royal Commission of Inquiry effected a revolution in Oxford's governing institutions. The Victorians launched four Royal Commissions with parliamentary powers to stir up England's two ancient universities. Parliament set Oxbridge free from the Church of England and in so doing cut the university's official tie to the British state (Ward 1965). Released from religious or political obligations, Oxford's teachers made the transition from clergyman to don (Engel 1983: 55–93). For the first time in its history, the university and its colleges became purely academic institutions.

After disestablishment in the 1870s, democratic powers in Oxford's colleges experienced a century of resurgence. A contemporary, Max Weber, the father of German sociology, characterized that type of academic organization as "functional collegiality" (1978: 272); it was not a form of organization he expected to last. In this regard, Oxford moved in the opposite direction from the general corporate trend of the age. Other collegial structures in cultural organizations, such as the nineteenth century's cooperative symphony orchestras of New York and New Haven, were destroyed and replaced by business corporations. In the early twentieth century, musicians' cooperatives were disenfranchised by wealthy patrons who, from boards of directors, controlled the symphony's affairs with professional managers (Couch 1983: 111–14; Moon 1995). In Oxford's colleges the cooperative form was revived in the late nineteenth and early twentieth centuries; there the cultural producers were also cooperative owners and management.

To some Americans, Oxford's twentieth-century self-government looked like a horse-and-buggy anachronism (see Rosovsky 1990: 283). There was nothing like it at any university of comparable status in the United States. American universities had distinctly hierarchical power structures with presidents and boards at the commanding summit, and with faculty members exercising direct democratic power at the departmental level. Furthermore, independent self-governing colleges did not exist at America's top universities, although there were superficial similarities between Oxford colleges and the residential units Harvard called houses and Yale referred to as colleges. By American standards, Oxford looked like a form of guild socialism.

Throughout its long history, Oxford had to face many external challenges; some of them strengthened Oxford's self-government and stimulated its intellectual activities, others did the opposite. Proceeding from the empirical evidence, one cannot construct an armor-plated generalization to describe the right relation of Oxford to external powers. It is simply not true that the university flourished best when left entirely to itself, or the opposite, that it fared better whenever outsiders meddled with it.

UNIVERSITY FINANCE AND INSTITUTIONAL AUTONOMY

All intellectual communities have complex and occasionally conflicting relations with their host societies. Some of those difficulties may spring from the obscurities of intellectual life, the esoteric or impractical habits of scholars and scientists. The expression "town and gown," which derives from a fourteenth-century bloody street battle between Oxford's students and townsmen, also denotes the frequent discomfort or hostility among those excluded from academe's garden. Serious strife, however, mostly tends to break out when conflicting demands are made on scarce resources.

The power of self-governance ultimately rests on material resources, especially cash. When academic rights are at issue, money matters. The paymaster sets the agenda, directly or indirectly. What David Riesman and Christopher Jencks have written of the public and private contrast in the United States was true throughout the twentieth century on both sides of the Atlantic: "The differences between public and private colleges seem to us to derive not from their boards of control but from their sources of financial support" (1969: 269). Where money comes from, how much, and with what strings determines the disposition of academic institutions even more than their formal governance arrangements.

The pattern of Oxford's external commitments and sources of financing changed in the 1870s, 1920s, and 1940s. With disestablishment in the 1870s, the university and its colleges became legally and financially more self-sufficient than ever before. Student fees, endowment income, and benefactions paid Oxford's bills. If there was a golden age of financial independence and self-governance for Oxford, it began in the 1870s.

Oxford's next entanglement with external authorities came in the form of public money. The university made its own way financially until 1922, when Parliament authorized the Treasury Department to give it recurrent grants. The government's funding offer came as a recommendation from a Royal Commission of Inquiry chaired by Herbert Henry Asquith, an Oxford graduate, Liberal Party leader, and former prime minister of Britain's wartime coalition government.

The Asquith Commission was established by the War Cabinet to authorize an anticipated postwar flow of public funds into Oxbridge (Cabinet and Cabinet Committees 1919). Before the war, state aid to either Oxford or Cambridge University was limited to small occasional grants to a few departments, such as forestry and engineering (*Parliamentary Papers* 1922: 34). But that changed after the government began providing the universities with money for war-related work.

The idea of regularizing a grant to Oxford was first raised informally by the Board of Education (the precursor to the Department of Education and Science) in November 1918. The suggestion was made at a meeting on postwar public funding to universities held between the chancellor of the Exchequer, the president of the Board of Education, and officials from

Redbrick universities. Redbrick universities had been recipients of modest grants from the Board of Education since the late nineteenth century. Under the wartime leadership of H. A. L. Fisher, himself a product of Winchester and Oxford, the board sought to consolidate its financial relations with the Redbricks and to extend its generosity to Oxbridge. The move was part of Fisher's general policy to undergird educational expansion by substantially increasing the state's provision of resources (Simon 1974: 20).

At Fisher's invitation, Oxford and Cambridge sent representatives to the November meeting. During the discussion on the size of the government's financial commitment to universities, Oxford and Cambridge were encouraged to apply for a recurrent grant (*Parliamentary Papers* 1922: 35). After some discussion, both ancient English universities chose to request public funding. In response the government appointed the Royal Commission chaired by Asquith to establish the legitimacy of Oxford's and Cambridge's applications, and to assess their administrative abilities to effectively utilize the funds. Within three years of its creation, the commission recommended to Parliament that along with the Redbrick universities Oxford and Cambridge should receive regular injections of public funds.

To distribute the public's money, and as an attempt to retain the traditional autonomy of Oxford and Cambridge, the University Grants Committee (UGC) was set up in 1919 as an intermediate body between universities and the state. It was the UGC's task to cope with the new paradox peculiar to all British universities of being academically autonomous yet financially dependent. By acting as a buffer between universities and the state, ensuring the freedom of the former while protecting the latter's generosity from abuse, the UGC was designed to inhibit the paradox from destroying the partnership.

Beginning in 1919, the UGC gave government money to Redbrick universities and Oxbridge without complication. Except for the war years, the central government awarded funds in the form of quinquennial block grants (UGC 1964: 172–79): five-year allocations of capital to help universities plan in advance without having to bother much about accounting for the use of the money. The size of each grant was set through a procedure described by the UGC as "the technique of informal consultation and discussion" (UGC 1948: 78). After its fraternal conversations with universities, the UGC would submit a grand total for all British universities to the Treasury; as the UGC 1964 report stated, "The Committee's recommendations were accepted, almost without question" (UGC 1964: 182). Between the UGC's inception in 1919 and the inflation of the early 1970s, the universities' block grant was reduced only once, in 1923, as part of a package of government expenditure reductions influenced by Sir Eric Geddes (Grieves 1989). Except for that singular moment, the Treasury provided the funds requested by the UGC without complaint or cuts.

The policies and practices of the UGC, viewed along a continuum with university self-sufficiency at one end and centralized funding at the other, have evolved since 1919. The weight shifted one way and then the other; yet a decisive shift toward centralization came in 1945. One might characterize the pre-1945 period as one in which institutional self-reliance was the norm; after 1945 the norm was institutional dependence on government.

The conventions and procedures of the pre-1945 UGC discouraged excessive reliance on government money. In the interwar period, for an institution to receive UGC recognition and become eligible for a government grant, the institution had to be able to cover two-thirds of its operating expenses through independent means (Shinn 1986: 67–70). For example, in 1928–29 British universities, excluding Oxbridge, received only 35.9 percent of their income as parliamentary grants; Oxford's percentage was lower at 30 percent, and Cambridge's was lower still at 25.6 percent (UGC 1929). There was a consensus that government patronage of higher education was legitimate and necessary but that it ought merely to supplement the fiscal resources of universities themselves. The UGC, government, and dons agreed that independent financial means provided the most secure foundation for academic freedom. In the aftermath of the Second World War the terms of consensus were reversed: thereafter the government would provide most of the funds, and universities would raise a mere supplement.

After 1946, British universities began to receive most of their funds for operating expenses from the UGC. Oxford was no exception. By 1952, the central government's grant covered over 60 percent of Oxford University's annual expenditures (*Oxford* 1956: 36; *Oxford* 1958b: 30); so there was much complacency inside Oxford over basic operating finances, as there was within all British universities. Universities could afford to be nonchalant about money because the state was there with an open purse.

The UGC's generous funding of universities' recurrent expenditures extended to support for new institutions of higher education. The New universities begun after World War II received most of their funds from the government through the UGC. From their inception they were dependent on the government. Before one could launch a new university, the UGC would have to give its blessing and pledge of perpetual financial support. For example, when the University of Sussex was given UGC approval in

1958, it received one and a half million pounds for building costs and could anticipate acquiring between 70 and 80 percent of its annual income from government grants (W. G. Stone 1970: 180, 186). Sussex "received its Royal Charter in August 1961," making it an "autonomous university," in theory free to run its own house, in practice all but completely reliant on government patronage (see Fulton 1970: 9).

What brought about this transformation in university funding patterns? The military requirements of the fight against Hitler did not directly cause a reevaluation of UGC conventions; rather, the postwar political and social consequences of the "people's war," as understood by the UGC and Whitehall, were responsible for bringing about the radical alteration (Sanderson 1987: 109). In a balance sheet on the relationship of universities to the government up through 1948, the UGC reflected that "in six years of war . . . no marked change occurred" (UGC 1948b: 11). Yet the effects of the war on British society had consequences for universities that were, the UGC wrote, "revolutionary":

> The war brought immense changes in political and social ideas; the trend towards a planned society and the welfare state was manifest; the Education Act of 1944 was bound to lead to a great increase in the number of students qualified for university education; the growing importance of science and technology, accelerated far beyond expectations by the war, would inevitably lead to increased demand for science graduates and for research activities. (UGC 1964: 183)

Anticipating the contribution universities would make to postwar reconstruction and the creation of a welfare state, the UGC proposed "doubling the annual grant" in 1945, and the Treasury and Parliament concurred. Thus, as the UGC stated, "It was not until 1945 that the dramatic change in scale took place" (1948b: 11). In one year, the relative proportion of government money in universities' budgets went from roughly one-third to over 50 percent.

Reflecting this dramatic shift in the absolute and relative size of the government's contribution to universities, Parliament revised the UGC's terms of reference. No longer merely an advisory body, the UGC in 1946 was charged with the responsibility "to assist, in consultation with the universities and other bodies concerned, the preparation and execution of such plans for the development of the universities as may from time to time be required in order to ensure that they are fully adequate to national needs" (Committee on Higher Education 1963b: para. 23). Since "national needs" were defined by the political climate, the creation of Britain's postwar welfare state greatly encouraged those who sought to enlist universities in reconstruction efforts.

After the war both the government and the public had great hopes for what universities could deliver. Right- and left-wing politicians looked optimistically to university science and technology for contributions to revitalize the economy. And university expansion was demanded by parents and left-wing politicians eager to see social opportunity improved through education. The climate of opinion tended to encourage a belief that postwar Britain could be a "New Jerusalem." British society should be, if not classless, at least affluent and open.

The "New Jerusalem" frame of mind was particularly well captured in a book advocating educational reforms written by an Oxford modernizer, Sir George Pickering.[4] Sir George served on the UGC from 1945 to 1954. He left the UGC and in 1956 became Regius Professor of Medicine at Oxford University and in 1969 master of Pembroke College, Oxford. Reflecting on those postwar dreams, Sir George stated:

> This post-war period was one of great hope and great ambition for all those visionaries and romantics who thought that we in Britain, having learned from the mistakes of the past, might create a world in which the rising generation could achieve, or approach, the ideal society. This was the hope of the governments which gave generously to university expansion, of the people whose taxes provided that money, and of the universities which used it.
> (Pickering 1967: v)

So the UGC set off in 1946 with dreams of a new Britain, and with a new executive role, to disburse twice as much money as in the previous year.

This intoxicating downpour of government money overcame all second thoughts about threats to academic freedom from excessive dependence on public funds. In its 1948 report the UGC declared, "We have seen no alternative to supplying by our grants a very much higher proportion of their total income than is ideally desirable" (1948b: 80). Regrettably, the UGC noted, with this qualitative escalation in government funding there must come "a certain measure of central planning." Yet the UGC felt confident that it could reconcile "the operation of planning with the maintenance of the essential academic freedoms" because, after all, this was Britain. In the UGC's considered opinion, political interference may not be "unknown even in countries in which the democratic principle prevails. [Nevertheless] we do not think we incur the charge of self-complacency if we say that in this country dangers of this kind are remote" (1948b: 81, 82).

Universities did not express any anxiety either about their compromised financial position or about centralized planning. Reversing their traditional posture, university leaders dutifully welcomed the prospect of government intervention. In July 1946, the Committee of Vice-Chancellors issued a statement granting to government the right to insist that universities serve the national interest effectively and efficiently:

> Universities entirely accept the view that the Government has not only the right, but the duty to satisfy itself that every field of study which in the national interests ought to be cultivated in Great Britain is in fact being cultivated in the university system and that the resources which are placed at the disposal of the universities are being used with full regard both to efficiency and to economy. (UGC 1948b: 77–78)

The government's prerogative to make universities accountable to its educational policies was voluntarily affirmed by university heads decades before Margaret Thatcher became prime minister.

Even in retrospect, the UGC and vice-chancellors' satisfaction over the wedding of universities to the state was not completely undeserved. The marriage was, in the main, a happy one. Universities retained their "autonomous" dignity in the outside world while vowing domestic submission to a state that promised to be, and was, magnanimous. The excitement of those early postwar years was even recaptured during the late 1950s and early 1960s expansion of higher education. This cozy relationship between government and universities continued without much disharmony for decades. Rough times did not come until inflation destroyed the quinquennial system in the early 1970s; yet neither partner publicly accused the other of malicious abuse until the 1980s. From 1945 until 1981, when Thatcher's minister for education and science, Sir Keith Joseph, imposed austerity, the arrangement worked amazingly well. That it worked at all, let alone as artfully as it did for more than 35 years, is more puzzling than its breakdown.

AN INTERNATIONAL COMPARISON: THE UNITED KINGDOM AND THE UNITED STATES

In the late 1940s, the British state's patronage of universities was hardly exceptional. Throughout the industrial world vast quantities of public money went into higher education after World War II. But the influx of public money, however comparable in proportionate size, had different consequences for universities in each nation.

For an international framework within which to understand national peculiarities, we can turn to Professor A. H. Halsey's work. Halsey classified national systems of higher education in the industrial world across a continuum with the United States and its academic free market at one end, and the former Soviet Union with its central plan at the other (Halsey 1986a: 3–8; 1987b: 5). Halsey placed the educational systems of Western Europe and Britain in the middle, between the Soviet and American categories. European countries tend to have a preponderance of centralized funding and decentralized administration. In Britain before Thatcher, the central government provided money, which universities individually decided how to spend; universities enjoyed administrative, but not fiscal, autonomy.

If, following Halsey's lead, we take the United States as an example of a higher education pattern most like a competitive free market, we find, remarkably, that America's level of public funding after the war matched Britain's. Research for the Carnegie Commission on Higher Education by Howard R. Bowen showed that between 1949 and 1964 American higher education, public and private combined, received over 50 percent of its income from government (Bowen 1968: 2). The differences between American and British universities were complex and multifarious, yet the percentage of total government subsidy in each system did not contribute to their divergence. Their levels of dependence on government money were nearly identical. As Table 1 shows, in 1946 British universities collectively received 58.3 percent of their income from government; in 1949 American higher education received 58.5 percent of its income from government.

Some chronological information is provided to illustrate the impact of 1945, the decisive year for increases in the size of the British government's contribution. The two American dates are there to demonstrate the proportionate consistency of funding sources throughout the period under review.

Into the early 1960s, the most important financial dissimilarity between the two systems was the concentration of funding from the central government in the British case, and the greater reliance on local funding in the American case. Each system received an equivalent percentage of its funding in public money. Counterintuitively, contributions from private benefactions and endowments provided a greater percentage of income to British than to American higher education.

TABLE I

*Sources of Income for Higher Education Institutions
in the United States and Great Britain, 1935–1964*

(percent)

Source	Great Britain 1935	Great Britain 1946	United States 1949	United States 1964
Endowments and private gifts	17.0	11.5	6.4	7.2
Local and state grants	8.7	5.6	30.2	30.4
Federal or UGC grant	34.3	52.7	28.3	27.5
Fees	32.5	23.2	21.3	24.1
Other	7.5	7.0	13.8	10.7

SOURCES: UGC 1948b: 79; Bowen 1968: 2

NOTE: The year 1945 was the decisive year for increases in the size of the British government's contribution. The two U.S. dates demonstrate the proportionate consistency of funding sources throughout the period under review.

In each national system there was a sizable fiscal tool available for political manipulation. Institutionalized safeguards against zealous politicians intent on imposing partisan agendas existed in each country, yet those safeguards were dissimilar: Americans protected their academic independence by fostering competitive pluralism, the British by protecting their cultural conventions. (The effectiveness of those defenses is not here the issue; sadly, both methods proved impotent against 1950s anticommunist hysteria in the United States and against a radical free-market prime minister in the 1980s in the United Kingdom.)

Academic freedoms in America have drawn some strength from the pluralism of government patrons, the large number of institutions, and the existence of a robust private sector. Public money flowed into institutions of higher education from the fifty state governments, hundreds of local governments, and a federal government that was itself divided into many separate departments. The multiplicity of government funding sources provided some academic maneuvering room. Additional protection from systematic political manipulation came through the considerable number of educational institutions. Even before the 1960s expansion of higher education in both countries, America had 141 universities, 756 liberal arts colleges, and 543 other higher-degree-granting institutions for a grand total of 1,440 (Committee on Higher Education 1963c: 275). In Britain by 1963 there were only 31 institutions on the UGC's grant list (Committee on Higher Education 1963a: 22). America's private sector also made a contribution to academic autonomy. In comparison with some state universities, private colleges and universities were relatively free from government meddling. And the private sector enrolled 50 percent of America's undergraduates up to the 1950s, when its percentage began to erode; nevertheless, by 1963 private institutions still enrolled approximately 36 percent of America's college students (Jencks and Riesman 1969: 272). Between 1960 and 1980 the state sector grew so large that the private sector's relative size declined further, from 36 to 20 percent (Kerr 1991: xv). Nevertheless, America's private universities carried a weight far beyond their numbers. As a 1987 Carnegie Foundation report stated, "Among the top universities, private ones loom large. With much stability over the last four decades, six or seven of the top ten rated universities have been private" (Clark 1987: 19).

Since higher education in Britain had neither America's large number of institutions nor a similar private sector, and most of its funds came from the central government, how did academic autonomy work before Thatcher? What restrained previous governments from imposing their will on universities? The conventional answer, in a word, was "culture." The governing class's culture, including its collective memory of Oxbridge, made the difference.

In summarizing this relationship, the political scientist Maurice Kogan has written: "The culture of government has, until recently [1982], enabled higher education institutions in Britain to make their own way. . . . The model of the Oxbridge College powerfully pervades the consciousness of those . . . in Whitehall itself" (Kogan 1984: 65). An Oxbridge-inspired governmental culture of respect for university autonomy facilitated comfortable relations between the two.

The culture of the British establishment, its values and conventional practices, made direct university accountability unthinkable. Except for Thatcher's administration, governments in the twentieth century were deferential to universities, working through dialogue and consensus, not confrontation and contract (Carswell 1985: 1–15, 107–18). Thatcher's secretary of state for higher education, George Walden, contrasted the pre- and post-Thatcher handling of university financing this way: "Decisions were made in a cozy, traditional, haphazard way. . . . [We formalized the process] and in response we tend to get a predictable reaction: 'Either you give us the money now, and as much as we want, or else you are against culture, you are against civilization'" (Walden interview 1987). Before Thatcher, political elites held universities in such high regard that they assumed the nation's interests were best served by leaving universities alone to be masters in their own house. As Edward Shils explained in an essay contrasting American and British governments' attitudes toward universities:

> The kinds of persons who governed Britain . . . stood in reverence towards Oxford and Cambridge. . . . Both the Treasury and the University Grants Committee taught successive governments that, come what may, the university had to be approached with great self-restraint. . . . The British government . . . [had a] tradition of respect for the universities as adjuncts of the aristocracy, Church, gentry and professional classes. (Shils 1982: 461–62, 483)

The culture of the governing elite, as well as Britain's general political culture, worked together to inhibit or repress the desire to manipulate universities (Rose 1965: 83–129).

Political scientists, sociologists, Treasury department men, and even government ministers agreed that culture played a mediating role in the relation of the state to universities. The collective memories and habits of deference acquired at university certainly contributed to the sensibilities of the power elites, but that was not the whole story. We will look into the matter in greater depth in Chapter 6.

After 1946, with the growth of public financing, Oxford University was effectively nationalized. Unlike members of America's Ivy League, in substance it ceased to be a private corporation and became, like Germany's Heidelberg University, a state institution. But the British ingeniously disguised and tempered this nationalization by keeping a clubbish association between the state and the universities. Between 1946 and the early 1970s, university dons received generous public funding, usually conveyed by Oxbridge alumni in the Treasury and Parliament.

The availability of public grants provided the foundation for Oxford's modernization. There was a dynamic relationship between, on one side, Oxford's reliance on the public treasury and, on the other, the growing social diversity of its undergraduate members and the recruitment of natural scientists to its faculty. How donnish democracy and government grants helped to change Oxford's social composition is the topic of the next chapter.

2.

The Making of Oxford as a Middle-Class Institution

ADMISSIONS CONTROVERSIES

This chapter documents and explores the dynamics of Oxford's social metamorphosis. Before the war, Oxford was close to being an extension of country-house estates much like Evelyn Waugh's Brideshead. It was a small, mostly wealthy and male, privileged world. If you were rich and your father had gone there, the doors would be opened wide. There was even a special category for you, "commoner" status, which could be secured without taking the rigorous entry exam required for a scholarship. The Oxford historian Jose Harris wrote that "virtually anyone who could afford it could get a commoner's place at Oxford in 1939" (Harris 1994: 247). Money and family connections nearly guaranteed one a place (Bowra 1967: 336–37). As one don confirmed from his college's files, "Up to 1939 . . . very few candidates for admission as a commoner were rejected. Names were put down at birth. . . . The [social] field drawn upon was well defined and regular" (Styler 1964: 57). More than two-thirds of the undergraduates were gentleman-commoners, usually public-school boys (Greenstein 1994: 46; University of Oxford 1962b: 30). They could socialize and participate in sports and do as much or as little intellectual work as they liked. And, if they were so privileged as to be completely indifferent to academic credentials, they could at the end of three years take an undemanding "pass" degree or receive no formal credit whatsoever. This undistinguished exit door was taken before World War I by perhaps 40 percent, and as late as the mid-1930s by nearly 25 percent, of all male undergraduates.[1] There were more than enough nonchalant gentlemen around to liven the tone of the place.

Alongside the gentleman-commoners, interwar Oxford had a contingent of "scholars." These were prize holders who constituted as much as 30 percent of the student body. Not only distinct in status from the 70 percent of undergraduates who were "commoners," the ranks of award winners were themselves divided into two social groups. Well over half of the prizes went to public-school old-boys, usually from families with the means to support them at university should they fail the exam path; the remainder of scholarships went to meritocrats who otherwise would have been unable to afford Oxford.[2]

These meritocrats from state-assisted grammar schools rather than the costly and snobbish public schools were middle- to lower-middle-class young men who had only their brains, test results, and hopeful sponsors to sustain them. Meritocratic scholars were about as numerous in interwar Oxford as African Americans, Hispanics, and Asian Americans were in the 1980s at Harvard (*Chronicle of Higher Education* 1991: 297). And although scholars were not as easily identified as racial minorities at Ivy League universities, their presence was visibly signaled by the distinctive academic gowns they wore to lecture or tutorial. Scholars were sometimes "embryo dons," to borrow an expression from Evelyn Waugh (1962: 29),[3] but socially they were the gentleman-commoner's poor relation. They were the serious, hard-working ones in a community that still placed a high value on the appearance of gentlemanly amateurishness.

Scholars and gentlemen often lived side by side, but there were distinctions among Oxford's 22 men's colleges in the space allotted to each group.[4] The more aristocratic foundations, such as Christ Church and New College, had relatively fewer award holders and more commoners than colleges with well-defined meritocratic traditions, such as Balliol, Jesus, and Corpus Christi.[5] (The term "foundation" comes from church history. It refers to an institution established with an endowment of property and wealth sufficient to ensure a perpetual income.) For example, in the entering freshman class in 1935, 76 percent of Christ Church College's new undergraduates were commoners and 24 percent held awards; at New College commoners were 73 percent and prize winners were 27 percent. But the scales start to tip the other way when one looks at Balliol College, where 34 percent held awards and 66 percent were commoners; and, even further, at Jesus College where 47 percent were prize holders and 53 percent were commoners. At Corpus Christi College, the scales weighed heaviest on the scholars' side. Corpus was unique as the only college with slightly more prize winners (51 percent) than commoners (49 percent) (*Oxford Magazine* 1935b: 26–29; *Oxford Magazine* 1935c: 62–66). Of variations in traditions among Oxford colleges, much will be said later, but now we turn to an exemplary case of a college scholar.

A central personality of this book, Oliver Franks was the embodiment of an intellectual's rags-to-riches story. Franks was a merit scholar who matriculated at Queen's College, Oxford, in 1923. The son of a congregational minister, Franks went on to become a philosophy don, the UK ambassador in Washington, a life peer, the head at different times of two Oxford colleges, chair of the university's major reform commission of the 1960s, and many other things.[6] Of his student days, he recalled:

> When I won a scholarship from Queen's in January 1923, there were no local government awards whatever. If you wanted to go into Oxford you had to do it under your own steam. Now my parents hadn't any money, my father was a congregational minister and there were four of us. . . . I got a scholarship of eighty pounds, a Deacon at father's church contributed another eighty, and I won a leaving scholarship at Bristol Grammar School for twenty-five pounds. I went up with a hundred and seventy-five pounds a year, and had to borrow from my father another fifteen pounds to get by at all. I had less than a pound for pocket money per term. (Franks interview 1988)

Of course, not every scholar was barely scraping by, and not all commoners were wealthy, but the poor scholar and the affluent gentleman-commoner were two classic Oxford types of the period.

There was abundant evidence and testimony on Oxford's social divisions before World War II. One authoritative comment came from another Oxford personality who appears frequently in this text, Cecil Maurice Bowra. Throughout his adult life, Bowra was a cognoscente of Oxford's most sophisticated circles. He was homosexual when the orientation, though illegal, held the status of an aesthete cult for his generation (Annan 1990: 98–124). As a classics teacher, Bowra was invited to guest-lecture at Harvard in 1936, an institution not known for its egalitarian social composition. Yet Bowra remarked that Harvard's "undergraduates came from . . . a wider range of social backgrounds than I should have guessed. Nor were the very rich much in evidence . . . the lines of demarcation were rather less obvious than in Oxford" (Bowra 1967: 311). Thirty years later, as a member of Oxford's governing council, in an affidavit to a formal inquiry, Bowra stated that, before 1945, "Oxford in fact imposed a wealth-qualification on its student-members" (Commission of Inquiry 1965b: 16).

Oxford's faculty rarely referred to their junior members as "students," but rather as "undergraduates" in recognition of their elevated and distinct status from other youths in education. Those socially privileged young men lived like nobility in college suites with separate sitting rooms and bedrooms, kept clean by obliging personal servants called scouts (Platt 1986). They ate in halls where real royalty and the likes of Thomas Hobbes and Oscar Wilde had once dined. They read books with tutors whose entire careers consisted of preparing men for final exams.[7]

The lives of many dons centered on Oxford. Overwhelmingly recruited from within, often selected for their own undergraduate exam results and given tenure very early, they were intensely loyal to the community that nourished them.[8] For some, Oxford was family. A significant proportion of Oxford's faculty were bachelors. Most tutorial dons, when not unmarried and living in college, resided less than a mile from their undergraduates' doors (University of Oxford 1966b: 398, para. 575).[9] About half of the paterfamilias of the colleges, the heads, were without spouses (Thomas 1994: 199).[10] The faculty's reading and dining area, called the Senior Common Room, was run by a steward who, Keith Thomas informed us, "was frequently a bachelor, noted neither for learning nor for the love of women" (ibid.: 198). A poignant measure of donnish devotion to Oxford is Holywell Cemetery, an obscure local burial ground dating from the 1850s, where one finds the resting places of "32 Heads of Colleges and over 160 Dons, Fellows and Professors," including the grave of Cecil Maurice Bowra (*Oxford* 1988: 49).

Oxford was a clubbish estate to which easy entry depended not only on wealth but also on gender. Overwhelmingly reserved for men, it was, if not misogynist, at minimum a very masculine society. Women were admitted near the end of the Victorian era, having been excluded for centuries, but their ranks were strictly regulated. In 1927, a quota limited the fraction of women to one-fourth (*Oxford Magazine* 1957: 221); when the restriction was quietly dropped in 1957, it made no difference because females continued to be segregated into five women's colleges or halls. Until the late 1950s the small assembly of women inside the university was excluded from many aspects of Oxford life. Through the late 1920s some lecturers went so far as to bar women from their classes; even in the 1950s, co-ed seminars were rare (Commission of Inquiry 1965b: 140). Whether in or out of their lodgings, female behavior was regulated by austere codes of social conduct and dress. Just as African Americans could not use "whites only" facilities in the pre–civil rights South, neither female dons nor female undergraduates could eat in the men's colleges (Howarth 1994: 346, 348, 356, 358). Even as faculty members, women were kept out of positions of university-wide authority. This world of Oxbridge gender segregation was the reference point for Virginia Woolf's *A Room of One's Own*.

Oxford's masculine environment promoted an antiquarian culture. Until the requirement was waived for entering science undergraduates in 1960, basic proficiency in Latin was mandatory for admission.[11] Along with the gate-keeping function of a Latin education, which mostly kept out those who had not attended expensive private schools, antiquity was the preeminent subject of high status and scholarship. The ancient world was studied at Oxford in the honors school of *literae humaniores*, also known as Greats.[12] As Jose Harris has noted: "There was a distinct hierarchy of academic esteem. . . . At the apex . . . was the faculty of literae humaniores. . . . In 1937 more than two-thirds of all Oxford fellows . . . had originally graduated in Greats" (Harris 1994: 232). Oxford was not just England's premier arts university; it was also its *collegia* of Latin learning. Even the faculty's news weekly, the *Oxford Magazine*, had two Romans on its cover, a warrior and a musician.[13] Dons directed their most brilliant undergraduates toward *literae humaniores* as the best place to receive an education suitable for politics and administration on the world stage. But by the early 1960s everything I have just described had changed.

Within twenty years of the war, Oxford's world of Latin letters and privileged leisure was dismantled. Wealthy gentleman-commoners were virtually driven out and replaced by hard-working scholarly meritocrats. Indeed, the conflict between old money and new talent broke out explicitly over the abolition of the commoner's entrance route into Oxford. Dons favoring meritocratic student selection achieved a partial victory in 1962; it was a formal compromise that they quickly turned into a triumph in practice.

The meritocratization of Oxford had two important effects. Equality of opportunity, especially the possibility for male talent from the lower classes to rise, came one step closer to realization. Oxford's working-class contingent came to constitute a respectable share of the student population. The lower classes were better represented at Oxford than at similar elite universities in France, West Germany, or the United States. And, in correlation with an influx of talent from new quarters, the dominance of privately educated students was broken. The meritocratization of Oxford came with a shift in the school backgrounds of undergraduates, from the private toward the state sector.

Unlike in the 1930s, Oxford in the 1960s was crammed, with twice the number of students.[14] (In this respect Oxford responded somewhat more vigorously to national needs for expansion than its trans-Atlantic cousin, Yale, which during the same period of time grew by two-thirds.)[15] Colleges that earlier could house individual students in multiple rooms had to divide up units and rely more on small "bedsit" accommodations in the city (Thomas 1994: 190–91).[16] Personal scouts, who were always men, were replaced by cleaning ladies who performed very specific chores and who were obliging only in the sense that one might be able to negotiate not to be bothered in the morning after a late night. Women were still accommodated in separate colleges, but most attempts to regulate relations between the sexes had broken down. And female dons had begun to play important roles in the university. (Anything resembling full parity for women inside Oxford did not arrive there, or at Harvard and Yale, until the 1970s.) Much of the prestige and popularity of *literae humaniores* was gone, and bright students began exploring contemporary fields such as modern history; politics, philosophy, and economics (PPE); and the sciences. By 1963, one-third of Oxford's undergraduates were reading science subjects, and 40 percent of the faculty were engaged in scientific research.[17] Oxford's scientists were in the middle of a Nobel Prize–wining streak. If Oxford continued to have the image of a leisurely republic of Latin letters, it was based more on collective memories of the 1930s than on 1960s reality.

How did these changes come about? What were the ideas, who were the actors, and which events were collectively responsible for Oxford's new social and subject mix? In the rest of this chapter we look at controversies over admissions requirements that affected Oxford's social composition, and the next chapter details the shift into the sciences.

THREE SOCIAL PHILOSOPHIES ON EDUCATION AND SOCIAL CLASS

One may ask why social class origins should matter to a university. What line of reasoning would make anyone inside or outside care, one way or another? Inequalities of wealth, power, status, and life chances were not a problem if one had a sort of Calvinist faith in predestination, where stratification expressed God's will. And there was little to worry about if one subscribed to a form of social Darwinism, whether sociobiological or free market. Either way, the best talent was selected by autonomous mechanisms and concentrated in a social-class-specific gene pool. But if one's faith was not in a wrathful God, selfish genes, or invisible hands, then the problem of matching merit with destiny for the individual, and of formulating institutional policies to advance the common good, was on the agenda.

Devising an approach for universities toward the problem of social class required addressing two different components of the system. Those components were the direct "consumers" of the university's pedagogy, the students, and the content of academic culture. For students, the university stood in the middle between their family status and their occupational aspirations. They came wearing the fabric of family and peer group and then refashioned themselves at university in anticipation of the constraints and opportunities of a job market. How a university recruited undergraduates and what it taught them was affected by its students' gender, class origins, and role destinations. In the past, Oxford had met this challenge simply by identifying an essential part of its mission as the selection and education of male undergraduates for positions of social leadership. Oxford's answer had been to draw from the male governing class and to send back to the governing class, a solution that became less acceptable after World War II.

The second element, academic culture, involved both scholarship and science. While the university must conserve and create cultural goods, those objects and ideas are themselves affected by social dilemmas: Was culture for the many or the few? Was culture's most natural ally the state, a free market, or a particular social group? Did culture need protection from commercial and mass pressures? Should it be cloistered behind high walls? How could intellectual institutions sustain cultural excellence and avoid capitulation to political or monetary forces? If there was not a thriving emporium for scholarship, and politicians had philistine agendas, then would universities be right to embrace an association between upper-class family dynasties and high culture as the price of excellence? Was there an indispensable bond between privileged classes and academic culture?

Even if there was an inescapable nexus between culture and class, the problems of appraisal still existed. How should a university determine which cultural elements were worth sustaining? What ought to guide the university's selections from among, to put it crudely, the bookish culture of the middle class, the ephemeral leisure activities of the lower classes, and the fine arts and elegance of the upper class?

During this period those concerns were articulated by actors using ideas derived from three social vocabularies: the social democratic, the organic conservative, and the democratic elitist. Those conceptual languages framed the available intellectual moves and provided an idiom for the debate. As rhetorical resources they informed the identification of problems and the formulation of solutions by actors in and out of Oxford. But one should not exaggerate the power of a discourse over individual actions or institutional outcomes. Ideas matter, but even in a university they are not the only important element. This is not an attempt to submerge the role of personality or the complexity of problems under intellectual scripts. Oxford's faculty did not split neatly into three partisan factions that then consciously fought the issues through to a resolution. Although most individuals were influenced by these social mentalities, and some even had temperaments that resonated well with one of the perspectives, the sketch of the intellectual logic of each position here is intended as a heuristic device. The following is a reconstruction of verbal and written statements and Oxford's institutional practices through the lenses provided by these three styles of social analysis.

One way to anticipate the direction of this narrative is to imagine the three styles of thought as vying for the allegiance of a generation. Many of the adult intellectuals who argued the pros and cons of those views in the 1950s and early 1960s had been student youths in the 1930s and 1940s. Their generation's sensibilities were influenced by historic events such as the depression, the Spanish civil war, and the fight against fascism. While most undergraduates remained as apolitical as ever, the times were propitious for the left. It was an era when the Communist Party at Cambridge University claimed upwards of one out of every eight undergraduates, and faculty leftism was not far behind (Annan 1990: 186–87). The London School of Economics was distinguished by its socialist-leaning professors, such as R. H. Tawney, Harold Laski, and David Glass. And "Oxford too could muster a formidable number of young dons on the left" (ibid.: 178). It would be the 1960s before campus radicalism was again so in vogue.

Although organic conservatism was on the way out, members of that interwar generation, according to Noel Annan, wrestled with the rival demands of social justice and intellectual excellence—the conflicting values identified here with social democracy and democratic elitism. The two impulses, while distinct and contradictory, sometimes fought for dominance within the same person. Borrowing language from Goethe, Annan described their condition in Faustian terms as two souls vying within the same breast:

Like Faust we discovered that *Zwei Seelen wohnen ach! in meiner Brust*. The first soul, the soul of justice, wanted more children to . . . enter higher education, wanted the disparities . . . diminished, . . . This was the soul . . . shocked to see how the scales were weighted against the poor. . . . The other soul, the soul of excellence, wanted the standards of entry to universities raised, . . . This soul dreamed of a society in which merit replaced privilege. (Ibid. 1990: 361)

After the war, some of those twenty-year-old social-democratic students would grow into forty-something democratic-elitist dons. The friction between the two perspectives was difficult to resolve, even within a single person.

Social Democracy

Social democrats were usually not Marxists. They did not advocate class war or the abolition of all private property. British social democrats could draw water from Fabian socialist and Christian socialist wells. What they tended to opt for was what T. H. Marshall, the London School of Economics sociologist, called "the hyphenated society" (Marshall 1981: 131). "Democratic-welfare-capitalism" was the postwar system in which political and economic rights were mixed with social rights, where political democracy and capitalism made the growth of public entitlements possible. The social democrat, whether Fabian or religious, objected on moral as well as cultural grounds to basic inequalities in society. Since the working classes had no means of survival other than selling their labor power for a meager wage, social democrats saw the proletariat's condition as inhumanely constrained. Lacking either the leisure time or the wealth to enjoy the fruits of civilization, the working classes experienced relative deprivation. Working people had their own dignity and ordinary culture but were manipulated by mass-market industries and suffered from a stigma of inferiority transmitted by a middle-class achievement ethic.[18] As long as society was capitalist, most working-class people would not rise into the professional middle or upper classes; to measure one's life by unattainable goals was to take inappropriate individual responsibility for a structural failure.

In the interwar period the clearest voice of social democracy was that of the economic historian R. H. Tawney. In his lectures on equality, given in 1929, the year of the stock market crash, and published in 1931, at the height of the world depression, Tawney argued: "Social well-being . . . implies the existence, not merely of opportunities to ascend, but of a high level of general culture . . . and the diffusion throughout society of a conviction that civilization is not the business of an elite alone, but a common enterprise which is the concern of all" (Tawney 1964: 108). Tawney eschewed the fashionable elitism of artists and intellectuals, such as those associated with Bloomsbury, as well as the evasion of universities that retreated from worldly engagement into the cloister.[19] It was not enough to cultivate citadels of cultural excellence to which one granted access to the talented few. For Tawney, meritocratic elite recruitment took second place to spreading the benefits of culture:

> The doctrine which throws all its emphasis on the importance
> of opening avenues to individual advancement is partial and
> one-sided. It is right in insisting on the necessity of opening a
> free career to aspiring talent; it is wrong in suggesting that oppor-
> tunities to rise, which can, of their very nature, be seized only by
> the few, are a substitute for a general diffusion of the means of
> civilization, which are needed by all men, whether they rise or not.
> (Ibid.: 108–9)

Everyone needed culture, and a truly humane culture needed the participation of all.[20] Gross inequalities of resources deformed culture by turning it into the private property of a particular class. When culture was too exclusive, too elite, it became debased into the ostentatious trappings and tinsel of oversensitive status groups; as such, cultural goods became objects for conspicuous consumption, the external symbols of privilege, and etiquette became just a means of invidious status competition.

In the 1930s and 1940s, while Tawney and others made the social democratic case outside Oxford, the socialist argument inside was advanced by some of the more prominent members of the university. Eminent dons with socialist ideals included the vice-chancellor and master of Balliol, A. D. Lindsay,[21] and Oxford's first professor of social and political theory, G. D. H. Cole.[22] Other notable leftists who influenced Oxford, especially in the 1950s and 1960s, included the Balliol historian with communist beliefs Christopher Hill;[23] R. H. S. Crossman, a socialist don at New College who formed a lifelong friendship with an undergraduate at Jesus College, Harold Wilson, the future Labour prime minister (1964–70 and 1974–76);[24] and Anthony Crosland at Trinity College, the chief theorist for social democracy in the 1950s and 1960s, as well as Wilson's education minister (Crosland 1956; 1962).[25]

Professor Cole was at the center of Oxford's social democratic network in the late 1940s and early 1950s. His basic views on education were published in 1939 as part of his program for a future Labour government. Cole stated:

> The British class system has its roots in economic exploitation; but it is powerfully reinforced by the structure and working of the educational system. This system, as it now stands, provides for a small minority of children an expensive kind of education from private preparatory school, through "public" school, to University, on lines definitely designed to train up a privileged governing class. (Cole 1939: 89)

By contrast, the social democratic policy would be to open up universities as much as possible, with wide access and vigorous outreach, taking university culture beyond its walls. This camp believed that education could promote equality of opportunity. As Tawney said, not everyone could rise, but by broadening the ranks of those with university credentials, education expanded the social range of candidates for professional and technical occupations, which helped reduce the barriers between classes. And by its transmission to students of aesthetic values and attitudes, the university could enhance the standards of ordinary life. Indeed, from the social democratic perspective, the positive influence of universities on their graduates' cultural values and leisure activities was one of the principal reasons why everyone needed higher education.[26] As Cole wrote: "The business of the University is to educate for life, and not merely for the art of earning a 'superior' living. Why should not an artisan or a clerk, if his bent lies that way, have as good a cultural education as anybody else?" (1939: 98). And given the general principle that culture ought to be spread around as widely as possible, the university should offer adult extension classes, especially for workers.

With the circulation of Cole's 1939 work, there began a "revival of the Fabian Society" in Labour Party and Oxford circles (R. H. S. Crossman 1952: xi). This intellectual group, at first preoccupied by the war, was uplifted by the Labour victory in the 1945 general election. With a Labour government running Parliament, Cole worked to refurbish the intellectual resources for social democratic postwar reconstruction. Crossman reported that in 1949, as chairman of the Fabian Society, Cole "persuaded a group of Fabians to spend a week-end" retreat working out an analysis of the postwar challenges. The question they attempted to answer, according to Labour's prime minister, Clement Attlee, was, "Where do we go from here?" (ibid.: xi, vii). Cole's group of twenty intellectuals, no fewer than ten of whom were affiliated with Oxford, published their preliminary answers in 1952 as *New Fabian Essays*. The book included chapters by Crossman on the values of socialists, by Crosland on problems of the transition from capitalism, by Roy Jenkins on Tawney's theme of equality, and by Margaret Cole, whose essay title was "Education and Social Democracy."

Cole's Fabians were not, at the time, the only ones at Oxford to address social democratic concerns; a small but influential group of Christian activists, eager for spiritual revival, also looked into the problems of education and social justice. They spoke eloquently of the dualist struggle identified by Annan, the conflict of two souls torn between equity and excellence. Organized into the Christian Frontier Council, participating dons worked with the Student Christian Movement to publish a pamphlet series on the problems facing universities. The dialogue in Christian circles was sufficient to inspire among them the notion of publishing a book of their reflections. The task of writing it fell to one of their most distinguished members, Sir Walter Moberly, the chairman of the central body for channeling government funds to higher education, the University Grants Committee (UGC) (Moberly 1949: 8–10).

Sir Walter, in addition to being the chair of the UGC for fourteen years, was a philosopher, principal of University College, Oxford, and, like C. M. Bowra, one-time president of the Classical Association. His presidential address to the association in April 1944 offered views on education that foreshadowed those developed under the stimulus of the Christian Frontier Council into a book, *The Crisis in the University* (see Moberly 1945). When it was published by the Student Christian Movement Press in 1949, Sir Walter had become vice-chancellor of Oxford. So here one had an active Christian highly placed to shape and set policy on universities.

A reviewer for the *Oxford Magazine* wrote, "There can be no doubt of the importance of this book. . . . [Its author] has unique credentials" (*Oxford Magazine* 1949: 548). Sir Walter presented a grave judgment on the times: The age was one of spiritual crisis. If Western civilization was not to languish, he said, it needed to revive those core values that communicated a sense of higher purpose. In this campaign the British university could perform a critical role, provided it renewed its own ideals; in particular, the university must revitalize its traditional mission to educate undergraduates for life and not just an occupation.

In this campaign, it was of some importance that Oxford and Cambridge, Sir Walter noted, "have come to embody 'the idea of the university' in the eyes of the nation" (Moberly 1949: 19). The national conception of the university involved several interconnected ideas. A British university of the Oxbridge type ought to provide a rounded education of the whole person that cultivates a love of liberal learning for its own sake, pursued within a family-like collegiate community (ibid.: 24, 33, 37).

In reality, however, the Oxbridge ideal was too exclusively upper class. As Sir Walter put it in a 1950 lecture summarizing his argument: "The chief aim of 'Oxbridge' has been to produce an elite of educated gentlemen. . . . University education, so conceived, must therefore provide for the continuance of such an elite by educating appropriately the younger members of the ruling classes" (Moberly 1950b: 9). After the Second World War, demands for more social democracy made it undesirable for universities to be ruling-class institutions. For the sake of institutional and spiritual renewal, Oxford needed to put its upper-class legacy behind it and embrace democracy, opening its gates to undergraduates from the lower classes. Sir Walter said as early as 1944 that "the motive-force of educational advance to-day is a passionate demand for social justice and equality of opportunity. Any culture must be suspect, whatever its intrinsic excellence, if in the nature of the case it can only be available for the few" (Moberly 1945: 22–23). In *The Crisis in the University*, he appealed to the dons to see that "if a university education is an advantage to the student, it ought to be brought as effectively within the reach of the son of a working man as of the son of a squire" (1949: 20).

The Christian reformist group inside Oxford joined ranks with Oxford's socialists to welcome working-class scholars into the community. At the same time, it fostered an attitude toward upper-class undergraduates that was, if not aloof, at least not obsequious. Dons influenced by either style of thought would be, as Keith Thomas put it, "suspicious of anything which looked like nepotism or social injustice" (Thomas 1994: 193).

Organic Conservatism

A response defending places for students from privileged social backgrounds came immediately from the pen of England's distinguished teacher of conservative philosophy, Michael Oakeshott. In the June 1949 issue of the *Cambridge Journal*, Oakeshott published an extensive rejection of the views expressed by Oxford's vice-chancellor, Sir Walter. Oakeshott's argument championed the notion that universities were not merely institutions for middle- and working-class scholars; they were also for educating the governing class. He wrote: "A university is not a contrivance for making scholars; its ideal is not a world populated solely by scholars. For about 400 years in England the education of the would-be scholar and of the man of the world has been the same, and this tradition belongs to our idea of a university" (see Oakeshott 1989: 100). By "man of the world" Oakeshott clearly referred to the upper crust, to those gentlemen whose family wealth gave them undergraduate leisure now and social power later.

The *Cambridge Journal*, which was edited by Oakeshott, allowed Sir Walter to reply at length in its January 1950 issue. In his response, Sir Walter acknowledged that Oakeshott "rejects scornfully my association of our university tradition with 'privilege' and a 'leisure class'" (Moberly 1950a: 200), but he was unwilling to give any ground on that point. On Oxonians before the war, he wrote: "Through no merit of our own we were members of a privileged minority . . . [in] a class-structure we took for granted" (ibid.: 201). Sir Walter tried to clarify his nuanced position to Oakeshott. Although he was not advocating strict egalitarian measures, such as one might expect from a Marxist, he did seek to address the problem of social justice. It was, he thought, an issue that Oakeshott wanted to ignore. Sir Walter wrote: "In this new situation, no more than Mr. Oakeshott, do I hold that the whole truth lies with the levellers, but I see a difficult moral problem where he apparently sees none" (ibid.: 201). Oakeshott complacently looked past the dilemma.

From Oakeshott's perspective, the viewpoint of organic conservatism, it was one of the essential responsibilities of universities to educate gentlemen of social privilege. This duty could be justified on grounds plowed by Edmund Burke. One could argue in good faith that cultural excellence and wise leadership were qualities one inherited as a whole way of life from one's family.

Although the political and cultural sides of the organic conservative perspective on education were articulated in the late 1940s by Michael Oakeshott and T. S. Eliot (to whom we will shortly turn), in each instance the full weight of the case stood upon foundations laid down by Edmund Burke. Just as the social democrat was indebted to Sidney and Beatrice Webb, and the democratic elitist to John Stuart Mill, so mid-century conservatives shared a language and a set of concerns with Burke. Hence, it was easier to feel the gravity of Oakeshott's and Eliot's views if one were acquainted with Burke.

Burkean conservatism is worth an excursus to prevent its confusion with late-twentieth-century conservatism of the Thatcher type. For a proper synopsis of Burke's convictions we shall turn to an Oxford philosopher, Anthony Quinton. Elevated to the House of Lords by his ally, Margaret Thatcher, Quinton was the college head or, to be precise, president of Trinity College, Oxford, when he gave lectures that proficiently summarized the core notions of British conservative thought (see Quinton 1978).[27]

Burke refrained from presenting conservatism in the form of first principles; he preferred to see it as a deferential and pragmatic temperament. Yet Quinton distilled from the conservative mentality three guiding, if not ideas, then Burkean prejudices: epistemological skepticism, traditionalism, and organicism (ibid.: 16–17).

From Burke's first prejudice, epistemological skepticism, conservatism articulated a philosophy of human imperfection. For conservatives, the most grave and recalcitrant of modern human sins was hubris: people are tempted toward error by an imprudent pride in their own abilities to rationally comprehend the social world without the aid of religious sentiment or conventional prejudice. Yet being mere humans, they cannot rise above defective reasoning and dubious morals except by deferring to the wisdom of collective experience as accumulated and embodied in immemorial customs and institutions. As Burke asserted, though the "individual is foolish . . . the species is wise," and its wisdom was found in tradition and community (Macpherson 1980: 41).

From Burke's rejection of the powers of individual reason to comprehend the character of society, the other two concepts follow. Burke's pessimism about man's rational abilities was counterbalanced by his faith in traditionalism, the second conservative principle identified by Quinton. For Burke, a traditional outlook, a deferential attitude to old arrangements, was the most prudent posture. If wisdom was a quality of collective experience spread over many generations, then it followed that the usefulness of existing institutions could never be rationalized in the sense of being reduced to first principles. Just as there was always more in laws, customs, and institutions than met the eye of critical reason, there was always a case for existing practices that was undiminished by anything that could be said against them by any living generation. So not only revolution but even rationalist social engineering was always folly. Human wisdom spoke most clearly in the voice of tradition.

For tradition to do its work, society could not be either an amoral marketplace or a rational bureaucracy; society needed to be a type of organic community. Hence, Quinton offered organicism as the third principle of Burke's thought. The wisdom of the species could be passed along only insofar as an unbroken, living continuity existed between generations.

For that to work, society was best thought of as a delicate living organism whose institutions and relationships served a higher purpose that could not be disturbed without doing violence to the fragile ecological balance.

What Quinton did not emphasize that was directly relevant to education and social class was Burke's view on inheritance and inequality. Those three notions—skepticism, traditionalism, and organicism—translate into an affirmation of inherited hierarchy. Society, for Burke, was a type of patriarchal extended family with power and property concentrated in the hands of the father. So to Quinton's three principles one must add a fourth, the notion of natural hierarchy.

Burke defended inequality and hierarchy with the rhetoric of family: Though all human beings are involuntary members of their families, it was nonsensical to think of that as anything but good. We receive all of our prerogatives and property "as *an inheritance from our forefathers*" (E. Burke 1968: 117). Burke insisted on the necessity of property, culture, and rights being passed along as an inegalitarian birthright: "The characteristic essence of property . . . is to be *unequal*. . . . The power of perpetuating our property in our families is one of the most valuable and interesting circumstances . . . which tends the most to the perpetuation of society itself" (ibid.: 140). Social inequality was, Burke told us, "the natural order of things" (ibid.: 138). Attempts to tamper with natural inequalities never worked; they all ended badly in force and violence, like the French Revolution.

In sum, property and leadership were passed along as a dynastic legacy. Between and within families there was an unequal distribution not only of material goods but also of experience with the exercise of authority. The wisdom required to lead could not be learned from a book; one could only acquire it through practical experience. An apprenticeship to father figures and the veneration of seniority were the essence of prudent social judgment. A natural respect for family and property led to a reverence for the sons of gentlemen. Oxford owed it to society, to the nation, to provide places to the masculine heirs of the upper classes. Or, as J. Steven Watson, a don at Christ Church, Oxford, expressed it, in selecting undergraduates, Oxford ought to respect both "the need to civilize those who are born to great responsibilities, [and] the desire to be tender to claims of loyal old members" (Watson 1960: 54).

What was true about the claims of social privilege on economic and political administration was even more valid, from the conservative perspective, in the cultural arena. T. S. Eliot wrote a defense of the union between culture and social class in the same year that Sir Walter wrote his. In 1949, Eliot's *Notes Towards the Definition Of Culture* conferred the authority of a Nobel Prize winner, and possibly the most eminent living poet in the English language, upon a conservative vision of culture and education. Even though Eliot was an American, educated at Harvard, after 1914 England became his adopted home. And by the Second World War, Eliot was in British literary circles not just an acceptable Anglophile with talent—he had become the consummate English poet. According to his biographer, Peter Ackroyd, Eliot became after "the death of Yeats in 1939 . . . the representative voice of the nation under threat" (1984: 256).

Eliot could write with an English sensibility enhanced by an intimate knowledge of Oxford. His ties to Oxford throughout this period stretched from his postgraduate-student days at Merton College before World War I to his fortnightly visits to Mansfield College during World War II to assist with the editing of the *Christian News Letter*. The periodical was an outgrowth of the Moot group, a circle of Christian intellectuals concerned with social and political issues who were brought together at a conference in Oxford in 1937 (ibid.: 54, 243, 257). Like Sir Walter's, Eliot's book on culture emerged from Christian discussions on the condition of the times. But unlike Sir Walter, Eliot drew very conservative conclusions from the dialogue.

In his essay Eliot made three basic conservative claims: that culture was derivative of religion, that it must be organically rooted in local conditions, and most important, that it must be particular to a social class. He wrote that the "transmission of culture . . . requires the persistence of social classes" (Eliot 1968: 87).

The class character of culture was inescapable for Eliot. Any culture worthy of the name could only be reproduced through the family. And families could not do culture's work unless they were structured into social classes with high levels of stability:

> If we agree that the primary vehicle for the transmission of culture
> is the family, and if we agree that in a more highly civilised society
> there must be different levels of culture, then it follows that to en-
> sure the transmission of the culture of these different levels there
> must be groups of families persisting, from generation to genera-
> tion, each in the same way of life. (Ibid.: 121–22)

In his view, class stagnation was a good thing for culture's sake. Furthermore, the delicate sensibilities required to truly appreciate and augment the fine arts and letters were nurtured best in families with generations of continuity in economic and cultural wealth.

It was pointless, the conservatives said, for educational institutions to attempt, as Tawney and the social democrats would have it, to spread the benefits of culture around and to promote social mobility. Culture could not be detached from class.[28] If universities tried to bring high culture to those whose family backgrounds did not suit them for it, it would simply fail in the attempt. And insofar as education advanced social mobility by providing passport credentials to the ambitious, it would only undermine the moral and cultural foundations of society. It would erode the under-pinnings of civilization and replace the healthy continuity of social class with an amoral meritocracy. Eliot wrote:

> The ideal of an educational system which would automatically sort out everyone according to his native capacities is unattainable in practice; and if we made it our chief aim, would disorganise society and debase education. It would disorganise society, by substituting for classes, elites of brains, or perhaps only of sharp wits. (1968: 177)

Eliot saw the social democrats' goal of replacing ascription with achieve-ment as a destructive and false utopia. No matter how offensive to con-temporary moral sensibilities, Eliot stood for culture and against social justice.

For organic conservatives, a university was not a vehicle of social jus-tice or vocational training; it was, rather, an activity of learning. As the topic of a civilized conversation set apart from practical affairs, it was not something everyone was interested in, or would benefit from; so the drive to expand university places was at best overly optimistic, at worst self-defeating (see M. Oakeshott 1989: 95–135).

If Eliot and Oakeshott joined Burke in a good-faith defense of class privilege, there was also a bad-faith case to be made for accommodating the upper classes. One could reject the Burkean identification of talent with property and assent to the opposite opinion expressed concisely by renais-sance humanist Michel de Montaigne, "that great fortune and ability are seldom found together" (1958: 61). And yet one could cynically accept that sons of the wealthy would call the shots tomorrow, so it was to the com-mon good to educate and polish them as best one could. Society stood to gain more by being ruled by an enlightened upper class than by a philistine one. Either way, in good or bad faith, universities should see the wisdom in making special allowances for undergraduates from the propertied classes.

Democratic Elitism

Ultimately, it was not the social democratic or the conservative argument that carried the day but the "amoral elite" mentality that Eliot feared. The democratic elitist perspective (labeled "meritocracy" by the sociologist Michael Young in 1958) had two advantages that neither the socialists nor the conservatives could claim.[29] First, it was entirely in harmony with Oxford's scholarly tradition. From the standpoint of intellectual excellence, one could ignore high- or low-class origins as long as academic achievement was served. Second, democratic elitists were swimming with the broad currents responsible for altering the composition of the upper classes in postwar Britain. While the war left British institutions still standing, the nexus between those institutions and the wealthy landed and commercial upper classes was coming apart. The old Tory establishment was near its end. For the upper crust in the 1940s, Eliot's fears that social class was being replaced by elites was fast becoming a reality independent of any educational policies.

Eliot's familiarity with the democratic elitist position came directly from his association with Karl Mannheim, one of its partisans. Mannheim, a Hungarian social theorist teaching in Germany, was forced to emigrate to England in 1933, shortly after the Nazi seizure of power. Mannheim had Jewish parents and a link with communism through Georg Lukacs and the abortive Hungarian Soviet revolution of 1919, and he was a sociologist; so the Nazis dismissed him in April 1933 from a professorship at Frankfurt University.[30] From 1933 until his premature death in 1947, Mannheim taught sociology at the London School of Economics and at the Institute of Education, University of London. Coincidentally, he and Eliot both belonged to the Moot group of Christian intellectuals who regularly converged on Oxford from 1937 to 1943. Eliot read and argued with Mannheim on precisely the issue of culture's relation to social groups. As Eliot acknowledged in the preface to his book on culture, "I recognize a particular debt to the writings of . . . the late Professor Karl Mannheim. . . . My debt to [him] . . . is much greater than appears from the one context in which I discuss his theory" (1968: 83).

When Mannheim fled central Europe for England, he intellectually journeyed away from Germanic idealist philosophy and problems in the sociology of knowledge and toward, as Lewis Coser put it, "a sociology of democratic planning and social reconstruction" (Coser 1977: 447). Mannheim was a theorist and an advocate of the emerging welfare-capitalist regime. He wrote copious essays from 1933 until his death on the challenges posed by modern democracy. In those writings he attempted to address the fundamental problems of the democratic elitist perspective.

Mannheim's contributions to the debate included essays, lectures, and books. His most notable works were the 1933 essay "The Democratization of Culture" (1971: 271–346) and two books, his 1935 *Man and Society in an Age of Reconstruction* and his 1943 work *Diagnosis of Our Time: Wartime Essays of a Sociologist.* Two chapters of *Diagnosis* were originally delivered as lectures in 1941 at conferences in Oxford; but more important, nearly half of the book was composed for and read to the Christian Moot group by Mannheim (Mannheim 1943: 100; Coser 1977: 448).

Mannheim thought democracy, equality of persons, was "our predestined fate, not only in politics, but also in intellectual and cultural life as a whole" (1971: 271). Yet if democracy meant the equal right of everyone to engage in politics and cultural life, it did not mean everyone could or should participate equally. Except in the minds of utopian radicals, political democracy did not require each person to act simultaneously as a citizen legislator and administrator, just as cultural democracy did not compel each to play the piano and sing. Systems of political representation and a division of labor among cultural producers were inevitable. Professional elites were an inescapable aspect of democratic social life. For Mannheim, "in politics as in culture at large: democracy does not imply that there are no elites—it rather implies a certain specific principle of elite formation" (1971: 279).

Aristocratic, bourgeois, and democratic society, according to Mannheim, each had its own type of elite. To engage in a comparative sociology of elites, one needed to pay special attention to three things: how the elite was selected, its social distance from others, and its cultural ideal. In other words, the modes of recruitment, the group's relation to nonmembers, and its collective ethos were Mannheim's essential criteria for analyzing different elite formations.

On enlistment strategies, Mannheim noted that in Western Europe's recent past elites had been chosen "on the basis of *blood, property,* and *achievement*":

> Aristocratic society . . . chose its elites primarily on the blood principle. Bourgeois society gradually introduced . . . the principle of wealth. . . . but it is the important contribution of modern democracy . . . that the achievement principle increasingly tends to become the criterion of social success. (1940: 89)

Elite positions in a democratic society, Mannheim believed, should go to those with talent, brilliance, and energy; elite authority ought to be due to individual merit, rather than family title or wealth. Although the entitlement to membership in the group should be clearly signaled by apprenticeship-like accomplishments, the arms of the guild should be open to those who sought qualification in the craft.

If selection were meritocratic, the group structure of a democratic elite should be inclusionary with a minimum of social distance and mystification between it and the rest of society. All aristocratic elites attempted to create high barriers, what Mannheim referred to as "vertical distance," between themselves and the people. They employed elaborate etiquette, stylized dress, and esoteric languages (as Mannheim noted, European aristocratic intellectuals especially loved Latin) and formal rituals of superordination whenever contact with lower social orders was necessary. In sharp contrast, he said, "Democratization means essentially a reduction of vertical distance" between the elite and others. Democracy endeavored to minimize, if not eliminate, prestige borders (see Mannheim 1971: 310, 311).

Vertical social distance was not primarily a feature of subjective culture, a type of psychological anxiety. It was objectively "created by power," the power embedded in the structure of "hierarchically stratified societies" (Mannheim 1971: 308). Without political coercion to enforce aristocratic stratification, social space could not be divided up into impassable enclosures. Democratic elites did not need, and should work to reduce, all vestigial social distance lingering around any aristocratic remnants.

Since democratic elites lived in an egalitarian, not a hierarchical, social world, they would tend to reject images of themselves as a superior social caste. Mannheim stated:

> Intellectual prowess which sets the elite apart from the uninitiated both in high and low social groups will no longer be treated as the supreme human value. The intellectual will no longer look down upon the manual worker, just as he is not looking up to the aristocrat. He will treat his specialty as being essentially on a par with other skills . . . not superior in . . . essential and qualitative terms, as the realization of a higher human type. (1971: 306)

Intellectuals as members of a democratic elite should eschew priestly pretensions, arcane incantations, and formal privileges that placed them above others.

Last, of Mannheim's three criteria, there was the matter of cultural ideals. What types of values could provide a guiding spirit and an ultimate goal for elite activity? For Mannheim, democratic intellectual elites had cultural ideals that differed from those of both aristocratic and bourgeois elites. Substantively, the democratic ideal was the antithesis of the bourgeois ideal; and, in predictable dialectical fashion, Mannheim saw that antithesis giving rise to a sharp struggle between bourgeois and democratic intellectuals.

The crucial postwar conflict, according to Mannheim, was between a bourgeois ideal of individual cultural perfection and a democratic ideal of social engagement through specialization. The distinctions Mannheim drew between the two concerned both the objects of intellectual inquiry and the social relations of scholars. Bourgeoisie and democrats divided over two questions: knowledge of what? and knowledge for whom? Bourgeois intellectuals pursued knowledge of the humanities for the sake of personal spiritual development; democratic intellectuals sought to specialize in a scientific subject, and from the interconnections of that discipline with other activities to "provide enrichment of life for broader masses" (Mannheim 1971: 332). The bourgeois aspired to become a unique personification of exquisite cultural sensibilities, a vessel of cultural grace. The democrat wanted to be a professional whose vocational competence enabled him to be an instrument of social progress.

The bourgeois cultural ethos was misrepresented by its partisans as an expression of universal and timeless values. It was articulated not as the ideology of a class but as humanism. Its humanistic ideal was "steeped in the values of classical antiquity." Along with dons in prewar Oxford, the bourgeois humanist found "in antiquity . . . those elements which [were] . . . best suited to developing harmonious, integrated and many-sided cultivated personalities." But the claim to cultivated universalism was fraudulent: the bourgeois scholar was not concerned with all things human, just sublimated art and literature. And this fine-arts cultivation was available only to the leisurely few, not to the many who must work for a living. The humanistic dream was "an ideal of ruling groups. . . . We find its devotees among sons of upper-middle class parents as well as among literati" (Mannheim 1971: 330, 331).

In opposition to all of that, the democratic intellectual was a specialist with a particular vocational calling. Whether as chemist or child psychologist, the democrat had a particular role in the social division of labor. He strove to be professional in performing his functions for peers as well as the larger society. While the bourgeois humanist in Mannheim's portrait may be a caricature of an Oxonian in *literae humaniores* before 1939, his democratic intellectual, not surprisingly, looked very much like a modern sociologist or natural scientist, neither of whom was much in abundance in prewar Oxford.

The democratic elitists' program for reforming Oxford included strict meritocratic entry requirements. They sought to dispense with the wearing of medieval gowns, the Latin language requirement, and inegalitarian forms of address and conduct. The tactic democratic elitism favored was not affirmative action for the working class, but higher entry standards for everyone. If gentlemen or sons of proletarians wanted to study at Oxford they could, but they would have to pass standards set by scholars. Finally, democratic elitists were eager to advance the standing of the natural and social sciences.

Before Mannheim, the English intellectual roots of the democratic elitist argument went back to John Stuart Mill and the philosophical radicalism of elements in the Victorian middle classes. Those members of the middle classes who were not entrepreneurs, or who did not, for example, run a family business in northern industrial England, sought to establish professional careers for themselves. They could do so by challenging the gentry's hold over the civil service, law, and other gentlemanly professions. The logic of meritocratic professionalization required a symbiotic relation between educational institutions and occupations (see Larson 1977: 80–103). Schools, colleges, and universities had to teach and administer competitive exams—and exam results had to become the basis for entry to professional occupations. Using those tactics, Victorian middle-class professionals strove to unseat the sons of the landed gentry from their governmental offices and then to replace them with those who attained high academic credentials.

The original goal, however, was more than just middle-class social mobility. Meritocracy was for J. S. Mill the preferred instrument of civilized progress. In Mill's most optimistic schemes, he sought to arrange political and social institutions to privilege the talented few in a competitive clash of ideas and lifestyles. If by multiple votes for intellectuals, proportional representation, female suffrage, and free speech society could institutionalize diversity, then the creative minority would be able to impel the majority forward to ever more perfect forms of civilization. The dangers of ignorance and conformism could be minimized and intellectuals could cultivate the higher faculties in everyone (Mill 1957; 1975). Civilization, understood as an active engagement with democracy and the intellectual arts, would triumph over despotism and vulgar pleasures, Mill thought, just as assuredly as "no intelligent human being would consent to be a fool" (1957: 12). Meritocracy was civilization's avant-garde.

With that digression on the three styles of thought on universities, culture, and class, let us now return to Oxford's history.

ADMISSIONS: THE POSTWAR RECORD, 1945–76

In the following, I use the three styles of social analysis as a scaffolding on which to reconstruct the views of participants in Oxford's admissions controversies. In addition to individuals who held opposing views, there were structural divisions. Within Oxford there were objective lines of cleavage between the colleges and the university, and between arts tutors and science staff. External institutional cleavages existed between types of feeder schools, especially private and state, between professional associations, and between government and university committees such as the UGC and the Committee of Vice-Chancellors and Principals (CVCP). Also contributing to the debate were economic and political pressure groups such as the Trades Union Congress (TUC) and the Labour Party, as well as individuals in and outside Oxford who were familiar with admissions procedures across the Atlantic, especially at Harvard and Yale.

The struggle to modernize Oxford's admissions raised, if it did not resolve, all of the important problems of democratic elites, including questions about social class (the position of gentleman-commoners, passmen, and fourth-class degrees) and the dilemma of Oxford's vertical social distance (entry exams, language requirements, gowns, nomenclature, and regulation of undergraduate social life). In the end, by 1976, explicit class privileges went by the wayside; the gender barrier was broken; and Latin, gowns, and social regulations were dropped. But considerable vertical distance remained, especially in the form of Oxford's separate entry exam. When Oxford ceased to be an upper-class club, it did not make a full transition to democratic elitism.

The 1920s and 1940s

Before 1945–46, Anglo-American "governing-class" universities on both sides of the Atlantic had faced their last admissions controversies in the 1920s. In that decade, the "big three," Harvard, Yale, and Princeton, imposed quotas on Jews, and Oxbridge did the same to women (Oren 1985; Karabel 1984; Farnum 1990a). The American universities' purpose was to avoid replicating in their own upper-class universities what they perceived to be an alarming decline in Columbia University's prestige. Columbia's difficulties were brought on by a wave of East European Jewish immigrants who arrived in New York City between 1880 and 1920 and quickly contributed approximately 40 percent of Columbia's undergraduates (Farnum 1990a: 60). Their enrollment led to phobic defections by upper-class Protestants. The lesson learned, Harvard, Yale, and Princeton circumscribed their Jewish admissions to 15, 10, and 5 percent, respectively (Synnott 1979: 64, 156, 196). Belatedly, Columbia imposed a limit on its number of Jewish students as well in the 1920s, but without effect. Already a weak competitor with the other three for upper-class loyalties, Columbia went from enrolling 25 percent of New York's undergraduates with Social Register parents to 4 percent (Farnum 1990a: 60, table 3.7). Richard Farnum's research showed that "Columbia's loss was HYP's [Harvard, Yale, and Princeton's] gain" (ibid.: 60). In the 1880s, HYP educated 53 percent of the New York Social Register's college youth; by the 1920s, the percentage was up to 84 (ibid.: 61, table 3.8). In England, the threat in the 1920s did not come from immigrants but from women. The decade of women's suffrage brought a slight increase in female numbers at university, which triggered pollution fears in the minds of Oxford and Cambridge dons. So Oxbridge's self-governing male assemblies voted to hold the line against women.

The successful barring of social undesirables left elite colleges free to accept every minimally qualified and wealthy male applicant. This situation did not change until after the next world war. Two American sociologists of education discovered that "although Harvard College began nationwide talent searches around 1937, a student of average ability and moderate wealth or enterprise could easily get in until the rush of veterans began after World War II" (Grant and Riesman 1975: 177). At Yale the timing was very much the same. According to historian George W. Pierson, "in 1946, for the first time, Yale found there were more 'satisfactory' applicants than could be accommodated" (1983: 100). And Sir Maurice Bowra said similarly of Oxford, "Until 1945 suitable entries seldom exceeded the actual places available. The Colleges, with very rare exceptions, took almost anyone who was thought good enough to get some sort of degree and able to pay his way" (Commission of Inquiry 1965b: 17). The admissions controversies after the war were generated by escalating numbers of applications from veterans. Government subsidies from the U.S. Servicemen's Readjustment Act of 1944 (the G.I. Bill) and the United Kingdom's Education (Butler) Act of 1944 brought university life within many more men's reach.

After Parliament passed the Education Act of 1944, there were more publicly funded scholarships for university-bound students. This intervention by the state allowed universities to choose the best candidates from a larger field. In response, without political pressure or institutional coordination, Oxford's colleges in the late 1940s began raising admissions standards. Tutors, many just home from the war, eager to attract the best brains to a particular college or to a new subject, got colleges to offer more scholarships of their own.[31] Even with this simultaneous growth in the number of subsidies and available places, the competition among applicants intensified. The entry of more and more lower-middle-class and working-class meritocrats constituted a social revolution.

Working One's Way Through College

One of the peculiar ways this new lower-middle- and working-class presence registered on the minds of Oxford's senior members was over the matter of summer employment. According to nostalgic tales, during the long vacation it had been customary for Oxford's young gentlemen to do some work from the syllabus, if not actually to go on a reading retreat. When in the summer months of the early 1950s the new breed of student took temporary jobs instead, some university faculty inside and outside Oxford expressed concern and objections.

Between 1952 and 1954, the *Oxford Magazine, Universities Quarterly,* the *Times,* and the Sunday *Observer* published articles, letters, and editorial comments on what they perceived to be a new hazard. But few articulated more trepidation than the editor of the *Oxford Magazine,* who wrote, "'Working one's way through college' is a fine democratic slogan, but it can conceal a most dangerous threat to academic standards"(*Oxford Magazine* 1953b: 127). Indeed, he concurred fully with the judgment submitted in a letter to the *Times* by another Oxford don that there was an "incompatibility between the present scheme of studies in this University and the mortgaging of vacations to non-academic activities" (*Oxford Magazine* 1954a: 141). The whole structure of undergraduate education was in jeopardy, they warned, if men did not devote their summers to books. The syllabus could not be properly covered in three years during Oxford's regular terms, not if undergraduates were to have a full extra-curricular life. Something had to give, and that something should not be intellectual quality. Paradoxically, the fact that the intellectual caliber of the average undergraduate was spiraling up went unrecognized, for the moment. And there was a symmetrical loss of memory on the prewar conflict between academic standards and gentleman-commoners. The vacations-devoted-to-academic-work narrative was a backward-looking conceit based on a few happy experiences;[32] fortunately, the anxieties behind the commentaries failed to take the form of new policy constraints on working students.

Other British universities experienced similarly swelling numbers. Government funds and an altered cultural climate after the war fueled the drive for university enrollment. To meet that demand, the expansion of existing universities and the creation of new ones was on the government's agenda. But until new institutions could relieve some of the pressure, the oversupply of viable candidates drove standards up and made the admissions process everywhere an administrative nightmare. In the midst of the summer employment flap, the universities' consultative council, the CVCP, launched an investigation into the possibility of centralizing admissions.

Toward Rationalizing Admissions

The proposal for a central office to receive and sort all candidates for undergraduate matriculation was first raised in 1949 by a Working Party on University Awards (*Oxford Magazine* 1954b). The concept was advanced again a few years later in conversations between the government and the vice-chancellors. Since public taxes were underwriting student enrollments, the chancellor of the Exchequer asked the CVCP questions about the system's capacity. Unable to provide detailed responses, in 1954 the CVCP authorized an inquiry into admissions under the direction of a sociologist from the London School of Economics, David V. Glass. Glass's effort evolved into a second inquiry in 1955, under the leadership of Dr. R. K. Kelsall, a sociologist from Sheffield University. Kelsall's investigation presented its findings in June 1957.

Those preliminary attempts to gather reliable data on university admissions were important because they led directly to the CVCP's creation of a permanent body to handle that issue, the Universities Central Council on Admissions (UCCA). The UCCA story was inextricably linked with Oxford's attempts to democratize its entry requirements. In the early stage of UCCA, Oxbridge colleges gave the effort considerably less than enthusiastic support, with the result that Oxbridge was left out of the initial scheme. Oxford dragged its feet for six years on UCCA, from 1958 to 1964, before it joined halfheartedly in 1965. Oxford's temporizing and conditional association with the method used by all other British universities for admissions increased the friction and, as Mannheim called it, the vertical distance between it and others.

There were signs that Oxford's colleges complained about research queries from Glass and Kelsall. The editor of the *Oxford Magazine* noted, "Senior Tutors and others have been somewhat perturbed by a request which has been made to the Colleges to provide information on the number of students admitted and rejected by Colleges" (*Oxford Magazine* 1953a: 89). A letter to the magazine by G. E. F. Chilver, a *literae humaniores* don at Queen's College, one of Oxford's more conservative foundations, expressed annoyance with and opposition to the entire effort.[33] According to Chilver, because the sociologists who designed the survey were insensitive and ill-informed about Oxford's procedures, the inquiry would produce only harmful misinformation. With the first part of the study over, Chilver found the exercise a conspicuous nonsense that deserved abandonment:

> It is perhaps true that irritation at the way in which a scheme devised by persons ignorant of Oxford practice was forced upon us without the smallest willingness to accept modifications is now passing. . . . It may also be true that the work involved seems less burdensome than it appeared . . . for so many of the questions are inappropriate that much of the forms can be left blank. But I would certainly have thought that the futility of the proceeding is more obvious now than it appeared six months ago. (Chilver 1954: 348)

Chilver's meaning was clear: Oxford's colleges should withdraw their consent to the inquiry.

Difficult though it may be to measure the strength of opposition within Oxford to national attempts to rationalize admissions, it is indisputable that the CVCP found it easier to proceed without Oxbridge. In the follow-up to Kelsall's research, in January 1956 the CVCP formed an ad hoc committee to formulate ways to restructure admissions throughout the university sector of higher education. Under the chairmanship of Sir Philip Morris, the vice-chancellor of Bristol University, the committee of twelve did not include a single member of Oxford University. Its first report, dated May 1958, specifically excluded Oxbridge from the committee's purview:

> We were agreed that Oxford and Cambridge, where the admissions procedures of the individual colleges often differ so markedly

in kind and timing from those obtaining elsewhere, should be regarded as outside the scope of this particular study; and in consequence no enquiries were addressed to either of those universities
or to the colleges. (CVCP 1958: 2)

The CVCP investigation and discussion went forward without inconvenience to Oxford's colleges. Chilver got his wish.

The Chilver Committee

One year after the CVCP's report, in March 1958, Oxford's Hebdomadal
Council authorized its own inquiry into the university's admission requirements. Under the chairmanship of the very same G. E. F. Chilver, the
committee worked in tandem with a team at Cambridge University. Chilver's group meet sixteen times, took evidence within Oxford as well as
from representatives of secondary education, and issued its report in January 1960.

Chilver's document cited the opinions of the public-school Headmasters' Conference and touched lightly on the just-released Crowther Report, a national probe into the education of teenagers.[34] But Chilver did
not even mention the CVCP's recent attempts to rationalize university admissions. Whether from caution against exasperating peevish personalities or from sheer indifference, the result was a report without a single reference to Kelsall's research or the CVCP's ad hoc committee.

Chilver's document recommended three reforms: one cosmetic, one
minor, and one quite significant. First, the committee proposed to eliminate Oxford's standard entry exam, called Responsions; in the future,
two passes at A level would suffice for admission.[35] In practice, the effects
of this proposal were negligible; previous applicants had bypassed Responsions by substituting for it five O levels, and admissions committees
already insisted on two A levels. The report acknowledged that two A
levels were requisite at all universities in England as well as in Oxford's
colleges:

> This requirement is demanded explicitly by all English universities
> other (so far) than Oxford and Cambridge; and a standard at least
> as high is in practice demanded by the colleges. . . . It seems to us
> unsatisfactory that the University's formal requirements should be
> so much lower not only than those imposed by other universities
> but also than those in fact imposed on candidates for admission to
> the colleges of the University. (University of Oxford 1960: 16)

Lawrence Stone, a history don at Wadham College, Oxford, bluntly dismissed the reform in a letter to the *Oxford Magazine*. The switch of two A levels for Responsions was "mere window-dressing for the purpose of public relations," in Stone's judgment (*Oxford Magazine* 1960a: 174).

If the first proposal was an inconsequential formality, the second was only a mild imposition. In the committee's opinion the writing skills of applicants, even those with A-level passes, were so poor as to warrant a separate "Use of English" paper requirement. This new test should be compulsory: "Its object would be to ensure that all candidates can understand and write English (with correct use of words, grammar, and punctuation) . . . it should be possible for anyone to pass the paper provided only that in all his school work, in whatever subject, attention has been paid to his use of English" (University of Oxford 1960: 8, para. 8). Whether schools were failing in their duties or students were coming from households where grammatically correct English was not spoken the report did not say.

Most controversial, however, was the third proposal, to exempt natural science and math students from studying Latin. The report spoke of Oxford's competitive disadvantage with Redbrick universities in attracting qualified undergraduates in the sciences and proposed a dramatic step to remedy the situation. It stated: "We are satisfied that the recruitment of scientists at Oxford has been hampered by the classical language requirement" (University of Oxford 1960: 10). The committee's evidence appears to have been entirely anecdotal. The lone dissenting member of Chilver's group protested: "I am doubtful whether any reliable and convincing evidence is available to show that the compulsory classical requirement has seriously hampered the recruitment of good scientists at Oxford. If such evidence does exist, it was not shown to or discussed by the committee" (ibid.: 13, para. 20, sec. a). Neither national studies nor Oxford data were cited. Presumably Chilver avoided annoying colleges with surveys like Kelsall's; as the report stated, the committee made "inquiries" but "We have not thought it right to address a systematic questionnaire to colleges" (ibid.: 16, para. 25).

In defense of the recommendation to exempt scientists from Latin, the report referred to two bodies of opinion, school heads and other universities:

> In fact, all three associations of school heads have given the scheme we recommend a wide measure of support. The Headmasters' Conference in particular at its meeting last October voted by a large majority that it would favour this solution. . . . We further note

that the adoption of such a system would bring Oxford requirements into general line with those of the great majority of English
universities. (University of Oxford 1960: 11, paras. 16, 17)

As the above shows, the report's rhetoric included words about bringing
Oxford in line with the standards of other English universities. In discussions and reports on admissions between 1946 and 1976, a convergence
of university policies was often aimed at but never reached.

The release of science and math students from an obligation to study
Latin would be a significant step. It would reduce the vertical social distance between Oxford and middle- or working-class students who specialized in those subjects and could neither see the need for Latin nor afford to attend the Headmasters' Conference schools that cherished the
dead language.

The publication of the report in the university's *Gazette* and its summary by the *Oxford Magazine* led to a flurry of letters for and against
Latin in correspondence columns. A number of Oxford's classicists
dusted off their armor and made ready for battle. Mandatory Greek had
been dropped in the 1920s; now Latin was to go for scientists as well—
how could civilization survive? Helen Gardner and Lord David Cecil led
Latin's Praetorian Guard.

Gardner and Cecil, organic conservatives on this and many other matters, proposed an amendment for Congregation's consideration on, as
they put it, "Latin as an essential requirement for entrance to this University."[36] They would not repeat the arguments made only the previous
June when this issue came up in Congregation; rather, they wanted to
"give Congregation the chance to express its view on this single issue un-
equivocally." For once, the ancient foundations of Oxford's culture would
be voted on as a matter of principle. Why was it so crucial? As Gardner
and Cecil explained: "Latin is both essential for an understanding of our
culture and unrivalled as an instrument for inculcating linguistic
skills. . . . If Oxford is to abandon not only its educational traditions but
also the educational traditions of all Europe, it should do so on a clear
majority decision" (Gardner and Cecil 1960: 172–73). The stand was
taken.

Of the many responses to Gardner and Cecil, none was more biting
than the sardonic column by the editor of the *Oxford Magazine*:

> It seems clear that on this question there is no last ditch. . . . The
> letter of Miss Gardner and Lord David Cecil . . . supplies a ripe
> example of that stupefying exaggeration which seems characteris-

tic of debate on the merits of Latin. What is proposed . . . is that a pass in Latin at "O" level should no longer be required of some (a minority) of those entering the University. What they [Chilver's committee] are represented as advocating is that Oxford should "abandon . . . its educational traditions." . . . Well, no doubt Oxford has an educational tradition; it certainly had, one might think, long enough to acquire one. But can it be suggested (with a straight face) that this tradition *wholly consists* in demanding that all entrants . . . should, . . . at one time *have* known, enough mechanical Latin to scrape through an elementary examination in that subject? . . . In fact what we have here is, surely, a case of what might be called "Classicist's Paranoia," the chief symptom of which is precisely to exaggerate without limit the claim to cultural significance of any shred, however tiny and residual, of classical lore. This is a highly respectable affliction, quite commonly to be found among the best people; all the same, its morbid character should not be overlooked. (*Oxford Magazine* 1960b: 181)

Even without reference to the discouraging effects of the Latin requirement on working-class aspirations toward Oxford, the editor's piece was incisive.

Chilver's report and the Gardner-Cecil amendment went to a vote in Congregation's assembly of February 23, 1960. The university's parliament sat in the Sheldonian Theatre, Christopher Wren's first architectural creation. It was designed, as if for the occasion, to be a replica of a Roman theater; and that day, approximately 400 faculty strode in to participate. For the Hebdomadal Council, Chilver introduced the report, and floor speeches pro and con were made. Whether scientists needed Latin, and what the educational effects would be if they did not have it, was the focus of debate. Reasonable cases were presented for both sides, but the cause of those who favored mandatory Latin probably was not helped by the truculent statement made by G. R. Driver, professor of Semitic philology. The *Oxford Magazine*'s account attributed to him the comment, "The scientists who had to mug up Latin [just to gain entry] . . . should be left to sink in their own asininity" (*Oxford Magazine* 1960c: 210). The amendment moved by the Latin conservatives went down to defeat, 111 to 290. Then all of Chilver's proposals were approved without additional opposition.

The significance of the delegitimation of Latin was tremendous. In the judgment of Jose Harris, a history don at St. Catherine's College, Oxford,

"It was a decision widely and to some extent correctly interpreted by the popular press as a major symbolic turning point in the intellectual history of Oxford" (J. Harris 1994: 225). Although Chilver was unfriendly to Kelsall's work, and he neglected to address the issues raised by the CVCP's ad hoc committee, the abridgment of Latin was a positive move toward democratic elitism. It reduced Oxford's vertical distance from lower-middle and working-class science students and from other universities. Other than Oxford's separate entry exam and the resources required to prepare for it, Latin was the most exclusionary barrier for students from families without university-educated parents. Chilver, ancient history don at Queen's, more in touch with the Headmasters' Conference than with research sociologists, nevertheless led the Hebdomadal Council's committee responsible for opening the door further to meritocracy. To Chilver's credit, he advanced a policy more in harmony with attracting high-caliber science undergraduates than with preserving a particular measure of cultural competence—a measure, moreover, with the markings of class privilege on it.

The Chancellor's Election

Within a fortnight of Congregation's vote to scrap Latin for scientists, Oxford's version of an alumni association, Convocation, held its election to select a new chancellor. While the vice-chancellor was Oxford's actual administrative leader, a type of institutional prime minister, the chancellor was the titular king of the university. His normal role was purely decorative and ceremonial; and his election was largely viewed by press and electorate as politically symbolic. This time the contest was between a Balliol graduate, the Right Honorable Harold Macmillan, the Tory prime minister in office, and the Queen's College scholarship graduate Sir Oliver Franks, former ambassador to Washington and then chairman of Lloyds Bank.

In and out of town most of his adult life, Franks commuted to Lloyds in London from his home in Oxford. He was, despite the banker's office, friendly to the Labour Party. Impressed by his reputation as an able administrator, nineteen college heads nominated Franks for the vice-chancellorship (*Oxford Magazine* 1960a: 181). Grasping an opportunity, Oxford's conservatives pulled off a reversal; they "presented . . . Macmillan as the anti-establishment candidate" (Brian Harrison 1994: 394). Whether or not those licking their wounds from the Latin battle joined forces with political conservatives, the margin went against the candidate who might be interventionist. The vote was close: 1,976 to 1,697. Franks lost by only 279.

In the week of Macmillan's election, the discussion of Chilver's report was still alive in the correspondence columns of the faculty's magazine. In his last contribution to the controversy, Lawrence Stone reiterated that Chilver's committee had not adequately addressed the substantial problems with sixth-form curriculum and university entry requirements. Toward the organization of the requisite campaign, Stone saw "no reason why Oxford and Cambridge should not give a lead" (Stone 1960b: 228). But Oxbridge did not lead—the ancient universities followed the CVCP's initiative.

Creation of UCCA

While the CVCP was attempting to create a national admissions system, the government was significantly stepping up its subsidies for undergraduates. In 1958, the Conservative government empowered a committee under Sir Colin Anderson to look into the funding of university students. The committee's report, "Grants to Students" (Anderson Committee 1960), was submitted to Parliament in 1960, and in 1962 Parliament acted to require all local education authorities to provide funds to everyone with two A levels and an offer from a university to study toward a first degree. As part of its social compact, the Conservative government extended the welfare state to university students; a fiscal entitlement for all undergraduates became the law of the realm. The spending did not cost the Conservatives any middle-class support. The economy was still expanding and Britain's baby-boom generation, the result of a postwar "bulge" in the birth rate, was just approaching the age for university. The 1960s would bring a significant increase in applicants to all universities.

In harmony with the government's initiative to use taxes to pay undergraduate fees, the CVCP published three reports on admissions that urged the creation of a centralized admissions council (Committee of Vice-Chancellors and Principals 1958; 1960; 1961). The CVCP formed first an ad hoc committee, then a working party, and finally the Universities Central Council on Admissions to move the process forward. They wanted to establish a rationalized system involving universities in England and Wales; it would take until 1964 for everyone to band together, and even then Oxbridge would remain half out. It was not a happy affair. The conflicts that arose over this process exacerbated the tensions between Oxbridge and Redbrick. And Oxbridge's failure to join the effort at the start became one of the examples widely cited to illustrate its public irresponsibility. The affair is worth reconstructing to record who was responsible for what and when. Both sides, the CVCP and Oxbridge, made mistakes that cast the latter in an unflattering light.

Even though Oxford and Cambridge had representatives on the CVCP, from the beginning Oxbridge was placed on the margin of its efforts on admissions. When the ad hoc committee was set up, Oxford was not on it. The research that went into the committee's first and second reports (May 1958 and June 1960) did not include Oxbridge. And each draft version of the new application form explicitly excluded Oxbridge. A prospective student would be able to fill out one application for up to three different Redbrick and New universities, but he would be instructed to apply separately to individual Oxbridge colleges, if possible two years in advance.

After the second report a working party was formed, which included Dr. Kelsall and five others, on which Oxford had only observer status. The ad hoc committee's third report (January 1961) advised the CVCP to establish a new organization, which became the Universities Central Council on Admissions, or UCCA.

UCCA's chairman was J. S. Fulton, vice-chancellor of Sussex, one of the New or Plateglass universities. Every university in the United Kingdom was represented on UCCA, including Oxford and Cambridge. Of the 68 voting members on its council, Oxbridge contributed ten (among them Dr. Chilver).

Those reports set the context for a meeting called by the CVCP in March 1961, to which all universities were invited. Oxford sent eight representatives to the conference. Three proposals were put forward, none approved. Unwilling to be frustrated by the initial absence of a collective resolution, the CVCP continued to work toward a consensus on the principle of establishing a national procedure for handling admissions. Each university was invited to formulate proposals for structuring the new system. Oxford's colleges agreed to participate in the discussion, and they were assured by the CVCP that "each college at Oxford and Cambridge would be regarded as a separate 'university institution' for this purpose"(*Oxford University Gazette* 1961: 124). At this stage the door seemed to be open for Oxbridge's participation in whatever arrangement emerged.

At the November 1961 meeting, UCCA proposed placing a centralized clearinghouse under its own administration. All English and Welsh universities would be included except Oxford and Cambridge. UCCA resolved, with Oxford's consent, to continue keeping Oxbridge at a distance. It appealed to Oxbridge to finish its selection earlier than was customary. If Oxbridge would schedule its entry exams and interviews in the winter and not extend them past January, all other universities would delay selecting their students until Oxbridge had done so.

Oxbridge was given a privileged and unique status outside UCCA (Universities Central Council on Admissions [hereafter UCCA] 1961b: 4–5). The chairman of UCCA explained that "the three months, November, December, and January, would provide 'a clear run for Oxford and Cambridge'" (University of Oxford 1962a: 10, para. 14).[37] Redbrick and New universities should wait to make their first offers to prospective students through UCCA in February and March, and second- or third-choice universities would have April and May to work with. UCCA would regulate the process by controlling the flow of information between candidates and non-Oxbridge universities. Universities would inform the central office of their decisions on applicants, which UCCA would then pass along on schedule. If a non-Oxbridge university tried to jump the queue, it would be warned that it could not oblige any student awaiting an Oxbridge letter to reply before January 31 (UCCA 1961a: 4). This arrangement could be viewed as a necessary compromise, one that acknowledged the political and administrative difficulties of coordinating Oxbridge colleges, which were private and independent institutions, with Redbrick and New universities. But the deal formally entitled Oxbridge to an aristocratic right of first choice which, once implemented, was widely resented.

After the November 1961 meeting, UCCA issued a confidential report spelling out the terms of the new system and the extraordinary arrangements with Oxbridge:

> In view of their special position, discussions are continuing about the part that the Oxford and Cambridge colleges would play in any new scheme. The Central Council cannot anticipate the outcome of these discussions; but it reiterates the opinion . . . that the immediate practical contribution . . . would be: . . . [for Oxbridge] to arrange their own admissions procedures so that their selections are completed by 31 January. (UCCA 1961a: 4–5)

UCCA and Oxbridge would negotiate, and in the meanwhile the two would synchronize but keep separate their own admissions processes.

Hardie's Working Party

The UCCA enticement for Oxford to complete its admissions by January 31 prompted the university's vice-chancellor to canvass all of the colleges for their reactions to the proposition (University of Oxford 1962a: 5). In response, the colleges agreed to form a Working Party, with eight members, including the ever-present Chilver, to be chaired by the vice-chancellor's choice, W. F. R. Hardie, president of Corpus Christi College.

Considering the difficulties involved, the Hardie Working Party moved quickly. Launched in February 1962, its inquiries and 26 sessions, including one with the Executive Committee of UCCA, took less then ten months to achieve a consensus, issue a report, win over reluctant dons, and organize a meeting of the colleges to ratify its proposals on November 15.

The Hardie report charted the first collective rationalization of Oxford's colleges' undergraduate admissions (University of Oxford 1962b). No longer would a male candidate for matriculation apply to one or more of 23 colleges, each with its own method for awarding scholarships and places. From then on a standardized entrance examination would "replace the present heterogeneous mass of scholarship and entrance examinations" (Thomas 1962: 1). With Oxford's own central clearing office and a uniform entry exam, one that "combined entrance and scholarship examinations" (University of Oxford 1962b: 31), as well as a schedule to meet UCCA's request, the Hardie proposals made it easier for state-school students, who were frequently working class, to apply. While the arrangement was not inconsistent with the goal of expanding the number of lower-class undergraduates, it was a clear triumph for democratic elitism. Meritocrats now had the machinery to control the entry gates to Oxford.

It was essential to the Hardie Working Party's success that it was a committee of Oxford's 23 men's colleges. Chilver's group was a creation of Council, a university committee. But if one were to effect substantial reform, one had to get beneath the university's structure into the organizational stratum of the colleges, where the real control of admissions rested.

On the surface, Hardie was about modernizing Oxford's admissions in time for UCCA to process other universities' applicants. Yet another and for Oxford more fundamental issue was on the table: the dilemma of dual entryways and status for undergraduates—in other words, the unresolved differences between scholars and commoners. The problem was acknowledged in the Hardie report, only to be downplayed by Hardie afterward; but it was the crucial contest, equivalent to the new policy on Latin, for moving admissions toward meritocracy.

Throughout the 1950s and early 1960s, the relative standing of commoners and scholars was a topic of discussion. Demographic changes,

government grants, and academics with egalitarian or meritocratic sentiments all eroded the privileges of wealth and family connections for men
at Oxford.

For centuries the university operated a dual system of admissions to accommodate both social privilege and brain power. Aristocrats and wealthy
boys were admitted in the category of fee-paying gentleman-commoner,
and the intellectual meritocrat was subsidized as a "college scholar." One
could argue that it was an equitable arrangement; wealth and brains could
trade on each other's advantages to their, and the university's, mutual benefit. The weight of numbers was solidly on the gentleman-commoners'
side; they were the many, while scholars were the few.

If meritocracy's first wave came in John Stuart Mill's day, its second arrived after World War II. After the war, there was a renewed struggle between old families and "talented new-arrivals," gifted individuals who
made their way up through institutions rather than class networks, to
shift the basis of legitimate authority from social to professional grounds.
As the social historian Francois Bedarida put it:

> Two concepts of the elite were competing, and one was gaining on
> the other. On the one side, the old aristocratic ideal held good, the
> ideal of the amateur, born with a gift for leadership, the "effortless
> superiority" of the Oxford man. On the other side, the modern
> ideal was ascendant: the competent professional, hard-working
> and efficient, whose worth was underwritten by merit. (1979: 283)

Bedarida was right about the contest, wrong about Oxford. He over-
identified Oxford with the social aristocratic ideal. Since at least the 1930s,
the Oxford community had been engaged in a debate within the British
"establishment" over which principle of leadership was more desirable,
social aristocracy or intellectual meritocracy. During this period, not just
outside but inside Oxford as well, the principle of meritocracy was becoming dominant.

In Oxford the lines of contention were drawn over admissions and
awards. Those who sought to advance meritocracy worked to increase the
number of scholars in college, while the defenders of aristocracy endeavored to reserve as much space as possible for gentleman-commoners.

The conservative guardians of class privilege resisted what they perceived to be a flood of state-assisted students who could offer college life
little other than ambition and amoral intellect. Anxieties had been expressed about this for a number of years. A particularly fine example was
the article "Numbers and Qualifications" by the master of Pembroke

College, Oxford, R. B. McCallum. With humble, nonstrident prose, Mc-Callum used the conversational language of organic conservatism to rouse the common sense of dons against allowing too many scholars into the colleges. Eschewing abstract reasoning about the problem, McCallum proceeded "to consider the matter comparatively and pragmatically." He reminded his readers that before the last war:

> University education was a commodity to be purchased by those who had the means to pay, subject to the qualification that endowed scholarships assisted in part many who could not otherwise afford it. The change which has turned the former trickle of state-assisted students into the present flood was a political decision. . . . The question that faces us is how we should select from the great number of applicants. (McCallum 1957: 38)

The existing practice, McCallum feared, was tilted toward the category of scholar because of the role played by the entry exams:

> Most colleges offer a double channel of admission, by open scholarship examination and by commoner entrance examination. It is possible to dispense with the commoner entrance altogether, and some colleges, I believe, have come near to doing this. In my own college . . . we could have filled the college three times over from our scholarship entry. Most colleges are probably in a similar position. . . . [Colleges could] take only those who win scholarships. . . . This has its advocates mostly amongst some of the younger dons. . . . Yet, on the whole, we shrink from so severe a rule. (Ibid.)

McCallum thought dons put too much trust in their methods of examination. It was possible that exams were a crude indicator of classroom promise, but they certainly were inaccurate measures of "the many qualities needed for success in public, professional and business life." Just as Burke would, McCallum implored his fellow dons to maintain "a rational suspicion of over-intellectualisation" (1957: 40). An excess of brains could do a college harm.

If scholars were not enough, then who else belonged in college? Mc-Callum eloquently reviewed the alternative categories of desirable undergraduates, leaving little doubt as to his preferences. One of them is worth repeating in full:

> It is said by many that there are young men and women who by their heredity and upbringing in more leisured and cultivated

homes have some special contribution to make and some particular capacity to profit by the education which we offer. Some will dismiss this with the plain word "snobbery." Yet even in the sixth decade of the twentieth century there are some who are ready to withstand this most terrible imputation. (Ibid.)

In other words, Oxford should not forget its unique relation to the upper class. Toward that end, it should retain a proper mix of class, culture, and fresh talent.

McCallum's message was that Oxford's colleges would be best off if they would house four types of undergraduate. The scholarship boy's intellect should be counterbalanced by three groups with different qualities: the upper class, who bring a touch of country-house civility; the alumni, who faithfully finance the old foundation; and "natural leaders," tomorrow's managerial and political elite, the governing class's heirs apparent, whose self-confidence exudes social authority. As the master of Pembroke, McCallum was positioned to ensure the desired equilibrium.

The basic steps in McCallum's argument were retaken by the admissions tutor for Christ Church, Oxford, J. Steven Watson. In the December 1960 issue of Oxford's alumni publication Watson reiterated the conservative case for balanced admissions (Watson 1960: 45–56). The editor of the *Oxford Magazine*, Keith Thomas, a history don at St. John's, was morally outraged by Watson's "reaffirmation of so blandly patrician an attitude," which was all the more perverse coming from someone otherwise known for liberal views (Thomas 1961: 143). But it was Hardie who wrote an article examining in detail the fallacies in Watson's argument (Hardie 1961: 240–43).

By the time Hardie's Working Party was formed, the balance between entry categories had shifted in the direction opposite from Watson's and McCallum's preferences. The hegemony of scholars in college was not total, yet they were on the ascent. On the topic, Lawrence Stone wrote in 1961: "For years middle-aged radicals like myself have struggled to dissuade Colleges from using school and family background as criteria for admission, for commoners as well as for scholars. Gradually this principle has begun to triumph, and is now generally accepted by most, though not all, Colleges" (1961: 28). Given the relative strengths of scholars, meritocrats could be magnanimous to conservative arguments on behalf of commoners. So, just as the Chilver committee found itself working to abolish Responsions after most colleges had in practice done so, Hardie's Working Party could afford to position itself above the conflict between commoners and scholars.

Conservative defenders of the rights of individual colleges to reserve places for gentleman-commoners could feel particularly reassured by certain passages in the report. For example:

> It was known that some colleges now wished to take all, or very nearly all, their commoners on scholarship examinations. . . . Other colleges remained convinced . . . that their exclusive use would shut out many candidates who have much to gain . . . and much to give to a college. . . . We have reflected on the arguments for these conflicting opinions. But we have not regarded it as our business to adjudicate between them. (University of Oxford 1962a: 7, para. 7)

To the rhetoric of compromise Hardie personally remained true. When Ralph Davis, the admissions tutor for Merton College, one of Oxford's most reform-minded colleges, hammered on this sore spot, Hardie took the time to deflect the blow.

Ralph Davis's article on the report identified the split over commoners and scholars as one of the "two main questions at issue." The other issue was UCCA's request that Oxford complete its admissions exams before January 31. Davis wrote: "The first . . . question of whether or not there should be different methods of admission for scholars and commoners, . . . is a question of basic principle on which we are so deeply divided that we have no option but to 'live and let live'"(Davis 1962: 37). Davis thought an Oxford divided on a matter of principle would not be well served by Hardie's proposals. The new single-route exam scheme recommended by the report would heighten tensions between the camps, and it would not make coordination with UCCA easy. Davis suggested as an alternative the use of A levels to evaluate candidates, the same as everyone else in UCCA, leaving it up to each college whether a separate scholars' exam would be offered in the winter.

Hardie's response to Davis both played down the schism between dons over commoners and scholars and defended the "flexibility" of the uniform examination scheme recommended in the report. Hardie wrote, "Mr. Davis . . . asks us to join him in a 'frank recognition' that we are 'deeply divided' on a 'question of basic principle.' This is the question whether, because 'we have two sorts of undergraduates,' there should be two different methods of admission." This was, for Hardie, a simplification; Oxford had many types of undergraduate. And there were "many opinions, not two, on the relative value of different criteria in the filling of places in a college." Moving away from the topic, Hardie rejected A levels as adequate substitutes for Oxford's own entry exam. There was, Hardie reminded Davis, a difference between necessary and sufficient conditions for entry: A levels were the minimum necessary, but they were insufficient for final selection. The majority of dons in Oxford were unwilling to work with only A levels. "Mr. Davis cannot . . . deny the plain fact . . . that most tutors would say that G.C.E. [A level] marks are an insufficient basis"; consequently, Davis's alternatives contained false premises and could not win a majority vote (see Hardie 1962: 54, 55).

Yet the Working Party's report told a somewhat different story. The schism over commoners and scholars was documented in the evidence gathered from the colleges and schools. The colleges clustered into three camps, meritocrats, conservatives, and compromisers. The report stated:

> Eight colleges would like to use scholarship examinations only. . . .
> Five colleges are declared believers in separate examinations for
> the selection of some, but not all, commoners. A third group of
> five colleges occupies an uncertain or intermediate position, either
> because of internal divisions of opinion or because they wish to
> except from a general use of scholarship examinations the recruit-
> ment of commoners planning to read certain subjects. (University
> of Oxford 1962a: 17–18, para. 29)

Although individual colleges were not named, likely candidates for those favoring a single meritocratic standard would be Balliol, Corpus Christi, Merton, New College, St. Catherine's, University, and Wadham; the five holdouts for separate paths probably included Brasenose, Christ Church, Keble, and Pembroke. On this question the line between progressive and conservative colleges cut across old and new, richer and poorer foundations.

Hardie's inquiries went outside Oxford to include secondary schools. Letters were exchanged and a meeting was held to elicit the views of the Headmasters' Conference (HMC), the public schools' exclusive organization, and the Incorporated Association of Headmasters (IAHM), whose ranks were filled by different types of grammar schools. Their opinions on Oxford's separate entry standards for commoners and scholars were also divided.

The report diplomatically noted and summarized the schools' conflicting views without lengthy elaboration or explicit classification of who stood where. But the line between public and grammar school was obvious:

> On the question whether there should be entrance examinations
> for commoners as well as scholarship examinations their replies re-
> ported, or implied, a range of opinions similar to the range of opin-

> ions in colleges. Mr. Smith reported agreement that commoners
> should not be selected exclusively on scholarship examinations, . . .
> Mr. Lunt reported a consensus . . . that . . . a boy . . . is probably
> not up to the standard of an Honour School unless he can make
> "a reasonable showing" on scholarship papers. (Ibid.: 21)

In other words, Smith argued for a separate method of entry for commoners, while Lunt saw the academic merits of exposing everyone to a
test of scholarship quality.

At the time, C. P. C. Smith was chairman of the HMC and master of
Haileybury, and the Reverend R. G. Lunt was president of IAHM and
chief master of King Edward's School, Birmingham. Haileybury and King
Edward's were not especially extreme cases; neither was the most or least
privileged of public or grammar schools. Yet the HMC with its aristocratic foundations, such as Eton, and the IAHM with its middle- to lower-
class northern grammars, such as Manchester, represented different social
groups and organizational cultures. On the Oxford divide in the early
1960s, public schools retained more affinities for gentleman-commoners,
while grammar schools could more earnestly embrace democratic elitism.

Where most types of schools could unite was in opposition to two in-
terrelated proposals. Nearly all headmasters did not want their boys to
have only one opportunity to gain entry; a majority, not including the
Reverend Lunt, did not want commoners and scholars sitting down to the
same exam. Hardie's scheme would channel everyone, would-be scholars
and commoners, through the same initial hurdle. If the student stumbled
and fell, he would be eliminated from the second stage of the exam, which
offered the possibility of a scholarship. Headmasters objected to this as
unfair.

The Working Party knew about these disagreements from its own investigations (ibid.: 22–23, para. 39) as well as from the results of a survey
by P. C. Bayley, the admissions tutor of University College. Bayley had
asked the headmasters of his college's feeder schools their preference
among one of three options: selection by scholarship exam; selection by a
joint scholars' and commoners' exam, the policy Hardie's report advocated; or selection of commoners by a separate exam. Of the 53 headmasters who replied, 4 favored a single scholarship test, 20 preferred the
joint arrangement, and 29 wanted to retain status quo, with a separate
commoners' doorway (see Bayley 1962: 336).

The Working Party also noted the position taken by the government.
In 1959, the minister of education endorsed the Crowther Report, which

urged Oxford to retain a mix of selection methods but to reduce the number of exams commoners had to take. Consequently, the state was associated with an evaluation that did not favor a uniform entry system.

On the Crowther report, Hardie's Working Party confessed: "We should feel uneasy if there were any major conflict between the conclusions and recommendations of [Crowther] . . . and our own proposals. . . . If 'a mixture of different methods' were amended to 'a mixture of different criteria', none of us would dissent from this [Crowther's] conclusion" (University of Oxford 1962a: 25). But how long would different criteria carry weight if all applicants took a single exam? How much space would tutors set aside for less able commoners when test results showed there to be so many well qualified to be scholars?

To conservative critics of the plan who thought "too much weight would be given to the intellectual powers which candidates can . . . display in examinations," the report's only reassurance was college autonomy (ibid.: 45). The system left the balance between scholars and commoners up to each foundation. "The decision as to the proportion of commoners to be admitted . . . would lie entirely in the hands of the individual college" (ibid.: 47). As long as conservative college heads or admissions tutors wanted commoners, they could get them.

According to the report, to play fair, no college was to subvert the plan by arranging to admit commoners who had not passed the first hurdle. This would be prevented by the moral solidarity of the other colleges, especially the way the scheme would group colleges together and monitor their relative performance, and the academic traditions valued by most tutors. The report clearly understood that "the majority opinion is at present in favour of the use of scholarship-standard examinations in the selection of most commoners" (ibid.: 30). Peer group disparagement would pressure a college with a disproportionate share of commoners, but there was little to work against the opposite.

Norrington Table

The Working Party's scheme was officially adopted by all of Oxford's colleges in November 1962. It established the machinery for meritocracy to become the regulative principle for admissions. Another proposal was made that same month to formalize a measure of the meritocratic competition between colleges through the "Norrington Table" (see Norrington 1962). The table provided an annual ranking of colleges according to their undergraduates' final exam grades. At the end of three years, undergraduates took intensive and lengthy exams that were graded by special university-wide committees. The marks a student received determined whether he or she graduated with a first-class, second-class, third-class, fourth-class (until its elimination in 1967), or pass degree. Colleges with the best exam results placed highest on the Norrington Table. Friendly rivalries between colleges over the exams were very old, and the faculty magazine in the past reported what it could about degree results. But this table gave the competition a reliable accounting system. Published yearly, the table provided material for endless Senior Common Room discussions on the relative merits of college tutors. In a community animated by academic values and the tradition of college autonomy, the table became an obsession. In this context, it focused even more attention on the scholarly caliber of the students and the teaching abilities of the tutors.

UCCA and Franks

If Hardie's reforms created the machinery for meritocratic admissions, and Norrington's Table helped direct attention toward degree results, the next stage, which involved UCCA and the Franks Commission, raised questions about Oxford's methods of judging academic merit. Did Oxford's exams, by virtue of being different from the requirements of other universities and the curriculum taught in most state schools, have social-class effects on its student body? Was it enough if the principle of achievement won against the principles of property and blood? Or could particular ways of evaluating achievement reintroduce unfair privileges? The social democratic subtext of the controversies over admissions became explicit with the Franks debate.

A history of the Franks Commission of Inquiry, its origins, workings, and effects, is covered in Chapter 5. Here I concentrate on just those aspects of the inquiry connected with admissions. The commission faced a situation framed by the terms negotiated between the colleges and UCCA for Oxford's participation in the scheme.

Approximately seven months after the adoption of Hardie's formula for working with UCCA, the issue of Oxbridge's position in the national system of admissions came up at a special conference in Cambridge. The master and senior tutor of Gonville and Caius College, Cambridge, convened a meeting in June 1963 between Oxbridge faculty and school masters. The discussion made it clear that "feelings ran high about U.C.C.A." (David 1963: 372). Different sorts of secondary schools were aligned with particular types of universities, turning education in England into a caste system. According to the conference's "scribe," Tudor David, conference participants felt that:

> The present system was dividing the schools and universities into two separate circuits. On the one hand were most of the maintained grammar schools with two-year sixth forms aiming at A level and then Redbrick; on the other the public and direct-grant schools geared to three years in the sixth, Oxbridge scholarships and then Oxbridge. . . . The establishment of U.C.C.A. . . . had served to strengthen this trend. (David 1963: 361)

One conference participant, Noel Annan, as Provost of King's College, Cambridge, drew attention to the way the educational schism reinforced existing social divisions. The caste system in education was based on the class system in society. Did the conference offer solutions to the situation with UCCA and the problem of state-school students "opting out of Oxbridge"? None that all could agree to. Yet the Caius meeting did reflect the fact that senior members of Cambridge were moving more quickly than their counterparts in Oxford on the problems raised by UCCA. Cambridge's leaders took the occasion of the Robbins report to press Oxford for a resolution.

When the Robbins report came out in October 1963, it was quickly noted that along with many other criticisms of Oxbridge, there was one related to UCCA. It stated that while there were reasons to make an exception for Oxbridge "at the outset," those considerations no longer held. Consequently, "we recommend that the arrangements [of UCCA] should be extended as soon as is practicable to cover all university institutions" (Committee on Higher Education 1963a: 83, para. 227). The government endorsed the report and Oxford and Cambridge were given, in effect, their induction notices for UCCA.

Negotiators from Cambridge and UCCA were already talking, but before Robbins, Oxford's leaders appeared to be satisfied to remain outside. After a meeting of the CVCP to consider the implications of Robbins, Oxford's attitude began to change. Oxford's vice-chancellor, W. F. Oakeshott, sent a confidential memorandum to members of the Hebdomadal Council that summarized the CVCP's discussion and drew attention to UCCA as a "matter which might become urgent" (Oakeshott 1963: 306).

Oakeshott noted that those who wanted to incorporate Oxford into UCCA, which officially included the government, might soon be able to wield additional pressure. That pressure would be due to Cambridge's willingness to go ahead alone:

> I understand from the Vice-Chancellor of Cambridge that the possibility of Cambridge joining the Central Clearing House is being actively discussed. A decision by them might force Oxford to reconsider its position. . . . the Vice-Chancellor of Cambridge told me to mention this as an item in the [Robbins] Report which might conceivably become "live" at any time. (Ibid.)

Oakeshott did not want Oxford left behind in a poor bargaining position. He wrote that week to Cambridge's vice-chancellor to suggest that "it would probably be of advantage to both universities if Oxford and Cambridge could act together in their negotiations with the U.C.C.A. over the terms on which the two universities joined" (Hebdomadal Council Papers 1963a: xcv). It was a sensitive situation. The Hebdomadal Council was thrown off balance by the Robbins view of Oxbridge. And it could not move Oxford into UCCA without confirmation from the colleges.

Between November 1963 and May 1964 when this issue was resolved, the Hebdomadal Council was entangled in controversies on how to respond to Robbins's broad critique of Oxbridge. Nonetheless, the vice-chancellor managed to set things in motion toward UCCA. The colleges were sent memos and consulted; joint negotiations were arranged between Oxford and Cambridge with UCCA. By January 9, 1964, Oakeshott could tell the Oxford and Cambridge Standing Joint Committee that "there was now general agreement at Oxford that there were strong political grounds for the colleges becoming associated with the admissions procedure of U.C.C.A. at a fairly early date" (Hebdomadal Council Papers 1964b: 151). Council could not, however, put forward a motion for Congregation to authorize entry into UCCA; the colleges needed to take that step individually and collectively.

Oxford's entry into UCCA was conditional on Oxbridge's keeping the privilege of first pick as well as a separate entry exam. A student could use a UCCA form to apply to Oxford and Sussex at the same time, for example. While his A-level grades, headmaster's reference, and interview might get him into Sussex, they would not be enough for Oxford. There he would still have to take the Hardie scheme's entry exam. Once past that hurdle, Oxford could offer him a place by January 31 or turn his application over to Sussex. The arrangement was unacceptable to a number of Oxford dons.

In early February 1964, a group of dons approached the vice-chancellor for permission to circulate a declaration in the university's business publication, the *Gazette*. Signed by 21 dons (eleven from Wadham, so I refer to it here by that college's name), it protested the conditions Oxford required to join UCCA. Oakeshott attempted to dissuade the dons from acting. He reported to Council:

> To give publicity to the point at the present stage in the negotia-
> tions might be unfortunate, and he had accordingly asked the
> signatories to discuss the matter with the Provost of Oriel as
> Chairman of the Management Committee of the Admissions
> Scheme. Such a discussion had been held, but they nonetheless
> still wished their fly-sheet to be circulated. . . . He did not feel able
> to refuse authority for circulation. (Hebdomadal Council Papers
> 1964g: lxviii)

The Wadham statement was distributed along with the *Gazette* to every member of Congregation; Oxford's Parliament would be aware of at least two ways to resolve the controversy.

The declaration took a position midway between democratic elitism and social democracy. Consistent with the former, the Wadham petition sought to eradicate all barriers between Oxford and other English universities; in sympathy with the latter, the dons wanted to make it easier for state-school students to get into Oxford:

> [Oxford's approach to UCCA] implies that Oxford and Cambridge
> *need* to be kept in some special position relative to all other uni-
> versities. Ignoring the political implications of this approach, the
> practical consequences are far from readily acceptable. . . . [We
> propose the simple alternative] of entering U.C.C.A. uncondition-
> ally. . . . This means, inter alia, that a boy in the second year sixth
> has a definite chance of coming to Oxford. Under the system
> which is now emerging, his chances are vanishingly small. (Dons'
> Petition 1964)

State schools, with lower-middle- and working-class adolescents, taught students for two years in a "sixth form" before they would complete their A-level exams. Then those students typically left school for work or a non-Oxbridge university. Middle-class youths who went to a public school or competitive grammar school could stay on after A levels for a third year in the sixth form to study for the Oxbridge entry exam. Class privileges combined with different school types to structure the youths' options.

The facts about Oxford's harvest of students who spent an extra year in the sixth form were known at the time. Oxford's Department of Education surveyed the entering class in 1962 and received 1,175 replies, a response rate of over 50 percent. Of those students Oxford picked for matriculation, 85 percent of the boys had done a third year in the sixth form; 91 percent of them had studied for a full year, not half a year. While half had worked mostly to prepare for Oxford's entry exam, the other half, in addition to that challenge, had taken A-level tests again. Of those who repeated A levels, 59 percent retook the same courses in order to get better grades. More public-school than state-school students were getting into Oxford, and 64 percent of those privately educated HMC boys repeated their A levels (see Peterson 1964).

Families willing to spend the money and time for their sons to have an extra year's education were winning the race to get into Oxford. Every Oxford requirement above what other universities demanded worked as a closed gate to those children whose families could not or would not pay the additional price of passage. The relationship between vertical distance and social exclusion was understood and articulated by members of Oxford's faculty in the early 1960s.

To most Oxford dons, however, the argument about standards spoke more persuasively than the analysis of social discrimination. Not enough dons backed the Wadham declaration to alter the terms of negotiation. The colleges of Oxford and Cambridge agreed in May 1964 to join UCCA effective July 6, 1964, with their relative privileges undiminished (*Oxford Magazine* 1964a: 329). Consequently, when the Franks Commission took evidence on admissions, nearly everyone expressed a position on Oxford's status inside UCCA as well as the legitimacy of its separate exam; to that evidence we now turn.

The Franks Commission and Admissions

When the Hebdomadal Council authorized its own Commission of Inquiry into Oxford, with Lord Franks as its chair, its terms of reference included admissions. The report to Council proposed that the inquiry investigate "whether the present methods of selecting undergraduates, including the system of entrance scholarships and exhibitions, are justified on educational grounds" (Franks, Wheare, and Brown 1964a). The phrasing was purely meritocratic, which was unfortunate, unless one hoped to keep things as they were. On educational grounds one could justify Oxford's entry exam system as yielding each year a cohort of the "best brains," but not if one stepped back from the language of excellence and looked at the social effects. Lord Franks, however, was sympathetic to the social democratic case for educational reform. His inquiry and report would look at admissions from the perspective of social justice as well as intellectual quality.

To gather evidence, the Franks Commission solicited testimony and statistics from all of the internal bodies in Oxford. The colleges, faculty boards, Council, the registrar—virtually everyone holding a formal position was asked to participate. From the outside, Franks made requests of the government, schools, unions, professional associations, industry, and others—a broad spectrum completely covering Oxford's world.

The following summary evaluates the evidence presented to Franks on admissions. The intellectual resources from our three modes of social thought (conservative, democratic elitist, and social democratic) are clearly discernible. We will survey the arguments of those partisans, and along the way we will examine some statistical data on schools and colleges.

Conservative Voices and Franks

Of the organizations and individuals whose views on admissions were written with a conservative vocabulary, the most interesting were those of Sir Maurice Bowra, Robert Blake, Lord David Cecil, and the Headmasters' Conference. In combination, they objected to UCCA, found the examination system excessive, and spoke with nostalgia for the days when Oxford nurtured the governing class.

The one with the most to say on the topic of admissions was Maurice Bowra. When Bowra gave evidence to the commission he was no longer just a *literae humaniores* don but master Of Wadham College, a longstanding member of the Hebdomadal Council, and a former vice-chancellor of Oxford. Moreover, in Lord Franks's estimation, Bowra was one of five elders who together governed the university in the period before the commission restructured Oxford's administration. (The other four were Lucy Sutherland, Kenneth Wheare, Walter Oakeshott, and Robert Norrington [Franks interview 1988].) If the university's old regime had a guiding inner circle, Bowra was in it.

Bowra's thoughts on UCCA dwelled on those boys who would be denied a second shot at entry to an Oxford college:

> Under the recent agreement with U.C.C.A. the Oxford Colleges agreed that all entry examinations should take place at the same time. This means that candidates have only one chance of competing for an award or place. This is manifestly unjust on those who from illness or some other inescapable reason are unable to take

part in the examination, and it is no less unjust on others who may just miss an award and might get one if they had a second chance. It is not clear why the Oxford Colleges accepted this scheme, and there is a strong case for examining the whole matter afresh. (Commission of Inquiry 1965b: 20)

Bowra's concerns were shared by the Headmasters' Conference. For teachers, parents, and boys who thought that university meant Oxbridge or nothing, a failure at one's only opportunity for admission was tragic.

The Headmasters' Conference also objected to "the elimination of the second chance." Some continued to resent the Hardie reform; they still felt strongly that scholars and commoners should not take the same examination. And they phrased a defense of the third-year sixth form with the language of standards. The third year was necessary, they argued, both to prepare boys for the entry exam and to make them capable of measuring up to the caliber of an Oxbridge education (see Commission of Inquiry 1965a: 45–46). But where would that leave the student whose school did not offer a third-year sixth form?

The Headmasters' Conference acknowledged that there were difficulties facing schools "which can only run a two-year sixth-form . . . but a third-year sixth is growing in all types of schools, and we are emphatically in favor of it" (ibid.: 46). The problem would solve itself, they implied, if the state invested more. But the government was not expanding state schools to provide an additional year; so families who did not pay for private education would continue to be disadvantaged. Bowra's idea was far less passive. The problem "can be met . . . by Colleges finding out how long candidates have been in the sixth form and making allowances for it" (Commission of Inquiry 1965b: 17). Just how to accomplish that, with colleges looking at the same exams for signs of intellectual promise, Bowra did not indicate.

Bowra did, however, situate the choices colleges must make to select undergraduates in the broad context of the university's mission. Contemporary Oxford had four general tasks: leadership education, research, the training of new scholars and scientists, and the transmission of civilized culture through the colleges. Leadership education was a legacy from Oxford's days as an institution of the governing class:

> Until 1914 it was commonly, and not unreasonably, held that
> Oxford provided a training for future leaders of the nation. . . .
> Without resorting to the word "leaders" with its unfortunate
> associations and its only partial relevance, we may still assume

that University men should be able to take a prominent and directing part in most kinds of work. (Ibid.)

The leadership functions of Oxford remained, even if its graduates filled
a wider spectrum of social roles than in the days before World War I.

On the second and third responsibilities, research and postgraduate
training, Bowra had little of substance to say. But on the fourth function,
he emphatically stated:

> No college can justify its existence unless its undergraduate mem-
> bers lead a full and vigorous life outside their academic obliga-
> tions. The essential idea of a College is that of a community in
> which the members share all kinds of interests. . . . In general they
> provide a highly stimulating and civilizing influence, and enrich
> an undergraduate's life in ways which lie beyond the scope of his
> academic work. (Ibid.)

As Michael Oakeshott had done, Bowra affirmed that the English ideal of
a university embraced more than scholarship.

On methods for selecting the right sort of undergraduate population,
Bowra approved of Oxford's keeping the scholarship examination for
picking scholars. But colleges needed "commoners who are not academically of this calibre," (and those should be chosen to fall into one of three
categories: artists, athletes, and "sons of old members" (ibid.: 19, 20).
Bowra favored a conservative balance of different parts. And given modern Oxford's ecumenical interest in intellect, Bowra was sensitive to the
discomfort this could cause ordinary commoners: "The danger is that
young men (and perhaps young women) who are chosen for not strictly
academic reasons may not feel entirely at home in a society of which the
members are for the most part chosen for their academic promise, and
this may be bad for their self-respect and self-confidence" (ibid.: 19). Colleges should be attuned to this dilemma. Bowra's sympathies lay with Oxford's traditional constituency—for example, the public-school boy facing his only shot at the entry exam.

Other conservative voices went further than Bowra's in discounting the
modern obsession with an examination-proficient meritocracy. Both Robert Blake and Lord David Cecil sought to revive Oxford's memory of its
glory days, when tutorials and college life cultivated "eminent people"
(ibid.: 33). Blake reiterated the opinion expressed by a Cambridge historian, that Oxbridge's prestige in the outside world derived primarily from
"the unpatronising care and attention . . . [devoted] to their academically

less than brilliant pupils" (ibid.: 14). Some of those formerly weak undergraduates, Lord David Cecil pointed out, were now very "distinguished people." Those notable people were not trying to get "firsts" in
their final exams; they spent their time at Oxford on other rewarding pur-
suits—such as social entertainment. Cecil must have shuddered at the
thought that "many would not even have got into the University today"
(ibid.: 35). It seemed to him that Oxford wanted to replace its adventur-
ous spirits of yesterday with timid souls who ground away on the exam
syllabi: "We now run the danger of choosing nothing but safe examinees
who, after they leave Oxford, will follow a useful and undistinguished career as teachers and minor civil servants. As a result the importance and
value of Oxford will be diminished. How this over-stress on examinations shall be checked it is not easy to say" (ibid.). Unless the shameful
obsession with exam marks was corrected, he implied, Oxford would become a place fit only for mandarin mediocrities.

Democratic Elitists and Franks

Those who posed questions and formulated answers within a democratic
elitist lexicon ranged from W. F. R. Hardie, who wanted to increase to
three the number of A levels required at all universities, to R. D. F. Pring-
Mill, who just wanted to replace the entry exam with "special," or S-level
papers. What they shared was the assumption that intellectual standards
were the primary value at stake.

Most democratic elitists developed arguments that converged on the
proposal to substitute S-level papers for Oxford's exam. For Hardie, it
was "a pity that the defence of the 'third year sixth' has come to be associated with the special interests . . . of Oxford and Cambridge" because
he thought that the minimum requirements for all universities should be
raised from two to three A-level subjects, followed by a special S-level
exam (Hardie 1965: 366). The S level could, in Hardie's opinion, displace
Oxbridge's entry exams, but only if three A levels were taken first.

Pring-Mill also liked the idea of using S levels. But he arrived at that
conclusion by reasoning that Oxford's "primary justification for not accepting candidates on the evidence of their 'A' levels" was faulty (Commission of Inquiry 1965d: 133). Oxford defended its own exam with the
argument that A levels only test what someone already knows about a
subject. They test achievement, what one can learn mechanically, even by
cramming at the last minute; while the Oxford exam was "concerned to
spot promise," to see if the boy could think. Pring-Mill suggested that the

dichotomy between achievement and promise was false. He noted, "It is quite possible to set papers testing 'promise' requiring far less 'achievement' than any 'A' level demands" (ibid.: 134). To reduce the tensions between it and other universities, he believed, Oxford needed to work within UCCA to admit students whose A levels demonstrated proficiency and whose S levels showed promise.

The Incorporated Association of Head Masters, the organization for state and direct-grant grammar schools, also contributed to the democratic elitist dialogue. It wanted to see some barriers dropped, such as Oxford's second-language requirement. And it approved of Oxford's joining UCCA. But a majority favored Oxford's keeping a separate entry exam of some sort, because A levels were too "standardised." Schools would attract a better teaching staff, and boys could work with more stimulating materials, if the Oxford exam continued to be there to cultivate "a candidate's potential and future possibilities" (Commission of Inquiry 1965a: 52).

Finally, Harvard's contribution belongs in the democratic elitist category. At the beginning of the discussion the director of admissions for Harvard College, Humphrey Doermann, wrote a long letter published in the *Oxford Magazine*, outlining his system. As at Oxford, "until World War II—a young man was admitted gladly to Harvard College if he looked as if he might survive academically . . . and if his moral character seemed adequate" (Doermann 1964: 304). In those days there had been little for an admissions director to do. But by 1964 the office had thirteen full-time staff and more than 1,300 alumni under its supervision. The task was to sort through 5,000 applications, each with personal essays, letters of recommendation, Scholastic Aptitude Test (SAT) scores, and interview notes often supplied by alumni volunteers. The system, Doermann explained, provided Harvard with an entering class drawn from the top 10 percent of SAT scores and school grades nationwide and with a sprinkling of slightly less cerebral alumni sons, young men with unusual talents, and athletes. It was simply a more meritocratic version of Bowra's balance.

What Doermann did not elaborate on was how Harvard arrived at this arrangement. At both Harvard and Yale, meritocracy's front-line troops were Jewish. Jews overcame much of Harvard's anti-Semitism, including its quota and use of exclusionary code words, such as "moral character," by the 1960s. Harvard's faculty played a part in 1960, with a major report and campaign to diversify the student body beyond "the very rich and the very bright" and to "scrutinize alumni sons with increasing rigor" (Karen 1990: 236; see also Lipset and Riesman 1975). The general pattern of recruitment activities organized by Doermann's office was set by those two forces. What appears to have impressed faculty at Oxford, however, was Harvard's administrative ability to orchestrate such a vast national effort, and to use what was then an uncontroversial SAT exam.

In sum, there were areas of convergence between the democratic elitist and social democratic vocabularies. As a style of analysis, each did object, albeit for different reasons, to old Oxford's relationship to wealth and property. But where democratic elitists looked to refining the tools of intellectual evaluation, which could include additional and more rigorous exams, social democrats wanted to find ways to throw down ladders to working-class youths. Democratic elitists did or did not take radical positions on the reduction of Oxford's social distance, but social democrats always did.

Social Democrats and Franks

Whether on vocabularies or political sympathies, the line between democratic elitist and social democrat was not always easy to draw. To provide a consistent reading, only those who explicitly referred to the value of social justice, to improving opportunities for the working class, or who used sociological arguments to champion state-maintained schools against public schools are included here in the social democratic ranks.

Among those who deployed social democratic questions and concepts in this discussion were the Trades Union Congress; R. Pedley, a supporter of the Labour Party; A. B. Clegg, education officer for West Riding Yorkshire; M. G. Brock, don at Corpus Christi, Oxford; John Vaizey, don at Worcester College, Oxford, and editor in 1964 of the *Oxford Magazine*; the Assistant Masters Association; and in the background some Oxford colleges, especially Merton and St. Catherine's.

Perhaps the most famous and unpopular proposal presented to the Franks Commission was Pedley's argument that the only way to escape the admissions dilemma was to turn Oxford into an exclusively postgraduate university. Oxbridge had been monopolized by public schools in the past, and competitive meritocracy threatened to exercise a different sort of exclusive ownership: "Stop. We don't want selection based on the old school tie, but selection on nothing but intellectual ability will make the race hotter and more desperate than ever. Instead, let's send everyone first of all to another university for the first degree, and keep Oxford and Cambridge for graduates only" (Commission of Inquiry 1965d: 123). Pedley's proposal focused on Oxbridge as a spot whose relative attraction would not diminish just by shifting the principle of selection from property to achievement. Oxbridge's historic inheritance, especially its architecture and resonance in the collective imagination, elevated it above other universities. Short of closure or demolition, Oxbridge could not stop being uniquely enchanting. Pedley's idea would lift the family curse from this legacy. It would spread intellectual talent around to other universities, take Oxford out of controversies about social class, and enable the university to be a research and graduate training powerhouse that rivaled any international competitor. Pedley had been circulating the plan since 1960, first in Labour meetings, then to the Robbins Committee, now to Franks. It was a rational and comprehensive solution—one that nearly everyone at Oxford rejected.

Another plan, put forward by Mr. Clegg, a local education officer, was being implemented by three Oxford colleges and a school council in Yorkshire. It was a quota system reserving a few spaces for working-class state-school students seeking entry to Oxbridge. The arrangement was made and reported to the commission by Clegg: "The purpose of the scheme is to find some solution, however limited . . . to the fact that children of working-class parents . . . do not gain admission to the university in the proportion which might be expected from their numbers in the population and their measured ability" (Commission of Inquiry 1965d: 26). Three colleges in Oxford (Merton, St. Catherine's, and University) and three in Cambridge (Churchill, Clare, and King's) were accepting working-class boys, with all the necessary A-level and language qualifications, on the nomination of their school's headmaster. The special program, a type of affirmative action, set aside only fourteen places at Oxbridge per year; to be effective, the quota would have to be multiplied many times over.

It may be useful here to digress briefly on the topic of individual college traditions. Among Oxford's colleges, the ones implementing this affirmative action scheme were, to use Lord Franks's expression, in "the van of reform" (Franks interview 1988). They were pushing to correct Oxford's imbalance in favor of public-school boys. St. Catherine's took the campaign a step further by setting aside half of its places for natural scientists, a group disproportionately drawn from state-school students with working-class backgrounds. St. Catherine's also pioneered soliciting applications from state schools, something that was just not done in the early 1960s (Bullock interview 1988).

Table 2 shows from which types of school Oxford's men's colleges selected their students in the 1960s. It illustrates the roles played by indi-

TABLE 2

Type of Secondary School Attended by Oxford Undergraduates, 1961 and 1965

(percent)

College	Independent[a]		Direct-grant[b]		State	
	1961	1965	1961	1965	1961	1965
Balliol	56.9	43	12.3	18	31.9	36
Brasenose	52.4	46	20.7	30	26.9	25
Christ Church	70.0	71	11.8	7	18.2	21
Corpus Christi	58.5	46	13.0	17	29.5	37
Exeter	45.3	31	13.1	21	41.5	46
Hertford	62.6	40	13.0	16	24.5	44
Jesus	41.9	27	13.5	18	44.7	55
Keble	48.6	42	14.4	13	36.1	45
Lincoln	61.2	38	11.4	17	27.6	41
Magdalen	54.5	45	11.9	21	33.6	33
Merton	52.9	32	18.8	21	28.3	47
New	66.1	56	9.7	11	24.2	33
Oriel	66.4	57	12.7	15	21.0	28
Pembroke	37.6	29	23.1	17	39.4	53
Queen's	37.2	25	23.8	25	39.1	49
St. Catherine's	30.4	23	16.5	17	53.2	59
St. Edmund	40.8	41	17.1	15	42.1	42
St. John's	50.4	53	14.8	17	34.8	31
St. Peter's	29.3	26	23.4	23	47.3	49
Trinity	80.6	62	5.2	12	14.1	27
University	50.6	36	17.0	13	32.4	48
Wadham	39.6	31	15.7	12	45.3	57
Worcester	64.7	40	11.9	24	23.4	35
Average	52.3	41	14.9	17	32.8	40

SOURCES: 1961 data taken from *Oxford Magazine* 1961: 306; 1965 data taken from University of Oxford 1966b: 62.

NOTE: For 1965 the total comes to 98 percent; the remaining 2 percent came from "other schools," mostly outside Britain.

[a]Independent schools were also called public schools (which in the United States would be called private schools). Most independent-school students were wealthy.

[b]Direct-grant schools were a type of grammar school with a socially broader range of students than the public schools.

vidual colleges as well as the early effects of Chilver, Hardie, and UCCA on admissions. In the four years from 1961 to 1965, the state contingent grew 7.2 percent, from 32.8 to 40 percent.

It may seem odd to dwell on individual college variations to this extent, but Oxford was then essentially a federation of independent col-

TABLE 3

Oxford College Freshmen from Clarendon Private Schools or Working-Class Families, 1920 and 1949 Combined

(percent)

College	Clarendon	Working Class
Christ Church	20	3
New	18	4
Magdalen	13	5
Trinity	13	1
University	12	12
Corpus Christi	10	10
Worcester	10	1
Brasenose	8	3
Balliol	7	7
Merton	7	7
Queen's	6	4
Exeter	5	7
St. John's	4	13
Oriel	3	8
Hertford	2	7
Keble	2	9
Pembroke	2	6
Wadham	2	9
Jesus	1	14
Lincoln	1	4
St. Catherine's	0	14

SOURCE: Dr. Daniel Greenstein provided the raw data; any coding errors are my own.

leges. When someone enrolled at Oxford he or she went to a college; from college one entered the university in a matriculation ritual, received a Bodleian library card, and returned to live in the college. Since the Tudor period, there has been considerable truth in the comment that the colleges are the physical body and the university the immaterial spirit of Oxford.[38] Tables 2 and 3 seek to illustrate that the separate identities and traditions of each college matter.

Table 2 displays individual differences as well as some interesting collective patterns. Of the 23 men's colleges in 1961, fourteen drew 50 percent or more of their entering class from the public schools, and only five had incoming cohorts of which state students were the largest contingent. In 1965 the figures are nearly reversed. By 1965 only five colleges had 50 percent or more of their entering cohort from the public schools, and thirteen colleges had state students as their biggest category of matriculant.

Table 3 shows that school and social-class differences among colleges go back at least to 1920. The table presents two indicators of high and low status for most of Oxford's men's colleges by contrasting the percentage of entering students from the elite Clarendon public schools with the percentage who were sons of manual laborers. The colleges at the top and bottom of the scale have been remarkably consistent over the years.

To return to our narrative on social democratic perspectives presented to Franks, the education officer from Yorkshire who designed the set-aside program, Mr. Clegg, also offered Oxford a profoundly penetrating insight into working-class attitudes toward Oxbridge. Across the United Kingdom, proletarian youths mostly opted out of the education system. Many different things, structural and cultural, worked against their staying in the race. To help Oxford's faculty better understand the cultural logic and psychological toll on working-class students of even the attempt to get into university, Clegg appended to his scheme an "account, written by a young sixth-former . . . of his problems as a working-class boy" (Commission of Inquiry 1965d: 27).

Under the title "Bilingualism," an anonymous Yorkshire working-class lad, less than eighteen years old, composed a poignant and concise explanation for rejecting sixth-form study for A levels and university entrance:

> The problem of speech facing a sixth-former in a working class area . . . may be the most prominent manifestation of his embarrassment and discomfort. . . . A child goes to a grammar school completely unaware that forces will be set to play on him which will force a division between himself and his parents and the world from which he came. . . . As the sixth-former becomes increasingly conscious of his inadequate vocabulary, lack of fluency, and lazy, slovenly speech (accent is unimportant), he may attempt to do something about it, but his normal social environment is not conducive to good speech. . . . When speaking in his usual surroundings, too, he may be ridiculed, and he feels that he is despised. People use such an opportunity as an excuse to deride someone of whose success they are jealous and who represents to them the personification of the working classes' traditional enemy. As he ascends each rung of the educational ladder . . . he leaves behind the life he has known, feels increasingly estranged in his new surroundings, and becomes increasingly embarrassed and

> confused. . . . Such are the emotional stresses experienced by a
> working-class sixth-former. (Ibid.: 31)

To judge from the paucity of commentaries alerting colleges to be aware
of this barrier between working-class youths and university, it appears
that even reformers in Oxford were inattentive to the psychological effects of academic culture on those they hoped to help.

Nonetheless, some members of Oxford themselves had lived versions
of the Yorkshire youth's description of psychological ambivalence toward
education. One example was Ralph Glasser, a "scholarship boy" in the
interwar period from the poor Jewish immigrant community in Glasgow
called "Gorbals," who thought of distant Oxford as "alien territory. Preserve of the boss class!" (1987: 106). Glasser, who did go to Oxford, was
aware of the reluctance of working-class meritocrats to enter the enemy's
turf. They were fearful that their new university mates from the upper
classes would dismiss them as grinds, lacking the proper vocabulary and
cosmopolitan seasoning. For the working-class undergraduate, his personal uprooting from family and community caused by academic success
was painful enough, as Richard Hoggart's portrait of the scholarship boy
illustrated, without the additional emotional injury that Oxford life could
inflict (see Hoggart 1962: 291–304). Why should the meritocrat subject
himself to feelings of social inadequacy at the hands of undergraduates
whom he perceived to be his academic inferiors?

The ambivalent emotions of working-class meritocrats toward Oxford,
a mixture of hostility and awe, when not channeled into moral indignation
sometimes found an opposite outlet in idealization. Oxford became a holy
grail, and the chance to matriculate there was, according to Glasser, "a romantic, heroic quest" (1990: 4). The quixotic Oxford was not just a path-
way to middle-class occupations but more important a citadel of higher
learning and culture. Oxford's gothic spires seemed to uphold Matthew
Arnold's claim that intellect enabled one to rise above social class in the
disinterested service of culture (see Arnold 1980: 518, 523, 538). That the
reality could fall far short of the ideal was the point of a critical book published by a coal miner's son who graduated from Oxford (Potter 1960).
Whether the proletarian youths carried a chip on their shoulder or ar-
dently identified with the institution, the psychological dynamics were
complex.

When Michael Brock, a fellow at Corpus Christi College, Oxford,
published a contribution to the Franks Commission's discussion in the
Oxford Magazine, he lightly touched on the dilemma. At the Caius Cam-

bridge conference on admissions Brock had asked a Yorkshire grammar-school headmaster why so few of his boys applied to Oxbridge. Brock remembered: "He replied 'It is a peculiar emotional feeling. They feel that Oxford and Cambridge are not for them and never have been'" (Brock 1965: 238). Brock passed silently by this "peculiar" psychological dimension of the problem; he mentioned it only to show that some barriers were not specifically due to Oxford's selection methods.

Following Brock's lead, we move from the psychological back to the structural aspects of the issue from a social democratic perspective. His interests in social class at university were framed by the Labour Party's attack on the supremacy of public-school boys in Oxbridge. Brock sympathetically monitored the Labour Party's debates. He noted that Labour's prime minister, Harold Wilson, had "pledged the Labour Party to 'end the system of college entrance at Oxford and Cambridge'" and that Labour's secretary of state for education and science, Anthony Crosland, was on record in favor of imposing an upper limit on the number of public-school boys Oxford could accept (see Brock 1965: 238). Both Labour and Brock evaluated the issue of working-class matriculation at a university as a matter of school origins. Public-school attendance signified that one was upper or middle class, while attendance at a state school (also called a "maintained" school) meant one was lower-middle and working class. The struggle was to increase the latter's proportion at Oxbridge, where undergraduates from state schools composed less than 37 percent of the total. Brock noted, "Our low percentage reflects, not the rejection of a great many maintained school candidates, but a comparative shortage of applications" (ibid.). The challenge was to raise the application rate from state-maintained schools.

Brock suggested that Oxford could not directly address some of the emotional constraints, but some impediments were built into the admissions machinery. He thought that entry into UCCA helped reduce the obstacles, but that an "important deterrent" remained in the form of the entrance and scholarship exams. Brock's solution was drawn from across the Atlantic. He wrote, "Oxford should at once start experiments . . . on a Harvard type scholastic aptitude test." Unlike A levels or Oxford's existing entry exam, it would not require a specific preparatory course. For state-school students there should be no other entry test. Brock thought a less precise exam "would be a small price to pay for convincing the maintained schools . . . that we meant to give them the fairest possible chance of admission to Oxford" (ibid.: 238, 240).

Of the organizations that used social democratic language, the Trades

Union Congress (TUC) and the Assistant Masters Association deserve mention. The TUC, in step with the Labour Party, advocated restricting public-school numbers in Oxford to their percentage of all sixth-formers in England and Wales. And the TUC thought admitting more adult students, such as those attending Ruskin, the trade union–affiliated college in Oxford, and more women were both important goals (Commission of Inquiry 1965a: 27–29).

The Assistant Masters Association (AMA) represented the teaching staff, not headmasters, in all secondary schools, public and state. Like most professional and trade union organizations, however, its strengths were in the state and not the private sector. The AMA came out firmly for UCCA and uniform entry requirements and against separate Oxford admissions exams; it wanted entry scholarships replaced with awards at the end of the first year and expressed concern over state students' fears about not fitting in socially at Oxford. Also the AMA thanked the commission for requesting its views, noting that the Hardie Working Party had refused to hear them (ibid.: 61–65). Hardie listened to the views of school heads, but not to the staff. The match of institutional position and policy perspective was strong: representatives of headmasters objected to Oxford's reforms, while delegates of teachers criticized it for not going far enough.

The Franks Report

With that review of the attitudes, questions, and proposals raised in the discussion, we now turn to what the Franks Commission of Inquiry wrote and recommended to Oxford. The language of the report was social democratic: "We are clear from all the evidence . . . that the admissions procedures of Oxford are not in all respects satisfactory. We do not think that they completely meet the two great requirements laid on all universities of academic efficiency and social justice in their arrangements for entry" (University of Oxford 1966a: 71). Franks distinguished between the "two souls" of academic merit and social justice and wanted to weigh each in the selection process.

For the Franks Commission, Oxford would not fulfill its duty to "national needs" if it used an exam that appeared to be neutral but in fact imposed a standard that only the privately educated could reach. It did not matter if Oxford was innocent of class bias in its evaluation of applicants, if the character of the requirements caused most state-school students to remove themselves from consideration. The commission's views on the social effects of Oxford's exam were not automatically shared by those who thought in conservative or democratic elitist terms.

The commissioners explicitly addressed the link between school type, social class, and entry requirements. On the working-class student and Oxford the report noted:

> Before 1945 money was the great obstacle to working-class boys and girls who had the ability to profit from Oxford. . . . Since that time, however, the financial aspect of the problem has disappeared. This being so, the business of Oxford is to ensure that its selection procedures draw upon the widest range of talent, and guarantee equality of treatment and opportunity to all those who apply. . . . The purpose of Oxford must be to relate its arrangements not to the class structure but to the structure of the secondary-school system. The solution does not lie in providing ways and means for poor scholars as of old, nor in the creation of "closed" methods of entry for working-class boys and girls. The key is to raise the application rate from the maintained schools by removing misconceptions about Oxford and by reforming the entrance examination. (University of Oxford 1966a: 78)

The Yorkshire set-aside program was discouraged. Franks's strategy was to remove the advantage for applicants who spent three years in the sixth form. To reduce those benefits, the report proposed in effect a two-track entry system; students with only two years in the sixth form should be tested differently from three-year students. "All entrance papers should have a section catering for entrants from the second year sixth" form (*Oxford Magazine* 1966: 375). A third-year sixth-form student would not take the two-year section of the exam, and vice versa. It was an attempt to place the state-maintained school on separate, and therefore fair, competitive grounds with the public schools.

It was forward-looking for Franks to make this proposal because Wilson's Labour government, with Crosland as education secretary, had just launched the reorganization of secondary schools into "comprehensives," all-in-one schools similar to American high schools. And comprehensives, even less than state-supported grammar schools, would tend not to have the resources to compete against public schools with sixth-form instruction for three years.

Proponents of the comprehensive reorganization of secondary education in the 1960s claimed that it would increase working-class access to higher education. Reducing the number of selective schools by transforming the government's grammar schools into comprehensives, Labour's educationists believed, would enable more working-class youths to stay on in school and qualify for entry to university. And getting proletarian youths to continue their schooling past the age of legal compulsion was, as we have seen, a major hurdle between the working class and higher education.

The Franks Report tried implicitly to take the government's comprehensive policy into account. An evaluation of its record was offered by Guy Neave of the Centre for Educational Sociology, University of Edinburgh, a partisan of comprehensive schools:

> The importance of these recommendations was twofold. First, it was a milestone in the recognition of changes taking place in secondary education. Second, it was important because the recommendations demonstrated that these changes would have an effect on the most privileged sector of the higher education system, and moreover, the recommendations stood out as one of the few examples of the university adapting itself to the *anticipated* effect of changes in secondary education. (Neave 1975: 82)

Neave praised Franks not only for introducing reforms at Oxford in advance of secondary schools reorganization, but also for the success of his proposals with working-class students in state-maintained schools. As a result of Franks's initiative, the number of working-class youths at Oxford went up. Neave noted: "In one sense the recommendations of the Franks Report *vis-à-vis* comprehensive schools seem to be borne out. It appears that the social reservoir on which Oxbridge can draw is, at this point, wider. . . . Whether it will be so in the future is a different matter" (ibid.: 88). We come back to this issue later.

It was an interesting twist that with Franks the thinking in Oxford came full circle, with a proposal to return to a dual-entry system, not for propertied gentlemen and lower-class scholars but for privately and state-educated youths.

Franks and Gender

The issue of women at men's colleges came up for Franks in the context of undergraduate admissions. If the debate on admissions cut two ways, one against Oxford's privileges as an institution set apart from other universities, and the other against Oxford's under-representation of state-school youths, women were still left out. While the subject of state schools was coupled with the issue of social class, the topic of female equality remained marginalized.

It is one indication of the depth of gender segregation that a self-governing intellectual community could argue for years about fairness and social justice with only occasional references to the status of women inside Oxford. At Oxford from 1927 to 1957, the number of women was limited to less than one-quarter that of men. The percentage of female undergraduates, at 16 percent in 1963–64, was significantly lower than the national average of 28 percent (University of Oxford 1966a: 51). Oxford's exceptional under-representation of women was not unrelated to their segregation into five "societies" and colleges. They faced statutory exclusion from the twenty-three men's colleges. It was an everyday form of apartheid that prevented even Professor Dorothy Crowfoot Hodgkin of Somerville College, Oxford, who won the Nobel Prize for chemistry in 1964, from eating in twenty of the men's colleges (see Vaizey 1954: 58). It was not that no one inside Oxford took notice; people did. But the condition of women never became the crux of a university-wide or inter-college investigation, such as the Chilver or Hardie reform efforts, between 1945 and the 1960s. No formal committees looked into this problem until the 1970s.

Yet there was a surprising proposal from the all-male governing body of New College, one of Oxford's oldest and most prestigious foundations: "New College declares its wish to amend its statutes to permit the admission of women to the College, and accordingly proposes to consult with the University concerning the possibility and implications of fitting a mixed college or colleges into the University framework" (Ste. Croix 1964: 4). The dons at New College had the legal right to unilaterally admit women. But they did not. Instead, they raised the issue with the vice-chancellor, who drew into the discussion the heads of the five women's colleges and Lord Franks.

While those in the inner circles of institutional power weighed New College's proposal to go "mixed," news of the radical idea was published in the faculty magazine and became a topic of conversation especially over dining tables in the Senior Common Rooms, which were open only to men. The views of G. E. M. de Ste. Croix, a don at New College, were supported in print by Miss Peter Ady, a don at St. Anne's College, and by John Vaizey of Worcester College, who was editor of the *Oxford Magazine* (Ste. Croix 1964: 4; Ady 1964: 138–140; Vaizey 1965a: 269; 1965b: 325).

Those who objected did so on a variety of grounds. One could argue, using a democratic elitist's vocabulary, that an increase in female numbers at Oxford would be bad because it would dilute the quality of the student body and change the mix of academic subjects being studied. Margaret Hubbard, a fellow at St. Anne's, warned against a "superficially egalitarian solution" that would boost female numbers while ignoring the fact that school girls mostly study arts subjects, such as French and English literature, while boys flock to the natural sciences and math. The space for females to read arts subjects was already filled, while vacancies remained in the natural sciences. Yet, she wrote, "we cannot take a girl to read a highly technical syllabus, for which her education has not prepared her." It would not bridge the gulf at universities between the two cultures of arts and sciences, "if one of the cultures is largely in the hands of women" (Hubbard 1965: 312, 313). If Oxford rushed to admit large numbers of female undergraduates, she feared, it would either reproduce the gender split in secondary schools between academic subjects or lower standards in the sciences.

Conservative opposition to the idea did not often surface in print, but Christopher McKnight, a scholar at New College, was sufficiently quarrelsome to have written: "Though it is perhaps a noble sentiment that education is an end in itself . . . the fact is that whereas men invariably take up careers women do not. Is it not then arguable that it is more useful to educate a second-class man than a first-class woman who marries immediately?" (McKnight 1965: 370). Oxford's priorities should reflect, rather than challenge, women's current social position.

The argument that carried the most weight with the Hebdomadal Council and the Franks Commission, however, was made by the heads of the women's colleges. Three of those leaders, Lady Ogilvie of St. Anne's, Dr. Lucy S. Sutherland of Lady Margaret Hall, and Dame Janet Vaughan of Somerville, submitted memos to Franks objecting to the notion that the men's colleges could resolve the problem of female numbers by becoming co-ed. They asserted the belief, as Dr. Sutherland wrote, that "women have the same rights and abilities as men and must be given the same educational opportunities" (Commission of Inquiry 1965b: 139). Nonetheless, in Lady Ogilvie's words, "co-education does not necessarily imply co-habitation"; single-sex colleges provided a refuge for serious work and recuperation from the "hurly-burly . . . in an undergraduate's life" (ibid.: 140). Ogilvie noted: "Anyone who has experienced the turmoil of a university Union at a provincial university will realize that a perpetually mixed society, while often enormously stimulating, can be infinitely exhausting and sometimes even boring, if there is no possibility of escape from it. [Single sex] colleges have provided this means of escape" (ibid.: 140). Gender-segregated colleges were a healthy device for insulating undergraduates from intrusions into their intellectual growth caused by the tensions between the sexes in society.

While pressing the case for women in higher education, the college heads moved the terms of the discussion away from opening up men's colleges to women to expansion at the women's colleges. As Sutherland urged:

> I should hope . . . that if the University aimed at an increase in the number of women students . . . the possibility of expansion at the existing women's colleges would be first of all considered. . . . Only if they were not able to expand . . . does it seem sensible either to undertake the great expense of building a new women's college, as at Cambridge, or to change the existing Oxford system radically by opening the existing men's colleges to women. (Commission of Inquiry 1965b: 171)

The core question, often unstated, was about the effects on the five women's colleges of actions by the men's colleges. One could argue that allowing the older, wealthier, and more prestigious men's colleges to matriculate women would attract the best talent away from the women's colleges, leaving those foundations to sink. In their oral evidence to the Franks Commission, the heads of the women's colleges urged a protective stance toward their collegiate homes. Those who worked so long to advance the cause of women inside Oxford, they said, should not be sacrificed to the presumptions of male dons.

The testimony of the women's college heads dismayed, among others, John Vaizey, *Oxford Magazine*'s editor: "As supporters of the New College proposal we regard the views of the women's colleges as presented to the Franks Commission as narrowly conceived. They are what the Negroes in the United States call *'Uncle Toms'—good negroes who know their place in a white man's world"* (Vaizey 1965a: 269). Their logic was to defend existing institutions rather than embrace a more abstract obligation to future female enrollments.

Lord Franks was convinced the women's heads were right. When New College's reformers were referred by the Hebdomadal Council to the commission, Franks kept the proposal off the inquiry's agenda. He personally responded to New College to safeguard that no action would be taken against the wishes of the women's colleges. To the warden of New College he wrote:

> If New College decides to proceed with the proposal and, in so do-
> ing, sets a fashion which several other men's colleges would wish
> quickly to follow, we believe that rapid action of this sort would in-
> flict great damage on the existing women's colleges. . . . if changes
> should come, we are clear that they should be gradual. . . . There
> should be immediate consultation . . . between the men's and
> women's colleges to reach a reasonable view on the extent and the
> timing of any proposed changes. (Franks 1965: 613–14)

When the commission's report came out, there was not one reference to
New College's initiative. The line taken by the inquiry was to strengthen
the women's colleges in order to increase their size. And, if necessary, it
"may well mean that at least one other college has to be founded" (University of Oxford 1966a: 52).

The role of the Franks Commission in smothering New College's initiative was puzzling. Not only was Lord Franks personally interested in
social justice, but he had made a request of the vice-chancellor, Oakeshott,
to include women in his inquiry from the start (Franks interview 1988).

One of the commission's two women was Jean Floud, a sociologist
whose work included research on social class and education. When asked
about the commission's evaluation of New College's proposal and the issue of female students, Jean Floud stated:

> The whole question of admissions was gone into very carefully.
> The very astonishing thing about that is that we were within spit-
> ting distance of women's liberation and the opening up of colleges
> to women. But it never entered into any of our heads. We always
> talked about the foundation of a new women's college, that more
> women were needed . . . but never was there so much as a suspi-
> cion that we might go mixed. (Floud interview 1988)

And in correspondence to clarify and double check, Floud wrote: "My recollection is that we did not take the New College proposal seriously. . . .
we did not entertain the idea that the existing men's colleges should admit
women. Had we done so, we would surely have discussed the wider implications of such a development and this would have been reflected in the
drafting of Vol. 1 paras. 101 ff [in the report]" (Floud 1988). Both Floud's
memory and the published records concur that genuine consideration of
the advantages to women of eradicating gender segregation in some of the
men's colleges was not sincerely explored.

Whether it was due to the gender bias of even the social democratic vocabulary on social justice, class being misunderstood as exclusively a masculine thing, or to the vested interests of the leadership of the women's colleges, the results were the same. The issue was kept off the commission's agenda, and the report's position was against men's colleges becoming co-ed.

HISTORICAL AND STATISTICAL RECORDS

Before we draw up a balance sheet on the relative weight of internal and external influences on Oxford's policies and practices, we need to review the statistical record on shifts in social class and school backgrounds during this period. Demographic trends, independent of institutional policy or political debate, certainly contributed to the balance of class forces inside Oxford. To provide a broad perspective on those demographic shifts, we begin with a brief review of poor scholars and wealthy gentlemen at Oxford in the Middle Ages.

Medieval Plebeians and Modern Proletarians

From the twelfth to the twentieth century, the proportion of upper and lower social classes at Oxford has gone up and down. In Oxford's first three centuries, it was an "open-access community" without strict entrance requirements, where boys of modest means prepared for careers in the church: "In England, the aristocracy remained largely aloof from the universities until the fifteenth and sixteenth centuries. It is only as they were in the post-Reformation period that Oxford and Cambridge can to some degree be described as vehicles of class privilege" (A. Cobban 1988: 16). After the sixteenth century, scions of privilege intermixed at Oxford with the offspring of relative poverty and then went their separate ways. Medieval sponsorship, college scholarships, and work-study arrangements (whereby plebeians took employment as "servitors," college servants, for wealthy students or dons) financed the education of poor boys (Stone 1974: 9, 21). Poor scholars mostly pursued careers in religion or education, while sons of privilege, especially those younger brothers not in line for an inheritance, ambled into the gentlemanly professions (see Stone 1974: 9; Stone and Stone 1984: 228–39).

Whether Oxbridge continued to host a mixture of social classes as well as promote meritocratic advancement over the course of the past three centuries remains a matter of controversy. Lawrence Stone has argued that with the rise in the nineteenth century of commercial-market rela-

TABLE 4

Oxford's Male Undergraduates by Father's Occupation, 1900–1967
(percent)

	1900–1913	1920–1939	1946–1967
Oxford's declining establishment			
Gentlemen, land, clergy, and law	44.4	27.0	10.5
The new men			
Industry	10.4	11.8	18.8
White- and blue-collar working class	5.6	10.0	19.4

SOURCE: Greenstein 1994: 56.

tions and egalitarian sentiments the lower classes were pushed out of scholarships by the middle classes and excluded from college employ. The vestiges of any premodern sponsored-mobility ladders for plebeian boys were allegedly kicked away by the Victorians. On this Stone has written, "Oxford was never so socially exclusive as it was in the second quarter of the 19th century" (Stone 1974: 63). But more nuanced assessments of Oxbridge's role suggest that things were never as inclusive or exclusive as Stone found them (see Rothblatt 1981: 29–93; Rubinstein 1986). In the eighteenth and nineteenth centuries, more plebeian undergraduates were from the lower middle class than from the bottom rungs of English society. And lower-class meritocratic mobility was never shut down. Stone's conclusions on Oxford's class composition in the nineteenth century are probably too bleak.

While the sources of evidence for the nineteenth century may not afford a resolution of all controversial questions, we do, fortunately, have an alternative authority for the years after 1900. Dr. Daniel Greenstein has provided us with a measure, both as subtle and as consistent as one is ever likely to get, of fathers' occupations for Oxford undergraduates from 1900 to 1967.

With Greenstein's data, one can glean indicators of the social flux inside Oxford. A gradual social transformation took place between 1900 and 1967, when undergraduates with high-status fathers in agrarian and establishment occupations were displaced by low-status youths whose parents had urban occupations. While the number of recruits from all other occupational groups changed very little, there was a fall and rise among two related social clusters. First, sons of gentlemen, landlords, clergymen, and lawyers decreased; second, the numbers of offspring of manual workers, clerks, small shopkeepers, and boys with fathers in industry increased. Oxford's establishment declined and new men took their place.

This transformation is highlighted in Table 4, which displays the percentages of Oxford's male undergraduates in those categories where significant changes occurred. Between the 1910s and the period after World War II, the size of Oxford's gentry-clergy-law establishment shrank 76 percent; those whose fathers worked in industry nearly doubled; and there was a quadrupling of junior members with lower-class fathers.

Oxford and the Peerage

Oxford's relation to the upper class and to the working class has changed significantly since the early twentieth century. The evidence is consistent with the hypothesis that there has been a restructuring of the British establishment from a system of class authority to a meritocratic elite—even though that shift may be disguised by the continuity of educational institutions. The available data do not, however, tell us how many of those classified as upper or working class are in the proper sociological sense family members of those social classes. For example, if a boy's father was a member of the working class but his grandfather and uncles had been middle class, then his structural class position would be proletarian, but he would not possess a living collective working-class memory provided by the reproduction of old kinship networks. He would be in the working class, but not of it; his class culture and consciousness would be ambiguous.

We have, however, one very reliable measure of the nexus between intergenerational family continuity and the pattern of upper-class matriculation at Oxford. Upper classes can be categorized in various ways, but following the lead of Shirley Williams we will take those British families with aristocratic titles as the topmost upper group. Williams's approach is supported by the finding that while income and occupation were used by the British public to distinguish between the working and middle classes, "the majority (65 percent) conceived of the upper class in terms of social status; that is, as those having some sort of hereditary title" (Marshall, Rose, Newby, and Vogler 1989: 146). Among those with any sort of title, the peerage, those 800 or so hereditary members of the House of Lords, are the best possible proxy for those stable families who provide continuity of culture and consciousness for the upper class. What shifts, if any, have occurred in the pattern of Oxbridge matriculation by the peerage? From changes in that group, we can estimate the extent of upper-class realignments within Oxford (see Table 5).

TABLE 5

Hereditary Lords by Birth Cohort, 1900–1969

	Birth Year				
	Pre–1924	1925–35	1936–46	1947–57	1958–69
	Approximate Years of University Attendance				
	Pre–1944	1943–55	1954–66	1965–77	1976–89
% at Eton	47	57	48	41	33
% at Oxbridge	50	45	31	21	16
% in other higher education	9	12	21	32	50
% without any form of higher education	40	43	48	47	33
Total number in each cohort	275	213	183	113	30

SOURCE: 1995 Debrett's, calculated from hereditary male Peers only, no Life Lords, women, or Lords Spiritual included.

NOTE: Total in data base: 814.

Until the birth cohort of 1958–69, the percentage of the peerage going to the prestigious Eton did not change nearly as much as their representation at Oxbridge. From the Second World War forward, the percentage of the peerage who passed through Oxbridge went down and their enrollment in other institutions of higher education went up. By the time of the Franks admissions reforms, fewer than half as many sons of lords attended Oxbridge as had done so before the war. Clearly, admissions reforms were having an effect. Upper-class membership was insufficient for Oxford matriculation. As Oxford became more meritocratic in the 1950s and 1960s, it became less and less the university of choice for the hereditary peerage. At Eton, family status and school remained coupled, while Oxbridge by the mid-1960s ceased to be an upper-class institution in the same sense.

This significant shift, from land and church to business and workers, reflected the downfall of the British aristocracy in the early decades of the twentieth century. Its collapse between 1910 and 1939 was one of the most monumental silent revolutions in European history. According to David Cannadine, two of its pivotal sources were "the impact of the First World War, in which a greater proportion of the aristocracy suffered violent deaths than in any conflict since the Wars of the Roses. And . . . the sales of land between 1910 and 1922 . . . amounted to a transfer of property on a scale rivalled in Britain this millennium only by the Norman Conquest and the Dissolution of the Monasteries" (Cannadine 1992: 704). By the 1940s, the aristocracy was no longer in command of the state or in possession of the most wealth in society. It finally ceased to be the dominant class. The effects of this loss on Oxford were portentous.

At Oxford in the twentieth century the shift was toward fewer entering students from landholding and professional families (the clergy and lawyers) and more from lower-white-collar and blue-collar backgrounds. If we think of Oxford as a "positional good" that children from different class backgrounds were competing for, then lower-class children gradually gained on the upper and professional classes. No matter that they began the contest considerably behind their competitors and that they had an enormous amount of ground to make up. From the perspective of the class balance at Oxford in the first half of the twentieth century, landed interests and professionals were the losers and lower-class students the winners of this contest.

From the 1920s forward, the mix of classes at Oxford improved, returning to something like its premodern social balance. By the late 1950s a don noted that as Oxbridge annually absorbed thousands of new men into the "Establishment" the university was again fulfilling "its old function of promoting an osmotic assimilation between the classes" (D. M. Smith 1956: 54). With approximately 19 percent of its undergraduates in the 1960s from the lower classes, Oxford may still have not been as open to the disadvantaged as it was before the sixteenth century, but it was drawing closer to medieval standards.

Oxford's proletarian contingent may seem modest, but not if one puts this figure in the context of similarly elite governing-class universities in France or the United States. In 1961–62, by Pierre Bourdieu's accounting, 2 percent of the students at the Ecole Polytechnique in Paris (one of Paris's Grandes Ecoles) had industrial working-class parents, and 8 percent had parents who did clerical jobs (Bourdieu and Passeron 1979: 10). Harvard's blue-collar sons, in the years for which we have reliable information, constituted 8 percent of the student body in 1935 and 5 percent in 1986 (Karabel 1984: 24; Thernstrom 1986: 125). In contrast, Oxford's postwar record was a significant accomplishment.

School Types and Social Class

In universities, as Franks stated, class was often expressed by the type of school one attended. The working class could not afford public-school fees, and until the early twentieth century those schools provided Oxford with nearly all of its students. It was only after World War II that the flow of applicants from the state sector, where the working class goes to school, accounted for even 19 percent of Oxford's matriculants.

The strength of the connections between public schools and Oxford reflected the historic weakness of the state system of schooling. England introduced compulsory schooling relatively late, in 1870, well after most nations on the European continent had done so. Throughout the nineteenth century many in the upper and middle classes sent their children to fee-charging public schools, while children of the working classes received little or no formal instruction. Oxford's colleges either had old entrenched relations with "feeder" public schools, or they cultivated those associations. For example some of the matriculants from Winchester who received degrees from New College, Oxford, would go back to teach more Winchester boys how to pass through Oxford's gates. It was the academic version of a big, cozy, extended family (see Bishop and Wilkinson 1967).

This relationship was not challenged until a Winchester and Oxford graduate, Sir Robert Morant, became head of the Board of Education. Morant crafted the Education Act of 1902 to require the creation of grammar schools that would ensure a flow of working-class candidates to Oxford and Cambridge. As education historian Michael Sanderson explained: "The main thrust of Morant's policies lay in the development of the grammar school. . . . Morant wanted to make the grammar schools genuine ladders for working class children to reach the ancient universities and the learned professions" (Sanderson 1987: 23). The flow of grammar-school students from the state sector to Oxford began as a trickle before World War I, grew into a stream during the interwar period, and then became a powerful river immediately after World War II.

The Butler Education Act of 1944 gave further impetus to the expansion and democratization of the education system. The Butler Act, in combination with egalitarian sentiments inspired by the fight against Nazi Germany, helped make the postwar cohort of state students at Oxford larger than ever before. In 1948 the state sector made its biggest single leap forward; however, it was not until the mid-1960s that state schools achieved parity with public schools for entry to Oxford (see Table 6).

The combination provided by public funds and admissions reforms correlated with a shift in the school backgrounds of Oxford's undergraduates. Before the war, 62 percent of its students had come from socially elite private schools and only 19 percent from the state sector. The greatest shift toward state students came in one decade, from 1938 to 1948, when their intake increased 16 percent. Over the next thirty-eight years

TABLE 6

School Type Attended by Oxford Undergraduates, 1938–1990
(percent)

	1938	1948	1958	1966	1986	1990
Independent	62.0	45.2	52.4	41.3	45.0	48.0
Direct-grant	12.6	14.9	15.4	17.1	—	—
State	19.0	35.0	30.0	40.2	47.4	44.5
Other	6.0	5.0	2.0	1.4	7.6	7.5
Total number	1,235	1,480	2,056	1,912	2,974	3,154

SOURCES: University of Oxford 1966b: 47; Cooke and Mellalieu 1990: 1; *Oxford University Gazette* 1990.
NOTE: Direct-grant grammar schools were abolished by a Labour government in 1976. "Other" includes foreign schools. The figures are for male matriculants only, except for 1986 and 1990.

to 1986, the state sector increased its share by only 12.4 percent, half in just the four years between 1961 and 1965, in the immediate aftermath of Oxford's admissions reforms, its entry into UCCA, and the creation of St. Catherine's. By the 1960s, the state sector had achieved parity with the private. (The scales moved back a little in the 1980s, a problem we will return to in Chapter 7.)

PROVISIONAL BALANCE SHEET ON INSTITUTIONAL CHANGE

What can the preceding account tell us about the process of reform at Oxford? Can we identify the external and internal forces that drive change or limit it? Did external shifts constrain or enable Oxford's reform efforts? Was there a logic of reform at work within Oxford independent of external forces?

The reform of Oxford's admissions regulations and procedures and the transformation of its social composition came about through an interaction of factors both beyond and within Oxford's control. The big driver of Oxford's class transformation was structural and from the outside. A demographic revolution in Oxford's social field was the precondition for shifts in the balance of class fractions within. The state played an indispensable role, materially enabling new social segments to afford a university education. The expansion of the state's funding of undergraduate education grew in a bipartisan fashion, from partial subsidies to complete financial aid between 1944 and 1962. The combined contributions from local and central government correlated with significant demographic shifts to raise objective challenges to Oxford's institutional practices. In turn, Oxford had the organization and actors to welcome those external developments. Oxford's organizational form was sufficiently flexible because of its diverse collegiate foundations, and there were adequate numbers of dons with democratic elitist or social democratic sympathies to make the institution receptive to the flow of demographic forces and to the opportunities afforded by government resources.

From the 1940s, individual admissions tutors with progressive social sensibilities responded positively to the changes. Those uncoordinated efforts on the ground floor circulated upward, generating controversy along the way. Oxford formally responded through internal controversies centered on committee reports (Chilver, Hardie, and Franks) that led to new official policies. In each case those inquiries initially trailed behind, then marched alongside, and ultimately took steps ahead of existing college practices.

The policy revisions that embraced and accelerated the process were occasioned by external forces. The three committees responsible for drafting Oxford's new policies were largely responses to the outside. Although Chilver was launched without the stimulus of direct external intervention, Hardie was the result of a request by UCCA, and Franks arose from a serious political threat.

If the instigation of the investigations came from the outside, the controversies surrounding policy formulation and implementation were internally generated. Not one of Oxford's three investigations (not Chilver, Hardie, or Franks) devised policies that acceded to the wishes or objective interests of the major external groups. Of the three most important players in Oxford's world, the public schools, other universities, and the government, not one of them controlled the agenda or held veto power over the program or practice of reform.

On Chilver's main accomplishment, the elimination of Latin requirements for scientists, Oxford's associates were neutral. The public schools, which one would expect to be unfriendly to the reform, were willing to accommodate. And the government was silent. The only vocal opposition came from inside Oxford, and it failed to obstruct the move. The gatekeeping hegemony of the classics fell in a fight that was internal to Oxford.

The Hardie and Franks investigations, launched in response to particular external pressures from UCCA or Robbins, went on to address issues far beyond the limits of those original concerns. Hardie began as an effort to harmonize Oxford's calendar with UCCA's. The committee proceeded to take a position on the dual entryways to Oxford that conflicted with the preferences of public-school headmasters, the recommendations of an Education Ministry's official report, and the wishes of Oxford's conservatives. With Hardie, democratic elitism won a decisive institutional victory over school and family background. Hardie's policies, once implemented, placed into the hands of college tutors the tools to build an exclusive meritocracy. The rhetoric of Hardie was compromise; the organizational effects were democratic elitist—not social democratic.

The Franks Commission was formed because Oxford's critics objected to Oxford's having procedures that were different from those of other universities. Yet Franks did not alter Oxford's arrangements to match other universities' or the government's requests. After Franks, Oxford's special position within UCCA and its own entry exam system remained. Yet with Franks, social democratic concerns came forward. The anxieties of headmasters and conservatives were disregarded. And the advantages left to the public schools offering a third-year sixth form were undermined. Franks's reforms to benefit state-school students, which would open up two exam routes into Oxford, were even ahead of the Labour government's policies on secondary schools. However, the Franks Commission blocked a viable internal proposal to increase the number and status of women within Oxford.

The university's moves away from social class and toward meritocracy were underwritten by state funds. Much of the Oxford community misunderstood the shift as a drift toward intellectual excellence. Oxford switched from a special relation to the governing class to a dependence on public resources. The only check on the discourse of academic autonomy was a concern for social justice.

Overall, what can be said of the pattern? The social transformation twirled its way into Oxford with only moderate internal recognition, while the external world remained mesmerized by the old myths. The formal process of reform began in response to external stimuli and then moved forward through a contentious discourse on Oxford's functions and traditions. Ultimately, meritocracy emerged on the ascendant, tempered by social democratic concerns and tarnished by gender biases. Oxford's collegiate and self-governing traditions, its organizational values, were reaffirmed. But the invisible hand supporting the process was attached to an arm of the state.

3.

Oxford Moves into the Natural Sciences

Another striking development, no less significant than Oxford's social metamorphosis, was its post-1939 expansion of resources, faculty, and students into the natural sciences. In the 1930s, Oxford was a community of liberal arts colleges. For investments in the natural sciences, Oxford was in the back ranks, behind such English universities as Cambridge and Manchester. By the 1960s, however, Oxford was a modern science university in step with other English universities and ahead of its trans-Atlantic cousins, Harvard and Yale.

This section investigates the mechanisms responsible for, and the extent of, Oxford's curriculum and research modernization. And we will probe the paradox that even in the 1990s, in the words of its premier sociologist of education, Professor A. H. Halsey, "Oxford could be represented satirically as the best liberal arts college outside or inside America," when it was actually more engaged with the sciences than either Harvard or Yale (Halsey 1994: 605–6). Despite its modernization, the vision of Oxonians as contemplative humanists, too unworldly to be cognizant of modern science, endured. We will examine when, how, and why it made the transformation. And we will explore the reasons why the rise of the natural sciences was a source of internal conflict and was not fully recognized on the outside.

SCIENCE FACULTY

The change in the composition of Oxford's university and college faculty after World War II was dramatic. Some sense of the transformation can be gained by contrasting two years on either side of the change, 1923 and 1974. In 1923, of college fellows and university faculty with teaching or research responsibilities, approximately 70 percent were in arts subjects; 26.6 percent worked on science or technology; and 3.3 percent were occupied with subjects that the British call social studies and that Americans classify as social science (*Oxford University Calendar* 1923–24).[1] By 1974 it was a different world; then some 43 percent of the faculty at Oxford were in science or technology, 38 percent taught arts, and 19 percent taught social studies (*Oxford University Calendar* 1974–75).

During the interwar period Oxford was still without question an arts university, yet by 1974 a plurality of Oxford's personnel were involved in the pure and applied sciences. Oxford's character had moved beyond the bounds of an "arts" designation (see Table 7).

The move by new university faculty into the natural sciences was most substantial between 1953 and 1963, years before the Robbins Report and pressures from Harold Wilson's Labour government.

One chemistry don, Dr. Robert Gasser, remembered the period fondly: "Those were the days of growth [for] . . . the natural sciences. . . . I recall vividly in the lab I worked in . . . I was the next appointment after Sir Rex Richards, who was appointed in the 1940s. As far as I'm aware, there was no college tutor or lecturer appointed until I was appointed in 1959. Then after that was a period of enormous growth in the sciences, in all sciences" (Gasser interview 1988). And Professor Denis Noble reminisced, "When I came to Balliol [in 1963] . . . I was the first fellow in physiology, but only in the decade before had they started to appoint fellows in physics" (Noble interview 1988).

Immediately following the Second World War, and until the financial retrenchments of the mid-1970s, Oxford increased its annual commitment of resources to science and technology. For example, building and equipment expenditures went from 183,000 pounds in 1956–57 to 1.2 million pounds in 1966–67. (These amounts do not include expenditures in clinical medicine or anything from the Historic Buildings Fund Appeal for restoration work.) Much of that money was spent on the Keble Road Science Triangle and on the new nuclear physics building. (The new zoology and psychology building was completed in the early 1970s.) University facilities, again mostly science laboratory space and lecture rooms,

TABLE 7

Oxford University Faculty by Broad Academic Field, 1923–1974
(percent)

	1923	1953	1963	1974
Arts	70	47	44	38
Social studies	3	23	15	19
Science and technology	27	28	40	43

SOURCE: *Oxford University Calendar*, various years.
NOTE: Percentages are rounded.

grew between 1956 and 1966 from 1.43 million square feet to 2.57 million square feet (*Oxford University Gazette* 1968).

At the level of faculty and fiscal resources, Oxford's commitments to the sciences have been equal to or above those of Harvard and Yale. For example, Yale has never had more faculty in the natural sciences than in 1991, when they constituted 37.5 percent of the university staff (Yale University 1992: 19). At Yale, the arts faculty were the largest single faculty group in 1991, with 40.8 percent of the total. In the natural sciences, Yale has not surpassed Oxford's record for 1963.

UNDERGRADUATES IN THE SCIENCES

In the 1950s and early 1960s, undergraduates switched in large numbers into the sciences, even though the trend lagged behind faculty growth in the field. In 1938, 59.1 percent of Oxford undergraduates read arts; 22.5 percent were in social studies; and only 18.2 percent worked in science and technology. By 1961 the swing to science and technology brought those subjects to 31.0 percent, while social studies remained much the same at 21.4 percent, and the arts went down to 47.5 percent. By 1992, however, the ascending preference of undergraduates for science and technology produced an entering cohort with a 42.5 percent plurality in those subject areas (*Oxford University Gazette* 1992b) (see Table 8).

Oxford's undergraduate scientists, who composed nearly one-third of the university's junior members in 1963, placed it in that respect ahead of comparable universities Harvard and Yale. In the early 1960s, fewer than one-quarter of Harvard students were studying the sciences, and at Yale the lab-coat division in 1962 amounted to 13.6 percent of the graduating class (see Table 9) (Leape, n.d.; Yale College Registrar's Office 1995).

TABLE 8

Broad Subject Areas Studied by Oxford Undergraduates, 1923–1991

(percent)

	1923	1938	1951	1961	1971	1981	1991
Arts	80	59.1	54.7	47.5	40.7	40.0	37.8
Social studies	0	22.5	19.0	21.4	20.0	21.8	22.7
Science and technology	20	18.2	26.2	31.0	39.1	38.0	39.3

SOURCES: University of Oxford 1966b: 5; Hebdomadal Council Papers 1963d: 343; *Oxford University Gazette* 1995d: 1336–37

Oxford's percentage of undergraduates in the natural sciences in 1963 reached a level not yet matched by the higher education system in the United States as a whole. In the second half of the twentieth century, fewer than one-third of U.S. bachelor's degrees awarded each year were in the sciences (S. Harris 1972: 318–19; Chronicle of Higher Education 1991: 30).

To summarize the basic facts of this section, a before-and-after statistical calculation reveals that in 1938 only 18 percent of Oxford's undergraduates had anything to do with science or technology—by 1971, 39.1 percent were working in those fields. Before the war against Hitler, fewer than 28 percent of the university's faculty worked in the natural sciences—by 1963, 40 percent did. The funds available to the university for science, which constituted the lion's share of government money funneled through the University Grants Committee, went from less than 100,000 pounds sterling in 1938 to more than 4 million pounds in 1964 (Commission of Inquiry 1965c: 1). By the early 1960s, Oxford had become a power base for the natural sciences. Finally, another measure of Oxford's turnaround was that between 1945 and 1973 its scientists won six Nobel Prizes, just one fewer than the entire nation of France (Morrell 1994: 262).

WHY THE SCIENCES TOOK OFF AT OXFORD

To what may we attribute the timing of Oxford's embrace of the natural sciences? The Second World War made England acutely aware of the importance of science and technology. The power of science was impressed upon the public by radar, jet propulsion, penicillin, rockets, and atomic

TABLE 9

Undergraduate Field of Study for Yale University
Seniors, 1955–1992

(percent)

	1955	1962	1972	1992
Arts	58.7	63.4	49.7	55.0
Social studies	25.2	22.9	31.1	27.7
Science and technology	16.0	13.6	19.1	17.2

SOURCE: Yale College Registrar's Office, 1995, courtesy of Dean John Meeske.

bombs. With popular opinion solidly behind it, in 1942 the British gov-ernment set up a Science Advisory Council to select and fund strategic projects. After the war various government reports focused attention on scientific and technological education (see Argles 1964: 149).

The push from the outside moving Oxford into the sciences took the form of special earmarked funds from the University Grants Committee to stimulate particular fields. After 1944, UGC committee reports (on med-ical education, technical education, and science and technology, for exam-ple) were presented to British universities with a package of fiscal incen-tives to expand those areas (Hebdomadal Council Papers, vol. 249, Octo-ber 1964: 70, 176–77).

The pull from within Oxford came from formal inquiries launched by the Hebdomadal Council and ratified by Congregation, such as the de-termination after the war to build a school of clinical medicine and the 1955 advisory committee recommendations to expand engineering (Roche 1994: 273). In addition to those initiatives from the center, scientists scat-tered around Oxford's periphery made concerted efforts to build discipli-nary empires. Before the war, when Oxford's sciences were relatively weak, some professors acted as entrepreneurs, individually raising the money for the equipment and recruiting the technical staff to assist with their experiments. After the war, scientists could look to government re-search councils for the initial funds to launch a line of investigation which, if it bore fruit, the UGC's recurrent grant would pick up and cover as a continuing expense. To the extent that scientists had to be like entre-preneurs after 1945, the state virtually eliminated the risk by acting as both venture capitalist and steady consumer. The government institution-alized a buoyant market for science.

With such plentiful external resources flowing to Oxford's gates, there were not enough jealous arts dons within the administration to obstruct entry. If institutionally powerful dons were intent on preserving a monopoly for the arts, they were ineffectual. It was possible for the Hebdomadal Council or the General Board of the Faculties to veto any particular project, yet except on a few rare occasions neither one did so. Each grant passed through both the council and the board, where it was voted on and recorded. For example, in September 1965, the Hebdomadal Council made resolutions accepting funding for 28 projects worth more than 200,000 pounds. The largest single grant was 41,000 pounds for a computing laboratory with one senior faculty post and six research assistants for two years. The smallest was 75 pounds for weather observations (Hebdomadal Council Papers 1965c). In the 1960s, projects and funds like those just discussed were processed several times a year.

In those exceptional instances when formal bodies inside the university blocked a new science project it was because the venture carried controversial repercussions for the whole of Oxford. Two virtually identical cases from the early 1960s involved the transfer of an existing research unit from another university to Oxford, Sir Hans Krebs's biochemistry team and Dr. D. C. Philips's molecular biophysics group. The catch was that each employed assistants at salaries 25 to 30 percent higher than Oxford's normal rates. The move would require annual salary reductions of between 400 and 600 pounds for those scientists. The controversy within Oxford was whether to make exceptions for those teams; the relevant faculties supported and the General Board was reluctantly in favor of pay flexibility, but Council and Congregation voted them down. Oxford was opposed to creating two pay classes, one for research scientists and another for everybody else. Whether the motives were democratic and egalitarian or conservative and stingy, the results set back Oxford's work in those areas (Hebdomadal Council Papers 1965f).

For many science professors the state's fiscal generosity was like the receipt of a long-dreamt-about rich inheritance. But not everyone was on the legacy list, and even those who were did not always receive the amounts hoped for. There were always limits to resources, even when the source was the British Treasury. In 1965, for example, when the UGC invited proposals for supplementary grants in technology, it received requests that, according to the UGC's chairman, J. F. Wolfenden, exceeded by "about six times . . . the amount of money which the Government had undertaken to make available" (Hebdomadal Council Papers 1965g: 346). Wolfenden wrote Oxford's vice-chancellor to explain that its request for

150,000 pounds to expand engineering had been turned down, but its metallurgy proposal procured 25,000. The money was used to cover the salaries of three new university lecturers and at least one technical staff person in metallurgy (Hebdomadal Council Papers 1965h).

Throughout the 1950s and 1960s, grants large and small filtered into Oxford, augmenting its faculty and equipment in the sciences. Within their labs professors had the powers of industrial bosses, organizing the production of experiments, commanding a staff outside Oxford's collegiate walls, and accountable only to their peers on grant committees.

All of this by the mid-1950s made Oxford University a world leader in nuclear physics, especially in the new field of superconducting magnets. Oxford's chemistry department had been for a time, and would continue to be, the largest in the nation. Metallurgy and engineering were taking Oxford into new areas of technology; and other fields, such as biochemistry, pathology and physiology, pharmacology, botany, and zoology, were growing (Roche 1994: 266–67, 269, 271–73).

Four elements made the transformation possible. First, the climate of opinion improved outside and inside Oxford about the importance of science and technology. Second, the state became more generous in its funding: the Treasury, Cabinet ministers, Parliament, and UGC were in harmony over the supply of resources. Third, the decentralized and dual organizational structure of Oxford made it possible for funds to circulate into myriad university projects without arousing the opposition of conservative arts dons in any of the colleges. And fourth, the energies of scientists received sympathetic support from those dons in Oxford's power structure who were influenced by social democratic and democratic elitist ideas. There was an affinity between the forces who pushed through meritocratization and the persons who worked to move Oxford in the direction of the modern sciences. By the time of the Franks Commission, distinguished scientists used democratic elitist arguments to articulate a program of radical reform.

THE MISRECOGNITION PUZZLE

If shifts in Oxford's resource networks made its rush into the sciences possible, the weight of the past and aspects of its organizational culture worked against widespread recognition of the transformation. It is a puzzling paradox that Oxford could become a science university and not receive public credit for doing so.

The puzzle grows when one realizes that Oxford was not the only institution accused of being averse to science and technology. During the government's postwar review of British science, the misperception spread that universities were deficient in the sciences and biased in favor of the arts. By 1959, Oxbridge and humanists throughout the university system were placed on the defensive by C. P. Snow's famous lecture "The Two Cultures."

Drawing on his experience of Oxbridge, Snow described a profound split in the academy between natural scientists and arts scholars. "Literary intellectuals at one pole—at the other scientists. . . . Between the two a gulf of mutual incomprehension." Although he acknowledged that there were those, such as Oxford's leader of St. Catherine's, "Alan Bullock and some of my American sociological friends" who defied either category, the two camps were on a treacherous fault line in intellectual culture (Snow 1964: 4, 9).

There was a convergence of the qualities of Snow's two cultures with the differences Mannheim attributed to bourgeois and democratic intellectuals. Scientists, according to Snow, were by vocation progressive democrats with "the future in their bones" who worked with analysis "usually much more rigorous, and almost always at a higher conceptual level, than literary persons' arguments" (ibid.: 11, 12). In contrast, the literary possessed a "traditional culture" that inclined them to be pessimistic and complacent about social problems. From more privileged homes and expressing more conservative political views than scientists, the literary were anti-industrial and fast "turning anti-scientific" (ibid.: 7, 10–11).

Snow predicted that as long as Western society was governed by arts men the odds that it would accomplish its "practical tasks in the world" were small (ibid.: 19). Horrible consequences awaited unless the humanities and the sciences recovered from their separation. The global gulf between rich and poor nations and the challenges unleashed by the scientific revolution, among other problems, would never be addressed.

Snow's portrayal of the two sides, democratic-elitist scientists on one and cultural aristocrats on the other, was without any pretense of nonpartisanship. The task of reconciliation, Snow implied, was up to the humanist, who had to become literate in scientific matters. Universities, Snow thought, relegated science and technology to a status subordinate to the arts; and time was running out on England's opportunity to reform its educational system to correct the bias.

F. R. Leavis, a Cambridge literary scholar, rushed to defend the humanities from Snow's attack (Leavis 1962). Unfortunately, Leavis's tone was anything but humane. Leavis, a self-appointed guardian of organic community, was crusading against the dehumanization of ordinary English life (Leavis and Thompson 1933; 1943). This was due, he thought, to commerce and the media's having sold England on an American-style consumer society. Behind Snow's adulation of the sciences Leavis saw "dark Satanic mills" belching cultural corruption.[2] Leavis's hostility to Snow was so similar to that inspired by liturgical zealotry that he caused sympathies to move away from the side he sought to defend (Trilling 1965: 126–54).

The perception that British universities were anti-science was false, and yet for decades after Snow's lecture the dispute refused to go away. The Robbins expansion of higher education merely added a new issue to the argument. Universities were allegedly guilty of promoting the "soft" social sciences to the detriment of the "hard" natural sciences in order to attract more undergraduates. Yet in Britain before the Robbins Report, John Carswell, the Treasury representative to the Robbins Commission, noted that "some 60 percent of all men going to universities were entering faculties of science and technology" (Carswell 1985: 45). Confirming Carswell's point, Michael Sanderson, a historian of British universities and industry, observed:

> There is a common misconception that the expansion of the universities from the 1960s has led to an imbalance in favour of the arts and social science subjects. . . . In fact the reverse is true and this in itself is a British peculiarity. Britain has a markedly lower proportion of students studying arts and a higher proportion studying science and technology than other leading competitors and comparable European countries. (Sanderson 1987: 134)

It is bewildering that before and after Robbins, British universities by international standards were uncommonly strong in the sciences, and yet journalistic and political recognition of that fact remained elusive.

Instances of politicians and journalists getting it wrong were numerous. In 1967, Labour's Anthony Crosland, secretary of state for science and education, acting according to those mistaken impressions, legislated a binary policy to create a new polytechnic sector of higher education. To correct the anti-science imbalance, the "polys" would be kept apart from the universities with their penchant for fluffy arts and soft social sciences. The polytechnics were placed under local governmental control, given a technological emphasis, and pledged to serve vocational goals. An example of the persistence of the journalistic misunderstanding was evidenced in a May 1990 "Viewpoint" column in the respected British daily the *In-*

TABLE 10

College Tutors and Lecturers in Science and Technology at Oxford, 1964–1989

(percent)

College	1964	1974	1989
Balliol	41	41	42
Brasenose	29	38	45
Christ Church	22	28	36
Corpus Christi	30	33	42
Exeter	33	32	38
Hertford	31	32	42
Jesus	32	31	38
Keble	23	34	43
Lincoln	33	29	42
Magdalen	30	30	31
Merton	40	27	41
New	26	31	39
Oriel	33	32	39
Pembroke	35	35	34
Queen's	23	32	38
St. Catherine's	56	42	45
St. Edmund	31	34	46
St. John's	35	38	41
St. Peter's	31	34	40
Trinity	32	32	42
University	32	37	45
Wadham	40	40	37
Worcester	36	26	40
Average	32.8	33.3	40.2

SOURCES: 1964 from Hebdomadal Council Papers, "Stewarts and Lloyds Professorship of Structural Engineering: Allocation to a College," Vol. 247, January 24, 1964: 135–36; 1974 from Oxford University Undergraduate Prospectus for 1976–77; 1989 from Oxford University Undergraduate Prospectus for 1990–91.

NOTE: In 1964, without St. Catherine's contribution the average would have been 31.8 percent. Compare the lag in the appointment by colleges of tutors in science and technology with the faculty statistics in Table 7. Percentages are rounded.

dependent (Faith 1990). In it Nicholas Faith claimed that'British science was weak because Oxbridge set a bad example. Force more scientists on Oxbridge, Faith urged, by withdrawing all government grants for the arts and social studies. Then Oxbridge will toe the line and other universities will follow.

The paradoxical gap between image and reality can be bridged intellectually when one ponders Oxford's history and its collegiate traditions. Oxford has educated a disproportionate share of Britain's governing class. Generations of politicians and authors have passed through its garden quads, taking little if any notice of science along the way.

When the university embraced the sciences, a division grew up between it and the colleges. The colleges stood aside and did not begin to welcome scientists into their cloistered homes until the mid-1960s. But the older, larger, and most prestigious colleges, such as Christ Church and Queen's, were unfriendly to science faculty until the 1980s (see Table 10).

Oxford's past practices fostered a collective mentality among the political and professional classes, who mistook a donnish disregard for science as a mark of cultural sophistication. John Pringle, a professor of zoology, pithily expressed this point in his submissions to Franks. The arts dons were science luddites who imprinted their prejudices on undergraduates, Pringle wrote: "The scientific illiteracy of college Fellows passes itself on from generation to generation. Oxford is to this extent directly to blame for the lack of understanding and application of science and technology in the government of this country, which is at the root of so many of our national problems" (Commission of Inquiry 1965b: 152). The myth that Oxford was anti-science was a legacy of Oxford's own creation.

SCIENCE AT OTHER UNIVERSITIES

Between the late nineteenth century and the early 1950s, when Oxford was relegating science to the back rows, other British universities were moving in more modern directions. The Redbrick universities, such as Birmingham and Manchester, were nineteenth-century manifestations of civic pride by the manufacturing middle classes. From the start, those institutions were solidly oriented to science, technology, and industrial concerns (Sanderson 1972). Cambridge too had been a science university since the end of the nineteenth century.

In 1922, the Royal Commission on Oxbridge expressed concern that Cambridge's sciences were so well developed that the humanities were at risk. The commissioners wrote:

> The growth of science at Cambridge since the era [nineteenth century] of the Royal Commissions has been perhaps the greatest fact in the history of the University since its foundation. . . . [Today the

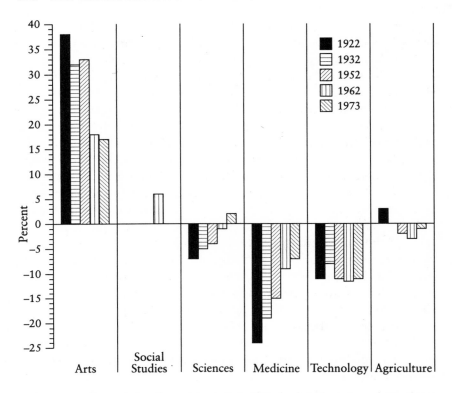

FIGURE 1. Over- and underrepresentation of Oxford students in undergraduate subjects, 1922–73 (percentage, in comparison with other British universities). Data are taken from University Grants Committee 1922–1974.

humanities] stand in danger of being overshadowed by the importance and popularity of science, and of falling behind in the matter of endowments which the state and private individuals are too apt to lavish solely on what is considered to be "useful" in some obvious sense. (Parliamentary Papers 1922: 33, 35)

By 1922, half of Cambridge's undergraduates were working in the sciences or technology. Cambridge's strengths, especially in engineering, gave rise to the saying that it produced Britain's scientists while Oxford turned out politicians. Behind that expression lurked one of the reasons for the persistence of the anti-science myth. Politicians who had attended Oxford thought they knew all about it; they assumed Oxford was an arts university and that other universities reflected the same priorities.

Until the late 1950s, the view that Oxford favored the arts was supported by the data. Figure 1 compares Oxford's representation in undergraduate subjects with that of other British universities.

SCIENCE AND OXFORD'S ORGANIZATIONAL CULTURE

While scientists poured in as university faculty and undergraduate specialists, the dons, those tutors with equal ownership and governing rights in their colleges, remained apart. In the decade after science arrived, Oxford had a deeply divided faculty. There had been differences in the past between university appointments and college posts: sometimes it was a division of labor between separate persons, other times it was a division of one person's responsibilities into two roles. Before the 1950s, however, those with only university positions were few; the weight of numbers went solidly with the colleges. Men with just university posts, in addition to being a small minority, were relatively deprived: the university was poor, and the colleges were rich. Near the end of the nineteenth century, for example, the university's income was approximately one-eighth of the combined annual income of the colleges (Commission of Inquiry 1965c: 20); not so after the expansion of sciences. With government funds, scientists made the university the wealthiest partner in the community by far. The colleges had their gothic quads, and now the university had more than just a library and a mailing address. The entire science area, in the northeastern part of Oxford, was filled with university buildings.

A committee chaired by A. R. W. Harrison attempted to make sense of the growth of the university independent of the colleges and proposed ways to reintegrate the two. Its report recognized that the new circumstances represented a near total reversal in the fortunes of the colleges and the university:

> We cannot emphasize too strongly . . . that the problem now facing "Oxford" is caused by a complete change in the size and functions of the University *which has already taken place.* . . . If the University ceased to exist . . . in 1920 the colleges would hardly have noticed. . . . Had the colleges ceased to exist in 1920, the University would have become little more than a book repository whereas today it could without overmuch trouble be made into a viable concern on its own. (University of Oxford 1962a: para. 4)

Oxford in the 1950s had a dual faculty structure. Some faculty had only university responsibilities, and others were fellows of colleges. Roughly half of the academics worked in the labs, the other half in the colleges. Properly speaking, only the latter were dons; the former were referred to as "nondons."

As a class, the nondons were a result of the rapid expansion between 1953 and 1963 of the science faculties in the university. The Harrison committee noted, "This expansion is commonly believed to have taken place within the college system whereas it has in fact in large part been achieved outside it" (ibid.). Nondons had university appointments but not college fellowships. The university's recruitment of new scientific talent outstripped the undergraduate colleges' desire and ability to provide for them. In 1955, the percentage of university science faculty in each field without college affiliations was, in chemistry, 36 percent; in physics, 40 percent; in biochemistry, 45 percent; in pathology and physiology, 50 percent; in pharmacology, 80 percent; in botany, 83 percent; in human anatomy, 87 percent; and in zoology, 89 percent (Roche 1994: 271). By 1962, there were 426 nondons in the Oxford academic community and 560 college fellows (University of Oxford 1962a: para. 2). Although nondons were in the university but outside the college system, they constituted almost 50 percent of Congregation, the university's highest governing body.

One offended nondon biochemist, a Dr. V. P. Whittaker, who received both his undergraduate and postgraduate education at Oxford, resigned his post in protest and left for a job at an American university. On the inequities of the system, he wrote:

> When I became a university teacher, it was speedily brought home to me that there are two grades of teacher in Oxford, the "haves" and the "have nots." By the "haves" I mean those possessing a college appointment and the good living which goes with it. During my seven years as a teacher, I can remember being invited to dine in college only five times. . . . The lavish food and wine and the quaint dining rituals struck me as anachronistic in post-war Britain; but I became aware that it was over the port that most of the decisions were made. I began to understand why university teachers had so little influence. . . . This complex network of class distinction among Oxford teachers is out of date, widely resented and inefficient. (Commission of Inquiry 1965c: 205)

Oxford's two cultures were divided not so much by different cognitive orientations or distinct temperaments as by social segregation. Scientists commuted from their homes to labs in the science area, while arts dons worked in colleges with dining halls and gothic quads.

Whittaker correctly targeted the three problems that faced scientists outside the colleges. They were without the material resources and club-like amenities provided by colleges; they lacked the symbolic dignity that follows from equality of status; and locked out of the informal networks that ran Oxford they were less powerful in institutional politics than arts dons. Scientists addressed the problem of facilities through a dining association called Halifax House; but the second and third problems could not be resolved without coming to terms with the arts dons in the colleges.

Halifax House, located in the science area, was a social club for Oxford's scientists, a few overseas visitors, and some graduate students. Begun in 1945, its membership had climbed to more than 700 by 1964 (Commission of Inquiry 1965a: 75, 77). Halifax's facilities were meager: it could offer only twelve beds for the night, yet it served lunch daily to more than 100 of its members, many of whom used its common room for coffee, newspaper reading, and conversation (Roche 1994: 285). At night smaller numbers used its dinner and drinks facilities. It was the gathering place for food and conversation preferred by most of Oxford's scientists, nondons and dons alike. The inhospitality of the undergraduate colleges, disproportionately on the arts side of C. P. Snow's cultural divide, and the propinquity of Halifax to the science labs caused even those scientists with college affiliations to opt for it. Consequently, it was the opinion of A. L. P. Norrington, the chair of a committee charged with looking into the nondon problem, that even if Oxford gave nondon scientists college memberships, "only a small number out of the 700 members of Halifax House [would] give up or even abate their use of its facilities" (Hebdomadal Council Papers 1965b: 183). If the two cultures were to be reunited, Oxford would have to do something other than subsidize a social center for scientists.

Nondons were kept on the margins of Oxford's formal and informal power structure in a variety of ways. Most obviously, they were denied the political resources available within the colleges. Colleges were small communities with abundant opportunities for politics. One could easily catch another don to pose a question, express a concern, or arrange to meet over lunch or dinner to discuss at length whatever one wanted to sort out. Conversation between dons in their rooms, halls, gardens, walkways, and Senior Common Rooms were a means for each to keep informed about and involved in Oxford's business. But the informal resources of college dons were not the only political disadvantage facing nondons.

Colleges were units of power in themselves. They admitted their own students, elected their own fellows, managed their own endowments, and oversaw the upkeep of college buildings and grounds. Within the university, each college was a distinct political entity. On controversial matters, each college's views as a corporate body were solicited by Council or by the committee working on an issue. The colleges were intermediate political societies standing between the individual don and the democratic powers of Congregation. The colleges gave each fellow a venue for exercising voice, separate from faculty groups, committees, Congregation, or the pages of the *Oxford Magazine*. Of possible ways to amplify one's voice, given Oxford's qualities as a traditional community, the colleges were the most effective. When a college spoke, its message was clearly heard.

The political handicaps that hindered nondons were not only those of grapevine or college governing body; nondons were actually ineligible for two of the university's most powerful positions: vice-chancellor and proctor. And even though nondons were not formally prohibited from holding other positions, they were grossly under-represented on all of the most powerful governing groups in the university. An article in the *Oxford Magazine* took stock of the nondons' exclusion from Oxford's political machinery: "There are in practice no nondons on Council, the Chest, the General Board, or five of the Faculty Boards." Barnes calculated that "significant seats of authority in the University may . . . be counted as 318. . . . Of the 318 places 266 go to dons" (Barnes 1962: 20). Dons were approximately 57 percent of the Oxford faculty, but they controlled 84 percent of the power structure.

The power of dons was itself not randomly distributed among Oxford's colleges. Rather, Barnes found that half of the colleges in combination controlled 85 percent of the 266 seats: "Ranked by size of share the first six colleges are Magdalen, All Souls, Balliol, Queen's, Christ Church, and New College. In short, disproportionate holdings of power within the University organs are acquired not merely by dons as against nondons, but also by stronger colleges as against weaker ones" (ibid.: 20–21). Dons in the older, wealthier colleges—those that drew heavily from the public schools—held more power than nondon scientists and reform-minded dons in the poorer and less socially privileged foundations such as St. Edmund Hall, St. Catherine's, Jesus, and Wadham.

If nondons were to gain power and status equal to that of dons, they would need to challenge the existing division between the haves and have nots. Barnes warned: "Apartheid of this pattern builds into the University structure a system of values . . . too parochial and too cross for the mental growth and moral education of leaders in the space age. . . . One way or another, don-supremacy will go before the turn of the century, perhaps well before" (ibid.: 21). Nondons should use their growing power in Congregation, Barnes intimated, to overthrow donnish power.

Oxford in the early 1960s faced a dilemma. The university and the colleges were coming apart. The schism came first at the level of faculty, but it was growing among the student population as well. Either the university would go its own way, becoming a natural science teaching and research institution, and treat the colleges as little better than pretty dormitories, or the university and the colleges would have to reintegrate themselves. But Oxford could not be a collegiate university if its sciences resided in labs and departments disconnected from its colleges. If Snow's two camps were not to overthrow Oxford's organizational culture, it would have to make significant adjustments.

In the struggle between the scientists and the arts dons, the former could draw upon resources from outside; the latter were most powerful within Oxford's organizational culture. The scientists could confidently call upon the backing of public opinion as well as the vast material resources of the state. Scientists both increased Oxford's dependence upon government money and became indispensable as brokers to bring in those resources. Furthermore, scientists could point to other universities and use their examples to urge the adoption of similar patterns. They could mobilize both normative and fiscal reasons why Oxford should become more like other universities. On the other side, the arts dons had the weight of tradition and the power of the colleges, their material and political resources. The colleges were resilient communities of living social traditions among whom the oldest, wealthiest, and largest were, as Barnes explained, in control of Oxford's political structure.

In the conflict between the arts dons and scientists to establish the authority of their descriptive and prescriptive vision, the dons could rely more upon Council, the nondons on Congregation. The dons could count on committees formed by the colleges, the nondons on university committees. The dons had their college governing bodies as platforms; the nondons could use faculty boards for leverage. And both could vie for space in the pages of the *Oxford Magazine*.

The nondons formed their own organization, the Committee of Non-Fellows, with Dr. W. E. van Heyningen as chairman. The committee pressed for nondons' rights and represented their voice in university politics. And its chair, Van Heyningen, was one of five scientists elected by Congregation to the Hebdomadal Council.

Council was itself divided by socio-philosophical sympathies and organizational loyalties. On Council the nondons could expect to receive the votes of not more than seven members, the democratic elitist scientists plus the social democratic master of St. Catherine's, Alan Bullock, and the principal of Linacre House, John Bamborough. The other thirteen members of Council were consciously conservative or simply too cautious to move quickly down reformist routes. Consequently, Council's divisions on controversial questions often broke down as six to thirteen or seven to twelve during the early 1960s.

The range of possible solutions to the growth of the sciences and the nondon problem included four options: do nothing and accept the split; abolish the autonomy of the colleges, turn them into dormitories, and make all of the faculty nondons; absorb the nondons into the existing colleges; take certain categories of nondons into the undergraduate colleges, and build new postgraduate colleges or societies for the others. Some diehard arts dons and radical scientists wanted the first or second response, but neither won sufficient support to place either on the agenda. Rather, the lines of division were drawn between complete and partial integration within existing or new colleges.

Formal inquiries by people inside Oxford to solve the nondon problem and bridge the cultural divide stretched over a decade, from 1962 to 1973. It took six committee reports to heal the split: the Harrison report of November 1962; the Norrington reports of January 1964 and November 1964; the Franks report of 1966; the Griffiths report of June 1970; and finally, the Bullock report of May 1972.

Those who favored complete absorption, the total abolition of two categories of faculty inside Oxford, were most encouraged by the Harrison and Franks reports. Both went on record favoring the institutionalization of a single class of faculty. For Harrison and Franks, Oxford was a collegiate university; it was a matter of principle that all university faculty should also be members of the colleges.

The Harrison report in November 1962, Council's first attempt to address the problem, took the following position:

> All members of the graduate staff of the University ought to
> have some form of affiliation with some form of graduate society
> [and] this cannot be fully achieved without the creation of new
> societies. . . . We make these proposals in the firm conviction that
> the members of the academic staff of a collegiate university . . .
> should have the opportunity of participating in something more
> than a "9 to 5 job" in the university department in which they are
> primarily employed. (University of Oxford 1962a: 15, para. 27)

If something like equal fellowship rights were not extended to the entire science faculty of the university, "then Oxford will cease to be a collegiate university and will become instead a university to which some colleges are affiliated; our proposals are designed to prevent this from ever happening" (ibid.).

The Harrison report and Franks worked for the principle of equal entitlement, that all university faculty with duties comparable to those of college tutors should have a right to a college fellowship. It would equalize the status and salaries of the university and the colleges, for although university faculty did not automatically have college positions, the reverse was true. Taking advantage of funds available to the university from the UGC, Council in 1950 "adopted in principle a scheme whereby it would be normal for every college tutor to hold a university lectureship" (Hebdomadal Council Papers 1967b: 122). With the status of a university lectureship for every don went money from the UGC for salary. The Franks report summarized this development:

> Before 1939 the majority of college fellows were in arts. They received their salaries from their colleges. . . . It is almost true to say that Oxford was not a collegiate university, as it now is, but only a confederation of colleges. After 1945, . . . colleges found it difficult to pay the fellows . . . out of their own endowment income and fees. The University then stepped in. . . . Thus the college fellow in arts became also a lecturer of the University, and his salary was paid from two sources. (University of Oxford 1966a: 132, para. 300)

Harrison and Franks wanted reciprocity from the colleges for the university's faculty in order to reaffirm the collegiate character of Oxford.

The principle of equal status, that all Oxford faculty should have dual positions, one in the university and the other in a college, was difficult to implement. The transmutation of a college don into a university lecturer was easy: the don got a new title and more money. But the metamorphosis of a university scientist into a don required granting membership privileges in a self-governing club. There literally had to be a place at the table for the newcomer; ideally, the fellows should actually want to converse with the scientists. Colleges did not inconvenience themselves rushing to invite scientists to dinner.

The opposition of the colleges to a total assimilation of the two cultures in the university was articulated twice by reports from committees chaired by Trinity's president, A. L. P. Norrington. In January and November 1964, Norrington's committees registered those criticisms of Harrison made by the colleges and presented counter-proposals. Norrington noted: "Colleges doubt whether it is desirable to insist, as the Harrison Report suggests (para. 16), on the linking of university appointments with college fellowships. . . . We do not think that all members of Congregation, at any given time, could reasonably or properly be made fellows of existing or future colleges" (University of Oxford 1964a: 5, para. 14, and 6, para. 19).

Although there were 426 nondons in the university, Harrison had recommended immediate action to affect the status of only 250 of them (University of Oxford 1962: paras. 2, 18). The Norrington reports, however, managed by a logic of exclusion to prune the number even further. First they excluded those with purely administrative or institutional duties in the university, such as librarians and museum curators (University of Oxford 1964a: 6, para. 19). Second, they cut out those faculty without tenure. In comments to Council on this, Norrington said, "It was encouraging that the number of non-Fellows concerned had been reduced to 150, from the 250 mentioned in the Harrison Report, mainly by the exclusion of those whose appointments had not yet been confirmed to retiring age" (Hebdomadal Council Papers 1964k: lxxxii). Equally important, the Norrington reports introduced a system of classification that established a priority list. The categories were defined by the perceived needs of the colleges.

Norrington grouped the 150 remaining nondons into three classes. The first, "numbering about 30," contained those scientists with so much international prestige that they would bring distinction to the undergraduate college. The second class, "about 60," were already teaching for a college; they were the ones "whose undergraduate tutorial teaching and experience makes them fitted for a fellowship." The last class, numbering at least 60, were neither world-famous nor involved in undergraduate teaching. They did not belong, according to Norrington's committee, at an undergraduate college. His report stated: "The absorption into *existing* colleges of class (III) . . . is neither feasible nor desirable. We are in no doubt that the right solution . . . is the foundation of new collegiate societies" (University of Oxford 1964a: 7, paras. 21, 23). The old colleges wanted you if you were prestigious, or if you taught their undergraduates. But if you were primarily a researcher or taught mostly postgraduates, you were put off to await a new foundation.

Both Harrison and Norrington affirmed the power of cultural traditions that placed the older undergraduate colleges at the top of Oxford's pyramid of prestige. In each report the relation of college arts dons to university scientists was framed as something like the assimilation of the nouveau riche into respectable society. Scientists might bring research money, but the colleges brought status:

> Some of the departments of the University have a world-wide reputation. . . . This, however, is a recent development, and it is still the case that "Fellow of . . . College, Oxford" carries more weight, both inside and outside the University, than "Lecturer, Demonstrator, or even Reader, in the Department of . . . Oxford." A college has in fact still the power to confer a greater status. (University of Oxford 1962a: 4, para. 6)

And the Norrington report emphasized how the nondon problem was less one of emoluments than of traditional status. The issue was not money, not benefits, but college status: "The root of the matter is *status*. Amenity ('club' facilities) and extra salary can be provided without a fellowship. Fellowship status belongs to a fellowship, and any substitute would be an inferior imitation" (University of Oxford 1964a: 6, para. 17). A fellowship, the crux of the issue for Norrington, gave one an identity that reflected Oxford's collegiate traditions. Norrington articulated the hegemony of the older undergraduate colleges in Oxford's hierarchy.

When the Hebdomadal Council solicited comments on Norrington's diagnosis, reactions were mixed. Most undergraduate colleges were satisfied, but the nondons, the librarians, the postgraduate colleges, and four of the poorer undergraduate colleges dissented. The Committee of Non-Fellows objected to Norrington's discussion of traditional status. In their submission to Council they wrote: "We must emphasize that the status conferred by a fellowship is not merely a symbol." And they worried about ambiguities in the report that might tolerate partial solutions. "It is essential that the existing colleges should absorb all the non-fellows in class (II), not merely 'many of them.'" If all nondons were to have homes, three new colleges would be needed; Linacre should become a proper college and Council should assist in the establishment of two more (Hebdomadal Council Papers 1964d: 234, 235). Additional criticisms were made by the head librarian for the university's depository collection, the Bodleian. He and his colleagues urged Council to include officers of the library in Norrington's class I and hoped "other graduates on the staff" also would be considered for college fellowships (Hebdomadal Council Papers 1964e: 237–38). Among Oxford's poorer foundations, Jesus College took the most inclusionary position by suggesting "the possibility of including post-doctoral research workers" and not just bona fide university faculty in the exercise (Hebdomadal Council Papers 1964d: 226–27). The science area employed large numbers of technical assistants and demonstrators, many of whom were in part-time or temporary positions even though they held doctorates. Those persons were an intellectual underclass, without formal representation in Oxford. And Jesus, with its own good record on admitting undergraduates from the working classes, extended its empathy to Oxford's technical staff.

The two postgraduate colleges, Nuffield and St. Antony's, and one of the women's colleges, St. Hugh's, objected to the creation of new colleges just as a way to provide space for nondons. Such creations would be neither proper undergraduate nor postgraduate colleges and would, in the words of Nuffield, "fall between all possible stools" (Hebdomadal Council Papers 1964f: 295). It would be a hollow settlement if Oxford were to build artificial societies just to sham the nondons. Another poor undergraduate college, St. Edmund Hall, also rejected the report's proposals, and instead advocated "measures . . . to enable the non-fellows of all three categories to be absorbed as fellows by the existing colleges" (ibid.: 298). St. Edmund's plan would have thoroughly erased the organizational barrier between the two cultures. St. Edmund's argument was reiterated (nine months later) by the Hebdomadal Council's assessor, Miss M. E. Hubbard, who "urged that colleges should receive grants . . . [to elect] fellows who had no teaching duties within the college" (Hebdomadal Council Papers 1964l).

Norrington's proposals went to Congregation, which voted in February 1964 to establish the principle of entitlement to fellowships for university faculty with responsibilities comparable to dons'. The legislation made Norrington's list of 150 eligible for fellowships; to accommodate them, Congregation voted to form new collegiate societies that would include students as well as faculty and that should move toward full independent college status as soon as possible (Hebdomadal Council Papers 1967a: 852). To implement those decisions, Council authorized the second Norrington inquiry, which issued its report in November of 1964. It projected two new colleges, St. Cross and Iffley (later renamed Wolfson) (University of Oxford 1964b: 8, para. 20). Following the report, Congregation passed new statutes in June 1965 that "established the principle of entitlement to fellowships for certain classes of university officers . . . and established two new societies, St. Cross and Iffley (now Wolfson)" (Hebdomadal Council Papers 1967a: 852).

Merton College, committed to the reform process, honored its pledge

If medieval Oxford's relation to the church may be understood through the story of New College, and Victorian Oxford's role in the British empire may be viewed through Balliol's record, then Oxford's involvement with postwar British society may be approached through the history of St. Catherine's. For the older foundations, the development of St. Catherine's pointed out the route they would soon travel. In a sense, St. Catherine's role in Oxford was to be an initiator. It could not advertise the historic strengths of the older colleges; rather, it had to focus on new challenges (Smith interview 1988). As a result of its self-appointed role, its former master Dr. E. B. Smith said that "St. Catherine's has become the cutting edge of the Oxford Collegiate system" (E. B. Smith 1989: 11). Practices that began at St. Catherine's spread quickly to the rest of Oxford.

Not only did St. Catherine's history foreshadow the direction of collegiate transition; but its creation illustrated one of the defining aspects of a social tradition, the principle of continuity. St. Catherine's creation fit a traditional pattern, centuries old, of preservation through alteration. Oxford colleges could be innovative because they were independent institutions. The colleges were by convention, law, and architecture tangibly distinct from the university and each other. From the twelfth to the twentieth century, Oxford had grown into a federation of 35 independent colleges, each expressing some particular interest of its time.[9] Whether designed for vocational training, as New College was, established to supply clerks for church and state (Bishop and Wilkinson 1967: 83), or founded merely to provide a home for students from a particular location, as was Worcester College (set up for men from Worcestershire),[10] each college has added, however modestly, to the spectrum of students or functions inside Oxford. Over the centuries, most major changes in student composition or educational activities have found a place first in a new collegiate undertaking. Every new foundation influenced other colleges and took on some common characteristics, so over time innovation and assimilation worked together—as they would in any living social tradition.

In the past hundred years the Oxford tradition to establish independent foundations for new categories of students and new academic fields carried over into the creation of women's and postgraduate colleges. Adding to a core of twenty undergraduate male colleges, innovators set up eleven foundations specifically for undergraduate women or postgraduates between 1878 and 1979.[11]

The five women's colleges (Lady Margaret Hall, St. Anne's, St. Hilda's, St. Hugh's, and Somerville) were creations of the late nineteenth century. In the period since World War II those colleges were less innovative than on the defensive. The women's colleges struggled to shelter their modest foundations from the trend favoring mixed-sex colleges, fearful that the wealthier colleges would siphon off their best talent and erode their viability.

The six postgraduate colleges (Nuffield, St. Antony's, Linacre, St. Cross, Wolfson, and Green) received charters between 1958 and 1979, during the same time as St. Catherine's creation.[12] So we shall turn to them for a brief overview following our account of St. Catherine's, Oxford's last under-graduate college.

The role of cultural authority and personality in the birth of St. Catherine's resembled their part in other Oxford experiences. At some point, each college benefited from Oxford's cultural status—for example, in the unsolicited appearance of a wealthy benefactor. The prestige of Oxford works like a magnetic force in attracting gifts and extraordinary persons. And whether a particular benefaction, person, or idea got moved along depended to an extraordinary extent on personality and propinquity. For inside Oxford's federation of small communities, face-to-face personal relations were all-important. Consequently, the founding of St. Catherine's was very much a story of individuals.

The occupations of the persons who shaped St. Catherine's may help to correct a common misunderstanding about Oxford. There was a widely held belief, which continued to draw support from the debate generated by Thatcher's education policies, that Oxford and the modern business community were antagonists. Yet without the timely advice and financial generosity of a number of leading business figures in London, St. Catherine's would not exist. As I will detail later, British businessmen paid for nearly half of the construction and endowment expenses of St. Catherine's. So, at minimum, one could say that Oxford and the business community were on cordial terms in the early 1960s.

The creation of St. Catherine's illustrates also something of what was meant by the Franks Commission's designation of Oxford as an international university. Oxford stands out from most other British universities by its capacity to attract students and funds from a great number of foreign countries. Only the University of London rivals Oxford's number of international students. And foreign money from continental Europe, Africa, and America have paid for significant expansions in Oxford's buildings and material resources. The money for St. Catherine's not supplied by British businessmen was provided by philanthropic foundations and businessmen from across the Atlantic.

In sum, the St. Catherine's story was similar to that of its elder Oxford relatives in the second half of the twentieth century: it exemplified a traditional pattern of continuity and innovation through collegiate expansion, and it was supported in part by a relationship to British business and foreign benefactors.

A NEW COLLEGE IN OXFORD

Oxford's youngest undergraduate foundation, St. Catherine's College, opened its doors in October 1962. Like other Oxford colleges, its character reflected a mix of societal needs and Oxford traditions. Alan Bullock, the founding master of St. Catherine's, desired to adapt the traditional benefits of an Oxford college to modern conditions, to build a medieval collegiate structure with contemporary materials.

Bullock thought that a collegiate institution could best address the challenges of the times by putting together a new mix of academic subjects and types of students. In past times, Oxford had been guilty of insularity by drawing too many of its students from socially privileged schools, public-school students who would work on arts subjects to the exclusion of the sciences. If the aesthete Brideshead legacy were to fade, the important thing was to strike a better balance in several areas: between C. P. Snow's two cultures of arts and sciences; between public-school boarding students and state-maintained or direct-grant day-school students; between Etonian aristocrats and Manchester grammar-school meritocrats; between the cloister and the worlds of industry and commerce. St. Catherine's took on the responsibility of developing a modern mix (Bullock interviews 1986, 1987; *Oxford University Gazette* 1962b: 111).

The St. Catherine's Non-Collegiate Society

In the 1950s, when public opinion and government policy favored a modest expansion in higher education and an increased focus on science (University Grants Committee 1964), the conviction grew among leading members of Oxford University that the best way to contribute to those two objectives would be to create a new college. No doubt there was an upper limit to the number of colleges that the Oxford community could accommodate without destroying its interpersonal qualities. But in the late 1950s, contrary to the words of a snobbish Oxford poem, heaven was not near to being crammed.[13] A new college was still a distinct possibility.

Within Oxford a fortuitous anomaly eased the way for a new foundation. In the mid-1950s St. Catherine's was a non-collegiate society consisting of hundreds of students all working toward university degrees but without a residential community.[14] St. Catherine's taught, but without benefit of its own rooms and halls. By the 1950s the obstacles that once justified a nonresidential association were no longer of consequence.

The St. Catherine's Society went back to 1868. Its creation was one of many outcomes of the Victorian penchant for reform. There were two major parliamentary debates and Royal Commissions in the nineteenth century on Oxford and Cambridge. Their combined effects were to pull the two universities out of their embrace with the Church of England and to open their gates and curriculum to the needs of the rising professional classes.

St. Catherine's seed was planted by the Royal Commission of 1850–52, which "met with bitter opposition in Oxford" (Engel 1983: 34). The commissioners understood Oxford's problems to stem from the oligarchic powers of the college heads. The masters held a monopoly over university matriculation that the commissioners hoped to break "by creating a new class of non-collegiate students" (ibid.: 35). The idea took sixteen years to assume legislative shape; by then advocates in Parliament and Oxford had additional reasons to offer in support of a non-collegiate system. With Gladstone's blessing and the backing of Balliol's famous master Benjamin Jowett, the partisans for non-collegiate students argued that Oxford needed a version of a Scottish university. They sought an arrangement that would break the monopoly of college tutors over instruction and restore a teaching role for the professorate. Further, they sought to provide a means whereby respectable middle-class parents could send their sons to Oxford without fear of the allegedly corrupting influences of everyday college life: boating, drinking, and whoring (Oxford University Commission 1852). Yet Scottish educational ideals and middle-class social prejudices did not survive long in Oxford. Soon the only element that remained of the original conception of St. Catherine's was its affordability. It was the least expensive option for parents who wanted to enroll a son in Oxford.

From 1868 to 1944, St. Catherine's stood as the poor man's doorway into Oxford (Bullock 1956: 98). Those students who wanted an Oxford degree but who could neither secure an academic scholarship nor afford the full fees and rents of a college, went to St. Catherine's. "Poor boys," by Oxford's standards, would live wherever they could as best they could while working with tutors to pass the university's examinations. As a way to gain an academic credential it worked adequately, but in virtually every other respect it was unsatisfactory. As an undergraduate guide book to Oxford written in 1879 put it, "the life of an unattached [St. Catherine's] student is isolated, and quite unlike the life of the college under-graduate" (Weatherly 1879: 4). By the 1950s, those Oxonians privileged to dwell in colleges referred to the St. Catherine's Society as "Cats" (Balsdon 1957: 78).

The financial barriers that kept an undergraduate without a scholarship from attending a "proper" Oxford college broke down, as described in Chapter 2, in stages. The culminating point came with the 1962 Anderson Report; it required all local education authorities to cover the entire cost of every undergraduate's university and college fees and provide an additional means-assessed subsistence grant.

Oxford students, regardless of class origin, were not above governmental or charitable subsidy. In fact, the large number of Oxford colleges offering their own scholarships put the percentage of undergraduates receiving some form of aid consistently above the national average. On the eve of World War II, when 41.1 percent of Britain's university students were receiving some financial assistance from a sponsoring body, Oxford's percentage was 43.7. In 1947, three years after the Butler Act's provision for government grants, the proportion receiving assistance in Britain as a whole climbed to 67.9 percent, while Oxford's percentage nearly doubled to 82.1 (University Grants Committee 1948b: 105). Of the 82 percent, it was estimated that 48 percent were supported by local education authorities, 40 percent by the Ministry of Education, and 12 percent solely by college scholarships (Longmate 1954: 164; University Grants Committee 1948b: 105).

By the early 1950s, St. Catherine's ceased to be a place for poor undergraduates and had become the spillover annex for the rest of the university. The university was in need of an overflow receptacle because Oxford attracted many more admissible applicants than it had room for. When a suitable student could not secure a place in a college, that student would then apply to St. Catherine's. But, as Alan Bullock noted: "If the problem is a shortage of places rather than poverty, it seemed reasonable to ask whether the University should not seek to meet this by the foundation of a new college rather than by the provision of a non-collegiate status which inevitably offers less to the undergraduate than a college can offer" (Bullock 1956: 98). Why should St. Catherine's continue in the same old way when the needs of Oxford had changed?

The call for change came from throughout the university. Within St. Catherine's, the undergraduates, whose formal academic status was equal to that of all other Oxford undergraduates but whose residential status was inferior, expressed an urgent need for reform. Outside the society, St.

Catherine's anomalous condition presented an affront to two of Oxford's traditions, its democratic and collegiate principles.

Oxford prided itself on being, as the Franks report affirmed, a "republic of equals" (University of Oxford 1966a: 235). Paradoxically, although Oxford was a highly selective and exclusive club, its senior members liked to think of themselves as a community of peers with shared governing rights and academic responsibilities. Its traditional ethos expressed a mentality that the German sociologist Georg Simmel described as one of superordination without subordination (Simmel 1950: 268–73). The condition identified by Simmel joined two apparently contradictory principles, egalitarian and elitist. By definition, superordination without subordination required a collegial association without sharp internal status differentiations that was, nonetheless, elevated above an external population. Historically such qualities were common to aristocratic governing assemblies, such as the House of Lords, and to professional guilds, like modern medical associations.

St. Catherine's position within Oxford was inconsistent with that elevated fraternity. Its undergraduates took Oxford degrees but lacked the tradition of communal life. St. Catherine's second-class position gave rise to status anxieties among its members that did not go unnoticed. Like the Bodleian Library and the Ashmolean Museum, St. Catherine's was under the jurisdiction of the university. As such, the Hebdomadal Council had to hear reports on, and bear a direct responsibility for, its welfare.

St. Catherine's peculiar status in the university gave it certain advantages and disadvantages. The disadvantages were evident. The society did not have its own endowment or quadrangles. It was not legally free to act without university consent; every society initiative was subject to university veto. The advantages were less clear; in substance they were whatever its leaders made of its relation to the university. In theory, St. Catherine's could draw directly upon the university's vast resources, including funds from the University Grants Committee. However, because the university's responsibility was vague, the extent of its participation in St. Catherine's affairs depended upon the attitude of the vice-chancellor and members of Council as well as the political skills of the society's censor.

The Office of Censor and Alan Bullock's Election

The office of censor at St. Catherine's was a post similar to college head. He was the man (and at that time it could only be a man) in charge of the society's affairs. But while a proper college head would perform ceremonial and administrative functions for a self-governing community of college fellows, the society's censor held a controlling position analogous to the rank of provost at a campus of a federated American university.

At the time of Alan Bullock's election, the St. Catherine's Society had only three tutors of its own. Lacking the daily participation of a residential body of collegiate fellows, the censor's efforts were subject only to periodic review by the society's delegates, a small group of Oxford figures who acted as an advisory body for the society. Most of the delegates were members of genuine Oxford colleges, which made a prior claim on their interests and energies.

As censor, Bullock found himself in a position of singular responsibility for the society's affairs. To a unique extent the direction of St. Catherine's depended upon the vision, skill, and energy of its censor. If the censor were eager to seize opportunities and bring about innovation, he would need allies, especially on the central administrative bodies of the university.[15]

St. Catherine's way to college status was smoothed by the vice-chancellor, Alic Halford Smith, warden of New College. Smith was responsible for placing Bullock in a position of authority on the Hebdomadal Council. That appointment made it possible for Bullock to begin translating anxieties about St. Catherine's into proposals for positive action.

Given Alan Bullock's unique role in the creation of St. Catherine's, one that exemplifies the importance of individual personality to the process of change in a decentralized collegiate institution, it is important to know about his record. Bullock was described by that chronicler of British society, Anthony Sampson, as a don with both feet planted in the outside world, eager to pull Oxford into the twentieth century (Sampson 1965: 229). A Yorkshireman with a Bradford direct-grant grammar-school education, he achieved a double first in modern history and *literae humaniores* while at Wadham College, Oxford. Soon after graduation he worked briefly as a researcher for Churchill during his "wilderness days" of political disfavor and social isolation before the war. After the Allied victory, New College at Oxford elected Bullock to a fellowship in modern history. He has had a long scholarly career producing political biographies, beginning with *Hitler: A Study in Tyranny* in 1952. In that year he left New College to become censor of the St. Catherine's Society. He joined the university's Hebdomadal Council in 1953 and served on it for more than twenty years.

Ever since his appointment to Council, Bullock was at, or near, the center of reform controversies inside Oxford. As a principled opponent of imperialism, Bullock led Oxford's opposition to the military adventure at the

Suez Canal in 1956 (*Oxford Magazine* 1956). While on Council his interests in reform included calling for a Royal Commission on Oxford's internal affairs in response to the criticisms made in the Robbins report. When
a Royal Commission did not materialize and Oxford set up its own investigation under Lord Franks, Bullock became the first elected vice-chancellor
under the new Franks statutes. As vice-chancellor from 1969 to 1973, he
was responsible for implementing many of the recommendations that came
out of the Franks inquiry. Outside Oxford, for education ministers, Bullock
in 1963 chaired the Advisory Council on the Training and Supply of Teachers; later, he led the commission on literacy that produced the 1975 report
A Language for Life. Knighted in 1972, in 1976 he became a life peer, a
member of the House of Lords.[16] In 1977, as chair of a government commission on industrial democracy, he recommended worker membership on
company boards of directors. He was a long-term member of the Labour
Party who signed the document announcing the center breakaway of the
Social Democratic Party. And, in the 1990s, he participated in a successful
campaign to "keep Britain green" by thwarting Conservative prime minister John Major's massive highway construction plans.

Whither St. Catherine's?

When Bullock became censor he had not given any thought to the obstacles standing between the St. Catherine's Society and full collegiate status.
"As the sixth censor of a rather unhappy Society," Lord Bullock remembered, my "first thoughts were to close it" (Bullock interview 1989). He
began to think about the society's metamorphosis into a college only after
he felt confident that government and public opinion favored university
growth.

   Government and official opinions on expansion varied in the early
1950s. The number of university students dropped in 1953, causing the
University Grants Committee to announce that the supply of available
places in universities matched student demand (W. G. Stone 1970: 176–
77). In 1954 the Parliamentary and Scientific Committee stated, "For the
time being there is no need to envisage any further expansion of the university student population" (ibid.: 177). Academics eager to see growth
were disappointed until 1955, when university enrollments and the birth
rate increased. In response, there seemed to be a perceptible warming of
the government's attitude toward increasing enrollment, so expansionists
took heart.

   Shortly after his election as censor, Bullock was brought onto the powerful Hebdomadal Council by the new vice-chancellor, A. H. Smith. How Bullock became a member of the Hebdomadal Council illustrates something of the nature of politics in a traditional university.

Traditionally, the value placed on continuity gave moral authority to those with seniority. Oxford University in the 1950s was governed by a group of elders on the Hebdomadal Council. Although since 1854 Council had been a body elected by Congregation, the parliament of resident Oxford dons, this assertion of democratic powers was tempered by a conventional practice that returned to Council large numbers of college heads. A Council with ten college heads, three professors, and thirteen college fellows, as recorded by the Robbins Commission, was typical in the postwar period (see University of Oxford 1966a: 223–30; Committee on Higher Education 1963b: 41, Table 14).

Under the pre-Franks statutes, the vice-chancellor was selected in rotation from among the college heads on Council. Fortuitously, the presiding vice-chancellor, A. H. Smith, had been warden of New College when Bullock was a tutor and dean there. During the long vacation (July to October) of 1953, Smith brought Bullock and John B. Butterworth onto the Council (Bullock interview 1989).[17] As a member of Council, Bullock could attempt to direct its attention to St. Catherine's anomalous and outmoded position.

A New Postgraduate or Undergraduate College, or Both?

Convinced that university expansion was on the political agenda and that the change in St. Catherine's role inside Oxford made propitious its transformation from a society to a college, Bullock's next thoughts went along postgraduate lines. Within Oxford, the creation of postgraduate colleges was in fashion. The society contained a large contingent of postgraduates, some of whom were there for the same reasons its undergraduates were, because the university was full; but a good number were there for administrative convenience. Many of the latter were actually working with the Permanent Private Halls, theological foundations affiliated with Oxford University. The practice of registering postgraduates at St. Catherine's was so routine that even Nuffield, before it opened its doors in 1958, processed its students through St. Catherine's. So one possibility open to the censor was to have the society gradually shed its undergraduates as it developed an identity as a postgraduate studies center (St. Catherine's College Archive 1985: 6).

The plan to turn St. Catherine's into a postgraduate college made good sense as long as the motive was to clear up the anomaly within Oxford of a non-collegiate society that could no longer justify its unusual status. But once it became clear that higher education faced two new challenges, to provide space for the postwar cohort of baby boomers and to accommodate the swing of school students into the sciences, Bullock's thoughts on St. Catherine's future turned toward an undergraduate foundation.

So, in April 1956, Bullock wrote a memo proposing to transform St. Catherine's into an undergraduate college. Thenceforward, Bullock employed a dual strategy for promoting the venture. Within Oxford he stressed the advantages of tidying up "what was an untidy situation," to remove the unnecessary ambiguity of St. Catherine's position (Bullock interview 1989). Outside Oxford he stressed St. Catherine's contribution to the expansion of places in higher education, to "allow many more science students to enter the University" (St. Catherine's College Archive 1985: 6). This two-sided case for the new college was designed to remove the objections of conservatives inside Oxford and modernizers outside—and it worked. No one in Oxford raised a voice against elevating the status of the non-collegiate students. And the possible contribution that St. Catherine's could make to science in the United Kingdom helped win political and financial backing from the outside.

Although the two sides of Bullock's argument in favor of a new college were largely intended for separate audiences, the externally aimed science pitch was important inside Oxford as well (Bullock interview 1989). The mid-1950s swing in schools to math and science alerted Oxford's elders to the gap between subjects read by its undergraduates and the subjects taken by students at A level. Discussions of the shift in undergraduate preferences took place in Senior Common Rooms and on Council and were reflected in the annual report on Rhodes Scholars written by Sir Edgar T. Williams.

Sir Edgar was a long-standing member of Council and warden of Rhodes House, the headquarters of the Rhodes Scholarship program. On institutional politics, it would be fair to characterize Sir Edgar as a conservative. In his 1956 yearly "Christmas Letter" to Rhodes Scholars the world over, he noted:

> In the sixth forms already, there is a marked change in the numbers of those specializing in science and mathematics: 49 percent. last May in the Independent Schools, 54 percent. in Direct Grant Schools, and 55 percent. in Maintained Schools; whereas here at Oxford the scientists *in statu pupillari* formed only a quarter of our company. (Williams, n.d.: 11)

Unless Oxford provided more places for science students, it would be in danger of losing its share of Britain's best brains. Influenced no doubt by Bullock's pleas on Council, Sir Edgar summed up his own thoughts on the challenge of increasing Oxford's science intake by suggesting to Rhodes Scholars: "Why not . . . make the undergraduate element in the present St. Catherine's the nucleus of a new College, increasing the number of scientists in both tutorial staff and undergraduate admissions" (ibid.: 12). Sir Edgar's letter reflected Bullock's solution to the problem.

Bullock's April memo urging collegiate status provided a basis for the censor to seek endorsement from Oxford's official bodies. The society's delegates, Council, and Congregation would have to pass concurring legislation. When the delegates met on June 6, 1956, to vote on the undergraduate foundation, the presence of the vice-chancellor, A. H. Smith, signaled Council's approval. He both chaired and addressed the meeting. The delegates passed the proposal unanimously (St. Catherine's College Archive 1986: 4–5).

On June 8, just two days after the delegates voted in favor, Council officially approved the undergraduate proposal. Congregation furnished its consent on October 23, which was as soon as the academic calendar allowed (*Oxford University Gazette* 1963: 119). There would be a new undergraduate college in Oxford, yet the postgraduate proposal was not forgotten.

Concurrent with the decision to cast St. Catherine's future in the direction of undergraduates, the delegates, Council, and Congregation all approved a plan to launch a separate postgraduate association. It would begin with the postgraduates on St. Catherine's matriculation list left after the theology students were split off to join Oxford's Permanent Private Halls. Officially recognized as Linacre House by the University in 1962, it became a college in 1965. Thus, Bullock could claim the unique distinction of having launched two Oxford colleges.[18]

The next crucial hurdle facing the censor was financing. How could he raise the huge amount of money necessary to build and endow a new independent college?

University and College Fund-Raising

Medieval foundations were endowed by the three wealthiest ranks of society: monarchs, religious officials, and great land owners. In the twentieth century money for higher education came predominantly from the "modern monarchy," the state. But the state reserved its patronage for old and new universities—not for old or new Oxford colleges. Recurrent government grants would compromise the legal independence and self-governing rights of Oxford colleges. St. Catherine's had to raise the money to construct its buildings from private sources.

The price tag on independence for an aspirant to collegiate status was high. To the college that bears his name, Lord Nuffield gave a benefaction in excess of 1 million pounds to build and endow it—and that was in 1937 (Chester 1986: 63). St. Catherine's needed more than twice that amount to achieve the same independence in 1956. Unlike Nuffield, however, St. Catherine's began without even one benefactor. Philanthropic foundations, corporations, and individuals would have to be approached—and soliciting money was not something on which Bullock, or any particular person in the university, could claim vast expertise.

By the late 1950s Oxford University had made public appeals for benefactions only twice in the century. The first was a 1937 Higher Studies Fund appeal for the extension and general improvement of the Bodleian library (see Chester 1986: 60–62). The second fund drive, the Historic Buildings Appeal for building restorations, was barely in the initial planning stage when money became an issue for St. Catherine's. Announced publicly in June 1957, its timing was unfortunate (*Oxford* 1958a: 7).

There were fears on Council and in the Chest, Oxford's financial office, that St. Catherine's solicitations would compete unproductively with the Historic Buildings campaign. Taking those anxieties into consideration, the society's delegates pledged to "neither launch a public appeal nor even campaign privately for donations without first seeking the approval of this [Historic Buildings] committee" (St. Catherine's College Archive 1986: 6). Apparently, Bullock would have to organize a money campaign with more constraints than assistance from official bodies. But the university's chief permanent official, the registrar, Sir Douglas Veale, came to his rescue.

In Oxford the post of university registrar was similar to the office held by a Cabinet minister's permanent civil service secretary. Selected by Council and approved by Congregation, the registrar acted as the secretary for Council, Congregation, and Convocation. He kept the minutes and files and generally facilitated the work of those three governing bodies (Oxford University 1931: 49–50). As the most important long-term official of Oxford University, the registrar had his own seat on the consultative association for U.K. universities, the Committee of Vice-Chancellors and Principals. Sir Douglas was described as "the most powerful man in the University" (Wheare 1974: 62) and as "the architect of the modern university in Oxford" (Bullock interview 1989). Yet the registrar's responsibilities were limited in accordance with the best traditions of the British civil service—he was there to serve, not to set policy. That subordinate relationship was very important in Oxford, where "university opinion has always had a peculiar dread of 'bureaucracy'" (Oxford University 1931: 12).

Fortunately, from the perspective of Oxford's collegiate tradition, Sir Douglas was the perfect man for the job. His personal inclinations fully matched the requirements of office; for, paradoxically, he was a university administrator who loved the college system, a "college man" first and last, uninterested in concentrating power at the university's center.

Sir Douglas was a former civil servant who cut short a promising career at Whitehall to return to Oxford as its registrar in 1930. He first joined the university in 1910 as a Bristol direct-grant grammar-school product reading *literae humaniores* with a scholarship at Corpus Christi College. According to a former Oxford vice-chancellor, Sir Kenneth Wheare, the experience at Corpus left a lasting impression on Sir Douglas: even as registrar, Sir Douglas's "first loyalty and deepest affection lies with his college" (Wheare 1974: 60). Upon his return to Oxford, Corpus made him a fellow, and his devotion to his college was such that, Sir Kenneth wrote, "Douglas never missed a meeting of the Governing Body or even of a college committee of which he was a member." Sir Douglas's sentiments for Corpus, in Sir Kenneth's opinion, "endowed him with the essential quality of a good Registrar—a profound attachment to the college system, a belief in it and an understanding of it" (ibid.: 61, 62). He used his post to strengthen rather than undermine collegiate independence. So when Bullock needed to raise funds and did not have a clue how to begin, it was characteristic of Sir Douglas to place at Bullock's disposal some of the best money connections then available to the university.

Sir Douglas offered to write on Bullock's behalf to two American philanthropies, the Rockefeller Foundation and the Ford Foundation, which had given generously to Oxford during his term as registrar. The decision to make a trans-Atlantic move to launch the St. Catherine's appeal was illustrative of an approach to funding that only changed after the implementation of Thatcher's austerity policies. For after World War II, Oxford University, in contrast to the colleges, had become accustomed to looking to the government to cover its annual costs and occasionally turning to private sources for special projects. Oxford's irregular need for large, one-time benefactions harmonized nicely with the predilections of its largest foreign component, its North American alumni.

Before Thatcher's cuts in the 1980s, most large gifts came in unsolicited, attracted only by Oxford's cultural authority. The university very rarely made public appeals, not only because the government provided for its basic needs, but also because its alumni did not expect to make, and were not cultivated for, donations. When raising funds, the key strength of a collegiate university turned into a weakness; for between the university and donations from graduates stood the colleges. Oxford graduates who made financial contributions tended to donate to their undergraduate college.

American alumni of Oxford, however, had a relation to the university that made them an exception to this pattern. For obvious reasons an American's experience of Oxford was quite different from the average British undergraduate's. As foreigners from a society that was often either admired or detested, too similar to British culture to be exotic and too wealthy and powerful to be unthreatening, Americans in Oxford received countless reminders of their national identity (Carter 1990: 197–212). Americans' distinctive perceptions of Oxford were also shaped by their academic status and accommodations. Most Americans were not undergraduates living inside a college but postgraduates living elsewhere in Oxford.

Whether as Rhodes Scholars or as candidates for second degrees, Americans provided Oxford with its second largest contingent of postgraduates, second only to those from the United Kingdom. In 1964–65, Americans were 28 percent of Oxford's foreign postgraduates, and by 1986–87 their numbers had increased to 39 percent (see University of Oxford 1966b: 25, table 17; University of Oxford 1987: 90). The university's report on its postgraduates submitted in October 1987 found that after Oxford, Cambridge, and London the fourth most represented university was Harvard (University of Oxford 1987: 121).[19]

Along with the majority of Oxford's postgraduates, Americans working for a second degree tended to live out of college. Oxford colleges mostly accommodated their undergraduates. The Franks report discovered that in 1964 a mere 15 percent of postgraduates lived in college properties (University of Oxford 1966b: 232, table 222).

After leaving Oxford, Americans were frequently employed in powerful institutions, such as Congress and philanthropic foundations, whose resources could be tapped for Oxford. Also, coming from a national culture where contributing to one's alma mater was customary, many Americans were inclined to donate privately to the university for special projects. Thus, the American response to university-wide campaigns was markedly better than the British, as the record of the university's public appeal in 1937–38 demonstrated.

Over the past hundred years, private American citizens and organizations made many highly visible contributions to the Oxford community. American funds were crucial in the creation of Ruskin College, Wolfson College, Templeton College, Green College, and, as we shall soon see, St. Catherine's. Grants from the Rockefeller Foundation made possible the New Bodleian Library and the new Law Library. The Ford Foundation got the Historic Buildings Appeal going and also gave generously to Wolfson College. Ford provided virtually the entire endowment for Wolfson College, a sum worth 4.5 million dollars in 1966 (Jessup 1979: 9). The Kellogg Foundation provided the money to recast Oxford's extramural studies. It would not be unfair to suggest that just as the state through its generosity made it natural for the university to depend upon public money for its recurrent operating expenses, Oxford's unique relation to the United States made it natural for it to look across the ocean for its special financial needs.

Invited by the Ford and Rockefeller trustees to present his case in person, in 1957 Bullock traveled twice to America. Each trip was a success: the Ford Foundation gave 100,000 dollars to St. Catherine's to endow five research fellowships (Bullock interview 1989). The Rockefeller trustees offered enough money to fund an office in Oxford to keep the appeal moving forward and came up with a singularly opportune proposition for a conference.

The chairman of the Rockefeller Foundation was Dean Rusk, a former Rhodes Scholar and later President John F. Kennedy's secretary of state. According to Alistair Horne, Harold Macmillan's official biographer, Rusk's "love for Oxford . . . had been overshadowed by some unpleasant experiences. . . . He was certainly no particular friend of the Special Relationship" between Britain and America (Horne 1989: 306).

Rusk was not in a position to offer a large grant, but he did have a surprise up his sleeve. As Lord Bullock recounted, Rusk said:

> "We've just accepted a white elephant, the bequest of a magnificent Estate in Italy which none of us has any idea what to do with. Do you think you could make use of it?" Visions of a Renaissance palace for reading parties raced through my mind, but it soon became clear that Dean Rusk meant for some sort of conference. "Of course," I said, and proceeded, off the cuff, to show our need to take the Fellows who had been appointed, but hardly knew

each other as yet, away for a ten-day meeting at which we could thrash out, away from every-day distractions, the sort of college we wanted to create. (Bullock 1987: 5)

Thus, the Italian Villa Serbellone became the site of a ten-day conference for the founding fellows of St. Catherine's to forge a common sense of identity and purpose.

Bullock's own thoughts on the character of modern institutions of higher education first came into focus when he accepted an invitation from the Advisory Committee for the forthcoming Sussex University to deliver a lecture entitled "The Purpose and Conditions of a University" (L. Stone 1964: 191). The talk was one in a series of six lectures given by Oxford luminaries to help Sussex come to grips with challenges it would face as a new university. In preparation, he read Newman's famous *Idea of a University* and found it not very helpful. For Bullock, a university fulfilled its mission best by avoiding the extremes of monastic retreat from, or total engagement with, contemporary society. The university had a moral compact with society. The university provided "basic research," which government and private business could utilize, just as it nurtured in its graduates a facility for independent thought that they should apply in life. Yet to perform those functions for society the university should have sufficient cultural authority and material resources to resist short-sighted manipulation by practical men and political zealots. University autonomy was a necessary precondition for, and not at odds with, a healthy relation to society (Bullock interview 1989).

More important for the success of the appeal than either a conference for college fellows or funds for an office was the connection to a single person. On his second trip to America, a chance conversation over dinner was responsible for the beginning of a friendship with a man who would supply the plan and know-how to raise most of the money needed by St. Catherine's.

Crossing the Atlantic on the *Queen Mary*, Bullock and his wife were seated at a table with two other British nationals, Mr. and Mrs. Alan H. Wilson. In 1957, at the time of the voyage, Alan Wilson was a director of Courtaulds, a textiles and chemicals firm that was among the top 100 British companies. Wilson went to Courtaulds after a career cut short at Cambridge University (he had been a fellow of Trinity College) to take charge of the Courtaulds research department; he went on to become the company's chairman.

During the voyage Wilson's interest in St. Catherine's did not immediately translate into a plan for raising funds. It was not until the spring of 1958 that Wilson put heavy pressure on Bullock to begin a public appeal. The reason for Wilson's sense of urgency was simple. He had learned of plans in the making by members of Cambridge University to create a college that would compete directly with St. Catherine's for funds. Like St. Catherine's, the Cambridge college would respond to contemporary anxieties on the economic utility of university science by leaning toward that subject area; but in addition, it would tap into the widespread veneration for Winston Churchill by presenting itself, with permission, as a monument to the man. The prospect of Churchill College's overshadowing St. Catherine's greatly concerned Wilson.

Before Wilson raised the alarm, Bullock and members of the St. Catherine's Society had acted with self-restraint in deference to Oxford's Historic Buildings Appeal. With their knowledge of Cambridge's plans, Wilson and Bullock thought that St. Catherine's should attempt to establish a claim upon individual and business charity before Churchill College won the lion's share.

Fortunately, Wilson also had a plan to address the challenge. Wilson's idea drew on his prior experience with the Independence Fund for the Advancement of Science in Schools. The fund was organized in 1955 by some of Britain's largest companies to provide public schools with the money and hardware necessary to educate more of their students in the sciences. The campaign ran parallel to government efforts to strengthen science education in the secondary schools. The fund approached the top 200 British businesses and raised more than 3 million pounds (Argles 1964: 119; Gathorne-Hardy 1977: 371). As a result, new labs for science and technology were built in approximately 60 public schools (Bullock interview 1989). Wilson proposed to appeal to some of the same companies to contribute to St. Catherine's, especially for the sake of Oxford science.

Thus in an ironic twist a new Oxford college with a desire to eschew public-school associations found itself indebted to a network set up by private corporations to reinforce the old-school tie. Bullock turned to a financial network begun to help public schools that had become, through the mechanism of a new Oxford college, of value to direct-grant grammar- and state-school students.

Bullock's fund-raising problems illustrated a dilemma all Oxford reformers faced. If Oxford was able to modernize, it could do so partially because of the marketable prestige gained through its centuries-long association with wealth and power. Reformers could raise money because of Oxford's old image even when its new qualities were being explicitly stressed. Oxford's inheritance ensured that the camp of internal reform had to live with ambivalent attitudes toward Oxford's legacy.

Bullock and Wilson put together an appeal letter and brochure for the business community that would draw attention to the science emphasis of the proposed college. If the funds were forthcoming, St. Catherine's would become, as Bullock said, "the first Oxford college to devote one-half of its places to science and technology" (Bullock interview 1989). To underscore St. Catherine's commitment to the sciences, the appeal letter was signed not only by Bullock and Wilson but also by two of Oxford's Nobel laureates in the natural sciences: Sir Cyril Hinshelwood, president of the Royal Society and a fellow of Exeter, and Sir Hans Krebs, a fellow of Trinity.

It helped to undermine objections from Council members and prominent individuals associated with the Historic Buildings Appeal that both the appeal and the St. Catherine's mailing did extraordinarily well. Within eighteen months of publicly announcing the Historic Buildings Appeal, the campaign could report that more than 1.7 million pounds had been pledged. The Ford Foundation promised 400,000; other trusts 250,000; British industry and commerce 400,000; Oxford graduates in the United Kingdom and North America 400,000; and the British government 250,000 (Bridges 1958: 7–9). The response to the St. Catherine's mailing was favorable enough to permit Wilson to schedule a meeting on June 10, 1958, between important corporate directors and representatives of Oxford University.

Meeting in the board room of British Petroleum, representatives of the business community and Oxford University drafted a compact for St. Catherine's benefit. The contributing corporations pledged an initial 500,000 pounds and promised to form a committee to raise additional funds with Sir Hugh Beaver, president of the Federation of British Industries and managing director of Arthur Guinness and Company, as chairman.[20] By 1961, and before fund-raising work among British corporations was over, St. Catherine's had collected approximately 1.2 million pounds from the committee. Generous donations from hundreds of companies made the British business community a collective benefactor of St. Catherine's.

Paradoxically, although the plans to establish an appeal for Churchill College spurred St. Catherine's fund-raising efforts, the Churchill appeal actually helped the campaign. Many corporations decided to give to both colleges, pledging to St. Catherine's half the money they pledged to Churchill (Bullock interview 1989).

Even with the help of Sir Hugh's committee, the financial problems of St. Catherine's were far from over. Before St. Catherine's doors could open, critical and significant funds would come from two unexpected sources: the University Grants Committee and a single American alumnus of the non-collegiate St. Catherine's Society.

St. Catherine's unique status as a department of the university gave Bullock an opportunity to approach Council for some money out of the university's grant from the UGC. Although Oxford colleges were ineligible for state funds, the departmental standing of St. Catherine's within the university opened the door for an initial injection: a one-time-only gift from the central government that would not jeopardize St. Catherine's legal autonomy. Should any offering incur for St. Catherine's a moral obligation to implement public policies, the science and state-school bias of the forthcoming college would discharge the debt. Despite some trepidation on St. Catherine's side, the UGC did not seem bothered by the moral or political complications of a donation. It got directly involved in the negotiations. The UGC's chairman, Sir Keith Murray, was a convinced expansionist (Carswell 1985: 14), so he generously found a way to provide the society with four grants totaling 372,250 pounds earmarked for land purchase, legal fees, construction, and furnishings (see Carswell 1985: 14; St. Catherine's College Archive 1986: 7, 11).

In January 1961, with the UGC's cash added to the money from American foundations and Sir Hugh's business associates, St. Catherine's had just over 1.74 million pounds (ibid.: 11). It was quite an accomplishment but, unfortunately, still 600,000 pounds short of the committee's minimum goal. Between January and June 1961 it became clear that the college could not afford to build on the scale and quality desired by Bullock and the college's architect.

The building plans for St. Catherine's were drawn by the famous Danish architect Arne Jacobsen. The selection of a non-British expert was another departure from established practice for the new college. Jacobsen had won the committee's approval for a plan with a distinctively modernist character. He designed everything for the college from its chairs and dining cutlery to its tower and moat. The undergraduates' rooms were, as was traditional in Oxford, in small clusters with separate staircases. But their style was to be Danish modern, not neo-gothic. The rooms were open and white and looked out, through a floor-to-ceiling glass wall, on English gardens. Jacobsen's materials were steel, slate, concrete, brick, and clear glass, not stone, tiles, mortar, and stained glass. When the college opened, the architect's vision and nationality were topics of controversy (Tojner and Vindum 1991: 92–102); by the 1990s, the college had been added to the National Trust list of historic buildings. In 1961, however, there were insufficient funds to build according to plan.

By June 1961, financial anxieties on the St. Catherine's Committee stirred up a proposal to drop Jacobsen's design. As Bullock recollected:

> I remember one particular committee meeting with the University officers at which this anxiety came to a head. Hugh Keen, the Secretary of the University Chest [the university treasurer], made a powerful plea for abandoning the idea of having an architect of Arne Jacobsen's standing, arguing that instead we should put up the cheapest possible accommodation. . . . Hugh was a good friend of St. Catherine's, and I believed him when he said: "I care a great deal about this new college, and I would love to see Jacobsen's plan carried out; but you are getting your priorities wrong. Look at Balliol (he was a Fellow of Balliol): its wholly undistinguished 19th-century buildings don't stop it being the best college in Oxford." I felt equally passionately that the buildings mattered more than anything else if St. Catherine's which, unlike Balliol, was a new college, was to achieve a distinctive identity and attract young people to it. . . . All I could do was to ask for an adjournment before we made any drastic decisions, to see if I could raise more money. (Bullock 1987: 5)

Within two weeks Bullock was rescued by Dr. Rudolph Light, an American graduate of the St. Catherine's Society.

Dr. Rudolph Light was a member of the non-collegiate society who had earned a medical degree from Oxford University; he had returned to America to work with the family firm, Upjohn Pharmaceuticals. Dr. Light's Oxford experience had been sufficiently formative to cause him, many years later, to move back with his wife and take up permanent residence in a house on the outskirts of Oxford. At St. Catherine's moment of need, and without foreknowledge by any member of the committee, Light requested an appointment with the censor. Bullock remembered: "I had no idea why he should want to see me. Even when he told me that he would like to offer us some shares in the family firm of Upjohn, I still did not grasp how much that offer would affect the future of St. Catherine's." However, after Light explained that he had in mind something on the scale of 20,000 shares of Upjohn worth approximately fifty dollars each, then Bullock "grasped that we were being offered a very large sum of money. As I stammered out our thanks, all I could keep on saying was 'It's an act of Providence.' And so it was, the perfectly-timed answer to the anxieties we had faced only a fortnight or so before" (Bullock 1987: 7).

The support of Dr. Light and his wife for St. Catherine's did not end with their donation of Upjohn stock:

> In all, including the further large sum left to the college on Rudi's death, we received the magnificent sum of two and a half million dollars, which not only provided the basis of our endowment, but allowed us to continue with Arne Jacobsen's plans for the building. If there is one name that should never be forgotten as long as St. Catherine's stands, it is that of Rudi Light. (Ibid.)

Thus, St. Catherine's was truly an outgrowth of opportunities actualized by a fertile combination of Oxford's cultural authority and a tradition of individual initiative for college innovation, encouraged and protected by Oxford's elders. By drawing on Oxford's traditions, a college with a new character was created independent of any external threats or political pressures. In the vice-chancellor's oration of 1964, Kenneth C. Wheare could claim that the founding of St. Catherine's confirmed the trustworthiness of Oxford's "folk wisdom" to shepherd good projects along without government interference (Wheare 1964: 52). Even the financing of the college was accomplished primarily without assistance from the government. Private American and British funds accounted in nearly equal proportions for St. Catherine's buildings and endowment capital. The contribution from British taxpayers, made for them by the UGC, subsidized barely 15 percent of St. Catherine's start-up costs. The university was both necessary for receipt of UGC money and useful for pointing Bullock toward America. Yet the bulk of St. Catherine's capital was gained from businessmen (including Rudolph Light), without university or government assistance. The raising of approximately 3 million pounds was an even more impressive accomplishment when one thinks about the relative value of the sum in 1957–63.

St. Catherine's Postscript

The founding master, fellows, and undergraduates were remarkably successful in achieving the desired blend of old and new. St. Catherine's was an innovative but nonetheless distinctively Oxford creation. Like the older foundations, St. Catherine's was a residential and self-governing academic community where tutorials and common meals regulated the rhythms of life. But unlike the older establishments, St. Catherine's was architecturally and spiritually open to the contemporary world, without formidable walls and closed quadrangles, where most dons and undergraduates worked in the natural sciences; indeed, in the 1980s, on average 53 percent of each first-year cohort studied natural science or technology (St. Catherine's College 1985–88). A substantial majority of students came from the state sector of secondary education; links with industry and commerce were robust and grew rapidly: in the 1980s, St. Catherine's opened its own consulting firm to organize the work of scientists for private industry ("Oxford Dons" 1988). And international relationships, key to the design and finance of its buildings, continued to thrive.

THE POSTGRADUATE COLLEGES

During the same time period as both the creation of St. Catherine's and the university's move into the natural sciences, Oxford's commitment to postgraduates grew. Between 1956 and 1966, while student numbers increased overall by 30 percent (from 7,000 to 10,201), postgraduate numbers more than doubled (from 1,110 to 2,609). For postgraduate studies in Britain, Oxford was second only to the University of London in absolute numbers as well as relative percentage (see Table 11).

The capacity of a decentralized collegiate organizational culture to facilitate Oxford's response to new challenges was nowhere better demonstrated than in the creation of the postgraduate colleges. The story of their collective origins highlighted the significance of Oxford's democratic organization. For on every level of Oxford's self-governance, whether as individual initiative, committee inquiry, or Congregation discussion and vote, the tradition of democracy contributed to the establishment of the postgraduate colleges.

By the 1970s, there were six postgraduate colleges in Oxford. In order of seniority they were: St. Antony's, Nuffield, Linacre, St. Cross, Wolfson, and Green. As innovative collegiate foundations established between the war and Thatcher's administration, they belong in this chapter.

The postgraduate colleges fell into two categories: those that specialized in a particular subject area and those open to students from any field. Nuffield focused on social studies, St. Antony's specialized in international subjects, and Green was a college for postgraduates in clinical medicine. The other three, St. Cross, Wolfson, and Linacre, had a mix of students from a variety of disciplines.

Nuffield's endowment gave credibility to the charge (discussed at length in Chapter 6) that Oxford was anti-industrial. The story told by Nuffield's

TABLE 11

The Oxford University Student Body, 1923–1990

(percent)

	1923	1938	1948	1958	1963	1976	1986	1990
Undergraduates	89	89	85	85	79	76	73	73
Postgraduates	11	11	15	15	21	24	27	27
Men	82	83	85	86	84	—	—	62
Women	18	17	15	14	16	—	—	38

SOURCES: For 1923–63, University of Oxford 1966b: 13, 23; for 1976–86, University of Oxford 1987: 5; for 1990, *Oxford University Gazette* 1990: 1012–13.

warden, Sir Norman Chester, was that members of Oxford were slowly building up a new curriculum in social studies when, in July 1937, Lord Nuffield (founder of the Morris auto works in Cowley) offered a benefaction for a new college. He wanted to create an engineering college, but the vice-chancellor, A. D. Lindsay, and the registrar, Sir Douglas Veale, persuaded Nuffield "that engineering was a subject best left to Cambridge" (Chester 1986: 67). Instead, a college devoted to social studies was established. After receiving its charter in 1958, Nuffield flourished despite Lord Nuffield's belated claim that he was "cheated" (ibid.). By the 1970s, one could say that of the six graduate colleges, Nuffield had the strongest reputation. It sponsored several significant studies of modern social mobility and voting patterns. And it maintained, through visiting senior fellows, regular links with the external worlds of business and politics.

The second postgraduate college launched (but the first to open shop) was St. Antony's. Made possible by a benefaction from M. Antonin Besse, a wealthy French merchant, St. Antony's became a new foundation on May 30, 1950. From the start, St. Antony's was designed to be a world center for the study of international economics and politics. According to the *College Record*, St. Antony's "specializes in international studies, with particular emphasis on Europe, the Soviet Union, the Middle East, Africa, Japan, South and Southeast Asia, China and Latin America" (St. Antony's College 1991: 1). Reflecting its international interests, St. Antony's had in residence more than 200 graduate students from more than 35 different countries (ibid.: 19).

Oxford's third graduate college, Linacre, established in 1962, was discussed earlier in this chapter in connection with St. Catherine's. Linacre's first students were the postgraduate members of St. Catherine's Society when it became an undergraduate college. The college owed its launch to Bullock, but its spiritual founder was a sixteenth-century medical scientist and humanist named Thomas Linacre. Located near Oxford's science area, the new postgraduate college acquired a reputation as a place for students, often in the sciences, from outside the United Kingdom.

With three postgraduate colleges in town, Oxford tried through the Franks report to take stock of its advanced students as a whole. In the process, Franks discovered that postgraduate education was an essential part of what qualified Oxford for its world-class academic status (*Oxford University Gazette* 1966).

The commissioners were greatly concerned about sustaining Oxford's international stature. They understood Oxford's global status to rest on its direct contributions to the academic world: research, new scholars, and scientists. As Lord Franks explained to Congregation: "To stay in the big league of international learning, what Oxford had to consider was the scale and the quality of its research, and the scale and the quality of its graduate education" (ibid.: 1489). Oxford's international standing required original thought and the nurturing of candidates for academia.

Before the war, Oxford's postgraduate students were few in number and light in relative weight. In 1938–39 there were 536 students in residence, constituting some 11 percent of the student population. After the war their numbers doubled, but their relative size in Oxford did not take off until the time of Franks. The commission projected "a large increase in the numbers of postgraduates" between 1966 and 1986 (University of Oxford 1966a: 34, para. 55). By 1966–67, the number of postgraduate students had jumped to 2,310, and they constituted 23 percent of the student body. And in 1986–27 their number had climbed to 3,530, or 27 percent (University of Oxford 1987: 5).

To accommodate them, Lord Franks discouraged American-style "great graduate schools" as out of harmony with Oxford's collegiate traditions (*Oxford University Gazette* 1966: 1487; University of Oxford 1966a: 35, para. 60). To embrace the American practice of enrolling large numbers of nonresidential graduate students in the arts and sciences would result in the training of new generations of academics without any experience of, or special affection for, the college system. The report's preference was for graduates to live and work in colleges. If necessary, said the report, new postgraduate foundations should be built to provide homes for the advanced students.

The origins of both St. Cross and Wolfson Colleges were covered in the section on Oxford's nondon controversy in Chapter 3; established to provide a space for Oxford's scientists without collegiate affiliations, they have continued to be heavily committed to the natural sciences. Wolfson's first president, Sir Isaiah Berlin, brought with him not only a liberal temperament and dazzling conversational skills but also the money from the Ford and Wolfson Foundations that provided the college's endowment.

The sixth postgraduate college, Green College, was an outgrowth of the development of Oxford's School of Clinical Medicine after Franks. The clinical school was one of Oxford's very few vocational programs (University of Oxford 1971: 24). Although the study of medicine in Oxford went back to the thirteenth century, clinical training dated to the mid-nineteenth century (University of Oxford 1971: 7). Oxford's medical student enrollment was very modest, at or fewer than 25 per year, until the time of the Franks report. By 1968 the clinical program had doubled in size (ibid.: 10). A 1971 report on the medical school noted the prerequisites for admission and the backgrounds of its growing student body. "All the students must have obtained an Honours degree in Physiology or an allied science before entering the school. . . . Slightly over half the students obtain their first degree in Oxford, most of the rest have Cambridge degrees" (ibid.: 16).

Funding for the program in the 1960s and 1970s was extraordinarily well balanced. Thirty-five percent came from an endowment donated by Lord Nuffield, 27 percent came from other benefactions and outside sources, and just 38 percent of the total came from the taxpayer through the UGC (ibid.: 18).

The practical side of students' training took place at local Oxfordshire hospitals, so they had to live in the area. But until Green College there were no accommodations for graduates in the clinical program (ibid.: 91).

From conception to delivery, the college took just four years to build. The idea to found a postgraduate college for clinical students was raised by a faculty board in 1975 (Green College 1991: 3). Dr. and Mrs. Cecil Green donated the funds for its construction and endowment after a 1977 visit from Texas. Dr. Green resided in America, held a master's degree from the Massachusetts Institute of Technology and a doctorate in engineering from the Colorado School of Mines, and acquired his fortune working for a corporation, Texas Instruments. But, as the Green College Handbook explained, he "was born in England and emigrated to Canada as a boy." The college housed its first cohort in 1979; by 1986 it was home to 132 graduate students (Green College 1991: 3; 1989: 29).

We see in these various foundations the expansion of the college tradition in Oxford. All of the St. Catherine's undergraduates, science nondons, students of clinical medicine, and some other postgraduates arrived in Oxford from outside the existing colleges. It would have been easier in every respect, less expensive and stressful, to leave the excess of undergraduates and postgraduates in city accommodations and the nondons in their science labs; but to do so would have undermined the community's tradition of small, self-governing colleges. With these students and nondons we see vivid proof that an organizational culture, the college tradition, was a vital resource within Oxford. It enabled modernizers to overcome the conservative mentality of habitual routine and economic calculations of material cost. Rather than sit by, stuck in unreflective routine, in time the Oxford community responded positively to these newcomers with a renewal of the collegiate tradition. This process of rejuvenation, begun in various colleges, spread throughout the university during the work of the Franks Commission—the topic of the next chapter.

Part Two

OXFORD EMBATTLED

5.

Labour Politics and the High Tide of Internal Reform

ACADEMIA CHALLENGED

Despite all of the preceding changes, Oxford's old architecture and its collegiate organization helped to disguise its metamorphosis. Politicians, journalists, and educationists in the late 1950s and early 1960s continued to speak of Oxford in terms appropriate to its prewar condition. Critics mistakenly attacked Oxford not only as an upper-class institution but also for its alleged inability to change. As a self-governing community with medieval traditions and a collegiate structure, Oxford was frequently depicted as one of Britain's most sluggish, selfish, and secretive institutions. Like the port-swilling Cambridge dons in Tom Sharpe's comic novel *Porterhouse Blue* (1976), Oxford's faculty allegedly stumbled along intoxicated and complacent, energetic only when resisting accountability to the outside world. Modernizers repeatedly made the plea to reform Oxford so that "progressive" Britain could come into its own. And reform must come from the outside, they said, because, as everyone knew, Oxford was infamous for its conservatism. Royal Commissions with statutory powers were necessary every time major changes were introduced to England's two medieval universities between 1850 and 1922. Why should the period after World War II be any different? The critical collective portrait of Oxford was of an entrenched and intransigent academic caste.

Public controversies over Oxford's privileged style of life and undergraduate composition flared now and then until the Robbins Commission brought things to a head. The Robbins report officially indicted Oxbridge for behaving in ways that were incompatible with the obligations of a state university. Oxford felt threatened and in 1964 organized the Franks Commission of Inquiry to respond to its critics as well as to identify areas in need of modernization.

THE ROBBINS REPORT

The publication of the Robbins report gave the higher education debate a focus (Committee on Higher Education 1963a). Lord Robbins, an economist at the London School of Economics with an impressive wartime administrative record, was asked by Harold Macmillan's government to evaluate the condition of higher education in Britain. According to John Carswell, the Treasury representative to the committee, the original motive for Robbins's inquiry was very modest. The government wanted to take stock of the expansion that had already taken place under the aggressive leadership of University Grants Committee chairman Sir Keith Murray (Carswell 1985: 17–19). But the climate of opinion made it possible for expansionists on the committee to go further. At a time when human-capital modernization theorists were excitedly announcing the economic importance of investment in education, when educationists were looking enviously at higher matriculation rates in foreign countries, and when parents with social aspirations were latching on to education as a vehicle of advancement, the Robbins committee came up with ambitious recommendations for the future size and character of British higher education (see Vaizey 1958; Carswell 1985: 26).

When the Robbins report was released on October 23, 1963, an ill Harold Macmillan had just turned over the prime minister's office to his colleague Sir Alec Douglas-Home. The new Conservative government issued a statement on Robbins that said, "This Report provides an opportunity to set the course of higher education in this country for a generation." The declaration went on to enunciate what became known as the Robbins principle: "The basic assumption of the Report is that courses of higher education should be available for all those who are qualified by ability and attainment to pursue them and who wish to do so" (Conservative Cabinet 1963: 301–2).

The doors to higher education were, in theory, thrown wide open. A ten-year plan for dramatic numerical expansion was set with a 1973–74 target of 390,000 students, of whom 217,000 would be full time in universities, and 173,000 in other institutions of higher education (ibid.: 302). In 1962–63, there were 216,000 students in higher education, of whom 131,000 were in universities. Within five years, enrollments for advanced degree work were far ahead of Robbins's schedule at 377,000 (Layard, King, and Moser 1969: 1, fig. 1).

The fundamental significance of the Robbins report was its open commitment to expansion. Britain was beginning to take steps that, if pursued vigorously, could effect a transition from a small elite and uncoordinated group of higher education institutions to an interconnected system of universities and other institutions for advanced study.

The report received wide praise. But critical opinion was divided between, on one side, the democratic elitists and conservatives and, on the other side, those who were more social democratically inclined. The former saw the scale and rate of government-sponsored expansion threatening the quality and autonomy of universities; the latter claimed that Robbins's embrace of the English ideal of a university would undermine or betray the social values implied by, if not the actual possibility of accomplishing, the projected expansion.

Clear differences were discernible in the educational loyalties of the protagonists. There were those whose vision of higher education was inspired by the old Oxbridge model and those whose vision of higher education came from Redbrick, Scottish, American, or technical educational models—all of which were believed by partisans to represent more egalitarian and socially responsive forms of higher education than Oxbridge epitomized. The argument was between those who saw the expansion as a threat to universities and those who believed Robbins's commitment to universities would undermine the promise of expansion. For many on the pro-university side of the debate, Oxbridge represented the quintessential British university; for almost everyone on the anti-university side, Oxbridge embodied all that was wrong with British universities.

On October 24, 1963, the day after publication of the Robbins report, the *Times* wrote an editorial "leader" defending British universities. Robbins, it said, was "just the sort of document for which those who are hungry to 'modernize Britain' have been waiting." But the *Times* would permit itself to act as "devil's advocate" because many of Robbins's assumptions and conclusions were questionable:

> When it comes down to the hard decision of the allocation of resources all the other desirable things about which the Robbins committee has so much that is so good to say . . . are (unless the world changes) fated to take their place in subordination to the politically overriding aim of putting up numbers. The Robbins rate of expansion, for all the cogency with which it is argued

and all the acclaim of which it is assured, is not proof against the criticism that it would work to dilute academic standards in the universities. They are worth holding on to. ("Robbins Report" 1963: 13b)

Between October 24, 1963, and January 3, 1964, the *Times* published seven editorials and major articles assessing Robbins. The commentators warned about the "dangers of docile acceptance" due either to a deference inspired by its detailed arguments or to political expediency (see "Dangers" 1963: 13b). Elections would be called soon, and because there were votes at stake in Robbins, hard questions would get pushed aside.

The *Times* challenged Robbins's most sacred principle, that all school leavers with two A levels should have a place in higher education. Two A levels were the minimum requirement for university matriculation, the *Times* reminded its readers ("Top Priority" 1963: 13b). And Robbins "could not show that the people for whom it wishes the universities to make room are particularly well suited to a university education ("Robbins Report" 1963: 13b). The *Times* repeated its fears that more numbers would drag down standards: "It remains permissible to doubt whether the Robbins target of one-sixth of the age group in higher education, 60 per cent of them in universities, is attainable within the advertised time without altering the character of British universities and without diluting their academic standards" ("Top Priority" 1963: 13b).

The "central weakness" of the report, according to the *Times*, was its failure to formulate a balanced policy on the type of higher educational institutions Britain needed. The *Times* editorial on December 4, 1963, argued that universities must be viewed through a synthesis of three perspectives: the organic, the instrumental, and the consumer's view. The organic view sees universities developing autonomously by advancing knowledge, teaching people to think for themselves, and preserving the cultural tradition. The instrumental view focuses on the development of national wealth and social fluidity. And the consumer's view takes account of student demand and vocational preparation. Government policy, it said, ought to strike a balance among all three. But in place of a rounded policy, Robbins had substituted an exclusively consumerist approach to education. The editorial predicted that this myopic perspective would merely facilitate the political expedient of putting ever greater student numbers above all other considerations: "A probable consequence of policies arrived at in that way is that the universities will be transformed, not just in size and number, but in character, aims, and emphasis as well" ("Dangers" 1963: 13b).

The editorial two days later presented a list of the positive attributes of British universities and especially praised their intensive tutorial Oxbridge-like qualities. It declared, "The debate, far from being over, should now begin" ("Questions" 1963: 13b).

The opposite social democratic view was presented immediately in a small magazine, *New Society*, by Eric Robinson, head of the department of mathematics at Enfield College of Technology. For Robinson, the report was too elitist: "The basic flaw of the Robbins Report, which leaves it open to attack from back and front, is that it implies the extension of elitist education to the mass. We should by now have learned from the history of secondary education in this country that this is no more possible than it is desirable" (Robinson 1963: 16).

Robinson argued that just as Sir Robert Morant's grammar schools (designed to prepare working-class youngsters for Oxford and Cambridge) reproduced all the bad elitist features of public schools (and both ought to be replaced by comprehensive secondary schools), British universities reproduced all the bad habits of Oxbridge. The alleged failures of British universities with working-class enrollments, applied science and technology, and community relevance arose from their slavish deference to and imitation of Oxbridge. The pull of Oxbridge status distorted the entire system of higher education. Robbins should have attacked, rather than supported, the Oxbridge model, Robinson believed.

Within four years, Robinson, as a member of the advisory team for Anthony Crosland (then Labour's minister of state for education and science) published a book, *The New Polytechnics: The People's Universities* (1967). It was a radical extension of Crosland's argument for creating the polytechnics. But unlike the original binary policy, which called for two sectors of higher education, one "public," run by local education authorities, and the other "autonomous" universities, Robinson argued for a single higher education system modeled on the polytechnics. Nearly twenty years later, Robinson's views had not mellowed. As director of Lancashire Polytechnic and vice-president of the Socialist Education Association, Robinson argued with A. H. Halsey about Oxbridge's abolition at a Labour Party education conference held in 1987 at Ruskin Hall, Oxford (see F. Jones 1987).

Sir Charles Morris, vice-chancellor of Leeds, Dr. A. H. Halsey, fellow of Nuffield, Oxford, and Professor Martin Trow of the University of California, Berkeley, all added their critical voices to the debate in a special issue of *Universities Quarterly*. Drawing attention to the former Colleges of Advanced Technology that had become the New universities and the alternative tradition of higher education they represented, Sir Charles Morris wrote: "The pattern of the future is by no means settled. The acceptance of Robbins means that . . . there will be more and more students. . . . But where they will go in the long run remains to be seen (Morris 1964: 128). Morris hoped to see the younger institutions rival or surpass the older universities, thus breaking the mold of higher education.

Halsey shared Sir Charles's wish to see a change in the pattern of higher education, but he was pessimistic about the odds. Halsey had just begun work with Martin Trow on a book about British academics, so he already had some sense of the strength of Oxbridge status throughout the profession (see Halsey and Trow 1971). With resignation he wrote: "The conclusion seems to be inescapable that competition for excellence in the wider system of higher education proposed by the Robbins committee will take place only within strata of the stable pyramid of institutions which has emerged from the history of the development of higher learning in Britain" (Halsey 1964: 135). The possibility that New universities, or even the older Redbrick universities, could dislodge Oxbridge from its position on top of the pyramid of academic prestige was highly unlikely. Robbins's hope that there would be no "freezing" of institutions into existing positions of authority was, in Halsey's opinion, unrealistic.

Professor Trow also addressed the problem of relative university status, and that key issue, as he saw it, reflected an internal contradiction in Robbins. "I have criticized the Report," Trow wrote, "not so much for its caution as for its unwillingness to accept the full implications of its own revolutionary principles" (Trow 1964: 150). The promise of providing space in universities for everyone with exam qualifications and the desire to learn could not be fulfilled in the existing system. According to Trow, Robbins could not stand for massive expansion and at the same time expect that expansion to take place inside British universities as presently constituted: "The Robbins Report projects . . . the present characteristics and balance of British higher education. The pattern it projects is that of an inverted pyramid, with the elite institutions . . . maintaining pre-eminence in numbers as well as prestige" (ibid.: 149). With Oxbridge and the University of London on top in size and status, the system of British universities would be too elitist and expensive to deliver on the "revolutionary" promise of equal opportunity.

The price of sustaining the elitist pattern would be very high. Modernization would be retarded. Trow predicted: "One price, certainly, is to slow the rate of growth of higher education, and to reduce its responsiveness to social and economic change" (ibid.). And another price would be

to abandon the report's "implicit principle," its commitment to social justice. There was, as Noel Annan put it, a social democratic soul struggling
within the report with its democratic elitist counterpart. Trow claimed
that in order to achieve Robbins's social goal of reducing "the wide
differences in opportunity and achievement among the several social
classes . . . I believe that either these principles will have to be sacrificed,
or that the recommendations regarding the size and shape of British
higher education embodied in Robbins will have to be revised" (ibid.:
150). Either new institutions, like America's state universities and community colleges, would be necessary, or the social program of Robbins
would succumb to the conflicting demands by dons for academic excellence and by government for economic accountability.

More evidence, from perspectives quite different from Trow's, that Oxbridge was the quagmire that threatened to undermine the Robbins report,
came from the editors of the *Spectator*, a quirky right-wing magazine, and
the editors of the *Economist*, free-market liberalism's authoritative news
weekly. Historians and sociologists have taken little notice, but even in the
1960s, conservative publications were among the sharpest critics of the
Robbins report and Oxbridge. On October 25, 1963, immediately after
publication of the Robbins report, the editors of the *Spectator* wrote, "The
Government has dodged the Oxbridge issue." Oxbridge was treated by
Robbins, according to the *Spectator*, as though there was "only a minor
difference between it and other institutions" (*Spectator* 1963: 511).

On the surface, it was an odd conclusion for the *Spectator*, given the
emphasis Robbins placed on exactly the opposite point. Internationally,
the report said, "there are probably fewer distinctions in Europe than in
Britain, where the prominence of Oxford and Cambridge are so marked"
(Committee on Higher Education 1963a: 36, para. 103). During the commission's labors, Robbins argued in favor of a separate inquiry of Royal
Commission stature to investigate and report on Oxbridge, precisely because Oxford and Cambridge were *not* like other universities (Carswell
1985: 31).

Nonetheless, Robbins seemed to be too soft on Oxbridge for the tastes
of fringe conservatives. The *Spectator* went on to list things that could
only embarrass Oxbridge: "Oxbridge differs from other universities in
the greater amount of money spent on its undergraduates, in the sort of
life they lead, and in the conservatism of some of its courses, and it is significant that its public school intake is again rising" (*Spectator* 1963:
511). If Oxbridge needed nudging, the *Spectator* was willing to push. But
it was left to the *Economist* to favor an inquiry by a Royal Commission.

On October 26, 1963, in its editorial leader, the *Economist* first praised Robbins's program for expansion and then grasped the nettle. If Robbins was serious about shaking up the status pyramid, Oxbridge ought to be held back, it said, and other universities built up, until an equal level was reached. There were intimations of this approach in Robbins, and the *Economist* drew attention to that part of the report:

> The real answer to their [Oxbridge's] excessive importance, it [the Robbins report] properly recognised, "is to be found in the deliberate development of other universities," by specially generous capital grants. But the higher pay of Oxbridge dons can surely not be justified; and it is obviously undemocratic that, while the proportion of entrants from state schools to all universities is now 70 per cent, the proportion at Oxford is only 39 per cent and at Cambridge only 25 per cent. . . . [These problems] have much to do with the existence of the autonomous colleges of these universities. The [Robbins] committee urges them to reform their own internal organization; and dangles the threat of an outside inquiry if they are unable to agree on how to do so. (*Economist* 1963: 355)

The editors in effect said, level the differences between Oxbridge, Redbrick, and new universities; reduce the social distance between them until nothing of substance separates one type of university from another.

There was a touch of historical amnesia to the *Economist*'s iconoclastic attitude on Oxbridge. The founding editor, Walter Bagehot, saw the secret of British government to be the division of labor between the practical and symbolic elements, what he called the efficient (read "Cabinet") and dignified (read "monarchical") parts of the English constitution (Bagehot 1976). The dignified component kept people distracted while the efficient component ran the show. The arrangement worked as well for a number of British institutions, enabling them to be both traditional and modern. Oxbridge obviously played a unique role in bridging the two parts. As a national institution, Oxford stood on the dignified and symbolic side of British life; but as a place that educated the governing class it prepared men for positions on the efficient side. Complete modernization would push Oxford onto the efficient side and undermine the symbolism Bagehot thought was necessary for effective administration. Given the intellectual caliber of the *Economist*'s staff, it is unlikely that they were ignorant of Bagehot's analysis. One can only conclude that they were no longer impressed by his notion that deference had utility and had replaced his faith in symbolism with a confidence in the unaided civilizing effects of market relations. Thus, the tension in Bagehot's theory, which represented a compromise between the deferential notions of organic conservative thought and the utilitarian rationality of market actors in nineteenth-century liberalism, was broken. One could conclude that the influence of Edmund Burke over the *Economist* had been, for some time, routed by the ideas of Adam Smith.[1]

As part of the "establishment," Oxford felt under indictment. Robbins, in a sense, was the court that found Oxford guilty. It seemed that the only thing left undone by the critics was to pass sentence. Pronouncing the terms of Oxford's punishment appeared to be the point of calling for a Royal Commission. In 1963, Oxford was closer to becoming the object of a government investigation than at any point since 1919.

ORIGINS OF THE FRANKS COMMISSION: MYTH AND REALITY

The events that led to the creation of the Franks Commission were instigated by the Robbins report. The report criticized Oxford's administration, its staff's pay levels, its undergraduate selection procedures, its difficulties providing standardized information about itself, and its general lack of accountability—all of which were deemed incompatible with public funding. The Robbins report saw many of these problems as "inherent in the collegiate structure of the two ancient universities" (Committee on Higher Education 1963a: 224, para. 687). Collegiate universities seemed unable to match a governmental desire for efficient bureaucracy:

> The number of times when it is necessary to except Oxford and Cambridge from general statements about British universities, the difficulty both universities have in reaching rapid decisions on matter of policy . . . the general obscurity in which so many of their administrative and financial arrangements are shrouded are not compatible with a situation in which they, like other universities, are largely dependent on public funds. . . . We recommend that, if Oxford and Cambridge are unable satisfactorily to solve these problems within a reasonable time, they should be the subject of an independent inquiry. (Committee on Higher Education 1963a: 224, para. 687)

Alarmed by the report, Oxford's Hebdomadal Council asked Lord Franks, then provost of Worcester College, to chair a committee to look into the points raised by Robbins and to determine which of those were already the object of an investigation, which ones were not, and whether a commission of inquiry was justified. This link between Robbins and the launch of Franks helped two misunderstandings to develop about the origins of the inquiry. One was that Franks was set up to prevent the creation of a Royal Commission. The other was that Franks was established out of fear of what a Labour government might do if given any excuse.

The Labour Party was out of office when Franks was commissioned, but elections were not far away. Important Labour Party figures were opposed in principle to the sort of educational privileges Oxbridge represented. In 1962, Anthony Crosland, who became under Wilson the minister of state for education and science, published *The Conservative Enemy*, based on a series of articles printed in 1960 and 1961 in *Encounter*. According to Crosland, poverty and social classes were aspects of the conservative enemy, but they were reinforced by a divisive educational system:

> University graduates (especially from Oxford and Cambridge) virtually monopolize the senior positions in the Civil Service, the bar, the church, the Conservative party (not to mention 40 per cent of the Parliamentary Labour Party), teaching, medicine, banking, scientific research [and so on]. . . . Those who can afford to purchase private schooling have a significant advantage in obtaining entry to Oxford and Cambridge. (Crosland 1961: 49, 51)

In the long run, the commanding positions of public schools and Oxbridge must be substantially reduced, Crosland said; in the short run, however, both should be opened up to lower-middle-class and working-class young people. Crosland proposed to break down the monopoly of wealth over public schools, if necessary through legislation (ibid.: 51). While only the public schools were threatened with parliamentary action in Crosland's essays, Oxbridge was warned of impending legal regulation by a series of statements made by Labour leaders in 1963.

As a member of Labour's Taylor Committee, a study group on higher education, Crosland helped write a pamphlet that proposed placing a quota on public-school entry to Oxbridge (see Labour Party 1963).

Access was Labour's first concern, but it had other objections to elitist education as well. Labour's shadow minister for education, R. H. S. Crossman, wrote an article that directly attacked Oxbridge college autonomy (Crossman 1964). And in a speech to Oxford's chapter of the Association of University Teachers about Labour's second thoughts on Robbins, Crossman praised Franks but ominously claimed "that without [the Franks inquiry] a Royal Commission on the University would have been inevitable" (*Oxford Magazine* 1964: 330).[2]

Certainly there were anxieties at Oxford about a Labour intervention. Looking back, fifteen months after Lord Franks's appointment, at the temper of the times when the commission's work began, the *Oxford Magazine*'s editor wrote, "Then the fear was that Mr. Crossman, bent on the abolition of privilege, would be Secretary of State for Education in a Government that would have a vast majority" (Vaizey 1965b: 373). The memory of that fear was alive in the minds of some Oxford fellows decades later. David John Wenden, fellow and bursar at All Souls and onetime chairman of the Estates Bursars Committee, remembered: "People were scared stiff that Crossman and the Labour Party would appoint a Royal Commission. And the Franks report was a do-it-yourself investigation to try and head off a Royal Commission" (Wenden interview 1988).

In retrospect, it was possible to see that those fears were unwarranted. Wilson's government, which took office in October 1964, did not assault Oxbridge; eleven out of 23 Cabinet members had Oxbridge degrees, and even though they were among those most outspoken about the medieval universities' faults, they found it easier to turn their attention to technical college expansion than to university reform.

Labour's objections to Oxbridge were displaced from universities and transferred to the constructive task of creating a new layer of higher education. When Crosland was minister of education and science, his think tank (which included Michael Young, Tyrell Burgess, and A. H. Halsey) came up with ideas for a "people's" sector of higher education. Thirty polytechnics, segregated from universities by an impassable "binary" line and directly under central and local government control, were the result. In addition, second-chance "adult" education in the home was offered by the radio and television courses of the Open University. So Labour began the new "university of the air," and consolidated a technological system of higher education, rather than translate its criticisms of universities into a punitive program.

Reflecting on the origins of the commission, Lord Franks had this to say about Labour-inspired fear:

> You couldn't say there was none, but you couldn't say that it was strong. People always can worry that government will make a lot of changes, but then they look at who will be in the Cabinet and see that they all come from Oxford, so to speak, then they wonder. I think that this is a bogey man on the horizon, rather than something which actually determines attitudes, thoughts, and actions. (Franks interview 1988)

Oxford's leaders seem to have taken reassurance from sociological reductionism, reaching the conclusion that Cabinet members with Oxford ties would not hurt them and that there was no need to be frightened by political leftists they themselves had educated.

In the pages of the *Oxford Magazine*, R. B. McCallum, master of Pembroke, offered an interpretation of Franks's origins that placed responsibility for the commission on insiders: "The spirit complained of was evident long before the Commission was mooted and indeed the Commission itself is a sign of the critical mood within the University. The Robbins report was more of the occasion than the cause of this organized effort at analysis" (McCallum 1965: 202). McCallum's opinion was slightly optimistic. The spirit of reform was alive in Oxford before Robbins, but it is unlikely it would ever have gone as far as Franks without outside pressure. Effective pressure, however, came not from Labour but from the Robbins committee, which was appointed by a Conservative administration.

It was true, though, that between 1960 and 1964, when the Franks Commission was established, Oxford's Hebdomadal Council authorized investigations into admissions, first and second public examinations, postgraduate conditions, teacher training, the integration of university faculty without fellowships into colleges, financial circumstances of the poorer colleges, university finances, and procedures in Congregation (Franks, Wheare, and Brown 1964a: 526). The desires of Council to adjust Oxford as a whole to the new standing of science and advanced research work, to make the admissions process more socially just and meritocratic, to effect curriculum innovations, to remove the large disparities in resources available to colleges, to ensure full participation by every academic person in both university and college life, and to make Oxford's self-government more effective—those desires were already the subject of internal investigations before the Franks Commission.

While it may not be possible to settle definitively the question of the role played by fears of the Labour Party, it is clear that Oxford's leaders were not motivated by a desire to head off another Royal Commission. The week the Robbins report came out the Hebdomadal Council began to carefully evaluate Oxford's situation. From the first discussion of appropriate ways to answer the negative points raised by Robbins until the final decision to approach Lord Franks, a majority on Council favored the establishment of a Royal Commission.

The response of the Hebdomadal Council to the Robbins report was structured by its internal politics. Just as Oxford as a whole had its conservatives, social democrats, and democratic elitists, so did Council. One could reasonably place the vice-chancellor, W. F. Oakeshott, with Kenneth Wheare, Maurice Bowra, Robert Blake, Sir Edgar Williams, and A. L. P. Norrington as Council conservatives. Alan Bullock was the only one strongly influenced by social democratic values. But democratic elitists included the scientists, Professor Pickering and Dr. van Heyningen, and the principal of Linacre House, John Bamborough. Of Council's twenty members, at least seven were conservative, five democratic elitist, and one social democratic. Under Oakeshott's leadership, Council's response to Robbins was irresolute.

When members of the Hebdomadal Council met in November 1963 to consider how to respond to Robbins, they had before them a memorandum by Oxford's vice-chancellor, W. F. Oakeshott. The vice-chancellor began his memorandum with praise for Robbins's expansion program, but he quickly moved from national concerns to the criticisms of Oxbridge. Oakeshott must have felt somewhat disappointed and defensive about Robbins's criticisms because he began by drawing attention to John Vaizey's comments on the report in the *Oxford Magazine*. It was, he said, "proof that many, even those with radical sympathies, find the references to Oxford and Cambridge not to their liking" (Hebdomadal Council Papers 1963b: 423). Of course, Oxford could change for the better, Oakeshott wrote: "No institution cannot be improved . . . and I cannot indeed remember a time when we seemed ourselves to be taking so seriously the case for change" (ibid.).

Unfortunately, in Oakeshott's opinion, the discussion stirred by Robbins was not so much over improvements as over different visions of what a system of higher education ought to embody. It seemed to reflect two fundamentally different perspectives, one that allowed for centers of excellence and another that wanted to make existing institutions more equal. The vice-chancellor expressed the typical conservative anxiety that expansion threatened the citadels of culture. He asked rhetorically:

> In the country at large [is there not] a basic difference of opinion between those on the one hand who think it essential to have a diversity of university institutions; to have some universities where the programme . . . remains rigorously academic; who believe that it would be a mistake to break up the great research groups . . . and those, on the other, who think that, in the interest of making such ability as there is go further, a major dispersion ought to be taking place immediately. (Ibid.)

Oakeshott feared that Oxford was under attack by the egalitarians. If it were to correctly defend itself—which would mean making improvements where they were warranted but standing firm on those things that reflected Oxford's vision of academic excellence—the job would have to be done by "some outside body." In Oakeshott's opinion, "a Royal Commission, or other independent external committee" should be asked to look into the issues (ibid., 423, 424). With the vice-chancellor's recommendations in front of them, Council attempted to develop a way to answer Robbins.

Council's discussion that afternoon was long and complex. There were many things to consider. Regardless of Council's wishes, the colleges were independent bodies and would require individual persuasion, and there was Cambridge University to deal with. Because of their shared qualities and history, no Royal Commission could investigate Oxford without reference to Cambridge.

Council agreed that something ought to be done, but a division emerged over whether to do it internally or to use an external commission. A. B. Brown, bursar and law tutor at Worcester, argued for an internal committee. But Dr. Chilver, who had chaired the committee that reformed the Latin requirement, brought things to a head with a motion "that Council should consider ways and means of securing the appointment of an outside commission." The motion was seconded by Alan Bullock and passed by a vote of eighteen to two. Then Council decided to appoint an ad hoc committee of five to report "on the form which an outside inquiry might take" (Hebdomadal Council Papers 1963c: cxxvi–cxxvii). The vice-chancellor along with the rector of Exeter, K. C. Wheare; the warden of Wadham, Sir C. M. Bowra; the principal of Lady Margaret Hall, L. S. Sutherland; and the senior proctor, J. H. Sanders, were asked to serve on the committee. So while Council's vote was for fast action toward an outside inquiry, the committee empowered to move the process along was in the hands of conservatives.

The ad hoc committee's report was available for the next Council meeting, on November 25. The committee presented two important recommendations as well as a sketch of the events leading up to the Royal Commission of 1919. They were convinced that "an inquiry by a Royal Commission or a committee with similar powers [was] desirable, and that . . . Oxford should take the initiative, with or without Cambridge" (Hebdomadal Council Papers 1963f: 527). And they thought that because Oxford's colleges "may hesitate to precipitate such an investigation . . . it would be necessary [especially if confidentiality is to be maintained] to take the first steps without prior consultations with the colleges" (ibid.: 527–28).

In his comments to the meeting, the vice-chancellor explained that Cambridge was reluctant but would go along with a Royal Commission if Oxford took the initiative. And of the five colleges he consulted informally, four favored Oxford's calling for a Royal Commission. The minutes did not identify the five, but those results suggest that there was not much collegiate opposition.

After considerable discussion, it was agreed that only a Royal Commission would do because only it would have the necessary authority to respond to Oxbridge's critics; it would be nonpolitical; it could include Cambridge; and it would have the power to request all relevant information. The proposal for a Royal Commission ought to come from Oxford, preferably with Cambridge's approval, but without it if necessary. Cambridge and the colleges should be consulted, and the records of the 1919 Royal Commission ought to be examined to see what role Council had played that time (Hebdomadal Council Papers 1963e: cxli–cxlii). So, as things stood one month after Robbins, Council was poised to request a Royal Commission, but again conservative voices prevailed that they should hold back just a bit longer to consult with Cambridge and a few more Oxford colleges.

At the next meeting, on December 2, 1963, the vice-chancellor informed Council that Cambridge was willing to act. The specter of a series of separate investigations had presented itself at a meeting of the National Incomes Commission on November 26. The Incomes Commission had made reference to Robbins's statements on the higher salaries of Oxbridge staff and had threatened to launch an inquiry. This contagion convinced Cambridge that it would be better to cover everything in one big Royal Commission than to suffer an indeterminate number of committees all responsible for different issues. So on November 28 the Standing Joint Committee on Oxford and Cambridge met to discuss the actions necessary to get a Royal Commission.

When Oakeshott reported back to Council, he had a series of specific steps to present. He proposed to send a delegation to the chancellor, Harold Macmillan, to ask him to approach the prime minister. Council was particularly concerned to gain the initiative; it wanted Macmillan to tell the prime minister, Sir Alec Douglas-Home, that if his government felt constrained Oxford "would wish to feel free to put the proposal forward in another way" (Hebdomadal Council Papers 1963g: clxiv). If the Tory government would not initiate a commission, Oxford would raise the question through other channels.

The delegation that went to see Macmillan was quite conservative, consisting of Oakeshott, Wheare, and the university registrar, Sir Folliot Herbert Sandford. Macmillan received them on December 5. Although Macmillan was willing to approach the government, he did not intend to go immediately to the prime minister. Instead, he suggested that the registrar communicate with the Cabinet secretary on some practical details while a London meeting was arranged for himself, Richard A. Butler, who was then the Cabinet minister in charge of the Foreign Office, and three representatives from each ancient university.

Pursuing his own connections, Cambridge's vice-chancellor had already talked with Butler about a Royal Commission. Butler, however, was unconvinced: "He wished to be told in more detail what the case was for a Royal Commission" (Hebdomadal Council Papers 1963h: clxxiv). Council took note of the situation and authorized the ad hoc committee to act over the holidays.

At the next Hebdomadal Council meeting on January 20, 1964, the news was not good. Butler had scheduling problems and could not even set a date for a meeting. The vice-chancellor, bothered by the delays, decided to return to conservative measures. He argued that "after discussion with the Vice-Chancellor of Cambridge and members of the *ad hoc* committee, . . . the University had, through force of circumstances, now missed the tide" (Hebdomadal Council Papers 1964a: xxiii). Oakeshott stepped back from pushing for a Royal Commission and advocated going along with Cambridge's idea to merely publish a statement responding to Robbins.

Council's progressives and centrist members were not persuaded. They rejected Oakeshott's proposal to issue a declaration as "quite inadequate." And they reminded him that since Michaelmas term Council was formally on record as favoring an external commission. If the government would not move on it, then "the University must be free to put forward the proposal in another way" (ibid.: xxiv). After an inconclusive discussion, further action was postponed until the next Council meeting.

In the meantime Council members tried to devise plans to implement the policy for an external inquiry. A number of schemes were put in circulation. To structure the discussion at the meeting on January 27, the vice-chancellor presented five alternatives for action: Oxford could sit tight; it could continue to work for the meeting that Butler had problems scheduling; it could go to the prime minister without Cambridge; it could present a motion in Congregation; or it could send a letter to the *Times* (Hebdomadal Council Papers 1964c: xliii). But before Council had an opportunity to discuss any of those proposals, the vice-chancellor expressed the hope that a motion by Alan Bullock would receive Council's full attention.

Bullock, as a very junior member of Council, and certainly the one most to the left, moved that Council as a whole sponsor a resolution in Congregation calling for an external inquiry or approach "a small number of eminent persons not being members of the University . . . to carry out an investigation" (ibid.: xliv). Since Bullock's proposals were not very different from the options outlined by the vice-chancellor, one can only speculate as to Oakeshott's motives for giving him the floor. Regardless, Council again talked at length but failed to achieve a consensus for action. It decided to postpone a definitive decision until February 3.

It was possible that some of those who suggested putting off a final decision for one more week knew of Macmillan's attitude toward a Royal Commission. But whether or not that was the case, Macmillan was the decisive influence on the next week's meeting.

All of the questions about an external commission were finally settled on February 3, 1964, three months after the Robbins report was issued. The vice-chancellor and the master of St. Catherine's had arrived at a compromise. They brought to Council a common proposal to establish an internal committee because "the time for the appointment of an external committee . . . had now passed" (Hebdomadal Council Papers, vol. 247, Feb. 7, 1964: lvii). The internal committee would be small, consisting of Lord Franks, K. C. Wheare, and Professor Sir Lindor Brown. Wheare represented the conservatives, but both Lord Franks and Professor Brown were progressives. The committee would go to work with the explicit understanding that it was to review Robbins's criticisms of Oxford and, if justified, make recommendations for a larger inquiry's terms of reference. The motion was passed without opposition.

Why the sudden consensus on an internal committee when for two months all but a few individuals on Council had favored an external commission? The scales were tipped against a Royal Commission by three factors: Cambridge's coolness to the idea, the government's unresponsiveness, and the opposition of one man, Harold Macmillan. The government of Sir Alec Douglas-Home had been unable to schedule a meeting in December or January. Butler spoke once about it when Cambridge brought the question up on December 8, 1963, but no other discussions occurred. Cambridge had never been keen on an external inquiry, preferring instead to publish a response to Robbins, which it went ahead and did, while awaiting events.

Macmillan was first consulted by Council on December 5, 1963. At some point between January 27 and February 3, 1964, Macmillan made it known, or gave permission for others to explain, that he was against a Royal Commission. Macmillan's personal authority was such that even Bullock, after learning of Macmillan's view, withdrew his motion (Bullock interview 1988). It may seem strange that Bullock and others were so willing to change their minds. But it followed from Oxford's position in relation to the conservative governing establishment in Britain. Whether from a sense of deference or pragmatic politics, a majority of Council were willing to concede to Macmillan's wishes. It would have been extraordinary if Council had chosen to ignore the opposition of a chancellor who until October 1963 had held the office of prime minister.

From the perspective of the Hebdomadal Council, the Franks Commission came into being not to prevent a Royal Commission, but because after months of effort Oxford had failed to get the government to launch one. The delay was due to Council's internal divisions as well as its desire to follow traditional procedures: to reflect on the context of the last royal inquiry, to confer with its sibling university, to work through dialogue and consensus, and to defer to the judgment of friends in government. And just as Oxford did not complacently ignore Robbins's criticisms, it did not set up Franks in a panic to escape public investigation. The Franks committee did the work of a Royal Commission, but under another name.

THE FRANKS COMMISSION: PROGRAM AND PERFORMANCE

Council's internal committee proposed in March to launch a full-scale public inquiry. Its three members, Lord Franks, Kenneth Wheare, and Professor Brown, took note of Oxford's traditionalist qualities and the need to defend them from radical attack. They wrote:

> Oxford, like other great traditional institutions, has to justify itself and its way of life. Oxford is un-accustomed to formulating its own aims and principles. . . . It appears parochial and complacent when the truth is that it has no consciously affirmed general policies. . . . [Yet, now, it must speak up or face] radical reforms being imposed from outside. If Oxford is silent or appears to be aimless, then the causes of higher education cannot be adequately pursued. (Franks, Wheare, and Brown 1964b: 3–4)

In this passage the authors expressed an understanding of Oxford's commitment to a whole way of life, its aversion to either central planning or radical change. And they affirmed Oxford's responsibility to the ethical mission of the university community. These were the sentiments and ideas of traditionalists attempting to maintain continuity while adjusting to novel challenges. From the document's language, one might assume that Wheare was its principal author.

The Franks Commission was unprecedented as a self-examination by one of England's oldest and most private of "establishment" institutions. Yet what, in the short or long term, did Franks accomplish? Was it a public relations show or a work of critical and substantive innovation?

The work of the Franks Commission was deliberately organized as a large public discussion of Oxford and its position in the nation (ibid.: 9; Franks interview 1988). Franks did not organize the inquiry as a cautious, closed-door, clubbish conversation. Rather, the investigation was as democratic and public as possible. Twice weekly, for an entire academic year, the committee "held public hearings" (University of Oxford 1966a: 14). All oral and written testimony, the results of two surveys of dons and students, and the responses to questionnaires sent to official bodies were published. Critics may dismiss this open and thorough discussion as a public relations gesture, but it was not designed as such.

The Franks Commission did its work as an open discussion because it could not imagine a better way to ensure positive results. Given Oxford's traditions of self-government, Lord Franks thought an open inquiry was the only way to proceed. In May 1966, Lord Franks told the *Oxford Magazine*:

> From the start . . . we thought our job was to place ourselves at the centre of debate and that this should involve external and internal participation. We believed we would learn a very great deal from this process and, with the democratic nature of Oxford, that the only way we could get the topics under active discussion was by holding these public sessions. (Franks 1966: 379)

Not everyone approved of the public debate. According to the *Oxford Magazine*, "The act of the Commission which has been most widely criticised by the faint-hearted . . . was the decision to take evidence in public" (ibid.: 379). Some apprehensive Oxonians imagined that criticism in public would inhibit candor and rational thought, yet the timid were missing the point. The commission believed that without an open discussion nothing of substance could be accomplished in this self-governing university. What was needed was a moral consensus, not legislative commands. As Lord Franks explained:

> We were trying to produce a degree of consensus. . . . We were
> taking evidence for a full year . . . and this was where, in a way,
> the most important work of the commission was done. It's where
> the work of conversion was done. . . . It was, I think, a very large
> process of self-education mainly because so much of the organiza-
> tion of Oxford . . . was by convention, by custom, by habit.
> (Franks interview 1988)

The public sessions and the published record ensured that, by the time the
final report was presented, there would be the broadest consensus possible. When Council submitted legislation to Congregation to implement
the report's proposals, it was already apparent which ones would and
would not receive approval.

The report's main recommendations related to:

the university's status as a world-class institution
the governing and administrative arrangements of the university,
    especially the roles of Council and the General Board
the establishment of a Council of Colleges to formulate common
    policy
the problem of science staff without college fellowships
the issues of college finance, especially the difficulties poor colleges
    face
admissions criteria and procedures
the creation of faculty centers and five "super faculty boards"
teaching, research, and examinations

The commission saw the international status of Oxford as its most
precious tradition and asset. For the university to continue its role in the
international community of scholars, a role that went back to the twelfth
century, it should retain its concentration of talent and resources. As discussed in Chapter 2, Oxford ought to renew its commitments to research
and graduate education. In response to Robbins, Franks stressed that if
Oxford were penalized for its past good fortune by reductions of its UGC
funds, the international stature of all British universities, not just Oxford,
would needlessly suffer. Britain could afford only a few universities of international standing, and it made more sense to keep Oxford as one of
them than to push it into decline by shifting resources elsewhere. Oxford's
world-class status was the general context in which the commission formulated its recommendations.

The commission's proposals on the university's governing and administrative arrangements were passed by Congregation. Oxford's Parliament resolved to replace the old arrangement whereby seniority among college heads determined who would fill the two-year post of vice-chancellor; from then on, the vice-chancellor would be elected to a four-year term in office, preceded by two years of preparation for the job. The General Board was to be "resurrected" (Franks interview 1988), and would have a two-year, full-time vice-chairman occupied with the allocation of resources. The commission resolved to abolish all but one of the legislative powers of Convocation, the assembly of all Oxford degree holders; in the future, Convocation would elect the chancellor, but all other powers would rest with Oxford's resident faculty and staff in Congregation and Council.

Oxford's democratic form of self-government was revitalized by a number of steps. Membership rights in Congregation were extended to Oxford's permanent administrative and library staff. Disputed questions were to be voted on by mail, and verbatim transcripts of Congregation's debates were to be distributed to ensure the widest possible participation in Oxford's affairs.

As explained in detail in Chapter 3, all members of the university were to be given collegiate homes. The university tried to integrate nondons, mostly scientists, into existing colleges. For those who could not be given the privileges of fellowship at an existing college, two new postgraduate colleges, Wolfson and St. Cross, were built to accommodate them. Furthermore, to enhance informal discussions, new faculty centers were projected in locations near the historic heart of the city (such as the one on George Street for social studies).

The commitment of the university to expansion and meritocracy was reaffirmed. The *Times* especially took note of Oxford's pledge to open wide its doors to talent. A headline on the commission read, "One-Third More Students for Oxford Urged, Ensuring Equality of Opportunity for Ability" (May 12, 1966: 10).

The commission put through an unprecedented solution for one of the problems of college financing. The poorer colleges in Oxford were in trouble. They were not well enough endowed to keep up with the university's appointments in new subjects. And they were becoming less able to afford a style of collegiate life in keeping with Oxford's traditions. Lord Franks recalls grouping colleges into categories of relative wealth and poverty and then persuading them to embrace a mutual assistance scheme:

> When we were inventing the college contributions scheme . . .
> we mentally divided the colleges into three groups, the peasants,

bourgeois, and the rich. The peasants had to be helped. The bourgeois, they were people whose financial position was such they had virtually no choices after just managing along. But the bourgeois had choices in ascending scale, as they became richer, and the rich colleges had many choices. Now, I reckoned Queen's was among the richest of the bourgeois. And I took my own college, Worcester, as the pivotal college in between the peasants and the bourgeois. Why? because it was a poorish college but it had just enough money to have a few choices. I thought it managed, it wasn't strapped on the wheel of necessity. And I didn't think it ought to be helped. I thought it was, using medieval terms, independent yeoman. And everything below should be helped, everything above should contribute, and more the richer they were. (Franks interview 1988)

The ranks of the poor colleges included the five colleges for women and some of the new colleges, such as St. Catherine's and St. Antony's. To rectify the situation, Lord Franks proposed taxing the wealthier colleges, such as Christ Church and Magdalen, to redistribute money.

The colleges went along with the plan for a mixture of reasons, ranging from Merton's reformist sense of empathy to Christ Church's fear of government control. Lord Franks explained:

Motives are always in practical life complex. The element of compassion was there, say in Merton. Without any question, they wanted to help because they thought that the state of life in these poor colleges was not what ought to be in an Oxford college. . . . [For others] the point at issue was whether if any college failed, went bankrupt, would it be allowed to sink? The argument was, the government would intervene. And if it did, there would be rules, but rules would be for all. And if they wanted to avoid that situation, then they had to help. Enlightened self-interest dictated generosity. . . . The college which had the most difficulty in seeing the light was Christ Church. I had many hours of direct personal argument . . . [there over] dinner. (Ibid.)

Through public dialogue with colleges as they were brought in groups to testify before the commission, and by private efforts, each became convinced that the plan was important to their long-range self-interest (ibid.).

With everyone on board, the goal was to build up the poorer colleges' endowments to make them self-supporting. Complete equality of wealth was not the point, but it was the goal to elevate "peasant" colleges to the rank of "yeomen" ones. The scheme, devised with the accounting assistance of Price Waterhouse, worked.

Among the report's recommendations there was a division between those that affected only the university and those that touched on college autonomy. The former were, with only one notable exception, passed by Congregation. The latter were only partially adopted. A member of Council for twenty years from the time of Franks forward, Michael Brock remembered:

> I think you have to make a clear distinction here . . . between those parts [of Franks] which concern the university . . . and those parts which really concern the colleges. Now on the first, I think there was little doubt that it was going to go through. . . . It was a necessary modernization. . . . What you get with all Royal Commission reports of this kind, and it was very like a Royal Commission, is really this. They put into one bag . . . two kinds of proposals. The first kind is the kind where they think that an immediate change can and should be made. The second kind is the kind where what they are really trying to do is to change the climate of opinion over the longer term. . . . The college proposals were really seen to be in the second category from the start. (Brock interview 1988)

The proposal affecting the colleges that did not stand a chance was Lord Franks's idea to create a Council of Colleges. The council would enable Oxford's colleges to speak with one voice and to arrange their relations by majority vote. A council seemed to Lord Franks necessary to make Oxford's collegiate federation more effectively democratic. A council would make the colleges more responsible and cooperative and less like an unruly crowd. But the colleges would not commit themselves.

From the first soundings on this idea, the Hebdomadal Council was opposed to the proposal, as were fourteen of the colleges. The opposition included all of Oxford's most wealthy and powerful colleges: Magdalen, All Souls, Balliol, Queen's, Christ Church, and New College. Of the others, five wanted some sort of additional collegiate coordination, three thought the idea might be worth trying (St. Peter's, Worcester, and Jesus), while only Merton and St. Catherine's favored it (Commission of Inquiry 1965e: question 11). Whether the proposal was rejected because policy would have been set by a simple rather than a two-thirds majority (for example), or just because it threatened college autonomy, it collapsed. When the conservative vice-chancellor, Sir Kenneth Wheare, failed to win the backing of his own college for the plan, it was clear the idea was going nowhere. Instead, the colleges formed a purely consultative body, the Conference of Colleges, in place of Franks's Council.

Another sore point was Franks's assessment of Oxford's only college without any student members, All Souls. The commission found that All Souls lacked a clear purpose. It was neither an undergraduate nor a graduate college, and its role as a research academy was obscure. It had approximately 57 fellows who enjoyed the amenities of the foundation (Caute 1966: 11). Of those, 26 supervised graduate students, and many more gave university lectures, but none had "a formal obligation to teach undergraduates" (Wilson 1966: 396). All Souls was old, architecturally distinguished, and immensely wealthy. It was viewed by outsiders as having nothing better to do with its resources than to serve as a daily club for its resident members and a weekend retreat for its London visitors. Matters were not helped by the temperament of its warden, John Sparrow.

According to his biographer and friend for forty years, John Lowe, the warden of All Souls was very close to Maurice Bowra. Both Sparrow and Bowra were conservative and intoxicatingly entertaining. John Sparrow "enjoyed all the little snobberies of the cognoscente" (Lowe 1992: 568, 570). Sparrow was not inclined toward the notion that All Souls should perform particular academic functions and thought that students or women around would just spoil the place. As Lowe put it: "All Souls was his [Sparrow's] favorite club. . . . While John had respect for some higher scholarship, he had neither sympathy for nor understanding of academic life and little real interest in the contribution that All Souls should be making to the intellectual life of Oxford" (ibid.: 571). When Lord Franks trained his austere attention on All Souls, the warden did all he could to evade the consequences.

When the issue hit the floor of Congregation, Max Beloff, the Gladstone Professor of Government attached to All Souls, rose to the college's defense. Rather than respond to the issues, Beloff rejected Franks's right to judge. Beloff stated that Franks did not have a legal mandate to interfere with the internal affairs of the colleges (Beloff 1966: 1493).

The colleges' governing body, its fellows, had to deliberate on and respond to Franks's criticisms. By feeding the colleges' fellows a "diet of insuperable difficulties" (Caute 1966: 8), Sparrow managed to fight a protracted battle of attrition. In reaction to Franks, Lowe explained:

[John Sparrow] was masterly, undaunted, and not a little Machia-vellian. He procrastinated through endless college meetings, allow-ing the fellows to debate four possible schemes, none of which John had any intention of implementing. The younger fellows were eager for change; the older mostly supported John's strategy to maintain the status quo. (Lowe 1992: 571)

When one of the younger dons, David Caute, resigned his fellowship at All Souls in frustration and published a disclosure of its inner turmoil (Caute 1966), he was denounced for telling "secrets" and spreading a slanderous "aspersion" on Sparrow (L. Butler 1966: 93–95). But Caute's account was sustained when, 26 years after the event, Lowe wrote:

This debate, within and without the college, went on for more than two years. Finally, because of outside pressure, John could procrastinate no longer. He had made promises that he had not kept, and, for better or worse, the fellows voted for the visiting fellows scheme. If nothing else, John could console himself that this hare had drawn the pack away from the odious possibility of disrupting the college with a new building and hirsute post-graduate students. And after all, one could use the visiting fellows scheme to slip in a few deserving, if not wholly academic friends, as temporary members of the club. (Lowe 1992: 571)

Sparrow assuaged the commission's concerns by establishing 25 new re-search fellowships to reinvigorate All Souls as an arts academy. There would be no students, but the college would elect and fund visitors; in fu-ture years, many of those guests, such as Yale professor of political sci-ence and sociology David Apter, would find the experience delightful. Others, such as Harvard professor of sociology Daniel Bell, mindful of All Souls' past, would turn the offer down (Bell correspondence 1993).

The "'Infirmity of purpose' at All Souls," as the *Times* headline put it (May 12, 1966: 10), attracted a disproportionate amount of public atten-tion. The problem was in a sense a side show, yet it was symbolically important because it confirmed some of the worst rumors about old, ir-responsible, hedonistic Oxford. From the perspective of public image, All Souls was at the center of Oxford's difficulties in adapting itself to the demands of the day. At the onset of the controversy, it looked as if the Franks Commission would get the upper hand; but the ultimate re-sult, the visiting fellows solution, was more in harmony with Sparrow's agenda.

A SECOND LOOK AT UNIVERSITY FINANCING: 1950–73

There were two crucial challenges on which the commission did not develop innovative proposals: women and university financing. As described in Chapter 2, the move toward women attending men's colleges was deliberately suppressed. In contrast, Franks encouraged a discussion of university financing, yet the dialogue did not settle on a positive program.

Almost everything about Oxford undermined its desire to launch an appeal to bolster the financial independence of the university. The disincentives included Oxford's relation to the state, its collegiate organization, and its collective mentality on academic autonomy.

To meet its financial needs, the university stood between the colleges and the state with palms outstretched in each direction. Unlike the colleges, the university did not have the properties and investments to give it a reliable income. And it had no students of its own. All junior members of the university were also members of a particular college that had first, and sometimes final, claim on the loyalties and bank accounts of its graduates. The university was financed by college contributions or, especially after 1946, by grants from the central government.

The colleges had a short-sighted interest in having the government shoulder most of the financial obligations for the university. Those burdens were growing because of the needs of natural scientists—and scientists were not especially welcome at many Oxford colleges. One can imagine, with slight exaggeration, a particularly complacent arts don being content to let the state pay for the university, since natural science research benefited the taxpayer. He might also willingly have tolerated scientists as long as they did not cost his college anything and he did not have to dine with them frequently.

There was also a growing consensus, across the political and intellectual spectrum, that the public purse should pay the basic expenses of British universities. For social democrats, education was a common good, from primary school through university, which should be the responsibility of public authorities to finance. From a conservative pragmatic perspective, it was conventional wisdom that the state's substantial contribution to universities could not realistically be replaced by private contributions. After the 1946 expansion of public funding, neither organic conservatives nor social democrats provided the intellectual grounds for a critique of institutional dependence.

The power of institutional interests and the weight of collective opinion did not work by choking off the formulation of alternative ideas but by their capacity to brush aside fund-raising proposals as ill-timed and inexpedient. The counterargument was made repeatedly between 1958 and 1968 by scientists and progressive reformers—but to no avail.

Before the establishment of the Franks Commission, Oxford had conducted three public appeals for money. The Higher Studies Fund (1937–43), which was used to build an extension to the university's main library, the Bodleian, resulted in raising money for social studies, geology, physical chemistry, and the Ashmolean Museum as well. The other two major fund-raising efforts, the Historic Buildings Appeal (1957–62) and the St. Catherine's Appeal (1958–61) (the latter being only a semi-public effort), were detailed in Chapter 4.[3]

The issue of public appeals was raised no fewer than seven other times between 1950 and 1967, always without effect. In 1950, opposition from the colleges blocked an effort aimed primarily at the United States (Registrar 1968: 106). Then in 1958, Professor Krebs got the Hebdomadal Council to authorize preliminary steps toward establishing an appeal that would be either general or linked to specific science needs. This time the chairman of the UGC, Sir Keith Murray, discouraged a broad public appeal. According to Oxford's registrar's files, when Professor Krebs spoke with the UGC chair, "Sir Keith Murray said that he was sure that the days for raising another Higher Studies Fund for general university purposes were over" (ibid.: 109). And since Professor Krebs and his scientist colleagues wanted to postpone any appeal specifically targeted to support the sciences until after the St. Catherine's campaign was over, nothing came of this initiative (ibid.: 110).

In 1962, when the St. Catherine's efforts were wrapped up and the topic of a general appeal was revived within the Hebdomadal Council by another scientist, Professor Brebis Bleaney—no one seconded his motion. So again the matter was dropped (ibid.).

In 1965, the problem was repeatedly put on the table for discussion. First, the chairmen of Oxford's natural science departments urged movement on the matter in a memorandum submitted to the Franks Commission: "It is suggested that the time may now be ripe to launch the general appeal for funds which was discussed some years ago, but set aside whilst the appeals for St. Catherine's and for the Historic Buildings were in progress" (Bleaney 1965: 409). Then in the pages of the *Oxford Magazine* Professor Bleaney drew attention to the scientists' memo and again made the case for professionalizing Oxford's finances:

As a member of the Hebdomadal Council, I advocated that the university should appoint an official with the status of a Vice-Chancellor, whose primary job would be to raise the university's endowment, and increase its financial resources. . . . At present, only one Curator of the Chest out of twelve elected members is a scientist. It is the scientist, who, to finance his research, is accustomed to plan ahead for a period of years. . . . In an academic community where considerable obloquy still attaches to "science" and much more to "science professor," it is unlikely that the University would accept a take-over bid from a consortium of active science departments. It might do worse. (Ibid.)

The magazine's editor, John Vaizey, endorsed Bleaney's analysis and called for a proper "fund-raising body" (Registrar 1968: 110) in June 1965. Immediately afterward, in July, a member of the Hebdomadal Council made a motion to launch an appeal:

Mr. A. B. Brown gave notice that he would in September move that the Hebdomadal Council appoint a committee of five . . . to consider and report, not later than the first meeting of Council in Michaelmas Term, on the desirability of making, in the calendar year 1966, a public appeal throughout the world for the general endowment of the University of Oxford. (Ibid.: 103)

When time came in September for Council to act on Brown's proposition, he was absent from the meeting and no one else addressed it. The matter lapsed.

A semi-official response came the next month in the *Oxford Magazine*. H. H. Keen, secretary to curators of the University Chest, Oxford's financial administration, wrote a reply to John Vaizey's favorable evaluation of Professor Bleaney's call for a general financial appeal. It was unfortunate, whether intended as a snub or not, that the article misspelled the science professor's name as "Bleamey" and that Mr. Keen's personal pronouns referred only to Vaizey.

With the habitual conservatism of an accountant, Keen sought to make "the discussion . . . realistic and sober" (Keen 1965: 8). While Vaizey thought 20 million pounds would unchain Oxford from the paymaster's tether, Keen believed the amount was wrong. It was too little to buy freedom and too much to be practical. Back in 1950, Keen calculated that Oxford needed 17 million to "make us independent of government grant"; by implication, in 1965 it would take considerably more. Although the St. Catherine's and Historic Buildings Appeal raised 4 million pounds in just over four years, Keen cautioned that Oxford should not aim to solicit more than 10 million pounds (Keen 1965: 8).

Why was he so pessimistic? Keen read Oxford's cultural and institutional context as insurmountable; given existing constraints, he believed, fund-raising efforts would achieve, at best, modest results, and could be futile, leaving Oxford no better off than before. Massive and continuous financial campaigns went against British traditions. Americans might regularly give to their alma maters, but Keen did not think that one could "transplant [that] habit of mind" to England (ibid.). Furthermore, the established arrangement made government, not individuals, accountable for university financing. Consequently, Keen reasoned, individuals would not give to increase Oxford's general endowment; they would only pay for special projects:

> The mean average donor is much more moved by a specific object—a library, a new college, a laboratory—than he would be by a general appeal for Oxford University which, he would remember, gets three-quarters of its funds from the government, which has assumed general responsibility for providing the country with the universities it needs. (Ibid.)

Plus, there would be a perverse catch. A successful campaign might give Oxford a quick fix, but it would not be allowed to benefit over the long term. If the university had sufficient cash to cover its ongoing expenses, that would only reduce its need for government money. The UGC would in time have to deduct some of that amount from Oxford's share of the government's grant for universities. So fund-raising would be a futile exercise, with much running just to remain in place. In sum, Keen painted quite a conservative portrait.

Six months later, when the Franks report was published, the commission included five paragraphs that touched on the topic of university fund-raising (University of Oxford 1966a: 128–30, paras. 289–92; 240, para. 548). Most of its comments were framed in terms of improving the capacity of departments to apply for money from governmental research councils. Its final thoughts on the matter, though, suggested that the vice-chancellor should have responsibility for external efforts: "Fund-raising from private sources should take up more of his time in the future than in the past" (ibid.: 240, para. 548). The idea was not extravagant. Franks's understated position was typical of donnish attitudes at the time. And it was a measure of Oxford's priorities that the commission could devote two chapters to problems of financing the colleges and develop a scheme for redistributing money from wealthy to poor colleges, and yet formulate nothing comparable on university finances.

In 1967 the problem resurfaced when the Labour government decided to charge higher fees to overseas than to domestic students. Members of Congregation, in a cantankerous if not egalitarian mood, moved to repudiate the government's action. It would be expensive for Oxford to defy the state since it would have to cover the increase from its own reserves. Consequently, some dons established the Oxford University Independence Fund, "to raise money which would be 'paid to the University for the financing of academic projects which the Government's action will otherwise curtail'" (Registrar 1968: 121–22). The initiators of the Independence Fund recruited Lord Franks to serve as its chair. A sizable number of dons, approximately 480, quickly contributed, but they gave modest amounts, scarcely averaging five pounds each (*Oxford Magazine* 1967a). While the amount could be thought of as seed money for a broader appeal, it was not enough to offset the university's losses.

When Lord Franks, on behalf of the fund, asked the vice-chancellor, Kenneth Charles Turpin, provost of Oriel, whether Council would back the organizers' efforts to amass a general reserve, he was told propriety forbade such a step. The registrar's comments on that exchange noted:

> During Michaelmas Term 1967 Lord Franks asked the Vice-Chancellor how Council would view a proposal from the subscribers that they should widen the fund to make it available for developments which the University would like to undertake but which cannot be financed from Government grants, and, on this wider basis, issue a general appeal. Council then recorded that it would be wrong for a general appeal for the University to be issued as a result of private initiative, but agreed that Mr. Vice-Chancellor should inform Lord Franks that Council would welcome his help with any appeal which Council itself decided to mount. (Registrar 1968: 122)

The vice-chancellor did not fall in line with this rank-and-file donnish initiative. But he did not cut off Council's discussion of the topic. On December 4, 1967, Council agreed to review the matter in early January.

When Council met in January 1968, it had notes from Alan Bullock on St. Catherine's financial campaign; it had another letter from a natural scientist, Professor Paul Beeson, which implored Council to act; and it had a comprehensive memorandum by the registrar on the university's record with appeals.

Professor Beeson's missive referred to the Franks recommendations and sought to draw Oxford's leaders' attention to the contrasting examples of Yale and Harvard. In 1967, Yale's sons were giving "annual unrestricted gifts . . . [of] $4,000,000." In addition, Yale's president, Kingman Brewster Jr., had just initiated a separate "fund-raising goal of $388,000,000 over the next ten years." Yale and Harvard were comparable institutions to Oxford, and they "certainly do not feel embarrassed or cheapened by making their needs known" (Beeson 1968: 133). Why should Oxford? Beeson wrote:

> I have heard some of the excuses given for Oxford's failure to appeal as a university—the collegiate system, the national economy, the nation's tax structure, et cetera. I question whether any of these is a really insuperable obstacle. In the time I have been at Oxford a considerable number of large gifts has been received . . . as a result of the efforts of individual "amateur" fund-raisers. . . . This only serves to show what *could* be done. (Ibid.: 134)

Beeson said that Oxford should ask its American cousins for advice and that it should employ professional fund-raisers to ensure the continued vitality of the university.

The registrar's memorandum took a less optimistic line. With civil service–type professionalism, the registrar set out for Council the "facts," as only a keeper of financial files could do. Consequently, when he turned, at the end of a lengthy document, to his summary of the situation, the registrar had persuasively framed the discussion in fairly narrow terms. "Past experience suggests," he wrote, "that it is easier to raise funds for building or to support activities for a limited period than for endowment in any form." It was "very doubtful" that Oxford's colleges would look favorably on a "general appeal." A specific campaign, rather than one for unrestricted endowment funds, was the way to go, he wrote. But if one sought money for particular purposes, one would "need to show that [those] particular activities cannot be financed by public or university funds, or that they should not properly be so financed." And even then the problems would not stop. One would also have to provide reassurances to potential donors that their gifts would not cause the government to reduce Oxford's share of the fiscal pie: "It is also desirable, though perhaps impossible, to show that in the middle and longer term Government grants will not be cut by the amounts raised from private sources." Oxford's big private sources were already tapped; most large foundations, American and British, and private industries have given sizable donations in the recent past. And, for unspoken but well understood reasons of prestige, the registrar concluded: "It will be necessary at all costs to ensure that the appeal is not a 'flop.'" If one had a sufficiently stout heart to proceed despite all of those caveats, then, as Lord Franks and Professor Beeson suggested, Harvard should be consulted and professionals should be employed; in fact, "offers have already been received" from professional fund-raisers (Registrar 1968; 122–25). But Council did not have the will to proceed, and the matter sank like a stone.

It was one and a half years until the next and final time (before the election of Margaret Thatcher) that Oxford's leaders weighed the pros and cons of a general appeal. It came during Alan Bullock's term in office as vice-chancellor. He was the first one elected under the new Franks statutes. And, more than any of his predecessors, he was the official with the will and ability to guide the university forward on this point.

By the time of Bullock's vice-chancellorship the leadership team for the university had undergone quite a transformation. Two old-guard conservatives on Council, Sir Kenneth Wheare and Sir Cecil Maurice Bowra, effectively resigned in 1967 (*Oxford Magazine* 1967b). And in 1969 another conservative member of the pre-Franks inner leadership circle retired, Sir A. L. P. Norrington, president of Trinity. Bullock was in office as a direct expression of the reformist trends that had been working through Oxford since the late 1950s, and he brought with him new men with a willingness to accelerate the pace of modernization.

With Bullock's administration, the financial prospectus was passed from scientists to some of the arts dons who guided the reforms of the previous decade. The process began in Michaelmas Term 1969, when Bullock assumed office. He formed a committee that included, among others, Lord Franks, then provost of Worcester; another elder savant at institutional reform, W. F. R. Hardie, president of Corpus Christi; and two of the new graduate colleges' presidents, Isaiah Berlin of Wolfson and John Bernard Bamborough of Linacre. Bullock wanted a general appeal and got Council, without opposition, to set the process in motion on December 8, 1969 (Bullock 1971: 586).

During the academic year the press of other business, which included a small wave of student protests, slowed things down considerably. The next time Council discussed the topic was February 15, 1971. Then, Council learned that Dr. John Thomson, chairman of Barclays Bank, had arranged a meeting for the following month between representatives of Oxford and leading members of the financial community in London. Also, the assistant registrar, Dr. Herrman, would be sent to Harvard to study its fund-raising methods. Bullock expressed the desire to launch an appeal during his term in office, which would end in 1973 (Hebdomadal Council Papers 1971).

The gathering with bankers in London took place on March 30, 1971. Dr. Thomson of Barclays organized the rendezvous as a dinner, in traditional Oxbridge fashion. It involved six leading Oxford figures, including Bullock and Lord Franks, "to test the reactions of a number of Oxford men in the City to the idea of an Oxford appeal" (Bullock 1971: 586). The target spoken of was near the figure recommended three years earlier by the registrar, approximately 10 million pounds. Even if one could imagine bankers being in a generous mood, the timing was all wrong. The London financial markets were not, as Wall Street bankers say, bullish: "The reception was critical and no one saw any prospect of the successful launching of an appeal. . . . My own conclusion was that there would be no prospect of an improvement in the circumstances until a decision had been taken on entry to the Common Market" (ibid.). The meeting was not a happy recurrence of the St. Catherine's experience.

It was a bad setback, but Bullock did not abandon the effort. Dr. Herrman returned from Harvard with ideas on ways to proceed. The plan implemented, however, was very different from American practices. It would not be organized by graduating classes or even as a public appeal to all Oxford graduates. Again, Oxford's collegiate structure worked against certain options. Rather, the university would pursue a strategy targeted at the elite. It would seek to tap only those former members who were "in a position to influence decisions on the allocation of industrial, foundation, and other corporate funds . . . the appeal would not be aimed at all Oxford men and women, but only at those in key positions" (ibid.: 587). Once Oxford's most elite graduates were recruited for the campaign, then the appeal would be taken overseas, especially to the United States. To identify the university's elite alumni, Dr. Herrman compiled a dossier on more than 1,200 of the largest corporations doing business in Britain. Herrman's files on those companies included names of Oxford's sons among boards of directors; sales and profits records; amounts previously contributed to higher education; and "the extent to which they regularly recruit Oxford graduates" (ibid.: 588). It was an impressive list. Council heard a report about Herrman's work in November 1971 and decided to go ahead (Hebdomadal Council Papers 1973).

In the meantime, objections were being voiced by some individual colleges within Oxford. To cope with the rumblings of conservative opposition, Bullock conferred with individual college heads. He wanted to avoid having the topic reach the floor of the Conference of Colleges where conservatives might be able to organize a consensus against the appeal. With or without the backing of Oxford's colleges, Bullock thought that Council would have to take responsibility for any decision on itself: "At some stage Council will have to decide whether the benefits to Oxford as a whole of a university appeal justify it in going ahead despite such objection from particular colleges" (Bullock 1971: 589). The Franks inquiry had been established by Council acting alone. Perhaps, in similar fashion, an appeal would get off only if Council provided the catalyst?

For more than a year, Dr. Herrman worked through his list of Oxford men on the boards of major corporations. But individual, discrete approaches produced virtually nothing. The economy seemed stalled. And the political climate on campus did not help. Business elites were, if not indignant, certainly cold to the student rebellions of the late 1960s and early 1970s. Benefactors did not line up to contribute to Oxford, even though it handled student protest with less indulgence than most institutions (Annan 1990: 379–81).

Dr. Herrman presented a balance sheet on the dismal situation to his Committee on a University Appeal, which then reported to Council. On February 22, 1973, Council decided: "The national economic situation is not propitious for a general appeal to be launched within the next two or three years" (Hebdomadal Council Papers 1973: 423). A small standing committee would continue to exist, at least on paper, but no further inquiries or solicitations would take place for the time being.

The committee's efforts and Bullock's determination came to nothing. It may have been a mistake for reformers to stick to elite corporate networks. Neither the economy nor politics worked in Bullock's favor.

Efforts to increase Oxford's financial chest were pushed forward at first by scientists, then by rank-and-file dons and Lord Franks, and finally by Bullock's team. In each case, roadblocks were thrown up by key players or unfortunate circumstances. Impediments came in 1950 from the colleges; in 1958 from the UGC's chair and from the St. Catherine's and Historic Buildings Appeals; in 1962 from Council's indifference; in 1965 from neglect by the Franks inquiry and from the registrar's pessimism; in 1967 from the vice-chancellor and Council's opposition; in 1968 from the registrar's skepticism and Council's irresolution; and finally in 1971–73 from Oxford's alumni in corporate board rooms. External circumstances were most favorable in the late 1950s and early 1960s, when, however, internally the will was absent; then, in the early 1970s, when Oxford's leaders were eager, the economic and political context worked against them.

The repeated failures left Oxford vulnerable, without room for maneuver, when Thatcher's cuts came seven years after Bullock's last attempt.

A SECOND LOOK AT UNIVERSITY WOMEN: ROBBINS AND OXFORD

Many critics of Robbins who doubted that the numerical goals for expansion or the enrollment targets for science and technology would be met saw the role of Oxbridge as the problem. According to the critics, the Oxbridge ethos, being elitist and focused on the liberal arts, would subvert Robbins's program. The critics' fears, however, reflected more the phantoms of the past than sober calculations of contemporary conditions.

By the 1970s the total enrollment in higher education exceeded Robbins's projections. There was a shortfall, but not in the total number. The gap between goal and performance was in the natural sciences and technology. Not enough undergraduates were working in those subjects to match the report's goals. Yet Oxbridge had little to do with the result.

Today the consensus is that gender divisions, and not Oxbridge, were responsible for higher education's failure to reach Robbins's goals in the sciences. If not sexism, then certainly a blindness to the effects of gender inequalities was the committee's undoing. As John Carswell testified, the Robbins Commission never once considered whether women's subject preferences would be different from men's. Yet its projections for the sciences were based on the assumption that female enrollment in those subjects would actually grow at a faster rate than men's. The assumption meant, Carswell stated, an "increase more than eightfold . . . in less than twenty years." Carswell went on to note that such a change would imply "a dramatic alteration in the pattern of studies in schools, in the attitude of the outlook of girls already in school, the attitudes of their families, and the habits of both sides of industry. The Report bears no stamp of awareness of these problems" (Carswell 1985: 44).

Halsey provided statistics that confirmed the importance of Carswell's point. There was, Halsey noted, a problem with enrollment in the sciences. Yet, "almost the whole of the short-fall in science/technology . . . is attributable to the absence of the women students who had been hoped for [by Robbins]" (Halsey 1988: 278). The final incongruity of the Robbins report discussion was that of the participants in the expansion debate ready to assign blame to Oxbridge, not one at the time questioned the projections for women.

If the growing number of female undergraduates had effects unforeseen by the Robbins committee, did Oxford fare any better? What were

the consequences of men's colleges going "mixed" for the balance between the arts and the sciences, and for the welfare of the five women's
colleges? How long did the process of gender integration take?

Six years elapsed between the Franks report and the creation of a
scheme for admitting women to some of the formerly men's colleges. Discussions between representatives of women's and men's colleges gave rise
to a university inquiry, report, and legislation in 1972.

As the *Report of the Committee on Co-residence* explained, from the
nineteenth century the women's colleges held an involuntary "monopoly
over the admission of women undergraduates" because the men's colleges
did not want women in the university (University of Oxford 1972: para.
5). The women's colleges were in effect academic ghettos, "greatly circumscribed as to numbers and laid under special restrictions unknown to
men" (ibid.). Their fellows were paid less and their undergraduates received lower scholarships so that the colleges could invest "their resources
in accommodation at the expense of building up their endowments"
(ibid.: para. 11). Doing everything possible to expand their enrollments,
they emphasized spending on new buildings. In the six years after the
Franks report, the five women's colleges provided enough new housing to
create "the equivalent of a sixth women's college" (ibid. 1972: para. 5).

If men's colleges were to begin admitting women, the committee urged
that it must not happen at the expense of the women's foundations.
The women's colleges heartily desired to enlarge the number of females
at Oxford; but if they were to survive the unknown consequences of
male colleges going mixed, they wanted a controlled, gradual process of
change.

The negotiations among the colleges produced a "closed experiment"
involving five men's colleges. Brasenose, Hertford, Jesus, St. Catherine's,
and Wadham would admit women as "new mixed colleges" beginning in
Michaelmas term 1974. (As Chapter 2 showed, these colleges were also
among the leaders in matriculating state-school and working-class undergraduates.) All other colleges would remain as before, and the effects
of the experiment would be evaluated in Hilary term 1977 (ibid.: paras.
7–8, 13).

To protect the women's colleges from a "brain-drain" of faculty to the
higher-paying mixed colleges, a convention was established to strongly
discourage migration (ibid.: para. 13). And demonstrating considerably
more foresight than the Robbins committee, the report posed relevant
questions: "What effect will the admission of women to mixed colleges
have on the balance of subjects? . . . Could it produce, for instance, a ma-

jor swing away from science to arts subjects?" (ibid.: para. 16d). The committee thought it would be impossible to answer those and other questions without some actual experience.

The five-college experiment worked well for a few years, and then government legislation against sexual discrimination overtook Oxford's timetable. By 1979 all of the men's colleges were going mixed, without much, if any, regard for the effects of the switch on the women's colleges. The women's colleges struggled to hold out as single-sex foundations at the same time that their fears about an undergraduate talent drain and a drop in their standing in the Norrington table came true. Gradually, most of them were compelled to go mixed as well; by the late 1990s, there was just one women's college left in Oxford, St. Hilda's.

What were the effects on undergraduate numbers and subjects? Working with data on "finalists," Oxford students who were completing their undergraduate examinations, Daniel Greenstein found a substantial increase in women and a decrease in men:

> Some time before the advent of mixed colleges, the proportion of women finalists begins to rise; the advent of mixed colleges causes this rise to accelerate. So much so, that the absolute number of male finalists actually falls fairly sharply from 2,029 in 1976 to 1,612 in 1986. The absolute number of women finalists, on the other hand, increases from 519 in 1976 to 1,024 in 1986. (Greenstein 1987: 4)

Mixed colleges were doing a good job selecting qualified females and turning down less-qualified males. The increase in the number of women overlapped with the period when Oxford's academic standards were on the rise. Women entering mixed colleges accelerated Oxford's meritocratization.

Yet the expansion of mixed colleges in the late 1970s brought additional gender stratification in subjects studied. Diverging from a recent trend toward proportional representation of men and women in the arts and sciences, more women and fewer men at mixed colleges were studying in the arts: "Women in the one-time single-sex men's colleges have taken the place of men arts students, thereby increasing the proportion of all men reading science subjects. . . . [After 1973] a smaller proportion of women and a greater proportion of men are taking science schools" (ibid.: 5).

When colleges became co-ed, the effects of divisive gender socialization became more pronounced. From 1973 on, more young men worked in the sciences, and more young women studied in the arts.

By the 1980s, women at Oxford were as unlikely to study science as their continental or American sisters (Organization for Economic Cooperation and Development 1986; K. Thomas 1990). Oxford's experience resonated with the findings of a Department of Education and Science survey of British schools that found: "Girls are more likely to choose a science, and boys a language, in a single sex school than they are in a mixed school" (Department of Education and Science 1975: 29). It would take more than university expansion to overcome the cultural and economic barriers to women entering the sciences and men entering the arts in equal numbers. Policy makers who ignored the effects of gender discrimination, as the Robbins committee did, did so at their peril.

Even with the setbacks represented by the collapse of the Council of Colleges proposal, as well as the failure to offer positive solutions for the problems of gender and university financing, the Franks Commission was quite successful. It won the support of most people inside Oxford for the majority of its ideas. Franks completely rewrote Oxford's statutes for the first time since the Laudian statutes went into effect in 1636. Franks pushed forward Oxford's extension of membership rights, the revitalization of its democratic powers, and its commitment to academic meritocracy. Among the most lasting effects of the commission were both the reendowment of the poor colleges and the resurrection of the General Board. Franks laid the foundation for Oxford's role in the second half of the twentieth century.

6.
Thatcher Politics

ACADEMIA DETHRONED

Governments often talk tough about shaking things up and then just tinker at the margins, introducing reforms that are more superficial than structural. That was not true of the Conservative government of Margaret Thatcher, which took office in 1979 and used state power to crusade against welfare dependency, blue-collar unions, professional associations, universities—the whole postwar "establishment." The Thatcherite new right, with different motives but similar claims as the Labour left, joined the denunciation of Oxford for the establishment's failings. In the view of the new right, if Britain had settled into senility and decline, a large share of the blame went to those Oxford-educated gentleman-amateurs who ran British institutions. The habits and values of Oxford gentlemen, according to Thatcher's supporters, were as detrimental to Britain's economic recovery as restrictive trade union practices. According to the new right, just as the power of union bosses over the labor force had to be broken, so the members of the Oxford club who monopolized positions of social authority should be purged and the clubhouse thoroughly renovated.

Pronouncements by Thatcherites on the antagonism of donnish values to the needs of Britain's new enterprise culture had teeth, unlike Labour's threats in the 1960s. Thatcher's policies on higher education were draconian. Her governments introduced fiscal cuts and administrative practices, codified by legislation, which destroyed the traditional relationship between the state and universities. She established the legal power and institutional means for the central government to control whatever it wanted to in higher education. She abolished tenure for all new faculty as well as for any extant faculty who consented to promotion or transfer to another university. And her inheritor, John Major, broke the guild monopoly of dons over degrees by bestowing university status on the entire polytechnic sector of higher education. In about a dozen years, Thatcherite politicians wrought havoc on a scale likened by Conrad Russell, among others, to Henry VIII's dissolution of the monasteries (Russell 1993: 3).[1]

Before we get into the substance of Thatcher's confrontation with universities, we should look at two unexpected developments in the period from 1973 to 1979 that influenced important aspects of Oxford's ethos and administration. The first was its rising admissions standards; the second was the new role played by Oxford's General Board.

A SECOND LOOK AT ADMISSIONS: 1970S ULTRA-MERITOCRACY

In the 1970s, Oxford became, in the words of Professor A. H. Halsey, "[a] stern meritocracy" (Halsey 1992: 82). Halsey, a Nuffield sociologist and former adviser to Labour's minister of education, Anthony Crosland, was among the first to draw attention to the meteoric rise in Oxford's undergraduate admissions standards in the 1970s. He feared that Oxford's ultra-meritocracy meant it would be, once again, less accessible to lower-class youths and more exclusively occupied by the progeny of privilege.

For sociologists, the 1970s revealed yet another dimension of the troubled relationship of education to social inequality. In the 1950s and 1960s reformers' attentions were focused on improving the life chances for members of lower classes by expanding opportunity. Policy makers hoped that a larger educational system would erode the connection between family wealth and how far one went up the educational ladder. After the 1960s, the problem seemed to be even more complex. Even with expansion, social divisions carried over into higher education. The criteria used by academics to measure qualifications themselves became suspect. New terms like "cultural capital" were employed to describe the resources used by privileged groups to retain their advantages. Symptoms of the problem were evident in the way Oxford's entry qualifications in the 1970s rose dramatically.

One could measure admissions standards in the 1970s by the A-level grades students earned in the sixth form before applying to university. Universities could evaluate their recruitment prowess by the percentage of students they attracted with very high A levels. In 1961 the percentage entering Oxford with top A-level grades was 43 percent; in other universities the average was below 22 percent. As the effects of expansion and secondary-school modernization were felt within Oxford, its share of high achievers went up dramatically: "Between 1970 and 1980 the proportion of undergraduates admitted with very high grades at 'A' level . . . was stable for the British universities as a whole at about 22%. In Oxford it rose from 58.6 to 73.5%" (Halsey 1982: 222). After 1980, the percentage was even higher. In 1983, for example, 82.4 percent of Oxford's entering class had top A-level scores; the national average was 28.9 percent (Oxford University Undergraduate Admissions Office 1984: 6). Without doubt, the meritocratic qualifications of Oxford's undergraduates surpassed those of students in other universities. Between 1961 and 1983, the percentage of Oxford students with the highest entering credentials almost doubled; four out of five undergraduates had nearly perfect records.

Objective measures of the triumph of academic meritocracy inside Oxford in the 1970s were matched by anecdotal evidence on changes in the admissions process. A person well qualified to judge was social historian Asa Briggs. From a northern working-class family, Briggs was a grammar-school scholarship boy who studied or taught at most types of British university: Redbrick, New, and Oxbridge. He became a lord in 1976 when the Labour government of James Callaghan elevated him to the House as a life peer. After more than a decade as guiding spirit and vice-chancellor of Sussex University, Briggs returned to Oxford in 1976 to be provost of Worcester College. When asked what had changed most about Oxford between the 1950s and the decade of his return, he singled out meritocratic admissions:

> If you talk about meritocracy . . . I do not have anything whatsoever to do with admissions to this college, nor in fact do most heads of colleges. . . . I get letters from old members of college about their sons and daughters, and I know perfectly well that if I were, for whatever reason, to press the claim of somebody . . . I would be counter-productive, even though there are people I know who would be very helpful to college for benefactions and things of that sort. . . . When I was in college in 1955, the provost [was] a very powerful figure in relation to admissions, which was one of his main interests. When I got back here, to my very great surprise, I found that the provost had nothing to do with admissions. It was a total change. Admissions are now essentially a delegated system. What happens now is that the tutors do, in effect, choose

> the people they want to teach themselves. . . . There is no dis-
> agreement at all with the view that you choose the people who
> seem to you to be academically the most promising. (Briggs
> interview 1986)

A college head in the 1950s could, if he were so inclined, act to preserve
organic conservative privileges, but by the late 1970s democratic-elitist
tutors were firmly in control of admissions. They looked for meritocracy,
and even with the inevitable imperfections apparently found it.

Oxford standards went up, however, not because tutors devised better
ways to select from a steady stream; rather, the waters had themselves
changed. Halsey explained that "Oxford and Cambridge . . . [found]
themselves, not necessarily through any merit of their own, faced with a
rising qualification in their average applicant" (Halsey interview 1988).
The spectacular escalation of Oxford's standards for admission was an unexpected by-product of educational expansion. More and better-qualified
students sought entry to Oxford in the 1970s. The race for a child to get
into Oxford had been intensified, apparently requiring increased family investments and ever younger preparation.

The prediction that this hothouse condition would emerge was the basis of Mr. Pedley's proposals to the Labour Party and the Franks Commission that Oxford be turned into a postgraduate institution (see Chapter 2). But his warnings were disregarded. And those education policy an-
alysts and scholars who did have influence with the Labour Party while it
was in power did not anticipate Oxford's entry heat.

In the 1960s, Halsey and other social democratic advisers to Labour
thought that new universities and larger enrollments in higher education
would not only expand access, drawing in lots of students from families
without any experience of higher education, but also shake up the old institutional hierarchy. Oxford would be forced to compete on a more level
playing field with other universities. Halsey offered this recollection of
Crosland's education policy unit:

> The pathway ahead was such that there would be a system of
> higher education which would compete on much more even terms
> than it had in the past. . . . There was strength in the new universi-
> ties as well as in the solid Redbricks that would get their chance
> in the future. . . . I think we were assuming that increased supply
> of qualified people from the secondary schools wouldn't necessar-
> ily choose to go to Oxford or Cambridge. As it turned out I was
> wrong. . . . I don't know the Cambridge figures, but the Oxford

"meritocratization," to use a ghastly word, through the '70s was . . . absolutely tremendous. (Halsey interview 1988)

The phenomenon was scrutinized and dissected by Halsey and others in the late 1970s and early 1980s, but it was not part of the stock of scholarly wisdom in the 1960s.

When British, American, French, and other systems of higher education doubled or quadrupled their size around the 1960s, the older elite institutions within them became magnets for those candidates, usually from wealthy or educationally advantaged homes, who wanted the most impressive formal qualifications. As more youths received higher education degrees, the value of a college education on the job market declined. If one wanted the best shot at a high-paying and prestigious job, it was not enough to get a college degree; one had to get one from the right place. So those with advantages aimed at Oxbridge or the Ivy League, while new social groups in the expanded educational system tended to end up at or near the bottom (Trow 1984: 132–40).

The paradox in England was that a small system had more room at the top for social diversity than a large one. From the 1970s forward, Oxford appeared to be less, not more, accessible to the lower classes. As Halsey explained about Oxford's institutional league: "There seems to be growing evidence that the Harvards and Stanfords, the Grandes Ecoles, the Japanese Imperial University . . . are all places that have increasingly become socially elevated, more restrictive socially than they were before the expansion began" (Halsey interview 1988). It was possible, though unlikely, that the escalation of entry standards was not accompanied by Oxford's becoming more socially exclusive. But in the late 1980s, the rise in Oxford's undergraduates with private-school backgrounds strongly suggested otherwise (see Table 6).

Solid evidence on whether Oxford's social composition changed after the 1960s was hard to come by. Ironically, the obstacles in the way of getting reliable data were due to expansion. After the state stepped in to finance undergraduate education and the Universities Central Council on Admission (UCCA) was created as an application clearinghouse, all British universities evaluated their applicants without any information about the income or education of their parents. A student's local education authority determined his or her economic need and kept the files on any grants awarded. The university would never know. The admissions tutors Lord Briggs referred to did not ask about a student's ability to pay or where a student's father attended college; it was not part of the process. One could not get access to data about parents' income or education within Oxford University. And the local education authorities were prevented by law from disclosing personal information. Consequently, since the late 1960s researchers on family backgrounds of undergraduates have had to work with proxy indicators, such as A-level grades, the percentage of privately schooled undergraduates, data from comparable institutions abroad, and data on social class in the entire British university system. Having already looked at entry grades and school backgrounds, we shall now see what insight the other two can offer.

UCCA kept track of parental occupations for the whole United Kingdom and reported class backgrounds using the broad employment categories of British census surveys. The categories used were: professionals; employers, managers, and lower professionals; white- and pink-collar service employees; and skilled, semi-, or unskilled workers. UCCA's records showed fairly consistent levels of participation at the top and low ends, with considerable variation in the middle (see Table 12).

The blue-collar working classes continued to slightly improve their standing, but white-collar applicants were squeezed. Two scholars, Howard Glennerster and William Low, have offered similar conclusions based on the General Household Survey data files for 1985. Given how the "social composition of the population has been changing . . . [there was] a relative *growth* in the chances of manual-class children going to university" (Glennerster and Low 1990: 71). But this did not mean, and they certainly did not suggest, that things in Oxford were moving in that direction. What was true of the whole was not necessarily true for each of its parts.

If Oxford's undergraduates since the late 1970s have not come increasingly from families with higher levels of wealth and educational credentials, they are the exceptions to an international tide. America's elite universities provide a useful window on the process. We know from comparative studies that Britain's patterns of social stratification have been quite similar to America's (Erikson and Goldthorpe 1992: 321). Major trends at America's elite universities suggest the possibility of similar developments in Britain.

Since 1980, Oxford's American counterparts, private, highly selective universities such as Harvard and Yale, "have become notably more economically exclusive" (Kingston and Lewis 1990: 113). In 1996, for example, 47 percent of all undergraduates at America's Harvards had parents whose annual income exceeded 100,000 dollars (Higher Education Research Institute 1996: 68); in 1980, only 19 percent of undergraduates came from similarly well-to-do families (Higher Education Research Institute 1983: 58). Even allowing for inflation, the growth in the very rich

TABLE 12

Type of Employment Held by Fathers of
Undergraduates in the United Kingdom, 1979–1993
(percent)

Employee type	1979	1986	1993
Professional	20	20	20
Employer, manager, or lower professional	38	48	45
White-collar or service class	21	11	12
Skilled, semi-skilled, or unskilled working class	20	21	22

SOURCES: Universities Central Council on Admissions, Statistical Supplements 1979, 1986, and 1993.

NOTE: The employee types are the categories used by the British Census. All percentages are rounded.

was significant. In addition to wealth, undergraduates at private, highly selective universities came from families who disproportionately invested beyond the baccalaureate level in advanced degrees. The old gap between students at state universities whose parents did not have bachelor's degrees and private university students whose parents did have degrees closed in the late 1970s. Then in the 1970s and 1980s, a new disparity separated students whose parents had graduate degrees from those whose parents did not. In Ivy-type institutions, undergraduate men whose fathers had graduate degrees in law, business, or medicine or from graduate schools in arts and sciences climbed from around 20 percent in 1968 to 45 percent in 1983, and to 55 percent in 1996. At state universities, the comparable statistics on fathers of male undergraduates were: 10.1 percent in 1968, 21 percent in 1983, and 26.2 percent in 1996. Elite investments in graduate education have run at nearly twice the non-elite rate (Higher Education Research Institute 1968: 22; 1983: 64; 1996: 77). The graduate degree gap did not close.

What this implied about Oxford was not a new role in the reproduction of the upper class; even America's private, highly selective universities were not responsible for all that. In the 1980s, being rich did not, by itself, get one into Yale; and America's Harvards did not ensure the persistence of class privilege. As Kingston and Lewis pointed out, in the 1980s approximately 87 percent of all undergraduates from families earning more than 100,000 dollars per year went to non-elite universities (1990: 114).

When only 13 percent of a social group passed through America's Harvards, it was not reasonable to accuse them of performing a special role in the intergenerational transmission of advantages for an entire social class. Yale's and Oxford's benefits are enjoyed disproportionately by wealthy families, and that may be a concern; but insofar as the rich "pass on privilege, they must often do so by other means" (ibid.: 116).

After 1976, Oxford's meritocratization was driven in no small part by the removal of gender barriers. As detailed in Chapter 2, when the men's colleges began admitting women, academically weak male students were replaced by better-qualified female applicants. The contribution women made to Oxford's rising standards must not be underestimated. Female undergraduates made Oxford academically stronger.

The effects of Oxford's 1970s meritocratization on the collective ethos of the dons, though, went beyond gender and class issues to touch on matters of guild pride. The materialization of meritocracy could be justifiably thought of as a vindication of the academic ethos. Oxford's historic advantages, a source of considerable ambivalence for socially conscious dons, had been successfully transformed into a virtually unassailable form of modern academic distinction. Especially after the admission of women, dons had little cause for continued anxiety over the conflict between social justice and excellence; the latter was by then unquestionably the dominant spirit. In the future, admissions tutors could all confidently pronounce, "It is true to say that all our students are admitted on their individual academic achievements alone" (Stein correspondence 1996.)[2] As the beneficiaries of candidates' rising credentials, dons could indulge their guild preference for the highest possible entry standards. The early 1960s critics of growth who said "more means worse" were certainly wrong about the top of the academic pyramid; at the summit, more meant better. Oxford had new grounds on which to stand above other universities. The fruits of academic autonomy, the pursuit of intellectual excellence for its own sake, seemed utterly justified. It would come as a surprise when Thatcher showed them that the authority of meritocracy was not enough.

THE RECONSTITUTED GENERAL BOARD

The other major development of the 1970s was, as Dr. Robert Gasser put it, "the decline of Council and the rise of the General Board as the central powerhouse of this university" (Gasser interview 1988). (Dr. Gasser was on both Council and the General Board from 1972 to 1981 and served as vice-chairman of the board in 1978–80.) During the pre-Franks era, and even throughout the 1960s, the affairs of the university were governed well or badly by members of the Hebdomadal Council. Then in the 1970s, Council's role was eclipsed by the General Board.

The General Board was responsible for the allocation of all university resources and any academic planning deemed desirable. It was placed in that position by reforms proposed by the Franks Commission and ratified by Congregation. After Franks, the board had a full-time head, called the vice-chairman; and its statutory powers put it alongside, not beneath, Council. The division of labor between Council and the General Board left the former to deal with external relations while the latter administered most academic matters within Oxford. Should a dispute arise between the two bodies, it would be settled by Congregation.

The General Board's work was organized by its vice-chairman. The full-time, two-year office came with a high salary and secretariat. The board convened on Friday afternoons, but the vice-chairman also attended Council's Monday sessions and numerous committee meetings in between. Sixteen of the other 22 members of the board were effectively selected by Oxford's sixteen faculties but formally elected by Congregation. The other seven members were there in some official capacity, such as the vice-chancellor and the assessor, or they were co-opted by the board.

The board's main duty was to distribute Oxford's budget, which in the 1980s was approximately 100 million pounds sterling per year. Of that 100 million, roughly 50 million was directly under the board's control; 30 million was administered by the board but came earmarked for specific projects; and 20 million was passed into the care of the Resources Committee, a joint committee of the General Board and Council responsible for buildings and miscellaneous items.

If the Franks reforms gave the board the capacity to direct Oxford's academic life, the long-term growth in the natural sciences, postgraduate education, and state funding gave the board its weight within the university. As the size of government's contribution to the university's activities increased, so did the responsibilities and powers of the General Board.

The role of the board differed in each decade between Franks and Thatcher. The 1960s were a time of resource amelioration that required very little supervision from the board. More and more state funds for new research projects and faculty appointments came in without any strategic coordination or effort from the center. Dr. Brian Smith, vice-chairman of the General Board in the mid-1980s, explained that expansion in the 1960s "was evolutionary, spontaneous . . . and while it was growing I don't think there was very much real coherent academic planning. There were movements about libraries and things, but . . . most of them arose from the periphery, the center gave very little guidance" (Smith interview 1988). With a constantly growing amount of money to share, there was little for the board to do except direct traffic.

Flush with cash, the board, as a university committee, administered a form of assistance to the financially strapped colleges. As legally autonomous bodies, Oxford's colleges were not entitled to direct government funding; nonetheless, taxpayers' money flowed into college accounts through student fees paid by local education authorities. And after the 1950s a second line of public financing was available through faculty salaries. The board oversaw the arrangement by which every college tutor received a joint appointment with the university and with that a spot on the government's payroll. Colleges could, in effect, appropriate university funds simply by giving someone a job. Christopher Kirwan, vice-chairman of the General Board in 1980–82, reminisced: "Let's say twenty years back a college could decide to have a fellowship. . . . The university of course didn't formally have to do anything about it, but we knew the university would simply create a CUF lectureship for this person. That was a formality." A Common University Fund (CUF) appointment would mean that "about 40 percent of [the lecturer's] total stipend [would come] from the university" (Kirwan interview 1988). Colleges with specific teaching needs could hire a tutor confident that the board would cover a significant part of his salary. There are no reasons to believe colleges abused this resource. They were cautious about adding new fellows to their governing bodies and did so primarily in response to increased student demand for a subject. The CUF arrangement helped the colleges financially, but it also tied their powers of appointment to the university's purse. It was a link they would be constrained by once the government's pocketbook snapped shut.

The expansion of the Robbins years slowed, sputtered, and then crashed in the 1970s. Financial growth decelerated in the early 1970s as the University Grants Committee (UGC) began to worry about costs (Shattock 1994: 9). The government's economic policy began to zig-zag, as inflation kicked in and undermined the UGC's five-year budget system. Then, after the 1973 oil crisis, "in 1974–75, . . . the quinquennial planning system was brought to an abrupt end" (ibid.: 16). The government ceased providing the UGC with the means to give universities secure funding. Inside Oxford, according to Gasser, "that was the end of the period of euphoria. After that, it was erratic, it was stop and go, and one got very frequent changes of direction from government" (Gasser interview 1988). Money was given out year by year with much difficulty and misdirection.

The General Board's new role in the 1970s, its second phase of development, was to manage Oxford's retrenchment. It had, in Gasser's opinion, "to educate faculty boards to a world in which resources were being taken away rather than added on" (ibid.). In the mid-1970s, the board did what it could to spread the misery around evenly. It did so without benefit of any sophisticated accounting tools or strategic plans. Rather, it discussed and evaluated previous distributions of funds and made what adjustments it felt were appropriate. But erratic resources from the government and inadequate information about what Oxford's faculties were doing made for a frustrating and messy situation.

The period of stop-and-go uncertainty lasted from 1974 to 1979. In the middle came "thirteen points for economy to the universities" from Shirley Williams, Labour's secretary of state for education and science in 1976 (Annan 1990: 383). A Labour government had first asked universities to tighten their belts. Although Annan believed universities "trashed" or merely "toyed" with Williams's proposals, Oxford's General Board devised a scheme in the next two years that went some distance toward rationalizing its expenditures.

When Dr. Gasser became the board's vice-chairman in 1978, he introduced a new "major instrument of policy." He decided to move the board into the modern age of quantitative measurements and centralized plans:

> It was during that period of stop-go that the need to evaluate departmental faculty support became clear, and this was something that I set myself really as a task when I was elected vice-chairman, that I wanted to try and put resource allocation procedures on a more numerical and quantitative basis, rather than purely looking at the history of it and saying "well, either there's a bit more for you, or everybody is taking a cut, so you take a proportional cut." (Gasser interview 1988)

Except when inquiries such as Franks were gathering information, Oxford had not tried to assemble, let alone keep current, accurate central records on its faculties and departments. So the first challenge was simply to amass statistics. Gasser compiled "all the factual data that I could: staff at different levels, students, graduate students, technicians . . . to try to get a numerical picture in summary of it all . . . telling you how the resources were being allocated" (ibid.). He was attempting to rationalize the entire distribution process.

At first, the goal was simply to apportion capital assets fairly among the faculties and departments so that the board could see whether a faculty had, relative to its duties, excessive or insufficient resources. Gasser explained: "I went through and analyzed the resources available to all the faculties, out of which it seemed to me that the physiological sciences as a whole, was, relatively speaking, generously provided for and would have to take a cut, along with others" (ibid.). Faculties with too much were told to cut back by a certain percentage and given an opportunity to devise a plan. If a faculty failed to administer its own reductions, the board stepped in and imposed cuts (ibid.); fortunately, that scenario was played out only once.

Gasser worked vigorously on the natural sciences and had not yet addressed the arts side of the university when he stepped down. A vice-chairman's term in office lasts only two years, a very short time to accomplish Gasser's goals. But when he passed the office on to Christopher Kirwan in 1980, Gasser left behind a new mechanism for the board's work. This level of administrative rationalization was new, and it raised the possibility of centralized academic planning and day-to-day management of a type not possible before in Oxford.

We will look at the role Kirwan's board played after Thatcher's cuts shortly. But for now the important thing is to see how the evolution from a period of growth (roughly 1946 to 1970), to one of stop-and-go uncertainty (1971 to 1978), to one of retrenchment and cuts (1978 to 1982) made central control by the board inescapable if Oxford were to minimize damage. The shifting economic ground of the state's relation to universities drove changes within Oxford's governing arrangements. When the fiscal mooring between government and universities came loose, Council effectively relinquished the helm to the General Board. As the cuts were implemented, it was the General Board that kept things shipshape.

OVERVIEW OF THE THATCHER REVOLUTION

While Margaret Thatcher was in office, between 1979 and 1989, the informal and formal framework that structured the postwar relation of all previous political administrations to universities was transformed in two stages. Those stages roughly correspond to the terms in office of Thatcher's two key education ministers, Sir Keith Joseph and Kenneth Baker. Phase one (1980–86) involved cuts without the imposition of detailed governmental directives upon universities. Phase two (1987–89) was interventionist and centralist; government gave itself the means to micro-manage universities.

From the beginning, Thatcher and Sir Keith Joseph, her close adviser and secretary of state for education and science, repudiated the deferential attitude of British political and administrative elites to the academic credo. Academics could think of themselves as self-regulating professionals in autonomous university corporations, but in fact they were employees of the state. It was the Conservatives' vision that one had to dismantle big government in order to reach their neo-Jerusalem, a land where wealth and freedom flourished through self-reliant individual competition in unrestrained markets. One had to slice away at the bloated state, force government to live on a tight budget, and enable individuals and corporate groups to find their way to productive freedom.

If, according to Thatcherite ideology, the government had to reduce levels of expenditure to balance the budget and to reverse the damage done by the careless expansion of the welfare state, then universities would have to suffer along with everyone else. There was nothing sacred about them. Thatcherites imagined that austerity would be good for universities because cuts in government grants to dependent institutions would stimulate positive behavior. At a minimum, cuts would increase institutional efficiency; at a maximum, they would spur universities toward free-market self-reliance. As Margaret Thatcher recorded later in her memoirs: "By exerting financial pressure we had increased administrative efficiency and provoked overdue rationalization. Universities were developing closer links with business and becoming more entrepreneurial" (Thatcher 1993: 598). So step one, for the recovery of universities, was to reduce their share of the public budget.

Between 1979 and 1986, when Sir Keith stepped down as secretary of state for education and science, government cut its budget for universities by approximately 15 percent (Shattock 1994: 20). The effects on individual universities varied in severity: some were slated for 5 percent cuts, others for up to 40 percent (Kogan and Kogan 1983: 53). The reductions were to be phased in over three years. In 1986, when the government released numbers on the budgetary effects of Sir Keith's cuts, the worst hit were Salford and Aston, which were cut 44 percent and 33 percent respectively from the baseline year of 1980. Two institutions, the London Business School and York University, were in the black. Thirty-six institutions suffered more, and thirteen less, than Oxford University's loss of 14.4 percent (Jobbins 1986: 5). Even then, Sir Keith's sword did not rest.

He announced another round of cuts in 1986 before stepping down, leaving the education office to Kenneth Baker.

It should be emphasized that Sir Keith was quite principled about what he was doing. He imposed cuts that reflected his evaluation of the universities' fair share of the burden of reduced public expenditures. He was not trying to tell universities what to do. Ultimately, he thought, the best solution might be for universities to be privatized, like British Telecom, the assumption being that they would flourish once they were set free of the government's apron strings. But emancipation, if at all, was a distant prospect. In the early 1980s, Sir Keith's message to the universities was, "Do what you will, but with less." Professor Denis Noble recalled a comment to that effect at a meeting of scientists with the minister. Noble paraphrased Sir Keith's words: "Gentlemen, we are not in the business of running United Kingdom Ltd. You ask us for a policy, we've got no policy. Indeed government should not have a policy. What we can tell you is what we can afford. And it's up to you then to work out what to do with it" (Noble interview 1988). It was left to the UGC to decide how to disburse the reduced funds; the UGC, not Sir Keith, imposed selective and in some cases traumatic cuts.

Under the strain of austerity, the UGC, like Oxford's General Board, became a very different body than it had been in the 1960s. The UGC went from being a passive buffer to being like a reactivated home office directing a restructuring of its branches. Academics on the UGC and its subcommittees were responsible for the distribution of the pain (Shattock 1994: 21–22, 26–28). If Salford feared bankruptcy and York was dancing, dons had made the choices that produced those results.

Phase one of the process involved cuts. Phase two directly addressed the culture of universities and the legal framework of governmental and university relations. The arguments of the second phase were foreshadowed by Sir Keith in 1985, but they were given definitive shape by Kenneth Baker's white paper in favor of legislation that became the Education Act of 1988 (see Department of Education and Science 1985; 1987). Universities were accused and found guilty of perpetuating anti-industrial and anti-entrepreneurial values. After 1985, government seemed unwilling to trust universities any longer to serve the national interest. With Kenneth Baker in the education office, government did not hesitate to claim the right to tell universities what to do. The UGC, tenure, and block grants all became things of the past. The UGC's replacement, the Universities Funding Council (UFC), would have a chairman and half of its members drawn from the business community. It would offer contracts with line-item funding for universities. Institutions whose performance failed to match the terms of their funding could be forced by the government to repay the grant (Department of Education and Science 1987; "UGC to Be Replaced" 1987). Reversing the historic priorities of the UGC, which acted until 1963 like a buffer between the state and universities, the new UFC was to act like a government enforcement agency (Shattock 1994: 27). Universities would be treated as if they were competing firms even if the market had only one buyer, the state. The new arrangement looked more like a version of Frederick Winslow Taylor's scientific management of piecework under monopoly conditions than like privatization and market freedom.

The transformation of the state's relation to universities raised two paradoxes. One would have expected Conservative politicians to respect traditional institutions and to favor decentralization, yet they did neither. Thatcher, Sir Keith, and Kenneth Baker, all Oxford graduates, did what Labour politicians had threatened but failed to do: they turned on their alma mater. Conservative Oxford graduates exposed the autonomy of British universities as a sham. The damage, however, went beyond battered prestige: universities suffered materially for their faith in the gentlemanly conventions that had governed their relations to Parliament and Whitehall. And even more important than financial cuts, the universities lost most of their means of protecting themselves from state interference. Between 1979 and 1989, Thatcher and the other Oxford alumni in her Cabinet espoused free-market liberal ideology while being responsible for placing in the hands of the central government the greatest concentration of powers over education ever seen in modern British history.

Why did a Conservative government abrogate the unwritten compact with the universities and replace it with an extension of centralized state power? Why did Thatcher's government pursue a confrontational program with Britain's scholars and scientists?

The Thatcherite Case: Oxbridge's Anti-Industrial Ethos

Much of the "evidence" for the broad Thatcherite indictment of universities came from books published in the early 1980s by two academics, Martin J. Wiener and Correlli Barnett. Each faulted Oxford and Cambridge for being aristocratic and anti-industrial. By being out of step with modern times, they said, Oxbridge nurtured the governing class's aristocratic ethos, which was greatly responsible for Britain's economic decline. The task for politicians and educators was to modernize elite institutions in order to revitalize and competitively equip the governing class.

Martin Wiener blamed public schools and Oxbridge for the cultural gentrification of England's middle and industrial classes: "If Oxbridge insulated the sons of older elites against contact with industry, it also gradually drew sons of industrial and commercial families away from the occupations of their fathers, contributing to a 'hemorrhage' of business talent. The educated young men who did go into business took their antibusiness values with them" (Wiener 1984: 24). This emasculation of the industrial classes began in the late Victorian era but continued to the 1980s. If anything, according to Wiener, the problem went from bad to worse: "As time went on, the larger the business the more likely it was that its leaders had attended public schools or the ancient universities. More and more in the twentieth century, the higher echelons of the larger businesses were dominated by men whose standards had been formed in the gentlemanly mold" (Wiener 1984: 138–39). Wiener argued that the public schools and Oxbridge attracted the leaders of each generation and taught them to be gentlemen. But because gentlemen did not dirty their hands with business competition, business was deprived of the best talent; and those second-rate Oxbridge graduates it did recruit, he believed, were disloyal to their employers.

Correlli Barnett agreed with the anti-industrial reprimand but highlighted the failure of British education in general, and Oxbridge in particular, to develop applied science. To summarize Barnett's core claims: Technology was the Achilles' heel of British education. There were three broad reasons for this deficiency: a businessmen's "cult of practical man," educators' romantic idealism, and everyone's antipathy to coherent organization (Barnett 1987: 209). But he lay direct culpability for this problem at the feet of Christian moralists. When the pattern for public-school and elite-university education was being set, technology was left out because a Victorian Christian revival was against it (Barnett 1987: 214). Although the Butler Education Act of 1944 presented an opportunity to correct the omission, once again Christianity intervened. The preoccupation of the Church of England with moral instruction, and Butler's desire to placate the Church, resulted in a bill biased against technology (Barnett 1987: 279–83). Until the Second World War, governing-class concerns with empire worked alongside a Christian eschewal of things technological to sustain and draw sustenance from an Oxbridge ethos of knightly nostalgia for the premodern world (ibid.: 221).

Wiener and Barnett had a sociological counterpart who drew the same conclusions. Geoffrey Ingham argued that Oxbridge was aristocratic and anti-industrial because of historic divisions within the propertied classes (see Ingham 1984). Drawing largely on the research of W. D. Rubinstein, Ingham noted that families whose wealth came from land, finance, or commerce intermingled through the Church of England, public schools, Oxbridge, London clubs, and Whitehall; but industrialists, largely northern and nonconformist, were isolated (by choice or by discrimination) from establishment institutions. Consequently, elite public schools, Oxbridge, the financial institutions of the city, and Whitehall—particularly the Treasury—were snobbish toward, and ignorant of the requirements of, modern industry (see Rubinstein 1977; 1981).

Wiener's book appeared in 1981, after the labor strife of the late 1970s and Thatcher's first general election victory, to an extraordinarily receptive public. Barnett's book came out early in 1986, during Thatcher's second term in office. Almost immediately upon publication, politicians, journalists, and university dons rattled by Sir Keith's cuts were reading and referring to Barnett or Wiener's diagnosis of British decline.

The universities' poor relations, the polytechnics, found comfort in Wiener's book as an explanation for their second-class status in higher education. The former chairman of the Committee of Polytechnic Directors, Dr. Raymond Rickett, director of Middlesex Polytechnic, expressed his wholehearted agreement with the anti-industrial indictment of British universities. On the controversy about universities and industry, Dr. Rickett offered these reflections:

> What interests me [has] to do with the way in which the anti-industrial bias of higher education has been caused by, or is cause of . . . the status attached to universities built on the backs of the perceived advantages associated with Oxbridge (for universities, in other words, read "Oxbridge") and the disadvantages perceived of associating with the lesser breed which is industrially buoyant, the polytechnics. (Rickett interview 1986)

Dr. Rickett was a Thatcher supporter working in higher education to bring about a cultural and social transformation of Britain. He wanted a more entrepreneurial, risk-taking, market-oriented society—a more American type of society—than Britain was in the 1980s. And he believed strongly that the polytechnics were better suited than universities to implement Thatcher's program.

Dr. Rickett was not the only Thatcher partisan engaged in the campaign to correct the anti-industrial bias in higher education. In 1986, Sir Keith became known as someone who subscribed to Barnett's analysis.

Evidence of Sir Keith's embrace of the Barnett thesis was provided at a seminar in Oxford on the government's policies in early 1986. Professor Denis Noble remembers the "Visitation" well (see Noble 1986: 5):

> He gave a seminar in a series which was normally run by the physical chemistry department; they gave up one of their seminars, normally on a scientific subject, and asked Sir Keith Joseph to explain science policy. . . . The meeting, of course, was packed out and I went to it. Sir Keith got up, he talked for about twenty minutes . . . and he said: "Well, what I've got to tell you is not very good news. Britain is not any longer a very strong power. The economy, though we are doing something about it, is not strong. And you people will have to realize that there can't be limitless budgets for science. I want to be honest with you, that's the state of play. And if you want to understand what I'm saying today, then you should read Correlli Barnett's *The Audit of War.*" I'm giving a caricature of the speech, but a pretty fair one I think. He left me feeling very very depressed. (Noble interview 1988)

Conservative politicians and educators embraced the Wiener-Barnett thesis that universities were anti-industrial, inefficient, and unmodern.

Logically, then, Thatcher's ministers subjected universities to relentless criticism. As Baroness Lockwood said in a House of Lords debate, those attacks inflicted "deep-down damage . . . to the morale and to the trust of the universities . . . damage caused . . . by the financial constraints and by the continual criticism of not being close enough to industry, not earning their keep and not possessing management skills" (House of Lords Official Report 1988b: col. 1395). But was there any substance to the charges? Was it true that university graduates generally, and Oxford's in particular, were anti-industrial? Were taxpayers being asked to support elitist students who did not assume productive positions in society? Had Oxford's graduates failed or sabotaged the economy?

Occupational Destinations

The vocational question was not just a Thatcherite issue. The type of education an institution provides affects the sorts of occupations its graduates may expect to assume. External vocational links influence the internal mission of the university. Of course, universities are more than mere vocational stepping stones; they also sustain cultural continuity and support the discovery of new knowledge. But the vocational connections of universities are often central to their relations with powerful political and economic actors.

The broad connections between occupational structures and educational institutions are fairly obvious. The *Economist* (1987) provided a crude but serviceable overview of the vocational linkages of European universities over the past three centuries. The eighteenth-century university was distinguished by its relation to the church, the nineteenth-century by its relation to the state, and the twentieth-century university by its relation to the modern economy.

Wiener and other modernization advocates who attacked Oxford's ivory-tower qualities alleged that its graduates eschewed productive occupations. Graduates preferred not to work in industry or commerce, critics claimed, opting instead to work for the BBC or the civil service. Those Oxford graduates who went into industry or commerce were accused of mismanaging British business because they were too arty and insufficiently scientific. What was the truth, if any, to those accusations? Where did Oxford graduates go? Which subjects provided graduates for the business world?

There are two important questions being asked here. First, did Oxford instill an anti-industrial bias in its graduates that deterred them from entering business? Second, were Oxford's graduates recruited by employers for positions of power for which their education ill suited them? As a result of Oxford's "antiquated" education, were its graduates mismanaging corporations and British institutions? In a phrase, were Oxford graduates anti-industrial and incompetent?

Was There a Talent Drain?

What was the historical evidence for Wiener's claim that an aristocratic ethos at Oxbridge and the public schools co-opted the business classes? On what did Wiener base his declaration that there had been a talent drain away from industry and commerce and toward the gentlemanly professions? Although, as previously noted, Wiener claimed Oxford's graduates were anti-industrial, his evidence was based entirely on public schools. Wiener provided just one citation for this argument, a book by T. J. H. Bishop and Rupert Wilkinson, *Winchester and the Public School Elite* (1967). Unfortunately, Wiener did not correctly interpret the reference (see Wiener 1984: 20).

The book by Bishop and Wilkinson provided a statistical analysis of the family and career patterns of public-school boys (known as "Wyke-hamists") from Winchester. The book had many strengths, but as Wilkin-son, one of its authors, noted, there were a number of "colossal interpre-tive gaffes" in it. Wilkinson explained: "I'm told that some sociologists use my book to demonstrate how false conclusions can be drawn from statistical data" (Wilkinson interview 1987). The Winchester study did not in any way substantiate Wiener's case.

In an essay on the debate over the merits of Wiener's argument, W. D. Rubinstein, a scholar of British elites, made exactly that point:

> The only source given as a citation in support of this statement in Professor Wiener's book is Bishop and Wilkinson's book. . . . On examining Bishop and Wilkinson's book however . . . I am regret-tably unable to find a shred of evidence which supports the state-ment. . . . The only relevant evidence on this matter . . . reveals that 11.1 percent of the Wykehamists' fathers were businessmen, while 16.4 percent of the Wykehamists themselves were business-men—in other words, precisely the opposite of the point made by Professor Wiener. (Rubinstein 1990: 81)

Rubinstein did his own research into this question and found: "There is certainly little or nothing in the available evidence which permits us to say that the public school *ethos* led its products away from business life" (ibid.: 83). Contrary to Wiener's thesis, Rubinstein found that the "out flow" of students to occupations did not sustain the anti-industrial charge.

To turn the question around: Was there any reason to think that Britain's business classes were particularly undereducated? When the anti-industrial problem allegedly surfaced in the nineteenth century, was the "in flow" of new blood into the business class in any sense diseased or unique in comparison with that of other industrial nations?

Harold James, a professor of history at Princeton University, investi-gated this side of the question and came to conclusions identical to Ru-binstein's. James inspected the comparative composition and reproduc-tion of different national business classes to see if the British pattern was atypical:

> Research on how business elites are recruited and on how wealth and status are passed from generation to generation . . . yield com-parable and rather similar pictures. The result of . . . rigorous and

TABLE 13

Occupations of First-Degree Graduates of Oxford and in the United Kingdom as a Whole, 1967–1986

(percent)

	1967–68		1970–71		1975–76		1985–86	
	Oxford	U.K.	Oxford	U.K.	Oxford	U.K.	Oxford	U.K.
Further study	27.9	22.1	21.9	18.1	19.7	15.2	17.4	12.3
Teaching	14.8	22.4	17.8	24.1	12.6	17.6	6.9	8.4
Government	6.2	6.9	6.6	9.5	4.4	6.6	4.1	5.8
Industry	19.8	26.7	17.4	20.8	12.2	17.3	9.5	16.4
Commerce	—	—	—	—	8.2	6.7	19.0	14.9
Accountancy	2.1	1.0	3.4	2.6	8.0	4.3	7.2	7.0
Law	3.9	2.8	4.6	3.3	7.5	4.7	7.3	3.6
Publishing and culture	2.9	1.2	2.6	1.0	3.0	1.1	2.7	1.7

SOURCES: Figures for 1958 (given in text) are calculated from University of Oxford 1966b: 191–92; 1967–86 are derived from University of Oxford 1958–87, "Appointments Committee Report," annual reports between 1968–87.

> quantified studies has been to show that the recruitment of busi-
> nessmen . . . proceeded in Europe and North America much more
> homogeneously than those looking for national differences would
> like to admit. . . . If it were true that business was so unpopular
> that the children of successful entrepreneurs went via Oxbridge
> into the professions, we should expect a lower than average British
> figure. (James 1990: 116, 117)

There was nothing extraordinary about the education or social reproduction of Britain's businessmen from the time of the industrial revolution to the Second World War. (After the war an educational deviation, which we will come to, did emerge.) James stressed: "This massive and international research on social mobility has, surprisingly, been utterly ignored by the adherents of the thesis of culturally induced British decline" (ibid.: 116).

If Wiener's argument was not supported by the Winchester data, or by the backgrounds of British entrepreneurs, was there any reason to believe that it described Oxford accurately? In the postwar period, when the British pattern varied from that of other leading industrial nations, and when Wiener claimed Oxford's pernicious effects on top business leaders were strongest, was there any evidence of a talent drain?

The Franks Commission found nothing to give credibility to Wiener's argument. Of male finalists in 1958–59 who took employment in the United Kingdom upon graduation, the largest single group, 31 percent, went into industry. The second largest contingent, 16 percent, entered commerce. And the combined Foreign Service, Home, and Overseas Civil Service intake that year was a modest 10 percent (University of Oxford 1966b: 192, table 171). (For occupational destinations in later years, see Table 13.) That is hardly the sort of breakdown one would expect from the principal source of anti-industrial bias in British society.

Were Latin Scholars in the Board Room?

If there was not a talent drain, then what of the claim that those Oxford graduates who went into industry were miseducated for their duties? Was there a stratified job market for Oxford's alumni that put arts graduates in positions of managerial authority and relegated science graduates to research?

The data available from the university's Appointments Committee does not sustain the allegation that Oxford graduates in industry were saboteurs. Most of those from Oxford who went into industry read science or technology; the arts graduates tended to enter commerce (University of Oxford 1958–87). So from Oxford's position, on the outflow side of the relation, the supply to industry was mainly educated in the sciences.

If there was a problem of arts graduates mismanaging technical enterprises, it could have resulted from industry's recruitment and promotion practices; industry may have been biased against the science graduate. The available evidence, however, does not support this view.

There are no compelling reasons to imagine that Latin scholars were running British industry into the ground. In 1978, the British Institute of Management published a survey based on responses from 4,000 of its members. It found that only 28 percent of British managers were university graduates. Of those managers with university degrees, a mere 8 percent read an arts subject, 10.7 percent read law or social science—and 81.3 percent held degrees in the natural sciences or technology (British Institute of Management 1978). The survey validated the assessment of Henry Tomlinson, a former personnel director of ICI and leading figure in the British Confederation of Business, that those large industries who did recruit graduates insisted on degrees in science or technology (Tomlinson interview 1987). Tomlinson read engineering at Cambridge University.

Since World War II, British industry's biggest problem with graduates, its national peculiarity, was not a misallocation of talent but an astonishing under-recruitment of university graduates from any subject area. For example, Japanese managers with university credentials outnumbered their British counterparts three to one ("Management Education Survey" 1991: 23). In Britain it was not only true that graduate management education, like that offered by Harvard's Business School, was undeveloped—even first-degree science and technology graduates were not aggressively recruited by industry, let alone arts graduates. So Wiener's fear that innumerate *literae humaniores* graduates were in executive positions, hampering the corporation's cutthroat zeal and high-tech vision, was groundless.

The Thatcherite adoption of the ideological Wiener-Barnett thesis was a self-deception that confirmed the anti-establishment populism of the radical right. The thesis inverted the reality—the role of culture as donnish safeguard—and stood culture on its head—as economic saboteur. The Wiener-Barnett thesis turned the *cultural authority* of Oxford, the fact that an intellectual institution had a high degree of autonomy and moral stature, into the crux of the problem. It was as if entrepreneurial values abhorred cultural pluralism and any alternative value orientation was a rival to vanquish. T. J. Reed, editor of the *Oxford Magazine* in the 1980s, summarized Thatcher's position as, "Anything that can claim to have a value or to be pursuing a value that's intrinsic and not a market value must come under attack by this government" (Reed interview 1987). Objectively, Oxford's crime was not that it subverted "the enterprise culture" but that it convinced anyone of the intrinsic worth of non-utilitarian activities.

Business Schools?

The condition of business education in Britain is an interesting issue in itself. Why did it take Britain so much longer than other countries to develop business schools? Why did the British equivalent of master's degrees in business administration (MBAs) never become trendy in the twentieth century? Were the universities at fault? Or was that slow development a reflection of business structures and attitudes?

In 1989, a scholar much concerned with wealth creation and educational systems, Robert R. Locke, published a thorough historical and comparative study of business instruction in five countries: the United States, Japan, West Germany, Britain, and France. Locke took as his departure point the Wiener-type argument that culture may decisively affect economic growth:

> The acceptance of business studies in each country depended on the ability of that country's culture to foster and to assimilate it. . . . Therefore, the historians who can deal with the specificity of this educational evolution can shed light, more light perhaps than scientists who ignore culture, on the relationship between business studies and economic performance. (Locke 1989: 55)

Yet he found Wiener's argument, that the character of education in nineteenth-century Britain was uniquely anti-industrial, to be false: "The British were not much worse than the French or the Germans in the nineteenth century" (ibid.: 69). Locke was confident that the British were not especially handicapped by their Victorian culture or educational system.

The problem Locke left open was whether the specific institutional traditions of British universities were responsible for retarding business studies in the twentieth century. To answer that question, Locke looked at the evolution of business education to see how different national academic cultures embraced or spurned managerial training. In the process, Locke reached the conclusion that Britain's social scientists did adversely affect business studies.

According to Locke, the formal education of businessmen in the twentieth century should be divided into two periods: the old paradigm before, and the new paradigm after, the Second World War. In the old paradigm, business training was practical; business management was taught as a craft. Administrative apprenticeships within firms were competitive with anything formal schooling could offer.

The second period for business education built upon the first but involved a rupture in the intellectual tools and training of management. The "paradigm shift" (a concept Locke used literally in the Kuhnian sense) (see Kuhn 1970) involved "integrating scientific method into the managerial decision process itself" (Locke 1989: 26): "The new paradigm in management studies . . . was really a matrix of interlocking, mutually conditioning scientific relationships in which no one science or discipline predominated, unless it was the instrumentality of mathematics" (ibid.: 24). The most important contributions, however, came through reformulations of neoclassical economics made possible by such innovations as linear programming, probability theory, statistics, and computers. All of these, and other components of the new managerial science, did not come together until after the Second World War, and did not take hold in universities and business schools until the 1960s (ibid.: 22, 26, 113).

In Locke's estimation, the "new paradigm" in business management required mathematical and analytical skills that could not be acquired indirectly. Neither on-the-job training nor a traditional university education would suffice. Rather, he believed, formal business education was the only way to cultivate the new science and train new managers in its techniques. Business schools were not, per se, absolutely essential; but the "new paradigm" must have a solid institutional home.

If a university or nation built business departments or schools only after the emergence of the "new paradigm," Locke implied that very little harm would come from this tardiness. In fact, Locke claimed that all of America's top business schools were disadvantaged by being elderly. He wrote that the "older business schools . . . that predated the new paradigm . . . would inevitably be behind" newer programs. Locke singled out Harvard for criticism. Elderly Harvard lagged behind, said Locke, because its great prestige was invested in an antiquated case-study method. Harvard's methods were inhospitable to the scientific requirements of the new paradigm (ibid.: 160). Among America's most prominent business schools, only the University of Chicago and MIT's Sloan School of Management appeared to meet Locke's standards.

In the early 1960s, when the new paradigm caught on inside academia, the British were setting up two national business schools. The recommendation to create the schools, one attached to London University and the other connected to Manchester University, came from a report commissioned by the British Institute of Management (Franks 1963). The chairman of the committee that did the research and wrote the report was Lord Franks. He finished that task in November of 1963, and only two months later agreed to chair Oxford's inquiries into its general condition. In the business report, Franks proposed creating elite institutions using the model of MIT's Sloan school rather than MBA-type programs. Franks's proposed business schools were built and have received mixed responses from British firms. At the same time, Oxford established a Centre for Management Studies that grew into Templeton College. Since 1963 it has offered executive education and graduate seminars for a small cohort of businesspeople and academics.

In Locke's view, Franks's recommendations were not wrong; they were just not ambitious enough. Britain needed more and bigger business schools than London, Manchester, or Oxford's Templeton provided. What was responsible for holding things up? Locke found the obstruction to be Britain's academic culture.

Locke placed a large part of the blame for the underdevelopment of business studies in Britain on the British "pure-science tradition." Academic purists, Locke argued, slowed down the growth of business studies just as they had retarded engineering studies in the nineteenth century. In both cases the academic objection to the new field was that the subject was too applied and insufficiently theoretical. In the case of business studies the snub was being given, according to Locke, by social scientists: "If engineering education suffered in Britain because of its subordination to the arrogant pure scientist, business education suffered more because the social scientist did not recognize its scientific respectability as much as the natural scientist did engineering's" (Locke 1989: 99). So in the end, Locke offered a modest version of Wiener's argument. If the British were not uniquely anti-industrial and anti–applied science in the nineteenth century, they nonetheless did less well with business studies in the twentieth century. The British lag in business programs, Locke argued, was largely due to the scientific snobbery of economists.

Locke may have a point for the years after the emergence of the new paradigm. But William Lazonick has offered a more persuasive explanation for the period before the 1960s. Lazonick's study of British economic decline de-emphasizes academic culture and stresses the role of entrepreneurial failure. Lazonick says that business studies followed along behind the transformation of corporate structures, rather than running ahead of them. In Lazonick's research, the "demand side" for MBAs came from the breakdown of family capitalism and the rise of large corporations (Elbaum and Lazonick 1986).

Lazonick's argument built on Alfred Chandler's work on managerial capitalism. On the association of business studies to the rise of large managerial hierarchies, one can consult Alfred Chandler's authoritative work *The Visible Hand* (1977), as well as his essay "The Emergence of Managerial Capitalism" (Chandler 1984). As the scale and complexity of firms grew, so did the layers of management. Those new managerial ranks gave the MBA its market. In America, the mecca of business schools, there was not a great demand for managerial studies until a large number of firms made the shift from family to corporate capitalism.

Chandler describes the sort of firm that demands MBAs as a "large integrated industrial enterprise administered through an extensive managerial hierarchy"; and in the United Kingdom that type of company "was still the exception . . . as late as 1948. . . . Britain continued until World War II to be the bastion of family capitalism" (1984: 495, 498). Chandler notes: "Apparently British industrialists wanted . . . to regard their companies as family estates to be nurtured and passed down to their heirs rather than mere money-making machines" (ibid.: 497). Firms did not usually hire university graduates, let alone persons with qualifications in business studies. If British capitalism did not stimulate business studies, Chandler implies and Lazonick explicitly argues, it was because business executives lacked an entrepreneurial vision and a drive to transform their small family firms into large managerial corporations.

Locke provided corroborative evidence of family capitalism's aversion to formal business schooling by documenting how British managers opposed the idea (Locke 1989: 97). Furthermore, a "Political and Economic Planning Report" published in 1966, based on interviews with 300 senior managers, showed that top British executives in the 1960s continued to express plenty of "resistance to management training and education" (Gater, Insull, Lind, and Seglow 1966: 265).

One can infer from Lazonick and Chandler that it was perfectly "rational" for British universities to ignore old-paradigm MBA-type programs. How rational would it have been for a university, in the face of that opposition, to set up a vocational course for which there was no market demand? To account for the history of business studies in Britain, Locke's argument may be relevant to the period after the 1960s, but Lazonick's and Chandler's analyses of the role of family capitalism before then are more powerful.

A final note on business studies. In 1993 Oxford University opened its first two-year MBA program. The graduate school strengthened Oxford's undergraduate business studies as well as the efforts of Templeton College. Oxford's commitment to the field should satisfy most of its pro-business critics. However, the difference the MBA will make to the economy remains in doubt. After World War II neither West Germany nor Japan, both of them economic success stories, had MBA-type programs. An Oxford MBA may have more symbolic than practical effects. Yet one can only wonder what difference such a degree, dating back to the 1960s, would have made to Oxford's defense against Thatcher. Harvard's business school may not apply Locke's new paradigm, but its prestige in the United States certainly reflects well on Harvard as a whole. Is it possible that the greatest damage done by the absence of Oxford MBAs was not to the economy but to Oxford's authority?

If the intellectual grounds for Thatcherite hostility to Oxford and the universities were illusory, the effects of government policy were not. Ideology justified a structural transformation of academic life. We now return to the chronology of government action and university reaction at Oxford.

THE EFFECT OF THATCHER'S POLICIES ON OXFORD

Margaret Thatcher's government imposed two rounds of cuts on universities, the first in 1980–81, the second in 1985–86. When the UGC applied the first, it sent to all universities letters of guidance, suggesting "a substantial reduction" in social studies, a "slightly greater than average cut" in arts, a "small increase" for business studies, and slight growth in most natural sciences and technology (Parkes 1981: 867–68). Edward Parkes, the chairman of the UGC, included in his letters the exact number of students each university should enroll in the three broad subject areas of "arts," "sciences," and "medicine," and the precise amount of money being granted. Oxford was faced with 8 percent cuts in its funds and a 4 percent reduction in the number of students it was to enroll. It was up to the General Board to cope with the crisis.

In 1980, Dr. Gasser had just stepped down as vice-chairman of the General Board and was replaced by Christopher Kirwan, an ancient-philosophy don at Exeter College. Kirwan picked up Gasser's quantitative policy tools and broadened their application from the science departments to the arts. Gasser recalled: "My successor, Christopher Kirwan, carried on this notion of the numerical thing to a considerable extent, and applied it pretty rigorously in the arts as well. . . . He carried . . . it with great intellectual force and conviction" (Gasser interview 1988). Part of the explanation for Kirwan's adoption of Gasser's method was philosophical. It allowed one to allocate resources in relation to student enrollment. Although undergraduate numbers alone were not the only basis on which resources were assigned, Kirwan was committed to a philosophy of education that prioritized the "demand" side, the student half of the equation.

Kirwan described himself as a sort of nineteenth-century liberal in the tradition of John Stuart Mill. He valued individual liberty, pluralism, and the notion that the purpose of a university was to educate individuals for life, not for a particular job. In Kirwan's opinion, Thatcher's ministers betrayed a basic "misunderstanding of what universities are for" when they attempted to harness education to economic ends and when they claimed the right "to direct universities in enormous detail" (Kirwan interview 1988). In a liberal society, he believed, the government should not be able to tell scholars what to teach and research or students what to study. The ends of education are not any employer's profits, but the enrichment of a particular individual's mind. Universities are, according to Kirwan, "for the private good of the students. . . . If it's worth supporting out of tax money, then that should be in the same sort of way as the health service is supported, not for the sake of the nation's economy, but for the private good of the beneficiaries" (ibid.). In other words, universities help individuals to pursue their own personal goals in life in the same sense that the health service provides for the lifetime needs of patients.

If the goals of education are "private goods" for individuals, then Kirwan believed that Oxford "should be led by the demand of its students" (ibid.). More than anything else, the preferences of individual students should determine how a university distributes its resources. Kirwan could apply Gasser's quantitative mechanism with great intellectual force and conviction because he used the device to advance the principle of student preferences. With it he could identify a fair student-faculty ratio as the standard with which to reduce or expand faculties. In a sense, Gasser gave the General Board the mechanism, and Kirwan provided it with the policy standard, for broadly managing its assets. Of course, the idea of being "demand led" was not uniquely Kirwan's, and he was not alone in favoring the normative standard of student-faculty ratios. But he was the first person in a position of power and with the technical means to put the notion into practice. He could, with that normative guideline, shift resources in response to general trends in student interests. It made, if not long-term, at least medium-term planning possible.

Under Kirwan's leadership, the board reacted quickly to the UGC's July letters. When the academic term began, it sent a "general resolution concerning the financial outlook" through Council for submission to Congregation to alert Oxford to its intentions and to receive the broadest authority for its efforts (*Oxford University Gazette* 1981a). It assured the faculty that the board would "proceed as slowly as circumstances may permit, in order to lessen the disruptive effect of rapid cuts," and toward that end the university's reserves would be cautiously drawn upon to fill in for emergency deficits (para. 8). The board warned that the UGC's imbalance between student reductions and fiscal cuts meant that "available resources per student will inevitably decline," putting the "standards of teaching and research . . . inevitably . . . under pressure" (para. 7). And it explicitly stated that "savings will have to be found wherever the opportunity is offered, in particular by not refilling most of the posts which fall vacant, even if in a particular instance the post is not one which would be abolished under the [board's] long-term plan" (para. 9). To meet the crisis, the board would have to freeze all vacant posts and control all faculty appointments. Congregation passed the resolution without opposition.

With the "general resolution" preparing the ground, the board proceeded to work the UGC's cuts into a form consistent with its long-term hope to balance student-faculty ratios. There was some marginal room within the UGC guidelines for the board to shift student numbers. Most subjects would have to restrict student admissions by the UGC's recommended 4 percent, using 1980–81 as the base year. But the board had a relatively free hand to adjust the consequences of the funding cuts on faculty numbers.

The General Board spent the better part of one academic year consulting with each of Oxford's sixteen faculty groups to devise and implement a long-term plan on the UGC cuts (Kirwan interview 1988). It looked for weaknesses in the faculties and found only one: the Honour School of Agricultural and Forest Sciences. The board proposed, and Congregation ratified, closing its doors to new students and phasing the program out as quickly as possible (*Oxford University Gazette* 1981b; 1981c). Then the board wrote and submitted to Congregation its report on the "long-term effects of an 8 per cent reduction in its resources" (*Oxford University Gazette* 1982a: 32).

This was the board's first fully rationalized and centralized academic plan. Kirwan explained:

> It was a fairly simple plan largely based on student numbers, but looking at the whole, at all sixteen faculties together, and dividing up the amount of money among the sixteen, that was something that I dare say the General Board had never done before. . . . What we allocated was numbers of posts. . . . That was the work of 1981–82, when we created what I suppose you would call a central plan. (Kirwan interview 1988)

The report offered a scheme for "permanent retrenchment" (*Oxford University Gazette* 1982a: para. 5). There was to be a "redeployment [of resources] . . . on a scale greater than has occurred in recent years" (para. 12). The UGC's reduction of Oxford's grant meant that 102 faculty positions would have to be abolished (para. 4). Those losses would be spread out in accordance with "student loads . . . [and] special circumstances and needs of each faculty" (para. 9). Reductions of any particular faculty were not at all reflections on their publication or teaching records; Oxford did not have moribund parts. The board wrote:

> The Board would wish to emphasize, however, that its assignment to a faculty board of a greater than average cut in academic establishment in no way implies an adverse or relatively adverse judge-

TABLE 14

General Board's Plan for Oxford University Student and Faculty Cuts, 1980–81 to 1984–85

Field	Percentage decrease or increase in students	Faculty posts
Anthropology and geography	– 4	– 2.0
Biology and agriculture	– 8	–21.0
Clinical medicine	+17	–11.9
English	– 4	– 1.3
Law	– 4	0.0
Literae humaniores	– 4	–16.1
Mathematics	– 4	– 3.0
Modern languages	– 4	– 6.5
Modern history	– 4	– 4.0
Music	– 4	+ 0.5
Oriental studies	0	–10.3
Physical sciences	– 2	– 2.0
Psychological studies	–11	– 8.0
Social studies and management studies	– 3	–19.0
Theology	–10	0.0
Educational studies	–10	– 2.0
Ruskin school	–15	– 0.3
Other	– 6	+ 5.0

SOURCE: *Oxford University Gazette* 1982: 34.

ment on the academic standard of the faculty, and would not be regarded by the Board as inconsistent with the opinion that the faculty was one of particular distinction. . . . It does not see these long-term retrenchment proposals as cutting out dead wood or lopping off pallid growths. On the contrary, the activities which will be affected are vigorous and valuable; the Board has selected them with regret; and it does not doubt that in imposing cuts on them it would be doing direct damage to the academic life of the University. (Paras. 12, 16)

The board certainly did not see the UGC's cuts as an elixir for restoring a diseased community to health. Tables 14 and 15 show the board's projections for student and faculty cuts.

TABLE 15

General Board's Design for Oxford Faculty,
1980–81 and 1984–85

Field	1980–81		1984–85	
	Number	Percent of total	Number	Percent of total
Natural science	482.5	38	444.6	38
Social studies	319.7	25	288.7	25
Arts	465.3	36	427.3	36
Other	11.3	1	16.3	1
Total	1,278.8		1,176.9	

SOURCE: *Oxford University Gazette* 1982: 34.

Honoring the spirit of the UGC instructions, the board proposed to decrease the number of students by approximately 467, with arts contributing 50 percent, social studies 30 percent, and natural science 20 percent of that total. The only area of growth would be clinical medicine, which would receive an increase of 58 students. The balance of faculty among the three fields (natural science, social studies, and the arts) was to remain the same. Natural scientists were before and after the largest single faculty group.

To keep track of faculty vacancies, Kirwan adopted a suggestion from William Smith of Balliol, a philosophy colleague and chairman of the Senior Tutors' Committee, an inter-college body in Oxford. The idea was to publish a "Register of Suspended Posts . . . to record what's there, still in existence, on the establishment, but unfilled" (Kirwan interview 1988). Then the board would be helping Oxford generally, and the colleges in particular, to be mindful of the scale and the distribution of the damage. The register was not for the 102 abolished posts, but for those positions that fell vacant. The board would review the register "each term and, when financial circumstances permit the release of any posts associated with a college, the Standing Committee of the Senior Tutors' Committee . . . [would] be consulted" (*Oxford University Gazette* 1982b: 69, para. 26). The board began acting as the gatekeeper, not only for university appointments but also for joint ones between the university and a college.

The register was both a type of casualty list and a symbol of the General Board's new sovereignty over the field of appointments. It became nearly inconceivable that a college would attempt to make a faculty appointment without the board's authorization. And if asked, "the General Board was very likely to say no, was presumed to say no" (Kirwan interview 1988). The gradual drift of powers in the recent history of Oxford away from colleges and toward the university, a process under way since the massive increase in state funding in 1946 and the rise of the natural sciences in the late 1950s, became distinctly visible to the dons.

Between the period 1946–73, when Oxford's budget was expanding, and 1982 "there was," Kirwan explained, "a revolution in the balance of power between the university and colleges. . . . We emerged in 1982 with colleges having no powers at all to command General Board money" (Kirwan interview 1988). The days of automatic Common University Fund lectureships for colleges to draw upon were gone. The joint appointment system that helped colleges finance their teaching obligations now constrained colleges from acting alone, even though legally they could. According to Brian Smith:

> The General Board took upon itself, without any opposition as I remember, essentially complete control of replacing of academic staff, which posts are to be abolished, which ones to be refilled now, and which ones to be deferred—not only for those which the university was paying the principal part of the salary but those for which the colleges were paying, and that was an enormous change. (Smith interview 1988)

In the 1960s, expanding resources strengthened decentralized powers in Oxford, and colleges and departments were able to take initiatives, confident of eventual support from the center. Retrenchment in the 1980s tied all of the parts of Oxford together in a new way: shrinking resources put the center in control. From an institutional perspective that was a serious abridgment of college independence, yet one they had to live with lest they risk depleting their own reserves.

The role of the board helped Oxford bid successfully for "new blood" posts. In 1983, the UGC convinced the government that, with appointments frozen by cuts, if it wanted any new scientific talent to be hired, government should provide special funds toward that end (Shattock 1994: 23). Oxford's board put in requests for 69 science, four arts, and seventeen information-technology posts. It received the second highest number of those positions awarded, just behind Cambridge University (Tapper and Salter 1992: 80). But the numbers were small. Oxford got seventeen new science faculty positions, one in the arts, and four in information technology (University of Oxford 1984; Kirwan interview 1988). The UGC funded a total of 312 for the whole United Kingdom.

Oxford endured the cuts with minimal discomfort; in comparison with those of Salford or Aston, its pains were indeed slight. Nonetheless, two years later, when Council attempted to grant Margaret Thatcher an honorary degree, Congregation was not in a conciliatory mood.

The Thatcher Honorary Degree Dilemma

By the time Congregation assembled to vote on Thatcher's honorary degree, there was not any way Oxford could come through the affair unblemished. Before Thatcher, every Oxford graduate in the office of prime minister had been given an honorary doctorate in law virtually upon occupation of 10 Downing Street. Yet with the whole education system in turmoil due to her administration's policies, with universities groaning from the pain of financial cuts, with Oxford's casualties recorded on its Register of Suspended Posts, whether the university followed tradition and voted a tribute to its graduate's ascent to the highest political office in the kingdom or voted to withhold that distinction, it would find itself accused of making a terrible mistake. A "yes" vote would outrage members of the education community and confirm accusations of Oxford's complacent disregard for those less privileged. A "no" vote would offend Thatcher's supporters and provide evidence of Oxford's anti-business snobbery. A negative judgment would also wound the sensibilities of those who valued convention as a form of civilized manners to be cherished above the muck of politics.

Thatcher took office in 1979, and Oxford voted on her in January of 1985. One can never know for certain, but if Thatcher had been nominated for the honor during her first year in office, it is likely that, except for some marginal protest, it would have gone through. The first puzzle, then, is to explain why the Hebdomadal Council hesitated for nearly five years before putting her forward.

Variations of the story are told in Oxford, but they all converge on the opinion that in 1979 Thatcher was too controversial. The fear was of a repeat of the embarrassment caused by Congregation's vote in 1975 not to award an honorary degree to its graduate Zulfikar Ali Bhutto, the late president of Pakistan, who many thought was implicated in the massacres in Bangladesh (see Hart 1985: 7). As Dr. Gasser, a member of Council, recalled, we "did not propose her for an honorary degree because there were still on Council [in 1979] all of the people who remembered the Bhutto affair" (Gasser interview 1988). Michael Brock, also a member of Council, related that, "When she first came in, people hoped it would get a bit easier next year. In fact, of course, it simply got harder next year, and harder the year after that" (Brock interview 1988). And T. J. Reed, an opponent of awarding the degree, remembered: "We were told that . . . those with responsibility in Council had a feeling that she was a bit in need of mellowing" (Reed interview 1987). But Thatcher did not soften in office.

While Council tarried, Thatcher implemented her program, rolling back the welfare state, breaking down trade union powers, and cutting the budget. Just when her popularity with the electorate seemed to slip, the war in the Falkland Islands assured her an impressive re-election in 1983. With a large parliamentary majority and a second term in office, Council's procrastination on Thatcher's degree became less and less tolerable.

Grumbles from the outside were heard in Oxford. However, the mounting pressure to act did not come directly from government; neither did the press publish a stream of letters or articles on the topic. Rather, the subject was nudged along through informal conversations, especially among Conservative grandees and businessmen in London. Michael Brock explained: "I think it was almost certainly what you might call 'club talk' among Conservatives saying 'she's a great prime minister, she's an Oxford honors graduate, what on earth are they delaying for?'" (Brock interview 1988). Gasser said that "it was thought to be doubly insulting that here was Oxford's first, the country's first, woman prime minister . . . and it was disgraceful that the university wasn't putting her forward for an honorary degree" (Gasser interview 1988). Then in October 1984, the Irish Republican Army attempted to assassinate her during the Conservative Party conference in Brighton. The cumulative effects of "club talk" and the bombing led Council to publish its intention to offer her name for an honorary degree in January 1985.

When Council chose to act, it was mindful there would be opposition in the university. "The people on Council who were really responsible for this did realize that they might not win. . . . [But] they thought that losing on a close vote would be better than not bringing it forward at all" (Brock interview 1988). Council, however, moved without benefit of soundings. On this, Council proceeded according to conventions that prevented it from trying out university opinion on the proposal. Once the matter was raised, Council members were silent on the topic outside their chamber. Consequently, they published an official notice of their intentions in December with only suspicions of, but no actual probes into, what they were up against (ibid.).

The response was immediate and largely negative. T. J. Reed recalled: "When you saw that thing in the *Gazette* you thought it cannot be true. . . . Everyone went around, as it were, for a little while, in a state of outrage. And then, I suppose, it just got around on the grapevine that somebody in Christ Church was going to call a meeting to discuss what we could do to prevent this" (Reed interview 1987). By word of mouth, a modest group assembled in Christ Church shortly after Christmas. Professor Denis Noble thought he was "probably the only scientist present" (Noble interview 1988). Thirty or so dons from the humanities and social studies and perhaps just one natural scientist gathered to air their thoughts on why and how to oppose awarding Prime Minister Thatcher an honorary degree.

Professor Noble was convinced that little would be gained from just showing up at Congregation to vote no. He remembered saying, "Given there was going to be a lot of difficulty over the issue . . . it was far better to go over the parapet and explain. . . . You will be misinterpreted anyway, but you may as well make the attempt to explain why you are doing it." After the discussion, according to Noble, "those who said that they wished to go public on the issue and say why they were going to oppose it were those who the media came to. Peter Pulzer and myself were immediately in the media" (ibid.). Since Noble was a physiologist, some of the media framed the issue as a confrontation between strapped natural scientists and a fiscal conservative.

While Noble and Pulzer were busy with the press, other dons from the meeting took steps to ensure the weight of the opposition would be felt in January. Most of those present at that first discussion were arts dons who wanted to draw into the debate as many members of Congregation as possible. So, as Reed explained, they "tried to get representation from all the colleges and all the departments" (Reed interview 1987). On January third, they were sufficiently successful in attracting additional faculty that they moved their assembly into a large lecture room at Christ Church. By this point the group had formed a consensus on the reasons for its opposition as well as on the next step:

> It was to be, as far as possible, depoliticized. And we were to argue the point that it was contrary to decency to award an academic honor to somebody all of whose policies had cut at the academic world. And by that we didn't mean Oxford, and we didn't mean universities; we meant the whole of education. We tried to insist that we were as much interested in schools,

right down to the level of nursery schools, as we were in universities. (Reed interview 1987)

The opposition was neither a Marxist conspiracy nor a gathering of scientists whose research had been directly harmed by Thatcher's cuts. Most
of the initial actors appear to have been motivated by the notion that Oxford should take a stand for the sake of the entire community of public
educators, scholars, and scientists.

Tactically, they decided to circulate a petition stating their convictions
to all of the colleges and laboratories in the university with the hope of
gathering approximately 60 signatures (ibid.). The statement would then
be submitted to Council for inclusion in the *Gazette* the week before the
vote in Congregation.

When the petition appeared, stuck between the pages of the *Gazette*
on January 21, 1985, it recorded (to its authors' amazement) the endorsement of 275 academics in Oxford to the following:

> We shall be voting against Council's resolution to confer an hon-
> orary degree on the Prime Minister, . . . on January 29. . . . Mrs.
> Thatcher's governments have done deep and systematic damage to
> the whole public education system in Britain, from the provision
> for the youngest child up to the most advanced research pro-
> grammes. . . . It would be inappropriate for any academic insti-
> tution to respond by giving its highest token of approval, and
> especially inappropriate for Oxford to do so. The University is
> widely perceived to stand at the pinnacle of British education. It
> is a representative, even a symbolic institution, and as such bears
> a special responsibility. If we were to confer this honour, it would
> be a bitter blow for everyone in public education.

Of the 275 who signed the statement, approximately 39 percent were in
the humanities, 29 percent were social studies faculty, and 31 percent were
natural scientists or mathematicians. (The remaining 1 percent worked in
Oxford's libraries and churches or could not be fully identified.) They
were a very respectable cross section of Oxford and included, as H. L. A.
Hart noted, "no fewer than ten Fellows of the Royal Society, Britain's
most prestigious scientific academy" (Hart 1985: 7). In the opinion of
Brian Smith, the effort was, without doubt, led by "pillars of society"
(Smith interview 1988).

Hart, Oxford's emeritus philosopher of law, published the definitive
eye-witness account of the actual debate in Congregation in the *New York*

Review of Books. In his estimation, the two most impressive speeches offering the reasons pro and con were given by Sir Patrick Neill, next in line to become Oxford's vice-chancellor, and Denis Noble, professor of physiology and fellow of the Royal Society. Hart recounted that Sir Patrick agreed with the opposition on the facts, but not on the principles. Thatcher's cuts "had caused the university great alarm and indeed [Sir Patrick] listed the numerous occasions on which the university had properly protested to her" (Hart 1985: 7). Nonetheless, he felt, the honorary degree was a different matter. In a very real sense, the award highlighted the dignity and calling of universities, and withholding it could not possibly help the cause of higher education. For Sir Patrick, "refusing . . . would be a petty, insulting gesture . . . it would be an unwarranted departure from established precedent and it would make the award of such honors a political matter and degrade them" (ibid.). To defend academic principles, the right course of action for the university would be to honor the convention and grant the degree.

Professor Noble's response disputed the appropriateness, in this instance, of Sir Patrick's deference to tradition. It was a matter for the assembled faculty to decide whether the university's cause was best upheld in this particular case by compliance or by departure from convention. Hart recorded Noble saying: "No one could have a *right* to an honorary degree. . . . For no convention should overrule the deep conviction felt by so many in the university that it would be utterly wrong." This was not business as usual for the university or for the country. Hart explained that "what motivated those who opposed . . . was great anxiety felt right across political party lines, because the policies to which they objected were causing possibly irreparable damage to the central purposes for which the universities and other educational and scientific institutions existed." Over half of the undergraduates in Oxford signed their own petition, and they were allowed one speaker to urge Congregation to reject the degree (see Hart 1985: 8). The momentum was impressive. It was as though unless Oxford protested, it would not be overlooking partisan flaws for the sake of a higher good; rather, it would be appeasing, without hope of reprieve, a mortal opponent.

On this issue Michael Brock, a progressive reformer in the 1960s, heartily agreed with Sir Patrick. "I voted for Mrs. Thatcher's honorary degree. I did so rather publicly, sitting behind the vice-chancellor. I'd do it again" (Brock interview 1988). Brock remembered Professor Peter Pulzer articulating the opposition's sense of alarm. According to Brock, Professor Pulzer, "a great friend, but I think he was quite wrong, he said

' . . . this is the last shot in the locker.' Quite wrong in my view, it couldn't possibly have that effect, did not have that effect" (ibid.). Things had not, in Brock's opinion, come down to a final warning shot, and pulling the trigger certainly would not alter the government's course.

Hart reported, "After a two-hour debate the dons voted by passing through exit doors marked "Yes" and "No," and the proposal was defeated by 738 to 319 votes" (Hart 1985: 7). It was the largest meeting of Congregation in the history of the university. In a restrained, donnish sort of way, Oxford's faculty experienced group effervescence. The moral sensibilities of their collective faith were, for both sides, each in its own way, reaffirmed. The external fallout started immediately.

The next morning's front page of the *Times* declared, "Oxford Votes to Snub Thatcher." The article reported the opposition of Professors Noble and Pulzer. It attributed to Noble the statement, "This may be the last chance for any serious academic institution to stop the catastrophe that we face as a scientific and educational nation [because] in two or three years' time it will be too late." It registered that Sir Patrick Neill moved the motion in favor, with the support of, among others, the conservative philosopher Lord Quinton. In reaction to Congregation's decision, a Downing Street spokesman was quoted as saying, "If they don't wish to confer an honour, she is the last person to wish to receive it" (*Times*, January 30, 1985: 1). The statement has been attributed to Thatcher herself; in the utterance, according to her biographer, "observers noted an undertone of contempt rather than bitterness" (H. Young 1990: 402).

The *Times* editorialized harshly and made outlandish assertions about the identities and motives of the actors involved. Under the heading, "Sale of Honours," it flatly pronounced, "There is no possible argument on which the decision . . . to refuse Mrs. Thatcher the proposed honorary degree is worthy of respect" (*Times*, Jan. 30, 1985: 13). Neither the grounds of the debate nor the people in opposition were legitimate, it said. Indeed, the *Times* alleged that "Marxist dons spearheaded the campaign" and, paradoxically, those left-wing militants managed to pervert the distinction into a cash transaction. "Oxford now sells its honours, giving doctorates when the government provides money enough, and not otherwise" (ibid.). The breadth of educational issues referred to by opponents was reduced to one: the size of the government's grant to the university.

For a week the *Times* printed articles and letters critical of Oxford. Nicholas Soams, personal private secretary to the chairman of the Conservative Party, called the vote "petty, spiteful and above all else political" (*Times*, Jan. 31, 1985: 2). David Watt rejected the presumption that Oxford spoke for the nation; rather it acted the fool (*Times*, Feb. 1, 1985: 12). Sir Ian Percival expressed the lament that "there can ever have been such reasons to feel ashamed of one of our great institutions" (ibid.). Nicholas Shrimpton, a don at Lady Margaret Hall, Oxford, characterized the action as "anti-female" and expressed his sense of shame (*Times*, Feb. 2, 1985: 6). Alistair Horne of St. Antony's College, Oxford, declared his "utmost revulsion to Tuesday's rebuff. . . . For folly and pettiness it is on a par with the infamous 'King and Country' motion which stigmatised Oxford in the 1930s" (*Times*, Feb. 2, 1985: 7). Professor A. A. Dashwood of Leicester University wrote: "Spitefulness and self-importance disguised by high-falutin sentiment are no strangers to academic transactions. Add to that the rage of an establishment whose comfortable defeatism has been successfully challenged and Oxford's decision to deny Mrs. Thatcher an honour granted in the past as a matter of course seems sadly predictable" (ibid.). And even the chancellor of Oxford University, Harold Macmillan, voiced his disapproval: "Nobody believes more strongly than I do in the right and duty of individuals in the university, and of its organs, to express criticisms of any government. But this is quite distinct from the traditional courtesies that have been observed" (*Times*, Feb. 4, 1985: 1). Yet there were at least four letters in the *Times* that either defended Congregation's vote or pointed out the absurdity of the claim that militant Marxist dons were behind the decision.

Generally speaking, journalists and letter writers across the spectrum of the conservative press, from the *Times* to the *Daily Telegraph*, maligned the opposition first as Marxists, then as selfish natural scientists. The press wanted to see subversion or narrow self-interest swaying those who voted no.

It is possible that more offense was taken by Thatcher's supporters in the press and the business world than by her or by members of the government. It is not that Thatcher was entirely unaffected, but, rather, as her biographer noted, "The vote confirmed quite a lot of what she already thought about the amply tenured and wholly uninvigilated members of Oxford University" (H. Young 1990: 402). If the government exacted any retribution for the affront, it was not a price paid by Oxford alone. A second round of budget cuts for universities was announced four months after the vote, but Oxford did not fare badly in comparison with other universities. Members of Council and the General Board were in a position to judge whether there were repercussions, but none reported any from the government. Rather, what fallout there was came, according to Brian Smith, "from people in the City," where the indignity influenced bankers (Smith interview 1988). Michael Brock said, "I remember being shown a cutting which I think was from the *New York Times* . . . which said that these chaps shot themselves in the foot. That was the reaction I remember well from various great donors who were great admirers of the prime minister and were very put out. One very big project . . . was certainly put at risk by it. That was the sort of reaction that I remember, not a governmental reaction" (Brock interview 1988). Oxford alienated some wealthy potential benefactors, but the affair did not deter the government's commitment to radical reform.

One of the direct effects of the degree debate was that Oxford's leaders decided to resurrect the *Oxford Magazine*. The faculty's in-house publication had been discontinued in the doldrums of the 1970s, but the cuts and controversies of the 1980s demonstrated the need for the university to have a medium in which to talk about issues outside the dining hall and common room. Its first new editor, T. J. Reed, explained:

> It was after the Thatcher thing that people in responsible positions, like Council, thought that the university badly needed a forum in which it could discuss things so it could get a sense of its own opinion without giving itself a sort of public airing, disagreeing with itself over such a very visible thing as an honorary degree for a prime minister. (Reed interview 1987)

Oxford's democratic capacities were certainly strengthened by the magazine's rebirth.

What, broadly, did the vote on Thatcher signify? It served notice on the depth of disaffection between Thatcher's administration and the cultural establishment. It is doubtful that any other modern prime minister had so dramatically alienated the academic community. In her campaign against academia, one could not help but notice the imbalance of the contest: Oxford's powers were symbolic, while Thatcher's were the powers of the purse and Parliament. Dons were not political activists or even adept as lobbyists. Perhaps, as Hugo Young stated, "It should have come as no surprise that . . . a representative body of dons lifted their puny fists and shook them at a powerful leader whom they had reason to regard as their enemy" (H. Young 1990: 403). The affair demonstrated how educational issues in Britain had become thoroughly politicized. There would be no safe retreat to the cloister; for the foreseeable future, universities would have to participate in the public debate. It was too early to judge whether donnish interventions were, or would remain, "puny." It was certain, though, that the vote signified how far Oxford and government had traveled away from the cozy pre-1940s world of privilege and gentlemanly civility.

Oxford 1985–86: Cuts and Assessment Exercises

Four months after Oxford's vote to deny Margaret Thatcher an honorary degree, the government announced another round of cuts. In May 1985, the UGC sent out more warning letters to universities. Oxford faced an additional 6.4 percent cut, for a total reduction between 1981 and 1986 of 14.4 percent. The Register of Suspended Posts listed around 100 frozen posts. Most other universities were doing less well. Part of the explanation for Oxford's relative comfort was the new philosophy of the UGC. Selectivity and differentiation were goals now, as the UGC moved toward the option of a three-tiered university system, with rounded research and teaching faculties at the top, universities with research strengths in just a few areas under them, and teaching institutions on the bottom (Shattock 1994: 67–69). Most of the government's resources would go to the top, with lesser amounts doled out to the others.

To rate the research qualities of each department in every university, the UGC conducted a "selectivity assessment exercise." The results were made public in May 1986. Oxford came out at or near the top in every department. In first place was "Cambridge, outstanding in 35 areas, Oxford outstanding in 32, while Bristol rated 14, Manchester 11, Leeds 10, Edinburgh 10" (Crequer 1986: 1). Keele and Bradford were at the bottom. In the field of clinical medicine, only Oxford and the Royal Postgraduate Medical School were "outstanding." The entire exercise was an unfortunate affirmation, but one worth underscoring, of Oxford's status as a research science university. Old myths continued to disguise the reality, but if Oxford was not, along with Cambridge, a modern science university, then there simply was not any such thing in Britain.

There were three other memorable events that May. The UGC, the Committee of Vice-Chancellors and Principals (CVCP), and the Association of University Teachers (AUT) all warned government that some universities were on the edge of bankruptcy. It was a moral and perhaps legal duty for government to caution prospective students, as the UGC said, "that some universities to which they might apply this autumn could be forced into bankruptcy before they complete their degrees" within the next three years (Crequer and Scott 1986: 1). In addition, a "working party" for the Advisory Board for the Research Councils (ABRC), led by Professor Peter Mathias of Oxford University, notified government that the private sector was uninterested in replacing it as the financier of basic science research in universities. Professor Mathias's conclusions stated: "It would be wholly wrong for Government to seek to divest itself of much of its present responsibility for the funding of long-term basic research in the universities . . . and to look instead to industry, commerce, the charitable foundations and wealthy philanthropists to meet part of this need" (Hall 1986: 1). It was a month of yellow flags in the government's face. Also in May, Sir Keith announced his resignation as secretary of state for education and science. His replacement was Kenneth Baker, a man "whose task was clearly to turn education from a vote loser to a vote winner in the next General Election" (Shattock 1994: 134).

That September, Baker gave a speech to the CVCP in Edinburgh in which he promised not to close any university, announced that research selectivity was "here to stay," said that all university resources had to be managed better, and cautioned universities to keep "new tenured appointments to the minimum." Tenure was a problem he had his eye on. "People outside who don't have such a privilege find it utterly incomprehensible" (Baker 1986: 13, 15).

"Saving" British Science

Late in 1985 and early 1986, a significant new voice for scientists emerged. From the perspective of Thatcher's opponents, one of the more positive effects of the honorary degree vote was to rouse many British scientists to enter the policy debate arena. As Professor Noble put it, "I think it is true to say that the political consciousness of scientists in Britain was activated by the Thatcher debate, no doubt about that" (Noble interview 1988). The episode led, twelve months later, to the launch of a group called Save British Science (SBS).

Within weeks of its debut, Save British Science had thousands of members and was an active lobbying organization. Since its submission of evidence, *British Science in Decline*, to the House of Lords Select Committee on Science and Technology in June 1986, SBS has been regarded by scientists, industrialists, government ministers, and civil servants as a serious voice in the field of science policy.

It emerged in late 1985 when, Noble recalled, "a number of people, about eight I think, met over dinner in Balliol—not all Oxford people, one from St. Andrew's, Scotland, one from Imperial College—we discussed in a very general way whether there was some way of getting round the fact that the ordinary means by which the interests of science in the United Kingdom could be represented to government and the public" were entirely inadequate (Noble interview 1988). The British Association for the Advancement of Science and the Royal Society were hardly up to the challenge. They were all too established to act as advocates for Britain's hard-pressed scientific community.

The dinner conversation hit upon the idea of soliciting funds from colleagues for an advertisement in the *Times* about the plight of British science. The response was considerably stronger than the eight anticipated. Noble recounted their steps:

> We then decided that what we might do was . . . send around a kind of pyramid letter . . . to see whether we were able to raise twenty pounds from each person, enough money to pay for a half-page . . . in *The Times*. We calculated that we needed 300 of our colleagues around the country to do it. . . . By the time that advertisement appeared, something like six weeks after deciding to go . . . we got 1,500. And by something like a fortnight after the advertisement appeared we were over 2,000. And of those, something like 200 were fellows of the Royal Society, and a majority of the Nobel Prize winners in Britain had signed and paid their checks. . . . we had vastly more money than was necessary to pay for the advertisement . . . so we decided that the best thing to do was to use the . . . extra [money] . . . to launch a more permanent organization. And that's how SBS got off the ground. (Ibid.)

The advertisement appeared in the *Times* on January 13, 1986, almost exactly one year after the Thatcher vote. SBS quickly became a kingdom-wide organization, with thousands of members, an executive committee of fifteen, and an advisory council of twenty.

In the new political environment, there was little point or need for Oxford to dominate SBS. Its chairman was Professor J. Lamb of St. Andrews, the treasurer Dr. J. Leggett of Imperial College; just the secretary, Dr. J. Mulvey, and two members of its executive committee were from Oxford (ibid.). As an organization, it represented active laboratory scientists. Although its roots were in the Thatcher affair, it would be wrong to assume that SBS endorsed Congregation's action. There were, Noble said, scientists on "its council who disapprove[d] strongly of the way the vote went" (ibid.). All that members of SBS agreed on, as its advertisement in the *Times* put it, was the importance of getting basic science research investment back to a level comparable to that of Britain's "main industrial competitors in Europe."

SBS viewed itself as an advocacy organization for scientists. It protested and presented detailed evidence at each step in the government's path toward lower levels of investment in research and development (R&D). But it was doubtful whether government programs were affected. No amount of reasonable discussion with Whitehall or dinner conversation with politicians seemed to protect scientists and scholars from the government's policies. Thatcher's ministers broke with convention by refusing to be deferential to universities. As George Walden, while secretary of state for higher education under Thatcher, put it: "We are not going to be deflected from pursuing these policies because of their [academics'] short-term pains or protests" (Walden interview 1987). And protest they did, but with little effect.

While the government was undeterred by dissenting academics, some of Thatcher's supporters have never forgiven Oxford for denying her an honorary degree. Even five years after the event, the head of Britain's Institute of Directors, Peter Morgan, raised the episode at a business convention like a bloodied battle flag. The news daily, the *Independent*, gave front-page coverage to Mr. Morgan's attack under the headline: "Enterprise Culture 'Sabotaged.'" According to the paper, Morgan "described the decision of Oxford University not to award an honorary degree to Margaret Thatcher as the 'spiteful, petulant action of dons caught in a time warp'" (Harrison 1990: 1). Morgan claimed that Oxford and the rest of the establishment were responsible for Britain's economic decline. Despite the establishment's eroding moral authority, it was not, as it should be, contrite and repentant. The article stated: "Peter Morgan . . . laid the blame for 100 years of decline on the 'pernicious' propaganda fed out by the British Establishment through the class-room, the pulpit, the Press and the stage. The Establishment, he claimed, had lost its authority but failed to renounce its anti-enterprise attitudes" (ibid.).

On the unwillingness of Oxford's dons to confess their sins, Morgan had a point. Most members of the Oxford community continued to regard the effects of Thatcher's policy on higher education as disastrous. Given the opportunity to recant in 1987 during the election of a new chancellor, Oxford reaffirmed its dissent. The Tory candidate was rejected in favor of Roy Jenkins, onetime labour minister and a leader of the center split from the Labour Party in 1981 that created the Social Democratic Party. Jenkins was "the politician who," as Thatcher's biographer Hugo Young put it, "more than any other might be said to epitomise the era and the values which Mrs. Thatcher stood against" (H. Young 1990: 410).

Academic opinion condoned Oxford's unrepentant behavior (Kogan and Kogan 1983; Scott 1989: 198–212; Porter 1990: 497–99, 720–22). Even a professorial advocate of competitive capitalism from across the Atlantic, Michael E. Porter of Harvard's Business School, saw Thatcher's education policies leading to irreparable damage. In *The Competitive Advantage of Nations*, Porter wrote that the policy of "gaining control over decision making" while cutting funds "threatens to drive away good teachers and permanently reduce the quality of both research and teaching" (Porter 1990: 721). This was, Porter argued, the opposite of what Britain needed: "While hardly an original observation, it must be emphasized that Britain will not regain innovation-driven status without a world-class educational and training system. . . . The rate of social investment must rise substantially. . . . *This is perhaps the most pressing issue facing Britain and the area in which current policies provide the least comfort*" (ibid.: 720, emphasis added). By 1988, there was nearly a total breakdown between the Conservative government and academics.

The Education Reform Act of 1988: The Baker Bill

The next public conflict between Oxonians and the Tory administration came in the House of Lords debate on the 1988 education bill. Under Margaret Thatcher's leadership, ideas crafted for the Conservatives' 1987 re-election campaign were revised, in Kenneth Baker's name, into legislation. On the election's message, the prime minister noted: "I like a manifesto which contains a limited number of radical and striking measures. . . . Education would, we all agreed, be one of the crucial areas. . . . We [presented] our reforms as the third stage of a rolling Thatcherite programme" (Thatcher 1993: 570, 572).

Among the bill's radical proposals, elementary and secondary schools would be given a core curriculum and the opportunity to opt out of the existing state system; the Inner London Education Authority (ILEA) would be abolished; the UGC would be replaced by a University Funding Council, with contracts supplanting block funding; tenure for new or promoted faculty would be eliminated; and vast new powers over the educational system would be given to the secretary of state. The House of Commons, where Conservatives held a majority, passed the bill, leaving it to the House of Lords to amend some of its most controversial aspects.

It is an under-appreciated truism of British political life that the kingdom's unwritten constitution leaves Parliament, or more specifically, the House of Commons, sovereign. Unlike the United States, Britain has no constitutional safeguards that balance or incapacitate (depending on one's views) the executive against the legislative and judicial branches of government. In Britain, if the ruling party's majority in the House of Commons is sizable and voting discipline effective, it can act with relative impunity. It can legislate at will on, to mention an example implausible in the United States, mandatory religious instruction in schools. As the legal framework for the European Union grew, its governing body in Brussels provided some counterbalance. But in 1988, the only immediate check on what an elected majority in the House of Commons could enact was the power of revision exercised by the unelected House of Lords. Thus what anxious champions of pluralism, such as Alexis De Tocqueville and John Stuart Mill, feared as the danger of tyrannous rule by majority faction was partially restrained in Thatcher's Britain by lords and baronesses.

In the 1980s, the lords numbered around 1,170, of whom approximately 800 were hereditary; 24 or so were bishops of the official state religion, the Church of England; and approximately 345 were life peers, a special category created by Prime Minister Harold Macmillan in 1958, two years before he became Oxford's chancellor (Sampson 1984: 28). When the Tories were in office, given the conservative sympathies of most hereditary lords, debates would have been dull and prospects for passing amendments remote indeed were it not for the fact that most aristocrats could not be bothered to leave the countryside or wherever it was they liked to pass the day. Infrequent attendance by backwoods lords left life peers, who constituted less than one-third of the House, with disproportionate leverage. Life peers were appointed as a reward for extraordinary public service (such as Oliver Franks) or for political distinction (such as Labour's former prime minister James Callaghan) and usually in a manner that would ensure diversity in the House. Their ranks included a sufficient number of Labour Party members, independents, and fringe party supporters, as well as academics of all political persuasions, to uphold a high level of discussion and occasionally a legislative reform.

Members of the House of Lords voiced objections to many of the education bill's provisions. From the standpoint of university critics of Thatcher's policies, the two most important topics of dispute were tenure and the principle of academic freedom. Oxford's chancellor, the social democratic Roy Jenkins, led the only successful effort to amend Baker's bill on a matter related to higher education. He did not, however, challenge the government's plan to stop granting tenure. Rather, he took tenure's demise as his departure point and worked to include on the face of the bill an amendment codifying a legal status for academic freedom in Britain.

When Lord Jenkins offered his amendment, he said, "The abolition of tenure leaves a dangerous hole which needs to be plugged" (House of Lords Official Report 1988a: col. 444). The patch Jenkins proposed was a statement obliging institutions and government to respect academic freedom. But why not contest the bill's clause on tenure? On tenure's end, Jenkins thought:

> Broadly speaking, it is true to say that university opinion has not strongly resisted that abolition. I believe the restraint has sprung from a desire not to be too concerned with material self-interest. . . . It may be that this self-abregation [*sic*] has been carried too far. . . . In any event, it looks as though tenure will go and that there will be certain inevitable and undesirable consequences. But surely it cannot be intended that academic freedom should be imperilled with it in a kind of side wind. (House of Lords Official Report 1988c: cols. 444–45)

By the time the bill came to a vote, not one organized academic body had fought to retain tenure: not the Committee of Vice-Chancellors and Principals, not Save British Science, and not Oxford's leaders.

The acquiescence of the CVCP on tenure spoke very loudly in the government's favor (Committee of Vice-Chancellors and Principals 1988a: 2; 1988b: 1). The Conservative Lord Beloff, a retired professor of government from All Souls College, could respond to the bill's critics with the unchallenged statement that, "In fact there has been no pressure whatever from the vice-chancellors and principals to preserve tenure" (House of Lords Official Report 1988c: col. 511). Given the United Kingdom's employment regulations, perhaps the CVCP was unalarmed? Perhaps the committee saw it as a necessary concession in exchange for public funding? Or, maybe it was subdued by the deeply problematic nature of tenure in a public educational system?

There were some in the House of Lords, such as Lord Peston, Earl Russell, Baroness Seear, and Lord Swann, who adhered to the aristocratic guild view, arguing that most university faculty deserved, for the sake of their duties, early tenure. For them, tenure and the academic craft were inextricably tied. As Earl Russell put it, "the only proper defense of academic freedom is tenure itself" (House of Lords Official Report 1988a: col. 1408). Others were more reluctant to contest the opinion that something about tenure had to be changed.

One predicament undermining the case for a necessary connection between tenure and the vitality of the academic vocation was that so many of the profession were bereft of it. In 1988, the entire polytechnic sector of higher education lacked a tenure system. One could allege, as Conrad Russell did, that polytechnics were teaching and not research institutions and hence did not enjoy the rights or merit the title "university" (Russell 1993: 106). But if tenure ought to be justified on the grounds of active research, the truth was that university inquiry relied to a great extent on untenured contract scientists. On that subject Professor Noble said, "The vast majority of the scientists who SBS write about are not tenured anyway. They are on short-term contract" (Noble interview 1988). Statistics compiled by a House of Lords Select Committee indicated that, in 1988, UK universities employed roughly 30,000 tenured academics and 15,000 untenured contract research staff (McCready 1996b: 13). Oxford was no exception; research there was breeding another underclass of nondons. In the mid-1980s, approximately 600 contract research workers, most of whom held doctorates, were employed by Oxford. A study by the local chapter of the Association of University Teachers drew attention to the fact that "the staff employed to do Oxford's high-rated research in the sciences and social sciences are increasingly employed on fixed-term contracts" (McCready 1996a: 2). Should the government oblige taxpayers to cover the additional expense of extending lifetime job security to all research workers in universities as well as to staff in the former polytechnics? If not, was it credible to claim that the preservation of tenure for some secured the job prospects and intellectual integrity of those without it? How meaningful were the academic freedoms of a 34-year-old biochemist working with a two-year contract on a project designed by a tenured university professor?

If tenure could not be given to everyone, then, rather than abolish it, why not make it more selective? Some lords sought a compromise position, at some remove from the aristocratic guild view or the government's position. They drew attention to the functional virtues and cost-effectiveness of keeping tenure for some fraction of the profession. Lord Dainton warned that the government's formula would generate perverse effects, that the bill would reward stagnation since "either promoting a member of their own staff or offering a higher or similar grade post to someone from another university [would deprive] him or her of a benefit of tenure already held under his or her existing contract" (House of Lords Official Report 1988b: col. 1377). Recruitment from abroad also would be handicapped. As Lord Adrian said, "I believe that it will become even more difficult to attract someone—from the United States, for example—occupying a tenured position, . . . and receiving a substantially higher

salary" (ibid.: col. 1389). Tenure was cheaper than merit raises or indus-
trial-scale salaries, and it helped to keep UK universities competitive.

Few appeared more distressed by the problem than Lord Annan. He
was "more disturbed than the vice-chancellors by the abolition of tenure"
(ibid.: 1988a: col. 1274). There was a matter of fairness, Annan said: "I
have always felt that it was reasonable to give people who were devoting
their lives to the study of sometimes very abstruse and difficult subjects,
the study of which does not qualify them for any other profession or activity, security of tenure for a certain number of years" (ibid.: 1988c: col.
480). And he agreed entirely with those who believed the eradication of
tenure would hinder the capacity of British universities to recruit world-
class professors. Annan asked: "Is there anything in the Bill which pre-
vents a university from saying to a distinguished American academic,
'Come and join us. We will give you tenure to the retiring age'? . . . I can
see no reason why one cannot give tenure to specified people on one's
staff provided that the whole lot are not granted tenure" (ibid.: col. 484).

The lord chancellor, the Tory leader in the House for this Bill, an-
swered Annan negatively:

> As regards the point raised by the noble Lord, Lord Annan, Clause
> 174(1)(a) requires that the statutes of the university should have
> inserted in them a provision enabling an appropriate body . . . to
> dismiss any members of the academic staff by reason of redun-
> dancy. In other words, if the university was hit by hard times it
> would be possible to dismiss anyone. (Ibid.: col. 484)

The Conservative case against tenure articulated in the House of Lords
rested on two claims: that tenure was an anachronism, an unjustified privilege not enjoyed elsewhere; and that with tenure, "changing economic
conditions" could bankrupt a university. The lord chancellor stated: "The
difficulty is that if the university or other institution is met by changed
economic circumstances it is hoised by those circumstances if all its staff
have tenure" (ibid.: col. 485). What was left unsaid was that Parliament
had the power to oblige universities to discontinue tenure because they
were state institutions, funded by the public. Consequently, if "hard
times" hit a university, it would be because the government was cutting
back on funding.

It would have been consistent with a Thatcherite free-market perspective for the government to have compromised and accepted a form of selective tenure such as existed in the United States. In America, if one included in the ranks of academia all staff in junior colleges, four-year

teaching colleges, and research universities, only half of those were even in full-time tenure-track slots (Clark 1987: 209); of those, perhaps half held tenure (Chronicle of Higher Education 1991: 58). In the British context, if a comparable percentage, approximately 25 percent, of higher education faculty were tenured, would the Treasury be unfairly burdened? Whether academics in the United Kingdom would find the U.S. system of competitive late tenure as congenial as the old British system of early tenure was another matter. Attrition rates among American academics were higher than those in the medical, legal, and architectural professions (D. Burke 1988: 119). Although the rewards may be great, the odds of reaching tenure are comparatively unfavorable.

The American competitive solution, however, was raised not by Thatcherites but by the bill's critics. The government's intransigence on the matter suggested that something other than purely economic considerations were at work. Consequently, even lords sympathetic to the bill were disturbed by the government's posture. The Lords Allen of Abbeydale, Blake, Beloff, Butterworth, Croft, and Flowers, among others, criticized tenure, welcomed the bill, and yet urged that some reassurance to scholars and scientists be made in the form of a statement endorsing academic freedom. Lord Blake said: "I do not believe that the Government are popular in academic circles; I do not suppose they are under any delusion on that point. I cannot see why a reference to academic freedom cannot appear on the face of the Bill. It would relieve the resentment and the depression that is felt by a great many dons" (House of Lords Official Report 1988a: col. 1277).

Oxford's leaders had been working hard to extract a compromise on this point. In private conferences with Conservative leaders, Oxford's vice-chancellor, Sir Patrick Neill, brought his legal training to bear in negotiations over the formulation of an amendment. The masters of Oxford's colleges wrote to old members in both the House of Commons and the House of Lords urging them to pass such a resolution. In the debate, two lords, Broadbridge and Wedderburn of Charlton, with degrees from the modern colleges, St. Catherine's and St. Antony's, read from their Oxford communications.

The government resisted. The lord chancellor felt that "academic freedom" was too abstract to become a legal statute:

> It seems to me that putting a specific reference to academic freedom in the Bill could result in some considerable difficulty. . . .
> Any reference . . . might lead the courts to conclude that since Parliament had deliberately mentioned it in the Bill, it must mean

something quite distinct from justice and fairness, concepts with which they are familiar. (Ibid.: 1988b: col. 1366)

Lord Beloff, with typical feistiness, challenged his fellow Conservatives to stop equivocating:

Many of us on this side [the government's side] . . . find it very difficult to understand why after six months of discussion, representations from the universities and negotiations with the Committee of Vice-Chancellors and Principals it is still not possible, unless the noble and learned Lord can delight and surprise us, for the Government to meet the unanimous wishes of the university community. (Ibid. 1988c: col. 452)

Lord Jenkins, taking his cue from Beloff, pressed for a vote on an amendment that committed the lords to the inclusion of some statement. The room divided as those who agreed with Jenkins passed out through one door and the chancellor's supporters went through another. Lord Franks and Lord Bullock walked together behind Jenkins. The government was defeated, 152 to 126 (ibid.: col. 460). When the lords resumed, Jenkins was able to read his version of an academic freedom clause into the bill (col. 471). To some extent, it was the dons' second vote against Thatcher.

WHAT MOTIVATED THE THATCHERITE ASSAULT?

Why did Thatcher force her policies on an increasingly alienated academic community? How can we explain the motives and support for the Thatcherite assault? What social conditions and collective beliefs made its anti-don bias possible but not inevitable?

This section offers an argument on the conditions and dynamics that gave Thatcher's attack on higher education its cultural significance. It is an attempt at a sociologically informed interpretation of Thatcher's logic and her supporters' belligerence toward universities.

To begin, let us look at what Thatcher's hostility to universities was not based upon. It was not related to a *petit embourgeoisement* of the Tory party, as Julian Critchley, a witty Tory "wet," suggested:[3] "As Mrs. Thatcher has gone up in the world, so the party has come down. . . . The *petit embourgeoisement* of the Conservative Party and its reversion to a form of nineteenth century Liberalism have gone hand in hand" (1985: 29, 50). Flattering as it may be to Tory wets, this social transformation never took place among Conservative members of Parliament. The occupations of Conservative members of Parliament (MPs) over the years 1951 to 1987 were remarkably stable (see Butler 1988: 317).

To move from occupational to educational backgrounds, the assault on universities was not led by nongraduates or even non-Oxbridge products. As earlier passages showed, there were just as many Oxbridge MPs and civil servants on Thatcher's team as in previous administrations. If her program was philistine and brutish, it was not for lack of members with a bit of Oxbridge polish.

Was Thatcher's education program caused by, or the cause of, a value shift in the views of the general British public? Not if opinion polls and the analysis of Essex University professor of government Ivor Crewe were anything to go by. He demonstrated that, "quite simply, there has been no Thatcherite transformation of attitudes or behaviour among the British public" (Crewe 1989: 241). Public opinion, generally, did not become neo-Victorian in Thatcher's likeness.[4]

And Thatcher's effect on universities was not some sort of "functional" correction of systemic problems faced by British business. On issue after issue of contention, the Thatcherite position was at best an exaggeration, at worst pure fantasy. British universities generally, and Oxford and Cambridge in particular, were not anti-science or anti-industrial in any meaningful sense. So Thatcherism cannot be understood as the political program that suited the "objective needs" or solved the "objective problems" of British industry.

If there was a voice that reflected objective and systemic "functional" needs, it was that of the Council for Industry and Higher Education. Its membership, drawn from the 200 largest companies in Britain, spoke for big business (Coldstream interview 1987). While the Confederation of British Industry was supposed to represent the entire business community, the Council for Industry and Higher Education offered the perspective of Alfred Chandler's managerial capitalism. Since its public launch on April 1, 1987, the council had been critical of Thatcher's restructuring policies. Instead of cuts, it proposed an ambitious program of expansion in higher education. It did not propose to extend the Oxbridge model, but did leave room for it in an expanded system that emphasized competitive skills. As its director, Patrick Coldstream, said: "We don't worry much about Oxford; it does an excellent job. What we want is more students, and more investment in higher education" (ibid.). The council pointed out that the continued growth of university students in the sciences "needs more public investment, since arts courses are cheaper to run" (Coldstream 1987:

11). It wanted more basic, not applied, research from universities. Its 1987 manifesto stated: "Companies have unanimously told the Council. . . . they wish to see neither a reduction in the overall science base nor any significant shift by the universities toward applied work which is easier to 'sell'" (ibid.: 17). The agenda the council presented was very much like the suggestions offered by Michael Porter. Those proposals more accurately addressed the educational needs of industrial capitalism than Thatcher's.

Finally, was Thatcher's education program merely an extension of state power—the reflection of a dynamic of bureaucratization and centralization that preceded her by decades? Two political scientists in Britain, Ted Tapper and Brian Salter, offered this interpretation (1987; 1992). The broad outline of their theory has been that the growth of a strong central state was a self-reinforcing process. In higher education, it was a dynamic whose center was the Department of Education and Science (DES) and whose local agents were the administrative bureaucrats running universities.

Although it was obviously true that the central government had more control over higher education in the 1980s than at any other time in the twentieth century, the chronology of the process did not suggest that a bureaucratic-centralist dynamic was the vital causal agent. All of the political and financial means necessary for government to impose its will on universities have been in place since 1946. Nevertheless, the working nature of the relationship did not change dramatically between 1919 and 1973. There were troubles along the way. In the 1970s, inflation and economic problems made five-year block grants impossible, but civility and supplementary funds saw the universities through. And there were foreshadowings of Thatcher's policies in previous administrations: in 1972, the Conservative prime minister Edward Heath sought to push the universities' scientific research into areas selected by the government (Shils 1982: 459–60). In 1976, the Labour prime minister James Callaghan launched the "Great Debate" on the economic relevance of education with a speech at Oxford's Ruskin College (see Salter and Tapper 1981: 189–220). In 1977, Labour's secretary of state for science and education, Shirley Williams, proposed efficiency measures for universities. But those steps were just that—steps, not a total reorientation of the government's relation to universities. Thatcher's policies represented a break from her predecessors. For the centralist-dynamic argument to be persuasive it would need to explain why state–university relations worked so well between 1946 and 1973. Without a broader sense of historical context and cultural forces, Tapper and Salter's theory is just too mechanical to be a strong explanation of the events.

If Thatcher's assault on universities was not because Tory MPs were more petit bourgeois and less educated in the 1980s than in the 1950s, or because big industry wanted it, or because the DES had masterminded a bureaucratic takeover of academia, then what did Thatcherism draw upon? Although motives and opportunities are messy things, two factors were crucial.

First, if there was a government department pushing cuts and regulations, it was the Treasury department rather than the DES. As Michael Shattock argues, "the story of the reorientation of British government between 1975 and 1985 is largely one of an increasing dominance of the Treasury over spending departments, most notably those that dealt with education, health and social services" (Shattock 1995: 24). The Treasury's efforts to make each expenditure area fully accountable was driven by the state's fiscal problems after the international recession of 1973. Of the items on the Treasury's balance sheet, universities were among the most vulnerable. Higher education had a smaller constituency than either health or social services. That academia touched so few in Britain prepared the ground for the second factor.

Thatcher's strongest electoral base, and greatest ideological appeal, was with the self-employed and those members of the rapidly growing managerial and supervisory occupations who were without university degrees (see Heath, Jowell, and Curtice 1985: 20, 67). The Robbins expansion of universities in the 1960s did not go far enough to include Thatcher's fractions of the middle class. This was what made Britain's middle class unique among industrial nations: its members were not exposed to higher education. When John Goldthorpe of Nuffield College looked at education and the salaried middle class (which he refers to as the "service class") in Britain, he found that only 7 percent of administrators and 5 percent of business managers had university degrees (Goldthorpe 1982: 174). And the results of Thatcher's 1983 election victory showed that the salaried middle class in Britain "is far more divided by education than it is by sector or occupation. . . . Higher education is not only associated with liberal values but also with a vote for the [centrist] Liberal (or Social Democratic) party" (Heath, Jowell, and Curtice 1985: 65, 67). Thatcherism helped articulate a new line of division in British society. The conflict was within sections of the middle class: the champions of the marketplace against meritocratic professionals.

This middle-class battle was over social prestige, whether society should esteem intrinsic cultural merit as well as external material accomplishment. It was a British variant of a common middle-class rivalry between money and culture. As Pierre Bourdieu schematically stated of the French, there was a conflict "within each class between the fractions richest in cultural capital and poorest in economic capital and the fractions richest in economic capital and poorest in cultural capital" (Bourdieu 1984: 39). On one side was an aristocracy of culture, the winners of the contest for academic credentials; on the other side were the bourgeois commoners, the self-employed or self-made who held white-collar positions without the benefit of a university degree.

This status conflict within the middle class was part of a schism between mentalities best characterized in religious terms as "low" and "high" church. John Carswell, the Treasury representative to the Robbins committee, described the "high church" and "low church" attitudes thus:

> "High church" . . . stresses autonomy, faith in the capacity of the
> institution as such to see the light, along with a certain charm
> and elevation of style which implies a degree of detachment. Con-
> trasted with this is the position ["low church"] founded on the
> belief that education should serve social ends and hence (on the
> congregational principle) should be accountable. One is prelatical,
> the other evangelical. One emphasises the church and its necessary
> privileges; the other the text, its mission and its consequences.
> (Carswell 1985: 53–54).

In those terms, Thatcher was a low-church Puritan offended by Oxford's high-church Anglican style. Between the two was a gulf on what counted as education. Thatcher was congregational and practical—any environment where there was a lab and test tubes would do to bring science to the student for the purpose of wealth creation. Oxford was priestly and idealist—education required the right sort of traditions and had no particular end outside itself.

It did not help the two sides to communicate that Thatcher had been a chemistry undergraduate at Somerville College, Oxford, in the mid-1940s. Both women and chemists were marginalized at Oxford in those days. One can hardly expect a fiscal conservative, committed to wealth creation not social expenditures, and who studied chemistry at Somerville to sympathize with the pains of discomfited dons.

Thatcher's instincts on academics matched the mentality of her core constituency. The Baker education bill that did most of the damage was designed to be a vote winner. And though most of its appeal was supposed to come from its policies on secondary education, those without university degrees were expected to applaud the stern lessons being taught to academia.[5]

This is not intended as a reductionist argument. Without Thatcherism to organize it this sentiment could smolder indefinitely without ever manifesting itself as a political program. Thatcherism provided an ideology that resonated with those self-made middle-class elements and gave them a standard to rally around. The self-made market actors resented and felt superior to university youths. They perceived undergraduates to be children of privilege having fun at the taxpayers' expense, without the real cares and risks of life.

The fact that the self-made had no university experience explained why it was so easy to fight this ideological battle with images that were completely outdated. The critics of Oxford offered visions of the place that may have been accurate before World War II but certainly not after. The self-made formed their impressions of university life from the media. They had no real experience of university with which to evaluate the images fed to them by the tabloid press. The tabloids read by the Thatcherite sections of the middle class such as the *Daily Telegraph*, the *Daily Mail*, and the *Daily Express* had in 1980 a joint circulation eight times greater than the combined run of the *Times* and the *Guardian*, which were quality dailies read by the established professions (and whose coverage of universities was slightly better informed than the tabloids') (see Bradley 1982: 18–21, 28, 47; Butler and Butler 1989: 494).

The perverse twist was that the Thatcherite attitude toward university culture was an inversion of the facts. It was doubtful that academic culture made any significant contribution to Britain's industrial problems, but it was certainly true that governing-class culture provided the peculiar foundation upon which British academic autonomy was based between 1919 and 1973. Cultural convention, the Thatcherite scapegoat for economic decline, was the only thing standing between the state and universities. Thatcher's campaign to free industry from the pernicious effects of university culture was actually the cover under which the state broke free from its traditional relation to universities.

Conclusion

7.

Dilemmas of Academic Authority

Oxford from the turn of the century to the interwar period was a loose federation of colleges where scions of the upper classes, with public-school backgrounds, pursued gentlemanly studies in the humanities when they were not playing cricket or boating. It would be safe to assume that more dons knew about Aristotle's ethics than about James Clerk Maxwell's electromagnetic theory of light. Until World War II the university received less than 25 percent of its funds from the government; the colleges collectively, and some individually, had an income greater than that of the university. By the 1960s Oxford was a meritocratic university where the single largest faculty contingent worked in the natural sciences. The social origins of Oxford's undergraduates were similar to those of students in Britain as a whole; and state-school students were a majority. In the late 1940s, the university ceased to be a privately financed institution and through an influx of government money in effect became a state institution. Since the 1960s, the university has received approximately 70 percent of its operating expenses from the government, making it by far the wealthier half of a partnership with the colleges. The key years of transition were between 1953 and 1966, when faculty and students moved into the natural sciences; when undergraduate recruitment from state schools increased considerably; and when government money for science and student fees surpassed private funds as the primary source of financial support for the Oxford community.

The process of institutional modernization was long and complex. There were conflicts, especially between the arts and sciences. Young research scientists without college affiliations butted heads with older arts dons comfortably ensconced in gothic quads. There was an agonizing incapacity to overcome gender inequalities. Some dons resisted replacing unintellectual gentleman-commoners with academic meritocrats. Structural tensions between the rights of colleges to go their separate ways and university-wide interests produced friction. Some colleges, such as Queen's and All Souls, obstructed modernization; others, such as Merton and St. Catherine's, were in the vanguard of reform. Nonetheless, the process of institutional transformation went forward. Oxford's reformers built empires of science departments and new colleges: St. Catherine's for undergraduates and five others for postgraduates. Dons with social democratic leanings worked with democratic elitists and scientists to transform admissions, to expand the faculty's democratic powers, to modernize the administration, and, assisted by outside pressures, to nudge and jolt Oxford into the second half of the twentieth century. The high tide of these reform efforts coincided with the work of the Franks Commission in the 1960s.

On balance, Oxford moved forward in areas of overlap between its internal culture and the social climate of the time. Oxford tried to strengthen itself as a scholarly community at the same time that it served the national interest. It became heavily committed to the natural sciences and hoped by raising its intellectual standards to help working-class and middle-class young men to gain entry to Oxford, thus simultaneously serving the causes of scholarship and social justice. To a great extent, those two goals were achieved. But, as is always the case, unintended effects emerged. Those inside Oxford who hoped to open opportunities to the lower classes in the name of social justice, very quickly got a narrow middle-class meritocracy of such high standards that the barriers between it and society were nearly as great as they had been when wealth determined a student's admissibility. Exclusion based on economic property was replaced by a new type of exclusion based on cultural competency. Senior faculty members, those who hoped to contribute more science to the nation, ended up, in the 1990s, being controlled by the funding agencies of the state in ways that they believed hurt British science.

It is important to see the extent to which developments in the natural sciences drove many aspects of the reform process inside Oxford. Oxford's modernization was largely a story of its transformation from a mostly arts to a predominantly science university. The Thatcher era strengthened the role of scientists at Oxford. Politically, they were pushed to the front by the rejection of an honorary degree for Thatcher and thereafter continued to play highly visible roles in the national debate on science policy. They were in the forefront of those who had to struggle with the new systems for awarding research grants and assessing university performance. And, in the process, the scientists carried much of the burden for upholding Oxford's reputation in government and industrial circles. The job they did was responsible for exposing Oxford's excellence in the sciences to a wider public then ever before.

Oxford came through the Tory restructuring of higher education bruised but not disabled. The government's efforts to make universities compete for research funding and to evaluate the performance of individual institutions did not harm Oxford as much as it did other universities. It may have been the wrong way to allocate resources, and time spent on departmental evaluations may have been time wasted, but after the reforms, Oxford, Cambridge, and the University of London were still thriving in a league by themselves. When the University Grants Committee's replacement, the Universities Funding Council, rated universities across all academic fields, Cambridge, Oxford, and London were ranked first, second, and third, each more "world-class" than any other British University (Walker 1993: 47). In the annual reports of the Science and Engineering Research Council, Oxford consistently placed second or third for total size of research grants won or science "studentships" awarded, again just behind Cambridge University and the Imperial College of Science of the University of London (Science and Engineering Research Council 1992: 75, 85). Oxford passed the government's tests and continued to be one of Britain's top three universities all around, but especially in science.

Another measure of Oxford's excellence in the natural sciences was offered by Tapper and Salter. They compiled their own data on Oxford's accumulation of science research grants between 1965 and 1990: "It would be difficult to deny that Oxford is *the* market leader. . . . The real success stories at Oxford are the fields of clinical and pre-clinical medicine and the Department of Engineering Science" (Tapper and Salter 1992: 189–90). According to the numbers Tapper and Salter amassed, Oxford "outperformed Cambridge" over the decades in getting science grants (ibid.: 183).

To identify Oxford as a modern science university was not to say that the arts were not excellent there as well, or that there was no longer any friction between the two cultures. However, scientists were predominant in their share of institutional resources; they received at least equal academic prestige for the rigor and success of their educational and research programs; and they increasingly set the tone for the university. One illustration of that came when the General Board sent a resolution to Congregation to move away from donnish academic titles. The nomenclature of Oxford's old colleges, where a fellow was more distinguished than a science professor, had been carried over into the 1990s. While 40 to 50 percent of most British faculty held the senior title of "professor" or "reader," and 50 percent were "lecturers," the ratio at Oxford was 23:77 (*Oxford University Gazette* 1995a: 663). Throughout their careers, most Oxford faculty were "fellows" and "lecturers." One could interpret that as either an attempt to maintain a "community of equal scholars" (*Oxford University Gazette* 1995b: 834) or the reflection of an insular and nostalgic attitude among arts dons. The controversy stirred up the old two-cultures "division between the Republic of Letters and the Empire of Research" (ibid.: 835). Many arts tutorial dons wanted to keep things as they were, while many scientists wanted change (*Oxford University Gazette* 1995a: 663). When the proposal was moved in Congregation the scientists won, 67 to 13 (*Oxford University Gazette* 1995b: 846). When the issue was put to the entire faculty in a postal vote, the result was 875 for, 595 against (*Oxford University Gazette* 1995c). In the future, when Oxford's scientists submitted research applications or participated in international conferences, they would have the same titles as their peers at other universities.

Given the magnitude of Oxford's twentieth-century renewal, it is peculiar that its changes and strengths should have been so widely misunderstood. The distorted understanding of Oxford was nearly a national conceit: of course Oxford was upper class, anti-science, anti-industrial, and incapable of changing itself—that's England. But the misperception was a disservice. The time when it was appropriate to designate Oxford as an upper-class arts university was over in the 1950s. Failure to recognize its new stature in the natural sciences reflected a basic misunderstanding of what a science university was, or an unwillingness to look beyond its gothic quads.

An institution of Oxford's age has experienced many periods of decline and revival over the centuries. Its renewal was always the same in the sense that traditionalism, organizational pluralism, and intellectual mission provided the means to innovate and conserve. Yet society's response to Oxford's renewal was not ever the same. In the nineteenth century the reform and renewal of Oxford brought about its "golden age." Oxford was never more autonomous, wealthy, and influential than in the period between the Victorian Royal Commissions and the Second World War.

Why did those changes add so much, and the more recent changes so little, to Oxford's authority? Part of the answer was vocational.

The work of the Victorian commissioners and their Oxford supporters was ultimately made successful by the symbiosis of two professionalization projects. Oxford's teaching dons were after professional status and job security; and, for undergraduates, administrative career opportunities were opening up. The Indian civil service, with its roots in the East India Company, had for some time based its recruitment on meritocratic criteria. Between 1853 and 1870, when the Northcote-Trevelyan reforms of the domestic civil service went into effect, thousands of administrative careers became open to talent. Thus, undergraduates with public-service ambitions had a need for exam preparation. Their newly acquired stake in intellectual work complemented the drive by Oxford tutors for official recognition and corporate power. Emboldened by a revitalized stream of undergraduates, Oxford's dons made common cause with Victorian reformers to professionalize and democratize the collegiate world. The "revolution of the dons," as Sheldon Rothblatt called the same process in Cambridge (Rothblatt 1981), resulted in an Oxford that was a federation of self-governing colleges engaged in undergraduate tutorial instruction (see Rothblatt 1981). College life organized around sports, common table, and weekly tutorials added up to an educational experience eminently suitable for gentleman-administrators. With the restoration of donnish self-rule came a renewal of Oxford's links to the governing class.

The link was the civil service. When, as at Balliol, upwards of one-third of one's college classmates were working in public service, the relevance of an Oxford education was obvious. And indirectly, the moral authority of the institution was enhanced. The external effects of Oxford's reforms in the nineteenth century would have been completely different without the professional aspirations and gentlemanly spirit of the Victorian civil service.

The late-twentieth-century gap between Oxford's image and reality, and its inability to harmonize the two, was an unintended effect of shifts in the social and political context. Oxford's problems were a result of the breakup of the class, occupational, and political networks that sustained it throughout the late nineteenth century and right up to the eve of World War II. Until 1939, Oxford was a clubhouse where country society and middle-class professionals mixed to mutual advantage, and most of Oxford's institutional prestige came from that association. The major source of the Thatcher-era conviction that educational institutions were responsible for sabotaging red-blooded capitalism by instilling gentlemanly values in British elites was the kinship-type relation that existed until the 1930s between the landed gentry and the professions on the one hand, and the public schools and Oxbridge on the other. As Chapter 2 demonstrated, there was a blue-blood extended family in residence at Oxford until after the Second World War.

Added to the underpinnings of social class were the links between Oxford and the professions. Until 1939 the three vocations pursued most often by Oxford graduates were in the establishment's trinity of church, state, and school. Over 60 percent of Oxford's junior members went into the clergy, government service, or secondary education (mostly in public schools) between 1900 and 1939 (Greenstein 1994: 68, table 3.4). In comparison with the heavy battalions that entered one of those three professions, law and medicine recruited tiny platoons. Whether in domestic or foreign civil service, church pulpit, classroom, or country house dining room, Oxford's prestige was affirmed. The nexus between Oxford and upper-class families, political power, and moral influence began to unravel in the 1920s, but it did not get set completely adrift until the war.

To the structural ruptures of class and career we must add a third break: the reconfiguration of Oxford's relation to politics and government finance. Until the mid-1950s, Oxford was home turf for the Conservative Party. Virtually every one of Oxford University's seats in Parliament, from 1832 until they were abolished in 1950, was held by a Conservative; MPs from Oxfordshire, the county, have been Conservative since 1918 (Harrison 1994: 378–80). Nearly half of all Conservative MPs with a university education went to Oxford, and there was an easy interchange between them and Oxford dons. In the 1950s, when Conservatives were elected and reelected to power, the *Oxford Magazine* published congratulatory lists of all the new MPs, arranged by their Oxford college and political allegiance. In 1951, Oxford's graduates contributed 99 Conservative, 38 Labour, and one Liberal Party member to Parliament; in 1955, it was 106 Conservative, 31 Labour, and still one Liberal (*Oxford Magazine* 1951: 48, 50, 52; *Oxford Magazine* 1955: 378, 380–82). Oxonian Tory MPs outnumbered their former classmates sitting in Labour's parliamentary seats three to one. This special relation's farewell performance came when the Conservative prime minister Harold Macmillan was elected over a former Labour Party ambassador, Oliver Franks, to Oxford's highly politicized position of symbolic leadership, chancellor of the university. (Four of the five chancellors before Macmillan had been Conservatives as well.) Oxford's relation to establishment politics started to come undone during the years of Labour's rule in the early 1960s and then fell completely apart in the late 1970s with the changing of the Conservative leadership from the old-guard Tories to Margaret Thatcher's new men.

Overlapping with the period of conservative Oxford politics, there was nothing less than a total revolution in the institutional relation of the state to universities in general, and to Oxford in particular. After 1946, the money flowing into Oxford came increasingly not from its own endowments or student fees, but from the central government. These developments completely altered Oxford's institutional capacities. A university cannot be autonomous if it no longer finances itself.

Oxford's authority had always been related to its class, vocational, and political links. In the past the university had been, in a sense, insured by those connections. It became vulnerable after World War II when it took its own rhetoric about a Republic of Letters seriously, forgot the nexus of that idea with a propertied upper class, and neglected to play politics. If one becomes a state university, one has to be there in the political arena pressing one's interests or be prepared to cope with the paymaster's pleasures.

It was an odd historic twist that when Labour or Conservatives criticized Oxford, they were working with images that, once more or less accurate, were by then out of date. When Labour went after Oxford's class composition, it had already changed; when the Tories attacked Oxford for being insufficiently scientific and relevant to the economy, its faculty were heavily scientists and its graduates were going to work for British industry. Oxford's political critics seemed arrested by images 30 years out of date. Fortunately, Labour was never seriously after university reform; unfortunately, when Conservatives were, Oxford was without powerful external allies.

If Oxford had had any social or political insurance, what form could that have taken in the second half of the twentieth century? From the standpoint of vocations, the challenge facing Victorian reformers was to divorce Oxbridge from the church and wed it to the state. The challenge confronting Oxford after the Second World War was not so clear cut. Oxford had to redefine its relation to the state and, at the same time, discover a role for itself in the modern economy. Only there was nothing comparable to the civil service in the economy. Creating MBAs for managerial capitalism was not the option in Britain it was in America. Teaching became, by default, the only alternative candidate. Yet it did not carry the cohesion or social power that it did before 1944. The loyalties of teachers were divided by the distinction between state and private schools. And the political attempts to improve social mobility by restructuring state schools demoralized many teachers. The denigration of vocational education at Oxford did not help it work through the challenge of finding occupational links. Whether it was teacher training or business studies, Oxford did not rush to cultivate it.

If a vocational link did not present itself, what of a connection to a particular social group? One of the consequences of Oxford's becoming a meritocratic and state-funded institution was its new disregard for potential family donors. It did not have to make that move; other elite universities combined intellectual achievement with the maintenance of family ties. America's Harvards were not doing themselves or education a disservice when they took family background into account in admissions.

The most selective private institutions in America work with academic "floors" that they will not go below, and those "floors" are actually quite high (Karen 1991: 361). One measure of their altitude is provided by SAT scores. For example, no institution had a higher average combined math and verbal SAT score for students entering in 1990 than the California Institute of Technology at 1400 (a perfect score is 1600). In 1990 Yale's SAT average was 1350, Stanford's was 1370, and Harvard's was 1370 ("Best Big Universities" 1990: 118). Even with Yale holding a top-floor admissions position since the 1960s, its "legacies," those undergraduates with at least one parent holding a Yale degree, have constituted, on average, 20 percent of the student community (Pierson 1983: 85, 87–88, 94–96, 98–99).

"Legacies" at private highly selective institutions do receive an edge in the admissions process, but not one that undermines academic standards. We have very reliable data to illustrate the point because Harvard's admissions practices were investigated and absolved by the U.S. Department of Education in 1990. Using Harvard's record as a proxy for similar institutions, one can say that legacies have SAT scores that average only about 35 points lower than those of nonlegacies (Lamb 1993: 496 n. 39, 505). Still, critics believe that legacies "receive an advantage greater than that enjoyed by any [affirmative action] minority student" (ibid.: 491). They clearly receive less preferential treatment than recruited athletes, however. Athletes, whose average SAT scores are 130 points lower than those of nonlegacies, receive the greatest boost of anyone in the admissions process.

Whether one opposes different standards for different groups depends on one's sense of ethics. If one embraces a single normative standard, such as meritocratic test scores, then one should object to any type of differential treatment. But if one sees the need for a university in a welfare-capitalist society to rely on a mix of criteria to achieve a desirable combination of goals (especially social equity, intellectual excellence, and fiscal self-reliance), then one can support flexible standards for different categories of applicants.

After graduation, Ivy league legacies disproportionately help with their alma mater's finances. They donate as members of their graduation classes and often also as members of America's top income group. Private colleges in America benefit from a practice of elite philanthropy that centers on higher education. Francie Ostrower's research on charitable contributions by the wealthy in 1988 shows that "education received [the] largest gifts from the greatest number of donors" of any recipient (Ostrower 1995: 39). The very rich, according to Ostrower, may give money to art museums out of a general love of art, but that logic does not apply to education. Contributors to colleges and universities give not because of their belief in education but out of a sense of solidarity with their alma mater (ibid.: 89).

College and university endowments did not grow naturally from some peculiarly American character trait; rather, they took years of organized effort to establish. The relationship between contributors and higher education has been methodically cultivated by the beneficiaries. In the 1990s, Harvard and Yale employed between them at least 100 full-time fund-raisers. In addition, they consistently drew upon graduation classes to organize reunion gifts. The fourteen Harvard classes holding reunions in 1998, for example, collectively donated $95,107,030 to the university (Harvard College, Graduate School of Arts and Sciences 1998: 3). In the years after graduation, legacies give millions of dollars that sustain university autonomy.

In Britain, with the public paying tuition for every undergraduate—rich and poor—Oxford could focus exclusively on meritocracy, without regard to family contributions. From a democratic elitist perspective that was an advantage, but one could object that when the public paid full tuition for the affluent that depleted resources better used elsewhere and left graduates unaccustomed to investing in education. And without steady donations from graduates, a university's capacity to be independent is undercut. A pure meritocracy, funded by taxpayers, benefits individual members of the middle class more than it enhances either social equity or institutional self-reliance.

Social groups, whether patrician or plebeian, can conflict with the purposes of academia. The university that was subservient to a particular social or economic interest would cease to be an effective community of scientists and scholars. Nonetheless, too many academics have been willing to posit a necessary connection between public funds and academic freedom, as though wealth and private interests were inherently antagonistic to the life of the mind. A plurality of funding sources, with the weight placed on the endowment and alumni, can provide a less precarious position than primary reliance on government. A private university with its own endowment can ignore any particular wealthy individual's displeasure.[1] But a state university that defies the existing government's will must either have constitutional guarantees backed by high courts or get electoral opinion behind it.

The dilemma facing universities is that they must defend academic interests with political tools or by cultivating alumni relations. Between the mid-1950s and the early 1980s, Oxford apparently ignored both options.

Why did this happen? The growth of the welfare state, the postwar consensus, the end of empire—all of these things made it unlikely that anything comparable to the political and social linkages of the nineteenth century would be available. Yet some responsibility falls on the shoulders of those who led Oxford's modernization. Most of the important actors in this narrative were grammar-school meritocrats. As beneficiaries of Morant's mobility ladder into the establishment, they were to an extent educational idealists. They thought of universities as national institutions that deserved public support. Why would any government think differently?

In the past the strength of Oxford was its ability to house both gentlemen and scholars. When the meritocrats won the admissions fight, they unintentionally undermined some of the grounds for institutional autonomy. As Andre Beteille, professor of sociology at the University of Delhi, has noted:

> An institutional order based on privilege and patronage might still have within itself considerable room for the recognition, cultivation and promotion of individual merit [and] the historical evidence quite clearly shows the capacity of institutions to accommodate contradictory principles. . . . Indeed, it is their capacity to accommodate such principles that gives to institutions their living quality and ensures their viability by enabling them to adapt themselves to changing historical conditions. (Beteille 1983: 132)

Oxford's modernization, no matter how true to its idealistic traditions, left class underpinnings and vocational connections too far behind. It was as though Oxford was suspended in a social vacuum, and the myths moved in to fill the abandoned social space.

If cultural authority and institutional autonomy are related in complex ways to wealth, social ties, and occupations, then Thatcher gave Oxford a blessing. Thatcher's policies motivated Oxford to launch an appeal to gain some financial independence. For a university of Oxford's caliber the financial campaign was a realistic alternative to total dependence on state funds. In going to the private sector, it could also look across the Atlantic for American contributions. This is not a strategy available to many universities; in fact, no other British university has Oxford's connections or prestige. While it will take time to judge whether Thatcher really damaged higher education as a whole, it is already apparent that she helped her alma mater. It was help that Oxford's dons would have preferred to go without, but given Oxford's position in the 1980s, it was not help they could refuse.

Reference Matter

Notes

INTRODUCTION, *The Oxford Myth*

1. The data on these matters are presented in detail in Chapter 3. But in 1992, Oxford's first-year undergraduates divided into subjects as follows: 42.5 percent in science and technology; 36 percent in the arts; and 21.5 percent in the social sciences (*Oxford University Gazette* 1992b: 173).

2. The misperception of Oxford as an upper-class arts university extends beyond the circles whose impressions of it are filtered through the mass media into the narrow ranks of scholarly experts on British universities. A book on Oxbridge published in 1992 stated, "Oxford remains to this day predominantly an arts-based university" (Tapper and Salter 1992: 145).

3. I refer to those values and customs that various scholars identify as relevant to national character. (For examples, see Robert Bellah et al. 1986; Liah Greenfeld 1992: 3–21; Ronald Inglehart 1990: 26, 422.) For a case of including Oxford on a short list of England's national institutions, one can turn to the memoirs of the mid-nineteenth century's most perceptive analyst of national temperament, Alexis de Tocqueville. According to his biographer, de Tocqueville's journal from his first trip to Britain "contains images characteristic of traditional England: a session of the House of Lords, an election in London, Oxford with its colleges and its fellows, a day in the court of a justice of the peace" (Jardin 1988: 199).

4. Jill Ker Conway, the Australian- and Harvard-educated historian, recalled of her Oxford stay in 1963, "I was irrationally irked by . . . the easy confidence of all concerned that they lived at the center of the greatest intellectual community in the world" (1994: 93).

5. "Public school" was the customary term used to refer to England's private, expensive, and often socially exclusive secondary schools. After the unrest of the 1960s, public schools referred to themselves as "independents" in a move to deflect calls, particularly from the Labour Party, for their public regulation or legal abolition. The best known of the public schools are those investigated by the 1861 Clarendon Commission: Eton, Winchester, Westminster, Charterhouse, St. Paul's, Merchant Taylors', Harrow, Rugby, Shrewsbury, Marlborough, Cheltenham, and Wellington. A list of comparable elite prep schools in the United States would include: Phillips Academy, Phillips Exeter Academy, St. Paul's, Lawrenceville, Groton, Hotchkiss, Choate Rosemary Hall, Middlesex, and Kent.

6. "Oxbridge" is a collective noun that refers to the universities of Oxford

and Cambridge together. It suggests a slight deference to the seniority of Oxford, rather than the expression "Camford" which, despite its use by some Cambridge dons, has never really caught on.

7. The second paragraph of Sir Keith's report proclaimed, "The Government believes that it is vital for our higher education to contribute more effectively to the improvement of the performance of the economy." And paragraph six warned "higher education establishments . . . to beware of 'anti-business' snobbery" (Department of Education and Science 1985).

8. For centuries the term "dons" has been used to refer to Oxford's faculty. Sheldon Rothblatt believes the word may be a corruption of "dominus." Over time "don" has become the informal tag attached to any British university teacher.

Most published evaluations of the period substantially agree that among its effects, "university autonomy as it was understood for much of the twentieth century is dead" (Tapper and Salter 1992: 242). For other examples, see A. H. Halsey's book (1992) and a report from the Center for Higher Education Policy Studies. The center's study concluded that Conservative legislation, "for the old universities . . . must surely signal the end of autonomy, a near complete defeat in the battle between state and university that has been waged over the last fifteen years" (Brennan and Shah 1994: 314).

9. According to the late Lord Ashby, the role of a university as a governing-class "nursery for gentlemen, statesmen, and administrators" was invented by Oxford and Cambridge (1958: 68). In the United States, Yale and Harvard have been very self-conscious about their responsibilities for educating society's "leadership class" (Trillin 1993: 6, 32–33). The relation of elite universities to the "leadership" or "governing" class is a theme in Chapter 2.

10. The numbers for ministers are from Butler and Butler 1986: 95–134; and Butler 1988: 319–20. The estimates on an average House of Commons are calculated from a table provided by W. L. Guttsman (1974: 35).

11. An equally expansive formulation, that "Oxford is to the mind what Paris is to the body," was offered by Richard Ellman (1988: 37).

12. Mary Warnock, head of Girton College, Cambridge, pointed out that the "television adaptation of *Brideshead Revisited* . . . was taken by many of its viewers as a literal and accurate depiction of Oxford as it is today" (1989: 138).

13. It is conventional to refer to different types of British universities by their architectural styles: gothic for Oxbridge, redbrick for late-nineteenth-century civic university, and plate glass for the new universities built in the late 1950s and early 1960s. "Redbrick" is the term commonly used to refer to the urban universities founded in the late nineteenth century. Established as expressions of civic pride, they developed in commercial and industrial centers like Birmingham, Liverpool, and Manchester. Organized along departmental lines, with lay members on governing bodies, Redbricks owed more to the Scottish model of higher education than they owed to Oxbridge. The "New" universities were part of the first wave of postwar university expansion. Seven in number (East Anglia, Essex,

Kent, Lancaster, Sussex, York, and Warwick), they were projected by the UGC and given Treasury authorization in 1957. Because they were innovative and built by modernist architects, they were labeled as a group, "New," or "Plateglass," universities.

14. For Oxford data, see Chapter 2. On Harvard, see Thernstrom 1986: 125.

15. Hollywood may treat Harvard as a stock reference for nefarious figures in films such as *Timecop* (1994) and *Conspiracy Theory* (1997), but the book-reading public finds few examples of demonic possession at the nation's oldest college.

CHAPTER 1, *Academic Autonomy and Money Matters*

1. The original sociologist of money, Georg Simmel, even believed there was an affinity between the use of currency and intellectual abstraction (1971: 326).

2. Noel (now Lord) Annan was once provost of King's College, Cambridge University, and vice chancellor of the University of London. Of his many publications on British intellectual life, *Our Age* (1990) is most relevant to this manuscript.

3. The oldest continuously operating university in the world is Azhar in Cairo, Egypt. It was founded by a Shiite sect, the Fatimids, in the tenth century.

4. For a critical description of the "New Jerusalemites" in government and academic circles, see Barnett 1987; and Glasser 1990: 119. For a fictional account that explores some of the effects of Britain's New Jerusalem dream being deferred, see Mortimer 1986.

CHAPTER 2, *The Making of Oxford as a Middle-Class Institution*

1. Daniel Greenstein's research showed that in 1900–1909, 20 percent were "passmen," and another 15–20 percent took no degree. In 1930–35, those percentages were down to 10 percent passmen and 10 to 15 percent taking no degree (Greenstein 1994: 57–58). As Greenstein noted, "This group, which had not come to Oxford for narrowly academic reasons, vanished only after the Second World War"(1994: 59).

2. According to Greenstein's calculations, public-school students received nearly 60 percent of Oxford's entry scholarships. Yet he pointed out that "almost 90 per cent of the boys from fee-paying independent schools" could count on financial contributions from their parents, while 40 per cent of undergraduates from the state school sector had to depend on an Oxford award for support (Greenstein 1994: 47–48).

3. Although Waugh used the term in reference to a Winchester public-school product, it applies equally well to grammar-school scholarship students.

4. As yet, there are no published accounts of Oxford scholars in the interwar period living in separate areas of their colleges. But at Yale until 1948, it was standard practice for Jewish undergraduates to be segregated by room assignments (Oren 1985: 164–65).

5. J. V. Beckett noted, "Peers tended to congregate in certain colleges"(1988: 101).

6. Oliver Franks was born on February 16, 1905, and was schooled at Bristol Grammar School. After graduating from Queen's College, Oxford, he received a fellowship there to teach philosophy (1927–37). He then accepted a professorship in moral philosophy at Glasgow University, where he taught from 1937 to 1945. During the war he was at the Ministry of Supply (1939–46) and then returned to Oxford as provost of Queen's from 1946 to 1948. During the Paris summit responsible for the Marshall Plan in 1947, he was head of the British delegation. The Labour government persuaded him to leave Oxford to become ambassador to Washington (1948–52), where he was a central figure in the implementation of the Marshall Plan and the creation of the North Atlantic Treaty Organization (NATO). Back home, Franks became a director of Lloyds Bank in 1953 and then its chairman from 1954 to 1962. In 1962 he returned to Oxford as provost of Worcester College, where he served until 1976. Also in 1962 he was made Lord Franks, a life peer, for his services to the nation. And from 1964 to 1966, he chaired the reform commission described in Chapter 3 of this book. He spent most of the rest of his days in Oxford until his death in October 1992.

7. Obituaries in *Oxford Magazine* for the 1940s and 1950s often noted that a don's professional life had been consumed teaching tutorials in one of the university's colleges. For example, the May 19, 1949, issue of the magazine says about J. D. Denniston (1887–1949): "His whole career . . . was spent at Hertford College, where he became a fellow in 1913. He was essentially a College tutor" (p. 502). Also see University of Oxford 1966b: 368, para. 549.

8. In this respect Oxford was merely an extreme case of the patterns identified in Peter Blau's work. As he noted, "Inbreeding promotes faculty loyalty" (Blau 1973: 125).

9. According to statistics reported in 1946, 44 percent of Oxford's dons were unmarried, and 70 percent had been bachelors in 1896 (*Oxford Magazine* 1946: 81–82).

10. In contrast, in the Ivy League, by the 1980s having a spouse was one of the requirements for the job of college master.

11. As we shall see, this pattern was repeated again and again. A reform is introduced to accommodate scientists, and then it is generalized to the rest of the university.

12. Although the outside world may have misunderstood the relation of classics to public schools, Oxford did not. When an article in the *Times* mistakenly claimed that grammar-school boys were "fast outdistancing those of many old

public schools" in the race for classics scholarships at Oxbridge, the *Oxford Magazine* noted, "It may be of interest to give the actual figures for this year. Of 147 awards for Classics won from schools at Oxford and Cambridge, 111 were won from independent schools" (May 18, 1950: 468). According to numbers given in the same article, in 1950, public-school students won 50 percent of the scholarships at Oxbridge, but they won 76 percent of the classics awards.

13. It kept its Roman figures even when the cover was redesigned in 1957 (*Oxford Magazine* 1957).

14. Between 1938 and 1949, the number of entering freshmen in fourteen of the men's colleges increased by 50 to 100 percent (*Oxford Magazine*, November 17, 1949: 141).

15. Between 1931 and 1961, Yale's enrollment went from 5,915 to 8,129 (Pierson 1983: 9, 11).

16. A "bedsit" was a small, single, rented room where its occupant usually did little but sleep.

17. For data on growth in the sciences, see Chapter 3.

18. It was an intrusion powerfully evoked by the work of Richard Hoggart (1958). For a good example of the literature on this in the United States, see Sennett and Cobb 1972.

19. For example, see C. Bell 1928.

20. Tawney's lectures were, in part, an homage to Matthew Arnold's 1869 book, *Culture and Anarchy*. Arnold's work called to Tawney as a type of social-democratic manifesto on culture. For Arnold wrote that "[the men of culture know] that the sweetness and light of the few must be imperfect until the raw and unkindled masses of humanity are touched with sweetness and light. . . . [They] are the true apostles of equality" (1980: 498, 499).

21. Dr. Lindsay was 45 when he became master of Balliol in 1924, and 56 when he was made Oxford's vice-chancellor in 1935, a position he held until 1938 (*Oxford Magazine* 1935a: 1). His obituary noted that he was a socialist idealist who, "always a college man," valued teaching over research. In 1943 he lectured at Yale (*Oxford Magazine* 1952).

22. Professor Cole's inaugural lecture was delivered in All Souls College, Oxford, November 9, 1945 (*Oxford Magazine* 1945). His talk was reprinted as "Scope and Method in Social and Political Theory" (Cole 1950: 1–16).

23. In May 1950, Christopher Hill wrote a letter protesting the McCarthyite tone of a book review of a biography of Marx (Hill 1950: 512).

24. Crossman followed the path provided by William of Wykeham, who served King Edward III and later founded both New College, Oxford (in 1380), and Winchester College (in 1382). He went first to Winchester and then matriculated in 1926 at New College, Oxford. He received an Oxford M.A. in 1933. When Harold Wilson enrolled in Jesus College in 1934, Crossman was a don at New. Crossman was a close friend of Wilson's and served in his Cabinet.

25. Anthony Crosland went to Highgate, a modest public school, and was a

scholar at Trinity College, Oxford. Trinity was his father's college. Crosland came from a middle-class professional family. Like Evelyn Waugh's family, the Croslands lived in Golders Green, a suburb northwest of London. His father, J. B. Crosland, had a distinguished career in the War Office; his mother was a lecturer at Westfield College, University of London. His parents were members of a religious-ethical sect that combined the commitment to moral and intellectual things that characterized the "intellectual aristocracy" discussed by Noel Annan. For more on this, see S. Crosland 1983; N. G. Annan 1955.

26. Whether the effects of higher education on cultural activities is a good thing continues to be a contentious issue. But the positive correlation between higher education and the public's participation in the arts is not in dispute. Attendance at performing arts events, museum visits, and book reading increase with university education. The definitive evidence we have on this comes from the United States, where the tensions between an expanded system of higher education and the penetration of everyday life by mass media and markets are much greater than in the United Kingdom (National Endowment for the Arts 1993).

27. One could also turn to a 1947 polemic by the City of Oxford's member of Parliament, the honorable Quintin Hogg. Hogg, the eldest son of Viscount Hailsham, was educated at the family institutions for his class, Eton and Christ Church, Oxford. Hogg successfully traveled a glittering path, becoming president of the undergraduate Oxford Union and after graduation a fellow of All Souls College. In 1947, following the Tories' defeat by Labour in the general elections, he wrote "The Case for Conservatism" (1947), to defend the party and its Burkean inheritance. Although Hogg was a representative figure at the apogee of conservative supremacy in Oxford, his presentation of the basic Burkean claims is less analytically rich than Quinton's. In 1976, Quinton was a member of a dinner club much admired by Margaret Thatcher, the Conservative Philosophy Group (H. Young 1990: 406–7, 575).

28. In this respect, if we take Eliot and Bourdieu as representative figures, there was a convergence between the conservative and the radical view on the class structuring of cultural capacities.

29. Michael Young's *The Rise of Meritocracy* explores fictionally the nature of a society in which everyone is selected for his occupation through a meritocratic system. The psychological consequences are terrifying because no one has any legitimate grounds for grievance about his lot in life. What sense do demands for social redress have in a perfectly meritocratic world? Young wrote, "Once all the geniuses are amongst the elite, and all the morons are amongst the workers, what meaning can equality have?" (1958: 115) In Young's novel the story ends with the overthrow of meritocracy by a revolt of the workers led by highly educated women. The success of meritocracy causes its downfall, and the moronic end up running society. Young's point was to show that meritocracy would not work; instead, Britain should strive for more equality.

30. According to Martin Jay, those first expelled from Frankfurt just three months after the Nazi assumption of power included the leader of the Marxist Frankfurt School Max Horkheimer, Karl Mannheim, and the theologian Paul Tillich (Jay 1973: 29).

31. Thirty-two percent of university teachers participated in either the military or the national service (UGC 1948: 18). Colleges continued increasing the number of awards right through to the Franks era in the 1960s. For examples in 1953 and 1963, see *Oxford Magazine* 1963.

32. Examples from before World War I can be found in obituaries of college tutors published by the *Oxford Magazine*. For one, see "Allan Frederick Walden (1871–1956)," November 22, 1956: 132–36.

33. Chilver was editor of the magazine from December 1951 to April 1953. On his familiarity with and affection for America's elite universities, it is worth noting that he wrote an article affirming Oxford's friendship with Yale. This was a special relationship, he said, because "Yale gave hospitality during the war to over 120 children of Oxonian parents"(*Oxford Magazine*, March 1952: 245).

34. The Crowther report from the Central Advisory Council for Education offered research and recommendations to the minister of education on the education of youngsters fifteen to eighteen years old. It found a "wastage of talent" due to children's leaving school early and documented the class connections between a father's occupation and children's school attainments. It was published in December 1959.

35. Secondary school students in England received examination certificates in particular fields, rather than high school degrees. It was normal for university-bound students to complete five ordinary or "O"-level exams and two advanced-subject or "A"-level exams.

36. For a personality sketch of David Cecil, at once flattering and scathing, see Amis 1991: 101–7.

37. The calendar for universities to take turns appears in para. 15, p. 11. The dates are repeated in UCCA's report (UCCA 1961a: 3–4).

38. Even in 1987, when individuals applied to Oxford University, although they sent their application to a central administrative office, most expressed a preference for a particular college. In 1987–88, 86.6 percent of the applicants specified one or two particular colleges, and of those admitted, 81 percent were accepted by their first choice (*Oxford University Gazette* 1989: 233).

CHAPTER 3, *Oxford Moves into the Natural Sciences*

1. Special thanks to Mark Curthoys, a member of the History of Oxford University Project, for his indispensable assistance in identifying the duties of obscure dons in 1923.

2. The expression comes from William Blake's poem on Milton.

CHAPTER 4, *St. Catherine's College*

1. One finds an example of this in C. S. Lewis's sympathy for foreign academics, to whom reading and examining "often becomes mere work" (Lewis 1961: 7).

2. Lord Woolton was initially the minister for food and later the minister for reconstruction in the coalition government's War Cabinet, 1940–45. He also held various ministerial posts in Churchill's Conservative Cabinet of 1951–57, and he was chairman of the Conservative Party from October 1946 to July 1955.

3. The contrast with that great denial of society's continuity with times past, the French Revolution of 1789, is striking. Mona Ozouf explained that one of the major problems that faced the organizers of revolutionary festivals was finding "a space without memory." They needed space that was open, uninterrupted, large, easily accessible, and without any historical associations. It had to be the opposite of aristocratic space, which is "enclosed, divided, and isolated" (as Oxbridge was) (Ozouf 1988: 128–29).

4. Among St. Catherine's famous alumni are three prime ministers of Pakistan, including Benazir Bhutto, who did graduate work there.

5. Although it has fallen into disuse, St. Catherine's had its own vocabulary known as "Catz speak."

6. A particularly vivid example of this is offered in the comments of Simon Winchester, a foreign correspondent to the *Sunday Times* and other British newspapers and a St. Catherine's old-boy: "Good old Oxford. . . . It is my home. It is the centre of my life. It is the place to which, above all others, I long to return when I am far away—the place of which I think fondly whenever I long to be away from this bazaar or that jungle, or on this desert waste or in that foetid city slum. Out there, the water is always ready to close above your head, the memories snap shut the moment you leave. But Oxford—it has this capacity for always remembering, for always keeping a place for you, long after you have gone" (Winchester 1987: 33).

7. Thackeray's essays on snobs were first published in the magazine *Punch* in 1846–47. His modern editor, John Sutherland, informs us, "The words cad and snob . . . originated, it seems, as neutral descriptions of humble artisans. . . . But cad at Oxford and snob at Cambridge were adopted as names for townees, and in passing through the mouths of the uppish young men of the university became charged with discriminatory overtones. In time they emerged as terms part-abusive, part-analytic, for articles which were somehow sham. Cads and snobs are society's false currency" (Sutherland 1978: 3). There are other nuances of meaning for the term "snob" than just Thackeray's definition; for examples see Judith Shklar (1984: 87–137).

8. Trevor-Roper presumably intended this passage to be ironic, because the article it appeared in expressed incredulity toward claims made about his own college. Yet the point stands.

9. Also, in association with Oxford University through the 1980s, there were ten Permanent Private Halls or theological colleges, plus a Centre for Management Studies and an adult residential college with trade union sponsorship, Ruskin College.

10. Worcester College began in the late thirteenth century as a Benedictine foundation with the name Gloucester College. When Henry VIII dissolved the monasteries he took control of Gloucester College as well. It subsequently decayed and all but disappeared until it was reestablished in 1714 with money from the baronet of Worcestershire, Sir Thomas Cookes. For more, see the account provided by J. C. Masterman when he was provost of Worcester College (Masterman 1952).

11. Twenty is the total number of men's colleges if one excludes St. Edmund Hall, St. Catherine's, and All Souls. Neither St. Edmund Hall nor St. Catherine's was an independent college before 1957; and All Souls, which has no students, stands in a category by itself. Although many senior fellows deliver university lectures and engage in tutorial instruction at All Souls, it is more like an academy for research in the arts than a conventional Oxford college.

12. A seventh postgraduate college, Templeton, dedicated to business studies and created with American money, received its Royal Charter in the late 1990s.

13. The poem included the lines: "We are the elite, the rest of you be damned. There's no room in heaven for you, for heaven can't be crammed."

14. In Oxford the colleges tutor undergraduates on syllabi designed for exams administered by the university at the end of the student's first and third years. The exams were graded by university-wide faculty committees, and the colleges competed with each other for the best results. The first exam determined whether a student should continue to work in Oxford, and the second determined the degree class with which the student graduated.

15. Bullock would not fit easily into any of the five types of academic politician identified by F. M. Cornford in a humorous monograph (1908). But he could be described as reflecting a particularly "dangerous" combination of the characteristics of an "Adullamite" and a "Young Man in a Hurry."

16. The Life Peerage Act of 1958 empowered the sovereign to give life membership in the House of Lords to individuals nominated by the political parties in the House of Commons. In this way, electoral politics, national concerns, and women could enter the House of Lords. Life peers make up about one-third of the House's approximately one thousand members.

17. The similarities between Bullock and Butterworth were remarkable. Like the censor and the vice-chancellor, Butterworth was from New College. He and Bullock were nearly the same age, and in 1953 they were the youngest members of Council. Each went on to become the founding head of an institution of higher education, in Butterworth's case Warwick University. Each would excel in raising funds from the business community for his university. As vice-chancellor

of Warwick University, Butterworth was so effective as a liaison to the business community that student radicals and leftist faculty denounced him for bringing capitalist values and management practices into the university (see Thompson 1970a, 1970b). And each eventually became a life peer.

18. Propinquity again came into play as Council selected John Bernard Bamborough, a don from Bullock's undergraduate college, Wadham, to become the head of this new postgraduate society (Bullock interview 1989; *Oxford University Gazette* 1961: 126; *Oxford University Gazette* 1962b).

19. Harvard's presence in England extended beyond Oxford. In April 1990 there were 4,000 Harvard alumni living in England, of whom 22 were members of the House of Commons (Fishburn 1990).

20. Today, the Federation of British Industries is called the Confederation of British Industry or CBI. According to Lord Bullock, Guinness in the 1950s was well thought of for its "wonderful help to artists in the Depression. It got this famous series of Guinness advertisements done by all the leading British artists who were hard up" (Bullock interview 1989).

CHAPTER 5, *Labour Politics and the High Tide of Internal Reform*

1. For a subtle discussion of some of the issues involved, see Pocock 1985: 193–212.

2. The Association of University Teachers was weak at Oxford, probably because self-governing dons felt little need for trade union representation.

3. In addition, the Ophthalmology Appeal (1943–45) was an unpublicized "private" effort between the Higher Studies Fund and the Historic Buildings Appeal, started by a benefaction from Lord Nuffield. The Ophthalmology Appeal sought to endow a department with the appropriate laboratory space and equipment to research blindness (Registrar 1968: 105).

CHAPTER 6, *Thatcher Politics*

1. Conrad Russell is a history professor at King's College, University of London, a life peer, and son of Bertrand Russell.

2. Every admissions tutor I spoke to or corresponded with, regardless of college, gave me a statement substantively identical to this passage. This particular one is from Professor J. F. Stein, tutor for admissions, Magdalen College, Oxford.

3. "Wet" was a label of Thatcher's for old-fashioned Tory paternalism and middle-path compromise politics. An American word with similar connotations would be George Bush's use of the word "liberal," or his opponents' characterization of him as a "wimp." For a discussion of the term "wet," see H. Young 1990: 198.

4. Crewe's interpretation was in line with the findings of Ronald Inglehart's

massive study of values in advanced industrial societies. Inglehart documented what he described as a "culture shift" from materialist to "post-materialist" values (Inglehart 1990).

5. Harold Perkin, the first person in Britain to become a professor of social history, came very close to this analysis in his book *The Rise of Professional Society* (1989). Perkin saw the trend of British society for the preceding hundred years to have been one of growing professionalization and the triumph of professional values. He argued that just as lord and peasant, capitalist and worker were the axis of conflict in the past, "so the struggle between public and private sector professions is the master conflict" today. Public-sector professionals were simply state employees, while private-sector professionals were those employed by corporations (Perkin 1989: 10, 11). For Perkin, Thatcherism was a political expression of private-sector professionals.

CHAPTER 7, *Dilemmas of Academic Authority*

1. For example, in 1995, Yale returned a 20 million dollar gift from billionaire Lee M. Bass for the study of Western civilization when Bass wanted, in exchange, some control over faculty appointments.

References

INTERVIEWS

Briggs, Asa (Lord). 1986. Interview in the Provost Lodge at Worcester College, Oxford, December 5.

Brock, Michael. 1988. Interview in his office at Nuffield College, June 10.

Bullock, Alan (Lord). 1986–89. Interviews in his office at St. Catherine's.

Coldstream, Patrick. 1987. Interview in the offices of the Council for Industry and Higher Education, London, June 8.

Floud, Jean. 1988. Interview in the Senior Common Room, Nuffield College, Oxford, May 11.

Franks, Oliver (Lord). 1988. Interview at his home in Oxford, February 11.

Gasser, Robert Paul Holland. 1988. Interview in Bursar's Office, Brasenose College, Oxford, June 22.

Halsey, A. H. 1988. Interview at Barnett House, Oxford, May 23.

Kirwan, Christopher. 1988. Interview at his room in Exeter College, Oxford, July 20.

Noble, Denis. 1988. Interview at Holywell Manor, Balliol College, Oxford, May 27.

Reed, T. J. 1987. Interview in his room in St. John's College, Oxford, October 16.

Rickett, Raymond. 1986. Interview in his office at Middlesex Polytechnic, December 17.

Smith, E. Brian. 1988. Interview at St. Catherine's in the Senior Common Room, June 9.

Tomlinson, Henry. 1987. Interview at the offices of Confederation of British Industry at Centre Point, London, May 11.

Walden, George. 1987. Interview in his office at Elizabeth House, the Department of Education and Science, January 12.

Wenden, David John. 1988. Interview at All Souls, March 2.

Wilkinson, Rupert. 1987. Interview in his London home, September 24.

Williams, Shirley. 1987. Interview at the Social Democratic Party National Office, January 19.

OTHER PRIMARY SOURCES AND SECONDARY SOURCES

Ackroyd, Peter. 1984. *T. S. Eliot: A Life*. New York: Simon and Schuster.

Ady, Peter. 1964. "Mixed Education and the Women's Colleges. *The Oxford Magazine*, December 3: 138–40.

Amis, Kingsley. 1991. *Memoirs*. London: Penguin.

Anderson Committee. 1960. "Grants to Students." Cmnd. 1051. London: Her Majesty's Stationery Office.

Annan, Noel G. (Lord). 1955. "The Intellectual Aristocracy." *Studies in Social History*. Edited by J. H. Plumb. London: Longmans, Green.

————. 1986. "The Case for Reform of Higher Education." Conference lecture and discussion, History of Education Society Annual Conference. West London Institute of Higher Education, December 12–14.

————. 1990. *Our Age: English Intellectuals Between the World Wars, a Group Portrait*. New York: Random House.

Argles, Michael. 1964. *South Kensington to Robbins: An Account of English Technical and Scientific Education Since 1851*. London: Longmans, Green.

Armstrong, John A. 1973. *The European Administrative Elite*. Princeton, N.J.: Princeton University Press.

Armytage, W. H. G. 1955. *Civic Universities*. London.

Arnold, Matthew. 1980 [1869]. "Culture and Anarchy." In *The Portable Matthew Arnold*, edited by Lionel Trilling. New York: Penguin Books.

Ashby, Eric. 1958. *Technology and the Academics*. London: Macmillan.

Bagehot, Walter. 1976. *The English Constitution*. Ithaca, N.Y.: Cornell University Press.

Baker, Kenneth. 1986. Speech to Committee Of Vice- Chancellors and Principals: Residential Conference, September 23, 1986." Department of Education and Science. London.

Balsdon, Dacre. 1957. *Oxford Life*. London: Eyre and Spottiswoods.

Baltzell, E. Digby. 1982. *Puritan Boston and Quaker Philadelphia*. Boston: Beacon Press.

Barnes, Leonard. 1962. "Authority in Oxford." *The Oxford Magazine*, October 25: 20–21.

Barnett, Correlli. 1987. *The Audit of War*. London: Papermac.

Bayley, P. C. 1962. "Admissions Procedures." *The Oxford Magazine*, May 31: 336.

Beckett, J. V. 1988. *The Aristocracy in England: 1660–1914*. New York: Basil Blackwell.

Bedarida, Francois. 1979. *A Social History of England: 1851–1975*. New York: Methuen.

Beeson, Professor. 1968. Letter from Professor Beeson to the Regius Professor of Medicine, December 18, 1967. Hebdomadal Council Papers, vol. 259, January 19: 133–34.

Bell, Clive. 1928. *Civilization*. London.

Bell, Daniel. 1993. Personal Correspondence. February 20.

Bellah, Robert, et al. 1986. *Habits of the Heart*. New York: Basic Books.

Beloff, Max. 1966. "Discussion by Congregation of Resolutions on Franks Report." Verbatim Report. *Oxford University Gazette*, Supplement (3) to no. 3284, Wednesday, July 20: 1493.

Beloff, Michael. 1968. *The Plateglass Universities*. London: Secker and Warburg.

Berryman, Jack W., and John W. Loy. 1976. "Secondary Schools and Ivy League Letters: A Comparative Replication of Eggleston's 'Oxbridge Blues.'" *British Journal of Sociology*, vol. 27, no. 1 (March): 76.

"Best Big Universities." *U.S. News and World Report*, vol. 109, no. 15 (Oct. 15): 118–20.

Beteille, Andre. 1983. *The Idea of Natural Inequality*. New Delhi: Oxford University Press.

Bishop, T. J. H., and Rupert Wilkinson. 1967. *Winchester and the Public School Elite*. London: Faber and Faber.

Black, Glen. 1988. "Admissions: The Truth." *Oxford Today*, vol. 1, no. 1, Michaelmas Issue.

Blau, Peter. 1973. *The Organization Of Academic Work*. New York: McGraw-Hill.

Bleaney, B. 1965. "University Finance." *The Oxford Magazine*, June 17: 408–9.

Bourdieu, Pierre. 1984. *Distinction: A Social Critique of the Judgement of Taste*. Cambridge, Mass.: Harvard University Press.

———. 1988. *Homo Academicus*. Stanford, Calif.: Stanford University Press.

Bourdieu, Pierre, and Jean-Claude Passeron. 1979. *The Inheritors*. Chicago: University of Chicago Press.

Bowen, Howard R. 1968. *The Finance of Higher Education*. Carnegie Commission on Higher Education. New York: McGraw-Hill.

Bowra, Cecil Maurice. 1967. *Memories: 1898–1939*. London: Weidenfeld and Nicolson.

Bradley, Ian. 1982. *The English Middle Classes*. London: Collins.

Brennan, John, and Tarla Shah. 1994. "Higher Education Policy in the United Kingdom." In *Higher Education Policy: An International Comparative Perspective*, edited by Leo Goedegebuure et al. New York: Pergamon Press.

Bridges, Edward Ettingdene (Lord). 1958. "The Historic Buildings Appeal." *Oxford*, vol. 16, no. 1 (December): 7–9.

Brierley, Peter. 1988. "Religion." In *British Social Trends Since 1900*, edited by A. H. Halsey. London: Macmillan.

British Institute of Management. 1978. "Survey of British Managers." Cited in Robert R. Locke, *Management and Higher Education Since 1940*, 214–16. Cambridge: Cambridge University Press, 1989.

Brock, M. G. 1965. "Admissions: The State of the Case." *The Oxford Magazine*, vol. 5, no. 14 (February 25).

Bullock, Alan. 1956. "The Proposal for a New College in Oxford." *Oxford*,
vol. 14, no. 3 (December).

———. 1971. "Memorandum by Vice-Chancellor on University Appeal."
Hebdomadal Council Papers, vol. 270 (September–December): 586–89.

———. 1987. "Alan Bullock Writes." *St. Catherine's Silver Jubilee Year:
1962–1987*. Oxford: St. Catherine's College.

Burke, Dolores L. 1988. *A New Academic Marketplace*. Westport, Conn.:
Greenwood Press.

Burke, Edmund. 1968. *Reflections on the Revolution in France*. Harmondsworth: Penguin.

"Business Schools for Oxbridge." 1990. *The Economist*, January 6: 27–28.

Butler, David. 1988. "Electors and Elected." In *British Social Trends Since 1900*,
edited by A. H. Halsey. London: Macmillan.

Butler, David, and Gareth Butler. 1986. *British Political Facts: 1900–1985*.
London: Macmillan.

Butler, Lionel. 1966. "Crisis in Whose Soul?" *Encounter*, vol. 26, no. 5: 93–95.

Cabinet and Cabinet Committees. 1919. *Minutes and Memoranda*. CAB series
23/11. London: Public Record Office.

Cannadine, David. 1992. *The Decline and Fall of the British Aristocracy*. New
York: Anchor Books.

Carr, Stephen, Mark Francis, Leanne G. Rivlin, and Andrew M. Stone. 1992.
Public Space. Cambridge: Cambridge University Press.

Carswell, John. 1985. *Government and the Universities in Britain*. Cambridge:
Cambridge University Press.

Carter, Ian. 1990. *Ancient Cultures of Conceit*. London: Routledge.

Caute, David. 1966. "The Crisis in All Souls." *Encounter*, vol. 26, no. 3: 3–15.

Chandler, Alfred D., Jr. 1977. *The Visible Hand: The Managerial Revolution
in American Business*. Cambridge, Mass.: Harvard University Press.

———. 1984. "The Emergence of Managerial Capitalism." *Business History
Review*, vol. 58, no. 4 (Winter).

Chester, Norman. 1986. *Economics, Politics and Social Studies in Oxford:
1900–1985*. London: Macmillan.

Chilver, G. E. F. 1954. "Correspondence." *The Oxford Magazine*, May 2:
348.

Chronicle of Higher Education. 1991. *The Almanac of Higher Education*.
Chicago: University of Chicago Press.

Cobban, Alan B. 1988. *The Medieval English Universities: Oxford and
Cambridge to c. 1500*. Berkeley: University of California Press.

Cobban J. M. 1969. "The Direct-Grant School." In *Fight for Education:
A Black Paper*, edited by C. B. Cox and A. E. Dyson, 39–42. London:
Critical Quarterly Society.

Clark, Burton R. 1987. *The Academic Life*. Princeton, N.J.: Carnegie
Foundation.

Cole, G. D. H. 1939. *A Plan for Democratic Britain*. London.

———. 1950. *Essays in Social Theory*. London: Macmillan.

"College Notes." 1953. *Oxford*, vol. 12, no. 2 (May): 53.

Collins, Bruce, and Keith Robbins, eds. 1990. *British Culture and Economic Decline*. London: Weidenfeld and Nicolson.

Collins, Randal. 1979. *The Credential Society*. New York: Academic Press.

Commission of Inquiry. 1965a. *Evidence: Part Three: Organizations*. Oxford: Oxford University Press.

———. 1965b. *Evidence: Part Four: Individuals*. Oxford: Oxford University Press.

———. 1965c. *Evidence: Part Nine: University Officials*. Oxford: Oxford University Press.

———. 1965d. *Evidence: Part Eleven: Individuals*. Oxford: Oxford University Press.

———. 1965e. *Evidence: Part Thirteen*. Oxford: Oxford University Press.

Committee of Vice-Chancellors and Principals of the Universities of the United Kingdom. 1958. "Report of an Ad Hoc Committee on Procedure for Admission of Students." London: Percy Lund, Humphries & Co.

———. 1960. "Second Report of an Ad Hoc Committee on Procedure for Admission of Students." London: Percy Lund, Humphries & Co.

———. 1961. "Third Report of an Ad Hoc Committee on Procedure for Admission of Students." London: Percy Lund, Humphries & Co.

———. 1988a. "Education Reform Bill: Briefing on Academic Freedom and Tenure." Distributed to members of the House of Lords. Unpublished handout.

———. 1988b. "Education Reform Bill: Progress to Date." Distributed to members of the House of Lords. Unpublished handout.

Committee on Higher Education. 1963a. *Higher Education*. (Robbins) Cmnd. 2154. London: Her Majesty's Stationery Office.

———. 1963b. *Higher Education Appendix Four*. Cmnd. 2145. London: Her Majesty's Stationery Office.

———. 1963c. *Appendix Five*. Cmnd. 2154. London: Her Majesty's Stationery Office.

Conway, Jill Ker. 1994. *True North: A Memoir*. New York: Vintage.

Cooke, Rachael, and Giles Mellalieu. 1990. "Off Target." *Cherwell*, Oxford, February 16.

Conservative Cabinet. 1963. "Government Statement on the Robbins Report." Hebdomadal Council Papers, vol. 246: 301–2.

Cornford, F. M. 1908. *Microcosmographia Academica*. Cambridge: Bowes and Bowes.

Coser, Lewis. 1977. *Masters of Sociological Thought*. New York: Harcourt Brace Jovanovich.

Couch, Stephen R. 1983. "Patronage and Organizational Structure in Symphony

Orchestras in London and New York." In *Performers and Performances*, edited by Jack Kamerman and Rosanne Martorella. New York: Praeger.

Crequer, Ngaio. 1986. "UGC Sends a Tough Message." *The Times Higher Education Supplement*, no. 708, May 30: 1.

Crequer, Ngaio, and Peter Scott. 1986. "UGC May Issue Bankruptcy Warning." *The Times Higher Education Supplement*, no. 707, May 23: 1.

Crewe, Ivor. 1989. "Values: The Crusade That Failed." In *The Thatcher Effect*, edited by Dennis Kavanagh and Anthony Seldon. Oxford: Clarendon Press.

Critchley, Julian. 1985. *Westminster Blues*. London: Macdonald.

Crosland, Anthony. 1956. *The Future of Socialism*. London: Jonathan Cape.

———. 1962. *The Conservative Enemy*. London: Jonathan Cape.

Crosland, C. A. R. 1961. "Some Thoughts on English Education." *Encounter*, July.

Crosland, Susan. 1983. *Tony Crosland*. Kent: Hodder and Stoughton.

Crossman, Richard. 1964. "Apartheid in Education." *The Observer*, January 26: 10.

Crossman, R. H. S., ed. 1952. *New Fabian Essays*. New York: Frederick A. Praeger.

Crowther Committee. 1959. *15 to 18*. Central Advisory Council for Education. London: Her Majesty's Stationery Office.

"Dangers of Docile Acceptance." 1963. *The Times*, December 4: 13.

David, Tudor. 1963. "Oxbridge Entrance: The Caius Meeting." *Universities Quarterly*, vol. 17, no. 4 (September): 360–76.

Davis, Ralph. 1962. "The Hardie Report." *The Oxford Magazine*, November 1: 37.

Department of Education and Science. 1975. *Curricular Differences for Boys and Girls*. Education Survey 21. London: Her Majesty's Stationery Office.

———. 1985. "The Development of Higher Education into the 1990s." Cmnd. 9524. London: Her Majesty's Stationery Office.

———. 1987. "Higher Education." Cmnd. 114. London: Her Majesty's Stationery Office, London.

Doermann, Humphrey. 1964. "Entrance to Harvard College." *The Oxford Magazine*, May 14: 304.

Dons' Petition. 1964. "University Admission." *Oxford University Gazette*. (Wadham) Petition signed by 21 dons, mimeo sheet, placed after Supplement 1 to no. 3186, February 13.

Drury, John. 1995. "The Whole Difference." *The Oxford Magazine*, no. 116, Eighth Week, Hilary Term: 1.

The Economist. 1963. October 26: 355.

Elbaum, Bernard, and William Lazonick, eds. 1986. *The Decline of the British Economy*. Oxford: Clarendon Press.

Eliot, T. S. 1968 [1949]. "Notes Towards the Definition of Culture." In *Christianity and Culture*. New York: Harcourt Brace Jovanovich.

Ellmann, Richard. 1988. *Oscar Wilde*. New York: Vintage Books.

Engel, A. J. 1983. *From Clergyman to Don, the Rise of the Academic Profession in Nineteenth-Century Oxford*. Oxford: Clarendon Press.

Erikson, Robert, and John Goldthorpe. 1992. *The Constant Flux*. Oxford: Clarendon Press.

Faith, Nicholas. 1990. "New Order That Could Change Oxbridge Bias." *The Independent*, May 31: 17.

Farnum, Richard. 1990a. "Prestige in the Ivy League: Democratization and Discrimination at Penn and Columbia, 1890–1970." In *The High-Status Track*, edited by Paul William Kingston and Lionel S. Lewis. Albany: State University of New York Press.

———. 1990b. "Patterns of Upper-Class Education in Four American Cities: 1875–1975." In *The High-Status Track*, edited by Paul William Kingston and Lionel S. Lewis. Albany: State University of New York Press.

Fishburn, Dudley. 1990. *Harvard University Board of Overseers 1990 Election*. Cambridge, Mass.: Harvard University.

Fleming, Ronald Lee, and Renata von Tsharner. 1987. *Place Makers*. New York: Houstings House.

Floud, Jean. 1988. Letter to author. May 17.

Franks, Oliver (Lord). 1955. *Britain and the Tide of World Affairs*. London: Oxford University Press.

———. 1963. *British Business Schools*. London: British Institute of Management.

———. 1965. "The Admission Of Women to New College: Letter from Lord Franks to the Warden of New College." Hebdomadal Council Papers, vol. 250, March 19: 613–14.

———. 1966. "Interview with Lord Franks." *The Oxford Magazine*, 3 Trinity: 377–79.

Franks, Lord, K. C. Wheare, and L. Brown. 1964a. "Report of the Committee Appointed by the Hebdomadal Council on 3 February 1964." Hebdomadal Council Papers, vol. 247, March 11: 521–530.

———. 1964b. "Report of a Committee appointed by the Hebdomadal Council to Consider Points Arising out of the Robbins Report." *Oxford University Gazette*, Supplement no. 7 to no. 3191 (March): 3–4.

Freud, Sigmund. 1959. *Group Psychology and the Analysis of the Ego*. New York: Norton.

Fulton, John. 1970. "New Universities in Perspective." In *The Idea of a New University: An Experiment in Sussex*, edited by David Daiches. Cambridge, Mass.: MIT Press.

Gardner, Helen, and David Cecil. 1960. "Entrance Requirements." Correspondence. *The Oxford Magazine*, February 4: 172–73.

Gater, Anthony, David Insull, Harold Lind, and Peter Seglow. 1966. *Attitudes in British Management: A P.E.P. Report*. Harmondsworth: Penguin Books.

Gathorne-Hardy, Jonathan. 1977. *The Old School Tie*. New York: Viking Press.

Gibson, Strickland. 1954. "The University of Oxford." The Victoria History of the Counties of England. *A History of Oxfordshire*, vol. 3. Oxford: Oxford University Press.

Glass, D. V., ed. 1954. *Social Mobility in Britain*. London: Routledge and Kegan Paul.

Glasser, Ralph. 1987. *Growing Up in the Gorbals*. London: Pan Books.

———. 1990. *Gorbals Boy at Oxford*. London: Pan Books.

Glennerster, Howard, and William Low. 1990. "Education and the Welfare State: Does It Add Up?" In *The State of Welfare*. Oxford: Clarendon Press.

Goldthorpe, John. 1980. *Social Mobility and Class Structure*. Oxford: Oxford University Press.

———. 1982. "On the Service Class, Its Formation and Future." In *Social Class and the Division Of Labour*, edited by Anthony Giddens and Gavin Mackenzie. Cambridge: Cambridge University Press.

Goldthorpe, John, and Clive Payne. 1986. "Trends in Intergenerational Class Mobility in England and Wales: 1972–83." *Sociology*, vol. 20, no. 1.

Grant, Gerald, and David Riesman. 1975. "An Ecology of Academic Reform." *Daedalus*, vol. 104, no. 1: 166–91.

Green College. 1989. *Green College Record*. Oxford.

———. 1991. *Green College Handbook, 1991–92*. Oxford.

Greenfeld, Liah. 1992. *Nationalism*. Cambridge, Mass.: Harvard University Press.

Greenstein, Daniel. 1987. "Gender Results: Men and Women in the Schools: 1913–1986." *The Oxford Magazine*, Fourth Week, Hilary Term: 4.

———. 1994. "The Junior Members, 1900–1990: A Profile." In *The Twentieth Century*, vol. 8 of *The History of the University of Oxford*, edited by Brian Harrison. Oxford: Oxford University Press.

Grieves, Keith. 1989. *Sir Eric Geddes: Business and Government in War and Peace*. Manchester: Manchester University Press.

Griffin, Jasper. 1966. "A Neglected Moral Function of the University." *The Oxford Magazine*, no. 2, Hilary Term.

Guttsman, W. L. 1963. *The British Political Elite*. New York: Basic Books.

———. 1974. "The British Political Elite and the Class Structure." In *Elites and Power in British Society*, edited by P. Stanworth and A. Giddens. Cambridge: Cambridge University Press.

Halbwachs, Maurice. 1980. *Collective Memory*. Introduction by Mary Douglas. New York: Harper and Row.

Hall, Nina. 1986. "Few Private Takers for Research." *The Times Higher Education Supplement*, no. 707, May 23: 1.

Halsey, A. H. 1982. "The Decline of Donnish Dominion?" *Oxford Review of Education*, vol. 8, no. 3.

———. 1986a. "Higher Education and Employment." Nuffield Seminar Paper on Education and Employment. Unpublished.

———. 1986b. *Change in British Society*. Oxford: Oxford University Press.

———. 1987a. "Social Trends Since World War II." *Social Trends*, no. 17. London: Her Majesty's Stationery Office.

———. 1987b. "Higher Education . . . " *The Oxford Magazine*. Second Week, Trinity Term.

———. 1988. "Higher Education." In *British Social Trends Since 1900*, edited by A. H. Halsey. London: Macmillan.

———. 1992. *Decline of Donnish Dominion*. Oxford: Clarendon Press.

———. 1994. "Oxford and the British Universities." In *The Twentieth Century*, vol. 8 of *The History of the University Of Oxford*, edited by Brian Harrison. Oxford: Oxford University Press.

Halsey, A. H., and M. A. Trow. 1971. *The British Academics*. Cambridge, Mass.: Harvard University Press.

Halsey, A. H., A. F. Heath, and J. M. Ridge. 1980. *Origins and Destinations: Family, Class, and Education in Modern Britain*. Oxford: Clarendon Press.

Hardie, W. F. R. 1961. "Admissions to Colleges." *The Oxford Magazine*, February 23: 240–43.

———. 1962. "Admissions—A Reply." *The Oxford Magazine*, November 8: 54–55.

———. 1965. "University Entrance." *The Oxford Magazine*, May 27: 366.

Harris, Jose. 1994. "The Arts and Social Sciences, 1939–1970." In *The Twentieth Century*, vol. 8 of *The History of the University of Oxford*, edited by Brian Harrison. Oxford: Oxford University Press.

Harris, Seymour E. 1972. *A Statistical Portrait of Higher Education*. Carnegie Commission Report. New York: McGraw-Hill.

Harrison, Brian. 1994. "Politics." In *The Twentieth Century*, vol. 8 of *The History of the University of Oxford*, edited by Brian Harrison. Oxford: Oxford University Press.

Harrison, Michael. 1990. "Enterprise Culture 'Sabotaged.'" *The Independent*, February 18: 1.

Hart, H. L. A. 1985. "Oxford and Mrs. Thatcher." *The New York Review of Books*, March 25: 7–9.

Harvard College, Graduate School of Arts and Sciences. 1998. "The Yard." July: 3.

Heath, A., R. Jowell, and J. Curtice. 1985. *How Britain Votes*. Oxford: Pergamon Press.

Hebdomadal Council Papers. 1963a. "Monday, 4 November 1963." Vol. 246 (November 8): xcv–xcvii.

———. 1963b. "Robbins Report: Memorandum by Mr. Vice-Chancellor." Vol. 246 (November 15): 423–24.

———. 1963c. "Acts, Monday, 18 November 1963." Vol. 246 (November 22): cxix–cxxvii.

———. 1963d. "Students in Residence: Table IV." Vol. 246: 343.

———. 1963e. "Acts, Monday, 25 November 1963." Vol. 246 (November 29): cxxxc–cxliii.

———. 1963f. "Committee Appointed to Consider Mr. Vice-Chancellor's Memorandum on the Robbins Report." Vol. 246 (November 29): 527–31.

———. 1963g. "Acts, Monday, 2 December 1963." Vol. 246 (December 6): clv–clxvi.

———. 1963h. "Acts, Monday, 9 December 1963." Vol. 246 (December 18): clxxiii–clxxxvi.

———. 1964a. "Acts, Monday, 20 January 1964." Vol. 247 (January 24): xv–xxvii.

———. 1964b. "Minutes of the Oxford and Cambridge Standing Joint Committee." Vol. 247 (January 24): 151.

———. 1964c. "Acts, Monday, 27 January 1964." Vol. 247 (January 31): xxxv–xlv.

———. 1964d. "Comments on the 'Further Report on the Closer Integration of University Teaching and Research with the College System.'" Vol. 247 (January 31): 225–36.

———. 1964e. "'Further Report on the Closer Integration of University Teaching and Research with the College System': Letter from Bodley's Librarian." Vol. 247 (February 7): 237–38.

———. 1964f. "Further Comments on the 'Further Report on the Closer Integration of University Teaching and Research with the College System.'" Vol. 247 (February 7): 293–300.

———. 1964g. "Acts, Monday, 10 February." Vol. 247 (February 14): lxviii.

———. 1964h. "Acts." Vol. 247 (February 17): lxxxviii, agenda point 22.

———. 1964i. "Appendix" to "Report Of the Committee on the Estimates." Vol. 248 (May 29): 469.

———. 1964j. "Hebdomadal Council Acts." Vol. 248 (July 1): cxliii.

———. 1964k. "Hebdomadal Council Acts, Monday, 26 October 1964." Vol. 249 (October 30): lxxxii, agenda point 25.

———. 1964l. "Hebdomadal Council Acts, Monday, 2 November 1964." Vol. 249 (November 6): c, agenda point 22.

———. 1965a. "Further Questionnaire from the Franks Commission: Communication from the Committee on the Closer Integration of University Employees into the College System." Vol. 250 (January 15): 127.

———. 1965b. "Letter from A. L. P. Norrington to Registrar." Vol. 250 (January 15): 183.

———. 1965c. Vol. 252 (September 17): 35–42.

———. 1965d. "Report of the Committee on the Closer Integration of University Employees into the College System." Vol. 252 (September 17): 55–59.

———. 1965e. "Permanent Private Halls: Inquiry from the Franks Commission." Vol. 252 (October 8): 180.

———. 1965f. "Molecular Biophysics." Vol. 252 (October 20 and 29): 215–21, 283–84.

———. 1965g. "Letter from the Chairman of the University Grants Committee to Mr. Vice-Chancellor." Vol. 252 (October 18): 346.

———. 1965h. "Earmarked Grants for Developments in Technology: Department of Metallurgy." Vol. 252 (October 8): 344–47.

———. 1967a. "Report of the Committee on the Closer Integration of University Employees into the College System." Vol. 257 (July 20): 852.

———. 1967b. "Communications from the General Board of the Faculties." Vol. 258 (October 6): 122.

———. 1971. "Acts, Monday, 15 February." Vol. 268 (February 15): lxxii.

———. 1973. Vol. 274 (February 22): 423. "Report of the Committee on a University Appeal."

Higher Education Research Institute. 1968; 1973; 1983; 1996. *National Norms for Entering College Freshmen*. Washington: American Council on Education.

Hill, Christopher. 1950. "Correspondence." *The Oxford Magazine*, June 1: 512.

Hirsch, Fred. 1976. *Social Limits to Growth*. Cambridge, Mass.: Harvard University Press.

Hogg, Quintin. 1947. *The Case for Conservatism*. London: Penguin Press.

Hoggart, Richard. 1958. *The Uses of Literacy*. Harmondsworth: Penguin Books.

Honey, J. R. de S. 1977. *Tom Brown's Universe: The Development of the English Public School in the Nineteenth Century*. New York: New York Times.

Horne, Alistair. 1989. *Macmillan: 1957–1986*. London: Macmillan.

House of Lords Official Report. 1988a. April 18.

———. 1988b. April 19.

———. 1988c. May 19.

Howarth, Janet. 1994. "Women." In *The Twentieth Century*, vol. 8 of *History of the University of Oxford*, edited by Brian Harrison. Oxford: Oxford University Press.

Hubbard, Margaret. 1965. "The Number of Women at Oxford." *The Oxford Magazine*, May 6: 312.

Ingham, Geoffrey. 1984. *Capitalism Divided? The City and Industry in British Social Development*. London: Macmillan.

Inglehart, Ronald. 1990. *Culture Shift*. Princeton, N.J.: Princeton University Press.

James, Harold. 1990. "The German Experience and the Myth of British Cultural

Exceptionalism." In *British Culture and Economic Decline*, edited by Bruce Collins and Keith Robbins. London: Weidenfeld and Nicolson.

Jardin, Andre. 1988. *Tocqueville*. New York: Farrar Straus Giroux.

Jay, Martin. 1973. *The Dialectical Imagination*. Boston: Little, Brown.

Jencks, Christopher, and David Riesman. 1969. *The Academic Revolution*. Garden City, N.Y.: Doubleday.

Jessup, Frank. 1979. *Wolfson College Oxford: The Early Years*. Oxford: Wolfson College.

Jobbins, David. 1986. "UGC Finally Hits Cash Cuts Target." *The Times Higher Education Supplement*, no. 710, June 13: 5.

Jones, Felicity. 1987. "Fabians Reveal Labour's Policy Rift." *The Times Higher Education Supplement*, no. 741, January 16: 1.

Karabel, Jerome. 1984. "Status-Group Struggle, Organizational Interests, and the Limits of Institutional Autonomy: The Transformation of Harvard, Yale, and Princeton, 1918–1940." *Theory and Society*, vol. 13, no. 1 (January): 1–40.

Karen, David. 1990. "Toward a Political-Organizational Model of Gatekeeping: The Case Of Elite Colleges." *Sociology of Education*, vol. 63 (1990): 227–40.

———. 1991. "'Achievement' and 'Ascription' in Admission to an Elite College: A Political-Organizational Analysis." *Sociology Forum*, vol. 6, no. 2: 349–80.

Keen, H. H. 1965. "University Finance." *The Oxford Magazine*, 1 Michaelmas: 8–9.

Kelsall, R. K., Anne Poole, and Annette Kuhn. 1972. *Graduates: The Sociology of an Elite*. London: Methuen.

Kerr, Clark. 1991. *The Great Transformation in Higher Education*. Albany: State University of New York Press.

Kingston, Paul William, and Lionel S. Lewis. 1990. "Undergraduates at Elite Institutions: The Best, the Brightest, and the Richest." In *The High-Status Track*, edited by Paul William Kingston and Lionel S. Lewis. Albany: State University of New York Press.

Kogan, Maurice. 1984. "The Political View." In *Perspectives on Higher Education*, edited by Burton Clark. Berkeley: University of California Press.

Kogan, Maurice, and David Kogan. 1983. *The Attack on Higher Education*. London: Kogan Page.

Kuhn, Thomas S. 1970. *The Structure of Scientific Revolutions*. Chicago: University of Chicago Press.

Labour Party, Taylor Committee. 1963. *The Years of Crisis*. London.

Lamb, John D. 1993. "The Real Affirmative Action Babies: Legacy Preferences at Harvard and Yale." *Columbia Journal of Law and Social Problems*, vol. 26, no. 3: 491–521.

Larson, Magali Sarfatti. 1977. *The Rise Of Professionalism: A Sociological Analysis*. Berkeley: University of California Press.

Layard, Richard, John King, and Claus Moser. 1969. *The Impact of Robbins*. Harmondsworth: Penguin Books.

Leape, Martha P. N.d. "Report on the Class of 1979." Office of Career Services and Off-Campus Learning. Harvard and Radcliffe Colleges, Cambridge, Mass.

Leavis, F. R. 1962. *Two Cultures? The Significance of C. P. Snow*. London: Chatto and Windus.

Leavis, F. R., and Denys Thompson. 1933. *Culture and Environment*. London.

———. 1943. *Education and the University*. London.

Le Goff, Jacques. 1980. *Time, Work, and Culture in the Middle Ages*. Chicago: University of Chicago Press.

———. 1993. *Intellectuals in the Middle Ages*. Cambridge, Mass.: Blackwell.

Lewis, C. S. 1961. *An Experiment in Criticism*. Cambridge: Cambridge University Press.

Lipset, Seymour Martin, and David Riesman. 1975. *Education and Politics at Harvard*. New York: McGraw-Hill.

Locke, Robert. 1984. *The End of the Practical Man: Entrepreneurship and Higher Education in Germany, France and Great Britain, 1880–1940*. Greenwich, Conn.: JAI Press.

———. 1989. *Management and Higher Education Since 1940: The Influence of America and Japan on West Germany, Great Britain, and France*. Cambridge: Cambridge University Press.

Longmate, Norman. 1954. *Oxford Triumphant*. London: Phoenix House.

Lowe, John. 1992. "John Sparrow, the Warden of All Souls." *The American Scholar* (Autumn): 567–74.

McCready, Shirley. 1996a. "Unsocial Contract." *The Oxford Magazine*, Second Week, Hilary Term: 2–4.

———. 1996b. "Letter to the Editor." *The Oxford Magazine*, Second Week, Trinity Term: 13–14.

McCulloch, Gary, Edgar Jenkins, and David Layton. 1985. *Technological Revolution? The Politics of School Science and Technology in England and Wales Since 1945*. London: Falmer Press.

McKnight, Christopher. 1965. "Letters to the Editor." *The Oxford Magazine*, May 27: 370.

Macpherson, C. B. 1980. "Edmund Burke's 1782 Speech on the State of Representation of the Commons in Parliament." In *Burke*. Oxford: Oxford University Press.

"Management Education Survey." 1991. *The Economist*, March 2.

Mander, John. 1963. *Great Britain or Little England?* Harmondsworth: Penguin Books.

Mannheim, Karl. 1940 [1935]. *Man and Society in an Age of Reconstruction*. New York: Harcourt, Brace and World.

———. 1943. *Diagnosis of Our Time: Wartime Essays of a Sociologist*. London: Routledge and Kegan Paul.

———. 1971. *From Karl Mannheim.* Edited by Kurt H. Wolff. New York: Oxford University Press.

Marshall, Gordon, David Rose, Howard Newby, and Carolyn Vogler. 1989. *Social Class in Modern Britain.* London: Unwin Hyman.

Marshall, T. H. 1950. *Citizenship and Social Class.* Cambridge: Cambridge University Press.

———. 1981. *The Right to Welfare and Other Essays.* London: Heinemann.

Martin, David. 1973. *Tracts Against the Times.* London: Lutterworth Press.

———. 1978. *A General Theory of Secularization.* New York: Harper and Row.

Masterman, J. C. 1952. *To Teach the Senators Wisdom or an Oxford Guide-Book.* London: Hodder and Stoughton.

Mill, John Stuart. 1957. *Utilitarianism.* New York: Macmillan.

———. 1975. *Three Essays: On Liberty, Representative Government, the Subjection of Women.* Oxford: Oxford University Press.

———. 1985. *Principles of Political Economy.* New York: Penguin Classics.

Moberly, Walter. 1945. "Plato's Conception of Education and Its Meaning for To-day." Presidential Address delivered to the Classical Association at St. Albans on April 12, 1944. Toronto.

———. 1949. *The Crisis in the University.* London: Student Christian Movement Press.

———. 1950a. "The Universities." *The Cambridge Journal,* vol. 3, no. 4 (January): 195–213.

———. 1950b. *Universities Ancient and Modern.* Manchester: Manchester University Press.

Montaigne, Michel de. 1958. *Essays.* London: Penguin.

Moon, Emmya. 1995. "New Haven Symphony Orchestra: Class and Culture." Senior thesis, Yale University.

Morrell, J. B. 1994. "The Non-Medical Sciences, 1914–1939." In *The Twentieth Century,* vol. 8 of *The History of the University of Oxford,* edited by Brian Harrison. Oxford: Oxford University Press.

Morris, Charles. 1964. "Second Thoughts on Robbins." *Universities Quarterly,* vol. 18, no. 2 (March): 128.

Mortimer, John. 1986. *Paradise Postponed.* Harmondsworth: Penguin Books.

Mulvey, John. 1987. *A Policy for British Science: Building on Success.* Belfast: British Association for the Advancement of Science.

Nairne, Patrick. 1987. "Reflections of the Master." In *St. Catherine's Silver Jubilee Year: 1962–1987.* Oxford.

National Endowment for the Arts. 1993. *Public Participation in the Arts: 1982 and 1992.* Washington.

Neave, Guy R. 1975. *How They Fared: The Impact of the Comprehensive School upon the University.* London: Routledge and Kegan Paul.

New Society. 1963. No. 23 (March 7).

Noble, Denis. 1986. "A Visitation." *The Oxford Magazine.* Noughth Week, Trinity Term: 5–6.

———. 1987. "Lloyd Roberts Memorial Lecture." London: Yelf Bros.

Noble, Trevor. 1981. *Structure and Change in Modern Britain.* London: Batsford Academic and Educational.

Norrington, A. L. P. 1962. "Letter from the President of Trinity." *The Oxford Magazine,* November 1: 40.

Oakeshott, Michael. 1962. "Political Education." *Rationalism in Politics and Other Essays.* New York: Basic Books.

———. 1989. "The Universities." In *Michael Oakeshott on Education,* edited by Timothy Fuller. New Haven, Conn.: Yale University Press.

Oakeshott, W. F. 1963. "The Robbins Report: Memorandum by Mr. Vice-Chancellor." Hebdomadal Council Papers, vol. 246 (November 1): 305–6.

Oren, Dan A. 1985. *Joining the Club: A History of Jews and Yale.* New Haven, Conn.: Yale University Press.

Organization for Economic Cooperation and Development. 1986. *Girls and Women in Education.* Paris: OECD.

———. 1990. *Higher Education in California.* Paris: OECD.

Ostrower, Francie. 1995. *Why the Wealthy Give.* Princeton, N.J.: Princeton University Press.

Oxford. 1953. "College Notes." Vol. 12, no. 2 (May): 53.

———. 1956. "Finance." Vol. 14, no. 3 (December): 35–36.

———. 1958a. "The Historic Buildings Appeal." Vol. 16, no. 1 (December): 7–9.

———. 1958b. "Finance." Vol. 16, no. 1 (December): 29–30.

———. 1988. "Holywell Cemetery." Vol. 40, no. 2 (December).

"Oxford Dons in the Market." 1988. *The Economist,* October 22: 66.

The Oxford Magazine. 1935a. "New Vice-Chancellor." October 17: 1.

———. 1935b. "List of Freshmen." October 17: 26–29.

———. 1935c. "List of Freshmen—II." October 24: 62–66.

———. 1945. November 8: 65.

———. 1946. "The Problem of the Married Fellow." November 14: 81–82.

———. 1949. "The Crisis in the University." June 2: 548.

———. 1950. Editor's "Notes and News." February 9: 290.

———. 1951. "Oxonians in the New House of Commons." November 1: 48, 50, 52.

———. 1952. May 8: 304–6.

———. 1953a. Editor's "Notes and News." November 19: 89.

———. 1953b. Editor's "Notes and News." December 3: 127.

———. 1954a. Editor's "Notes and News." January 21: 141.

———. 1954b. Editor's "Notes and News." May 20: 329.

———. 1955. "Notes and News." June 2: 378, 380–82.

———. 1956. "Notes and Comments." November 8: 81, 88–89.

———. 1957. "The End of the Women's Quota." January 31: 221.

———. 1960a. "The Chancellor." February 11: 181.

———. 1960b. "Latin Again." February 11: 181.

———. 1960c. "Congregation." February 25: 210.

———. 1961. "Survey of UK Undergraduates." April 27: 306.

———. 1963. "College Awards." June 20: 374–75.

———. 1964. "Notes and Comments." May 28: 329.

———. 1966. "The Principal Innovating Recommendations of the Franks Report." 3 Trinity: 375–76.

———. 1967. "The Independence Fund." October 27: 22.

Oxford University. 1931. *The Government of Oxford*. London: Oxford University Press.

Oxford University Calendar. 1923–24.

———. 1953–54.

———. 1963–64.

———. 1974–75.

———. 1984–85.

Oxford University Commission. 1852. Parliamentary Papers, vol. 22.

Oxford University Gazette. 1961. "Annual Report, 1960–1." Supplement 1 to no. 3095, October 5: 124.

———. 1962a. "Annual Report." Supplement to no. 3133, October 4.

———. 1962b. "Oration by the Vice-Chancellor." Supplement to no. 3133, October 4: 107.

———. 1963. "Annual Report." Supplement to no. 3171, October 7: 119.

———. 1964. "Report of the Keeper of the Archives, 1962–3." Supplement no. 4 to no. 3188, March.

———. 1966. "Discussion by Congregation of Resolutions on Franks Report." Verbatim Report. Supplement no. 3 to no. 3284, July 20: 1486.

———. 1968. "Report of the Joint Committee on the Size and Shape of the University." Supplement no. 7, June.

———. 1974. Supplement no. 3 to no. 3583, May 8.

———. 1981a. "Voting on General Resolution Concerning the Financial Outlook, Explanatory Note to Resolution." October 29: 171–72.

———. 1981b. "Congregation, 1 December." December 3: 256.

———. 1981c. "Verbatim Report of Proceedings in Congregation." December 21: 323–33.

———. 1982a. "Report on the General Board's Initial Assessment of the Long-Term Effects of an 8 Per Cent Reduction in Its Resources." September 30: 32–34.

———. 1982b. "Annual Report 1981–2. October 7.

———. 1989. Supplement no. 1 to no. 4157, October 30.

———. 1990. Supplement no. 1 to no. 4185, July 9.

———. 1992a. "Oration by the Vice-Chancellor." Supplement no. 2 to no. 4264, October 12.

———. 1992b. "Appendices." Supplement no. 2 to no. 4264, October 12: 173.

———. 1995a. "Promotions Policy for Academic Staff and Recognition of Academic Distinction." Supplement no. 1 to no. 4351, January 30: 655–65.

———. 1995b. "Verbatim Report of Proceedings in Congregation." Supplement no. 1 to no. 4356, March 6: 831–46.

———. 1995c. "University Acts." No. 4359, March 23: 914.

———. 1995d. "Student Numbers." Supplement no. 2 to no. 4369, June 26: 1335–42.

Oxford University Undergraduate Admissions Office. 1983. "Statistics Based on Places Given Through the Admissions Exercise October and December 1982." Oxford.

———. 1984. "Statistics Based on Places Given Through the Admissions Exercise October and December 1983." Oxford.

Ozouf, Mona. 1988. *Festivals and the French Revolution*. Cambridge, Mass.: Harvard University Press.

Parkes, Edward. 1981. "Letter from the Chairman of the University Grants Committee." *Oxford University Gazette*. Supplement 2 to no. 3852. July 8: 867–72.

Parkin, Frank. 1979. *Marxism and Class Theory: A Bourgeois Critique*. New York: Columbia University Press.

Parliamentary Papers: Reports, Commissions. 1922. "Royal Commission on Oxford and Cambridge Universities." Cmd. 1588. Vol. X (10)(4): 27–256.

Perkin, Harold J. 1969. *The New Universities in the United Kingdom*. Case Studies on Innovation in Higher Education. Paris: Organization for Economic Cooperation and Development.

———. 1989. *The Rise of Professional Society: England Since 1880*. London: Routledge.

Peterson, A. D. C. 1964. "The Sixth Form Experience of Oxford Entrants." *The Oxford Magazine*, February 6: 172–73.

Pickering, George. 1967. *The Challenge to Education*. London: C. A. Watts.

Pierson, George W. 1983. *A Yale Book of Numbers*. New Haven, Conn.: Yale University.

Platt, Christopher. 1986. *The Most Obliging Man in Europe: The Life and Times of the Oxford Scout*. London: George Allen and Unwin.

Pocock, J. G. A. 1985. "The Political Economy of Burke's Analysis of the French Revolution." In *Virtue, Commerce, and History*. Cambridge: Cambridge University Press.

Porter, Michael E. 1990. *The Competitive Advantage of Nations*. London: Macmillan.

Potter, Dennis. 1960. *The Glittering Coffin*. London.

"Poverty Ringed with Riches." 1989. *The Economist*, July 8: 53.

Proust, Marcel. 1981. *Remembrance of Things Past*. New York: Vintage.

Putnam, Robert. 1993. *Making Democracy Work: Civic Traditions in Modern Italy*. Princeton, N.J.: Princeton University Press.

"Questions That Must Be Discussed." 1963. *The Times*, December 6: 13.

Quinton, Anthony. 1978. *The Politics of Imperfection*. London: Faber and Faber.

Rae, John. 1981. *The Public School Revolution: Britain's Independent Schools, 1964–1979*. London: Faber and Faber.

Reed, T. J. 1994. *The Oxford Magazine*, no. 101, Hilary Term.

Registrar. 1968. "Appeals and the Raising of Funds for University Purposes: Revised Memorandum by the Registrar." Hebdomadal Council Papers, vol. 259, January 19: 103–34.

Robbins, Lord. 1971. *Autobiography of an Economist*. London: Macmillan and St. Martin's.

"The Robbins Report." 1963. *The Times*, October 24.

Robinson, Eric. 1963. "After the Honeymoon." *New Society*, November 14: 16.

———. 1967. *The New Polytechnics: The People's Universities*. Middlesex: Penguin Books.

Roche, John. 1994. "The Non-Medical Sciences, 1939–1970." In *The Twentieth Century*, vol. 8 of *The History of the University of Oxford*, edited by Brian Harrison. Oxford: Oxford University Press.

Rose, Richard. 1962. "Anatomy of British Political Factions." *New Society*, no. 2 (October 11): 29–31.

———. 1965. "England: A Traditionally Modern Political Culture." In *Political Culture and Political Development*, edited by Lucian W. Pye and Sidney Verba. Princeton, N.J.: Princeton University Press.

Rosovsky, Henry. 1990. *The University: An Owner's Manual*. New York: Norton.

Rothblatt, Sheldon. 1981. *The Revolution of the Dons*. Cambridge: Cambridge University Press.

Rubinstein, W. D. 1977. "Wealth, Elites, and the Class Structure of Modern Britain." *Past & Present*, no. 76 (August): 99–126.

———. 1981. *Men of Property*. London: Croom Helm.

———. 1986. "Education and the Social Origins of British Elites: 1880–1970." *Past & Present*, no. 112 (August): 163–207.

———. 1990. "Cultural Explanations for Britain's Economic Decline: How True?" In *British Culture and Economic Decline*, edited by Bruce Collins and Keith Robbins. London: Weidenfeld and Nicolson.

Russell, Conrad. 1993. *Academic Freedom*. New York: Routledge.

St. Antony's College. 1991. *St. Antony's College Record*. Oxford.

St. Catherine's College. 1985–88. *St. Catherine's Year*. Oxford.

St. Catherine's College Archive. 1985. "Notes from a Meeting with Lord Bullock, 30 January 1985." Oxford: St. Catherine's.

———. 1986. "Draft of the Chronological Aide-Memoire to Further the Organization and Replenishment of the College Archive." Oxford: St. Catherine's.

Ste. Croix, G. E. M. de. 1964. "The Admission of Women to New College." *The Oxford Magazine*, October 15: 4.

Salter, Brian, and Ted Tapper. 1981. *Education, Politics, and the State*. London: Grant McIntyre.

———. 1985. *Power and Policy in Education: The Case of Independent Schooling*. London: Falmer.

———. 1987. "Tarnish on the Ancient Glitter." *The Times Higher Education Supplement*, August 7: 12.

Sampson, Anthony. 1965. *The Anatomy of Britain Today*. New York: Harper and Row.

———. 1984. *The Changing Anatomy of Britain*. New York: Vintage Books.

Sanderson, Michael. 1972. *The Universities and British Industry: 1850–1970*. London: Routledge and Kegan Paul.

———. 1987. *Educational Opportunity and Social Change in England*. London: Faber and Faber.

Save British Science. 1986. "Save British Science." Press Conference Pamphlet. Oxford: SBS.

———. June 1986. *British Science in Decline*. Oxford: SBS.

———. 1987. "Civil Research and Development." Statement for House of Lords Debate, February 19. London: SBS.

———. 1987. *An ABC for Decline: Comment on the ABRC's "A Strategy for the Science Base."* London: SBS.

———. 1988. "Applause Is Not Enough." Evidence Submitted to the House of Commons Select Committee on Education, Science and the Arts. London: SBS.

Science and Engineering Research Council. 1992. *Annual Report of the Science and Engineering Research Council*. Swindon: SERC.

Scott, Peter. 1982. "Excellence and Uncertainty: The Future of Oxford." *Oxford Review of Education*, vol. 8, no. 3: 287.

———. 1984. *The Crisis of the University*. London: Croom Helm.

———. 1989. "Higher Education." In *The Thatcher Effect*, edited by Dennis Kavanagh and Anthony Seldon. Oxford: Clarendon Press.

Scrutator. 1952. "Is Britain a Great Power?" *The Sunday Times*, August 17: 6.

Sennett, Richard. 1990. *The Conscience of the Eye*. New York: W. W. Norton.

Sennett, Richard, and Jonathan Cobb. 1972. *The Hidden Injuries of Class*. New York: Vintage.

Sharpe, Tom. 1976. *Porterhouse Blue*. London: Pan Books.

Shattock, Michael. 1994. *The UGC and the Management of British Universities*. Buckingham: Society for Research into Higher Education / Open University Press.

———. 1995. "Britain's Nationalised Industry." *The Times Higher Education Supplement*, April 28: 24.

Shils, Edward. 1972. "British Intellectuals in the Mid-Twentieth Century." In *The Intellectuals and the Powers*. Chicago: University of Chicago Press.

———. 1982. "Great Britain and the United States: Legislators, Bureaucrats and the Universities." In *Universities, Politicians and Bureaucrats: Europe and the United States*, edited by Hans Daalder and Edward Shils. Cambridge: Cambridge University Press.

Shinn, Christine Helen. 1986. *Paying the Piper—The Development of the University Grants Committee: 1919–1946*. London: Falmer Press.

Shklar, Judith. 1984. *Ordinary Vices*. Cambridge, Mass.: Harvard University Press.

Simmel, Georg. 1950. *The Sociology of Georg Simmel*. Edited by Kurt H. Wolff. Glencoe, Ill.: Free Press.

———. 1971. *On Individuality and Social Forms*. Edited by Donald Levine. Chicago: University of Chicago Press.

Simon, Brian. 1974. *The Politics of Educational Reform: 1920–1940*. London: Lawrence and Wishart.

Smith, D. Mack. 1956. "The Changing University." *Encounter*, vol. 6, no. 5 (May): 53–58.

Smith, E. B. 1989. "Founders' Lunch Speech—Friday 3 March 1989." *St. Catherine's Year*. Oxford: Syndex Partnership.

Snow, C. P. 1964. *The Two Cultures and a Second Look*. Cambridge: Cambridge University Press.

The Spectator. 1963. October 25: 511.

Stein, J. F. 1996. Correspondence with the author.

Stone, Lawrence. 1960a. "Correspondence." *The Oxford Magazine*, February 4: 174.

———. 1960b. "Correspondence." *The Oxford Magazine*, March 3: 228.

———. 1961. "The Case for a Graduate College." *The Oxford Magazine*, October 26: 28.

———. 1974. "The Size and Composition of the Oxford Student Body: 1580–1910." In *The University in Society*, vol. 1, edited by Lawrence Stone. Princeton, N.J.: Princeton University Press.

———. 1981. "History and the Social Sciences." In *The Past and the Present*. Boston: Routledge and Kegan Paul.

Stone, Lawrence, and Jeanne C. Fawtier Stone. 1984. *An Open Elite? England, 1540–1880*. Oxford: Oxford University Press.

Stone, W. G. 1970. "Steps Leading to the Foundation of the University." In *The Idea of a New University: An Experiment in Sussex*, edited by David Daiches. Cambridge, Mass.: MIT Press.

Styler, L. M. 1964. "Admission to the Colleges." *Oxford*, vol. 19, no. 3.

Sutherland, John. 1978. "Editor's Introduction." In *The Book of Snobs* by William Makepeace Thackeray. St. Lucia: University of Queensland Press.

Symonds, Richard. 1986. *Oxford and Empire: The Last Lost Cause?* London: Macmillan.

Synnott, Marcia Graham. 1979. *The Half-Opened Door: Discrimination and Admissions at Harvard, Yale, and Princeton, 1900–1970*. Westport, Conn.: Greenwood Press.

Tapper, Ted, and Brian Salter. 1987. Paper delivered at a seminar on education. King's College, University of London, February 27.

———. 1992. *Oxford, Cambridge and the Changing Idea of the University*. Buckingham: Open University Press.

Tawney, R. H. 1964. *Equality*. London: George Allen and Unwin.

Thackery, William Makepeace. 1978. *The Book of Snobs*. St. Lucia: University of Queensland Press.

Thatcher, Margaret. 1993. *The Downing Street Years: 1979–1990*. New York: Harper Collins.

Thernstrom, Stephen. 1986. "Poor but Hopeful Scholars." In *Glimpses of a Harvard Past*, edited by Bernard Bailyn. Cambridge, Mass.: Harvard University Press.

Thomas, Hugh, ed. 1959. *The Establishment*. London: Anthony Blond.

Thomas, Keith. 1961. "Notes and Comments." *The Oxford Magazine*, January 19: 143.

———. 1962. "Notes and Comments." *The Oxford Magazine*, November 22: 1.

Thomas, Kim. 1990. *Gender and Subject in Higher Education*. Buckingham: Open University Press.

Thompson, E. P. 1970a. "Warwick: The Business University." *New Society*, February 19.

———, ed. 1970b. *Warwick University Ltd*. Harmondsworth: Penguin Books.

Tojner, Paul Erik, and Kjeld Vindum. 1991. *Arne Jacobsen: Architect and Designer*. Copenhagen: Danish Design Center.

"Top Priority for Numbers?" 1963. *The Times*, December 5: 13.

Topf, Richard, Peter Mohler, and Anthony Heath. 1989. "Pride in One's Country: Britain and West Germany." In *British Social Attitudes: Special International Report*, edited by Roger Jowell, Sharon Witherspoon, and Lindsay Brook. Aldershot: Gower.

"Toward the Multiversity." 1987. *The Economist*. July 11: 21–25.

Trevor-Roper, Hugh. 1989. "Hugh Trevor-Roper on the Peterhouse Effect." *The Independent Magazine*, December 9: 16.

Trillin, Calvin. 1993. *Remembering Denny*. New York: Warner Books.

Trilling, Lionel. 1965. "The Leavis-Snow Controversy." In *Beyond Culture*. New York: Harcourt Brace Jovanovich.

Trow, Martin. 1964. "Second Thoughts On Robbins: A Question of Size and Shape." *Universities Quarterly*, vol. 18, no. 2 (March): 150.

———. 1984. "The Analysis of Status." In *Perspectives on Higher Education*, edited by Burton Clark. Berkeley: University of California Press.

"UGC to Be Replaced by New Funding Council." 1987. *The Times Higher Education Supplement*, April 3: 3.

Universities Central Council On Admissions. 1961a. "Report on a Scheme for University Admissions." London.

———. 1961b. "Report on a Scheme for University Admissions" (second report). London.

————. 1979, 1986, 1993. *UCCA Statistical Supplement*. Cheltenham: UCCA.
Universities Quarterly. 1964. Vol. 18, no. 2 (March).
University Grants Committee. 1922–1974. *Returns from Universities and University Colleges in Receipt of Treasury Grant*. London: Her Majesty's Stationery Office.
————. 1929. "Returns from Universities and University Colleges in Receipt of Treasury Grant 1928–9." London: Her Majesty's Stationery Office. Cited in *The Government of Oxford*. London: Oxford University Press, 1931: 30.
————. 1948a. "Education in 1947." Cmnd. 7446. London: Her Majesty's Stationery Office.
————. 1948b. "University Development from 1935 to 1947." London: Her Majesty's Stationery Office.
————. 1964. "University Development 1957–1962." Cmnd. 2267. London: Her Majesty's Stationery Office.
University of Oxford. 1958–87. "Appointments Committee Report." Annual reports from 1958 to 1987. University of Oxford.
————. 1960. *Entrance to Oxford and Cambridge*. Oxford: Oxford University Press.
————. 1962a. "Report on the Closer Integration of University Teaching and Research with the College System," A. R. W. Harrison, chairman. Unpublished report.
————. 1962b. "Admissions to Colleges." Unpublished.
————. 1962c. "Admissions to Colleges." Report of a Working Party on Admissions. Oxford: Oxford University Press.
————. 1964a. "Further Report on the Closer Integration of University Teaching and Research with the College System." *Oxford University Gazette*, Supplement no. 1, January (Norrington Report).
————. 1964b. "Report of the Committee Appointed by the Hebdomadal Council to Make Detailed Proposals for Carrying Out the Policy Contained in the Further Report on the Closer Integration of University Teaching and Research with the College System." *Oxford University Gazette*, Supplement no. 1, November (second Norrington Report).
————. 1966a. *Report of Commission of Inquiry*, vol. 1 (Franks Report). Oxford: Clarendon Press.
————. 1966b. *Report of Commission of Inquiry*, vol. 2: *Statistical Appendix* (Franks Report). Oxford: Clarendon Press.
————. 1970. "Report of the Committee on the Long-Term Problem of Entitlement." *Oxford University Gazette*, Supplement no. 8, June (Griffiths Report).
————. 1971. "The Development of the Clinical School." September.
————. 1972. "Report of the Committee on Co-residence." *Oxford University Gazette*, Supplement no. 6, May.

———. 1987. "Report of the Committee of Inquiry into Provision for Graduate Students." October.

University of Oxford Undergraduate Prospectus, 1986–87.

Useem, Michael. 1989. *Liberal Education and the Corporation*. New York: Aldine de Gruyter.

Vaizey, John. 1958. *The Costs of Education*. London: George Allen and Unwin.

———. 1964. "The Nobel Prize." *The Oxford Magazine*, November 5: 58.

———. 1965a. "Mixed Colleges." *The Oxford Magazine*, March 11: 269.

———. 1965b. "Women." *The Oxford Magazine*, May 13: 325.

———. 1965c. "The Context of the Inquiry." *The Oxford Magazine*, June 3: 373.

Walker, David. 1993. "Cambridge Tops Rival Oxford in U.K. Research Rankings." *The Chronicle of Higher Education*, vol. 39, no. 20 (January 20): A47.

Ward, W. R. 1958. *Georgian Oxford*. Oxford: Clarendon Press.

———. 1965. *Victorian Oxford*. London: Frank Cass.

Warnock, Mary. 1989. *A Common Policy for Education*. Oxford: Oxford University Press.

Watson, J. Steven. 1960. "University Admissions." *Oxford*, vol. 17, no. 1 (December).

Weatherly, Frederick Edward. 1879. *Oxford Days; or, How Ross Got His Degree. By a Resident M.A.* London: S. Low, Marston, Searle, and Rivington.

Weber, Max. 1978. *Economy and Society*, vol. 1. Berkeley: University of California Press.

Wheare, Kenneth. 1964. "Vice-Chancellor's Oration." *Oxford University Gazette*, Supplement to no. 3209, October 2: 52.

———. 1974. "Sir Douglas Veale." *Oxford*, vol. 26, no. 1 (May 1).

Whittaker, V. P. 1965. Submission to University of Oxford Commission of Inquiry. *Evidence: Part Eleven: Individuals*. Oxford.

Wiener, Martin. 1984. *English Culture and the Decline of the Industrial Spirit: 1850–1980*. Cambridge: Cambridge University Press.

Williams, Edgar T. N.d. "Rhodes House Letter 1955–56." Oxford.

Willis, Paul. 1981. *Learning to Labor: How Working Class Kids Get Working Class Jobs*. New York: Columbia University Press.

Wilson, Bryan. 1966. "An Answer from All Souls." *The Oxford Magazine*, 4 Trinity: 396–99.

Winchester, Simon. 1987. "Home-Thoughts, from Abroad." *St. Catherine's Silver Jubilee Year: 1962–1987*. Oxford: St. Catherine's.

Woolton, Lord. 1959. *The Memoirs of the RT. Hon. the Earl of Woolton*. London: Cassell.

Yale Bulletin and Calendar. 1995. Vol. 24, no. 1 (August 28–September 4).

Yale College Registrar's Office. 1995. "Definitive Majors for 1955–1992." New Haven, Conn.

Yale University. 1992. "Report of the Committee on Restructuring the Faculty of Arts and Sciences." New Haven, Conn.

Young, Hugo. 1990. *The Iron Lady: A Biography of Margaret Thatcher*. New York: Noonday Press.

Young, Michael. 1958. *The Rise of Meritocracy*. Middlesex: Penguin Press.

Zweigenhaft, Richard L. 1992. "The Application of Cultural and Social Capital: A Study of the 25th Year Reunion Entries of Prep School and Public School Graduates of Yale College." *Higher Education*, no. 23: 314.

Index

In this index an "f" after a number indicates a separate reference on the next page, and an "ff" indicates separate references on the next two pages. A continuous discussion over two or more pages is indicated by a span of page numbers, e.g., "57–59." *Passim* is used for a cluster of references in close but not consecutive sequence.

Library of Congress Cataloging-in-Publication Data

Soares, Joseph A.
    The decline of privilege : The modernization of Oxford University /
Joseph A. Soares.
        p.   cm.
Includes bibliographical references and index.
ISBN 0-8047-3488-7 (cloth)
    1. University of Oxford—History—20th century.   2. Higher
education and state—England—History—20th century.   3. Universities
and colleges—England—Sociological aspects—History—20th century.
I. Title.
LF521.S63   1999
378.425'74—dc21   98-50865
                                                                            CIP

⊗   This book is printed on acid-free, recycled paper.

Original printing 1999

Last figure below indicates year of this printing:
08   07   06   05   04   03   02   01   00   99

Designed by James P. Brommer
Typeset in 10/13 Sabon and Sabon display